D1120662

Voices of 196

Read *Voices of 1968* to understand how, why, and where deeply rooted activist currents coalesced into a global uprising that changed the world. Filled with a treasure trove of first-hand accounts and raw materials, *Voices of 1968* transports readers to the front lines of local organizations and nationwide movements led by feminists, anti-imperialists, Black Powerites, and the New Left. Here are the transnational threads of hope and possibility desperately needed in an era of neoliberalism.

> Robyn C. Spencer, CUNY, author of *The Revolution Has Come:*
> *Black Power, Gender and the Black Panther Party*

This is a direly needed document collection of great value. To the best of my knowledge, this is the most comprehensive such publication on global 1968 in any Western language.

> Gerd-Rainer Horn, Institut d'études politiques de Paris, author of
> *The Spirit of '68: Rebellion in Western Europe and North America, 1956–76.*

This extraordinary collection brings together the great manifestos, political programs, and other original writings that inspired—and were inspired by—the movements and uprisings of 1968. There are documents here from France, Czechoslovakia, and the United States, of course, but also lesser known writings from Canada, Mexico, and Yugoslavia, among other countries. This volume is indispensable for anyone interested in the global upheavals of that *annus mirabilis*.

> Jeff Goodwin, NYU, editor of *The Social Movements Reader*, author of
> *No Other Way Out: States and Revolutionary Movements, 1945–1991*

Here are VOICES from the marvelous year of 1968, as they spoke then. Some speak to projects we still struggle to realise half a century later. If a few are slightly mad, most are empowering, we know them as our own. We are their inheritors.

> Colin Barker, Manchester Metropolitan University, editor of
> *Revolutionary Rehearsals*, author of *Festival of the Oppressed*

The many revolts and uprisings of 1968 have frequently been told through narratives which have depoliticized them. They continue to be recuperated as individualized youth protests which ultimately paved the way for neoliberalism. This valuable collection of original documents and writings reasserts the diverse forms of radicalism and struggles for radical change that animated this iconic year. From Derry's Bogside, to the Black Writers' Congress in Montreal, and to the National Strike Council in Mexico, the texts demonstrate both the reach and impact of the events. This is a much needed book which will be a significant resource for hope and struggle.

David Featherstone, University of Glasgow, author of
Solidarity: Hidden Histories and Geographies of Internationalism

These revolutionary texts, many translated into English for the first time, challenge the whitewashing of this extraordinary year of anti-imperialist, anti-capitalist, antiracist, feminist, and LGBT struggles.

Françoise Vergès, Chair Global South(s),
Maison des sciences de l'homme, Paris

Voices of 1968

Documents from the Global North

Edited by Salar Mohandesi,
Bjarke Skærlund Risager, and Laurence Cox

PLUTO PRESS

First published 2018 by Pluto Press
345 Archway Road, London N6 5AA

www.plutobooks.com

British Library Cataloguing in Publication Data
A catalogue record for this book is available from the British Library

ISBN   978 0 7453 3809 5   Hardback
ISBN   978 0 7453 3808 8   Paperback
ISBN   978 1 7868 0345 0   PDF eBook
ISBN   978 1 7868 0347 4   Kindle eBook
ISBN   978 1 7868 0346 7   EPUB eBook

This book is printed on paper suitable for recycling and made from fully managed and
sustained forest sources. Logging, pulping and manufacturing processes are expected to
conform to the environmental standards of the country of origin.

Typeset by Stanford DTP Services, Northampton, England

Simultaneously printed in the United Kingdom and United States of America

Contents

Acknowledgements

Following the spirit of '68, this project has been a collective one from start to finish. We could have never seen this book through to completion without the generous support of so many friends and comrades, colleagues and scholars, contemporary movement memory projects, academic libraries and archives, publishers and journals, and, last but not least, participants of the "long 1968" themselves. They helped us unearth primary sources, track down permissions, and navigate foreign languages. They reviewed drafts, provided background information, and offered advice of all kinds. We would like to thank: Sofie Abelsen, Astrid Nonbo Andersen, Simon Avenell, Alexander Aviña, Marie Groth Bastiansen, Sabine Dueholm Bech, Mark Bergfeld, Jens Berthelsen, Peter Bielik, Fabrizio Billi, Rasmus Lybech Bojesen, Jonathan Bolton, Chiara Bonfiglioli, Maja Hojer Bruun, Peter Bugge, Helge Buttkereit, Robert Cavooris, Irina Cerić, Marija Cetinić, the comrades of Chicago86, Ueno Chizuko, Sakura Christmas, Colin Coulter, Vinny Cunningham, Jens Dahl, Avril Dennison, Nicolai von Eggers, Sofía Eguiarte Flesher, Ana Margarida Esteves, Madigan Fichter, Marlon L. Fick, Joe G. Feinberg, Cristina Flesher Fominaya, William Gambetta, Bernadette Gardiner, Rebecca Geddes, Niall Gilmartin, Niels Mandøe Glæsner, Dennis Gould, Jessica Hanley, Julie Herrada, Fernando Herrera Calderón, the Irish Left Archive, Jan Palach: Charles University Multimedia Project, Steven L. B. Jensen, Einar Lund Jensen, Simon Jones, Zlatko Jovanovic, Thomas Ekman Jørgensen, Patrick King, Ivan Kraljević, Martine Lind Krebs, Mike Krebs, Poul Gerhard Kristiansen, Mads Kjærgaard Lange, Finn Breinholt Larsen, Nicole Ledl, Shi-Lin Loh, Alberto Arribas Lozano, Ben Mabie, Mariella Magliani (Biblioteca Civica di Padova), William Marotti, Rob Marsden (Red Mole Rising), Shannan Mattiace, Anna Mazzoldi, Luseadra McKerracher, Martin Melaugh (Conflict Archive on the Internet), Silke Mende, Silva Mežnarić, Flemming Mikkelsen, Jonas Mousten, Jiři Navrátil, Anne Engelst Nørgaard, Niklas Olsen, Nunni Navaranaaq Olsen, Theresa O'Keefe, María L. O. Muñoz, John Peto, Rudi Petrovič, Anthony Pratcher, Birgit Rehse, Donald Reid, Mathias Skærlund Risager, Ane Bonde Rolsted, Brian Rosenblum, Jakob Rosendal, Søren Rosendal, Jasmin Schenk, Jürgen Schröder, Alan Sears, Inge Høst Seiding, Sergio Serrao, Setsu Shigematsu, Noriko Shiratori, Patricia Steinhoff, Daniel Swain, Achim Szepanski, Emma Teitelman, Mikkel Thorup, Órfhlaith Tuohy, Thijs van Leeuwen,

Onno Rasmus Severin Vollers, Gavin Walker, Eric Zolov, and Camilla Zuleger.

We are especially grateful to all the translators. Many of these texts proved quite challenging, and translating them required considerable training, skill, and patience. We thank you for all your tireless efforts to make these rich documents accessible to a much larger audience.

In addition, our sincere thanks for permissions to republish these texts and images go to: Kheya Bag (*New Left Review*), Julieann Campbell (Museum of Free Derry), Siegfried Christiansen (OOA Fonden/smilingsun.org), Lia Dadduzio (*il manifesto*), the Deputy Keeper of Records (Public Records Office of Northern Ireland), Daniel Drache, Gretchen Dutschke-Klotz, Madigan Fichter, Joachim Frank (Staatsarchiv Hamburg), Krisztina Kós (CEU Press), Klaus Lankheit (Institut für Zeitgeschichte), Lucia Lischi (Pisa University Press), Elizabeth Løvegal, Axel Mayer (BUND), Margot Miriel (Éditions Gallimard), Chanel Nelson (Black Cultural Archives, London), Eoin O'Mahony (Workers' Party), the Family Percl and Croatia Records, Mgr. Světlana Ptáčníková (National Service Archive, Prague), Boris Shedov (*McGill Daily*), Inger Sørensen, Nick Victor (*International Times* Archive), Leni Wildflower, and Barbara Williams.

Also a special thanks to the authors and artists who have given us permission to translate or reprint their rebellious writings and graphics: Renato Curcio, Mariarosa Dalla Costa, Marlon L. Fick, Jim Fitzpatrick, Ole Grünbaum, Milan Hauner, Lisbeth Dehn Holgersen, Milan Knížák, Åse Lading, Aqqaluk Lynge, Vincent McCormack, Eilis McDermott, Tanaka Mitsu, Ninon Schloss, Marie-Louise Svane, and Peter Tatchell.

Many thanks to David Shulman for his enthusiasm and patience, and to everyone else at Pluto Press. Thanks to Slagmark Press for editorial collaboration. We also wish to acknowledge the assistance of the Maynooth University Publications Fund with translation costs. Bjarke is thankful for the support from Independent Research Fund Denmark (Grant no.: 7023-00011B).

More generally our students and colleagues, family and friends, and anyone we've forgotten.

What Was 1968?

Salar Mohandesi, Bjarke Skærlund Risager,
and Laurence Cox

On January 2, 1968, Fidel Castro ended his speech commemorating the ninth anniversary of the Cuban Revolution by calling for a deepening of the global revolution. "Our country," he promised, "will carry forward its internationalist policy of solidarity with the revolutionary movement throughout the world without hesitation of any sort." Looking back to the death of Che Guevara, symbol of internationalist revolution, and looking forward to the struggles that lay ahead, he presciently proclaimed 1968 the "year of the heroic guerrilla." "Let this year be worthy of its name, worthy of Che's example in every respect," he concluded.[1]

That year would surpass his, and indeed everyone's, expectations. Building on the many struggles already unfolding across the globe, the events of 1968 would push democracy in new directions, overturn social roles, challenge accepted forms of representation, and redefine the very meaning of politics. This cultural, political, and social ferment reached every corner of the globe, with each example inspiring new ones, each movement pushing further than the one before, giving rise to a crescendoing wave of activism in the late 1960s and 1970s. Many felt as if they were living through a kind of revolution.

Why did so many people turn to activism? What did they want? What did they do? Who participated? What challenges did they face? How were these different movements connected to one another? Did they succeed or fail? This book attempts to answer these questions by presenting the voices of those "heroic guerrillas" themselves. *Voices of 1968* is the first international reader of original sources from the social movements of the 1960s and 1970s, gathering over 80 documents from a dozen countries, with country surveys, text introductions, and suggestions for further reading. The texts—manifestos, speeches, letters, interviews, posters, flyers, song lyrics, images, and more—capture the energy, diversity, creativity, and limits of a wide range of movements from the time, while highlighting the rich transnational linkages that bound them together.

---

1. Fidel Castro, "Speech on the Ninth Anniversary," Plaza de la Revolución, Havana, Cuba, January 2, 1968, republished at http://lanic.utexas.edu/project/castro/db/1968/19680102-1.html.

The Long 1968

Regardless of one's political inclinations, when one thinks of the 1960s, or even the 1970s, the year 1968 is often the first that jumps to mind. After all, in dozens of countries some of the most spectacular—in every sense of the word—events of the decade took place in that year. In Vietnam, the Tet Offensive. In Britain, the march on Grosvenor Square. In Jamaica, the Rodney Riots. In the United States, the assassination of Martin Luther King, Jr. In Mexico, the Tlatelolco Massacre. In Tunisia, the protests at the University of Tunis. In France, the May events. In Czechoslovakia, the Prague Spring. In Senegal, the May student rebellion. We could go on.

But as many scholars have pointed out, a narrow focus on the year 1968 gives us an incomplete picture of the time. 1968 was not necessarily a high point of activism in every country. In fact, in many places, "1968" came years earlier or later—in 1962 in Guatemala, 1967 in Guadeloupe and Hong Kong, 1972 in Madagascar, or 1973 in Thailand. This is true even for those countries that are said to have had a "1968," like Italy.

Even when 1968 did stand out, the events of those years never emerged spontaneously from a vacuum. These were the culmination of years of thinking, organizing, and fighting. The eye-catching events of the year 1968 were made possible by earlier developments, though of course these varied from country to country. In France, 1968 would not have been possible without the Algerian War; in the United States, the civil rights movement; in Britain, the Campaign for Nuclear Disarmament.

By the same token, the events of 1968 did not abruptly end in December of that year. In fact, in many countries, activism not only continued, but escalated. It was after 1968 that radical ideas grew in popularity, protests became common, activists grew more militant, and movements more diverse, tackling issues that had not received as much attention, such as incarceration, settler colonialism, or homophobia.

In this sense, "1968," if the date is to be used, must be understood as a synecdoche: a part substituting for the whole, or vice versa. To underline the point, many scholars now employ the somewhat paradoxical term: the "long 1968." Following the most recent scholarship on the period, here we take the term to mean the period of contestation that stretched from the mid-1960s to the mid-1970s, with 1968 at its center.

The Global 1960s

1968, Ruth Wilson Gilmore has noted, was "a disorderly year, when revolutionaries around the world made as much trouble as possible in as many places as possible."[2] More broadly, the 1960s and 1970s saw marches, occupations, strikes, and even insurrections break out on every habitable continent. Political turmoil was so widespread that one might rightly ask which country did not have a "1968." Many of these movements consciously looked to one another across borders, exchanging ideas, images, tactics, even goals. Despite enormous national differences, some participants imagined themselves to be a part of the same wave of contestation.

Recent scholarship has belatedly started to reconstruct this astonishing simultaneity of struggle, with the term "Global 1960s" now becoming common. In this respect, understanding 1968 bears similarities to attempts to understand other historical waves of revolutions or social movements: the Atlantic Revolutions of the late eighteenth century, 1848 across Europe, the wave of struggles at the end of the First World War, mid-century resistance to German and Japanese fascism, postwar anti-colonial revolutions, the movements of 1989 or those of 2011 among others. It is more widely agreed *that* such waves happen than *how* we can understand or theorize them, or even *which* cases can be identified as waves and which countries should be included.

It is probably uncontentious, however, to say that all these waves were geographically uneven: they were strongest and most successful in particular global regions, and in particular countries within these—while typically being connected, and watched, far beyond. Part of what a wave such as "1968" means is that ideas developed in the struggles of one country could be picked up in another country, often sooner than they might otherwise have arrived, and sometimes find a ready audience. These same processes also often operated within individual countries, between the "advanced metropolis" and small-town or rural settings and conservative regions. The temporalities of women's or gay and lesbian struggles, for example, bear witness to this "uneven and combined development."

One of the challenges in thinking the "Global 1960s" is that in casting the net as widely as possible, it can become very difficult to adequately theorize what were in reality highly heterogeneous events. Movements may have broken out at roughly the same time on every continent, and many of their leaders may have been fully aware of events elsewhere, some even expressing shared aims, but this wave of contestation was not remotely uniform.

Certainly national historical conditions were radically different in the 1960s. The United States, the wealthiest country on the planet, had little in common with Cambodia, where over 80 percent of the population worked as rice farmers. Iran, where a monarch drew on oil revenues to pursue a

2. Ruth Wilson Gilmore, *Golden Gulag: Prisons, Surplus, Crisis, and Opposition in Globalizing California* (Berkeley and Los Angeles: University of California Press, 2007), 24.

modernization program from above, was very different from Angola, a Portuguese settler colony in the throes of a national liberation struggle. The People's Republic of China, engulfed as it was by the Cultural Revolution, shared little with Brazil, which fell to military dictatorship in this decade.

As a result of these tremendous differences, the struggles that unfolded in these countries were unsurprisingly also very different. In some places, like West Germany, many young people criticized what they perceived to be an over-industrialized, consumer-saturated economy, a world of abundance, but also one of emptiness and alienation; in South Yemen, by contrast, many people fought to industrialize in the first place. In Vietnam, militants rallied behind the banner of nationalism in their struggle to unite the country; by contrast, in other countries like Britain, many radicals, even those actively supporting the Vietnamese revolution, criticized the very idea of the nation-state. In the United States, some feminists sought to overturn the traditional family, gender roles, and heteronormativity in the 1970s; but in Laos, many women rallied around the family as something to be defended from imperialist violence.

This is not to say there were no links between these struggles, only that they were fundamentally different, and should be approached as such. This sharp diversity makes it difficult to understand what was so global about the 1960s. The more countries one includes in the survey, the more generalized, reductive, and ultimately unhelpful the analysis risks becoming. Too few, and we return to nationally-bounded historiographies that erase the global entirely. To move from description to explanation, analysis, and theorization, one must draw certain boundaries that help explain the global while still taking into account differences in specific contexts.

The Global North

There is another, and more material, reason for establishing boundaries— the impossibility of complete coverage. This book, to our knowledge the first of its kind, surveys a dozen countries and nine languages. This was a major effort for a three-person international, multilingual, and interdisciplinary editorial team, and no doubt we have our own blind spots. To reach beyond this to 24 countries, to say nothing of the whole world, would have required a doubling of editors, pages, cost, and production time.

For that reason, we have decided to narrow our scope to what is sometimes called the Global North. Of course, such a move is not without its problems. It seems to reorient the discussion back to North America and Western Europe precisely when the newest scholarship is uncovering lesser-known histories in Africa, Latin America, and Asia. To be sure, in limiting our analysis to the Global North, we are not saying this region is more important than others. Quite the contrary, some of the most trans-formative changes of the time occured not in North America or Europe, but in what is today called the Global South. In fact, in this book we argue that it was precisely the anti-colonial, anti-imperialist struggles in Africa, Asia, and Latin America that made possible the radical 1960s in the Global North. Struggles in what was then called the "Third World" generated new ideas, proposed different models, and acted as sources of inspiration.

We do not see the Global North as standing in for the rest of the world, but only as one of many, more or less, coherent, parts of that world. If we have selected the Global North, and not some other conceptual region, it is partly because it is the piece of the puzzle we are most familiar with. Our sincere hope is that others, with greater familiarity with the long 1968 in other parts of the world, will publish their own collections surveying these different pieces.

The concept of the Global North is far from perfect. In mapping patterns onto the globe, it tends to solidify boundaries that are in reality far more porous. There are, for example, countries in the southern hemisphere, like Australia, that would rightly belong in this category, while there are others in the northern hemisphere, such as North Korea, that do not. Moreover, it is well known that the division between North and South is not only traversed by innumerable transnational flows of objects, ideas, and people, but that there are, in a sense, pockets of the Global South in the Global North. The North, in other words, is neither separate, nor homogenous.

Nevertheless, we still find value in the Global North here as a working concept. Despite its limitations, it allows us to group together distinct experiences in a way that makes possible broader theorizations about the long 1968. In spite of their differences, the countries here share similar core features. In general, they are relatively wealthy, even if that wealth is unevenly distributed between and within them. Compared to most countries in the Global South in the 1960s and 1970s, the standard of living in the North was higher, populations were healthier, and infrastructure generally more developed. All the countries boasted comparatively robust consumer societies, even those non-capitalist countries in Central, Eastern, and Southeastern Europe, which at the time were collectively were known as the "East." Moreover, these countries all had relatively stable states, most of them exercising considerable international power, at least compared to the majority of states in the Global South. Lastly, although most were products of colonialism, none of these countries were transitioning out of direct colonial rule in the 1960s, something that radically distinguishes them from most other countries experiencing turmoil at this time. As a result of these common structural characteristics, the causes of discontent, the nature of the movements, and their trajectories shared meaningful similarities.

Not only did these countries share analogous conditions, most were ordered within the same international networks of power. American hegemony brought together North America, much of Western Europe, and Japan through a series of dense economic, cultural, political, and above all, military linkages, creating a kind of chain of advanced capitalist countries. In this period, many of those countries tended to trade more with each other than with the Global South. Likewise, Soviet hegemony brought together much of the "East" into its own competing internationalist chain. As a result, developments in one link could more easily reverberate across the entire chain. Furthermore, the Iron Curtain did not completely separate these two competing chains from one another. Indeed, social, economic, cultural, and even political relations between the two not only existed, but were in fact deepening over the course of the 1960s and 1970s. In the 1960s, the U.S.S.R. began importing American grain, East and West Germany drew closer together, and the two superpowers moved toward what would later be called be called détente. Because of these ever-denser linkages, people living in different countries, even those located in rival blocs, became much more aware of developments elsewhere. This, in addition to comparable structural features, helps explain why movements spread so rapidly in the 1960s and 1970s.

Of course, there are always important outliers. Japan, for example, is the only country in Asia included in this book. And yet, despite its distinct history, Japan had much in common with Western Europe: an imperial past, strong economic growth, representative democracy, and a vibrant consumer society that even surpassed some countries in Europe. And it was also, like Western Europe, brought into the same international order by American hegemony.

Mexico also differs in some respects from the other countries documented here. North American, but also squarely in Latin America; wealthy by the standards of the Global South, but not as much as the other countries in the North; sovereign for well over a century, but still subjected to imperialism. Yet here, too, Mexico experienced many of the same patterns of development, from economic growth to urbanization, the generation gap to consumerism, and gave rise to a range of movements that were profoundly similar to those taking shape elsewhere.

Northern Ireland represents another anomaly: the Irish Revolution had produced an independent, post-colonial state in the South while partition of the island left a Protestant, British-identifying majority in the North. The Catholic minority, discriminated against on ethno-religious grounds, saw themselves as under alien rule. The contradictions between membership of the UK (developments in welfare and education) and internal colonial relations within the Northern state would explode dramatically in these years.

Perhaps the two greatest outliers in this collection are Yugoslavia and Czechoslovakia. Neither were capitalist, neither were liberal democracies, and neither of them could be counted as an American ally. Admittedly, the differences here are sharp enough to warrant separate treatment, but there are enough parallels to justify their inclusion in this reader. This is especially true for Yugoslavia, which did not follow the Stalinist model, was not a member of the Warsaw Pact, enjoyed great independence on the international stage, and was the most Western-oriented country in the East. The same postwar trends seen in the other countries took hold here, and the movements of the 1960s shared much in common as well—intellectual ferment, antiwar sentiment, countercultural experimentation, internationalism, critique of capitalism, student revolt, university occupations, and attempted worker-student unity were all core features of Yugoslavia's 1968.

Czechoslovakia is the most distinct case. A state dominated by a single Communist Party, firmly aligned with the U.S.S.R., attempting to follow the Soviet path to communism. Here, the movement looked quite different, taking the form of a reformist push within the ruling Communist Party. Nevertheless, similarities can still be observed. Before 1948, Czechoslovakia had been culturally, socially, and economically integrated with the rest of Europe. Many Czechoslovak citizens continued to see themselves as such, with some scoffing at the term "Eastern European," pointing out that Prague was further west than Vienna. Additionally, Czechoslovakia experienced some of the same historical developments as its Western European neighbors, such as consumerism. In fact, in the 1960s there were more television sets per capita in Czechoslovakia than in France. Lastly, the Prague Spring, although different, unfolded in the same conceptual space as other countries in the Global North, and did share some similar elements.

In other words, there are still sharp differences even within this category of the Global North, but they contribute to the larger project of trying to understand the long 1968. Similarities across distinct contexts can allow us to discern the essential from the contingent; but so, too, can differences. This is the strength of historical and comparative analysis.[3]

Causes of Discontent

The wave of political unrest that rocked the Global North in the late 1960s seemed to come from nowhere. At first glance, the 1960s was a decade of

---

3. It goes without saying that even within these parameters there were many other countries that could have been included in this reader, and whose differences could have further enriched this collection. Unfortunately, for pragmatic reasons, it was not possible for us to go beyond a dozen countries in a single volume. Our hope is that they, too, will receive the proper scholarly treatment in years ahead.

relative prosperity, especially when compared to the horrors of the 1930s and 1940s. In North America, Western Europe, Japan, and even Central, Eastern and Southeastern Europe, standards of living were higher than ever, governments seemed stable, and a sense of optimism filled the air. Why, then, did so many people take to the streets at the same time?

The international context was of decisive importance. The Cold War, decolonization, the rise of new nation-states, and "hot" wars in Latin America, Africa, and Asia created a highly charged atmosphere. The single most important international development was the wave of anti-colonial revolutions that broke out after the Second World War. By the 1950s, much of Asia had won independence. In 1955, the newly independent countries met in Bandung, Indonesia to promote economic, cultural, and social cooperation. Soon after, national liberation movements made headway in Africa. By the early 1960s, dozens of countries across the world were either about to begin, were in the middle of, or were just coming out of revolutions of some kind.

But decolonization did not simply happen "out there," in the Global South. Decolonization struggles helped shape the political horizons in the Global North—in some cases, like France and later Portugal, they even brought down governments. They radicalized young people in imperialist countries, giving future activists their first experience with politics. Decolonization became a major source of ideas, with the writings of figures like Frantz Fanon, Che Guevara, or Võ Nguyên Giáp circulating across the globe. Immigrants from the Global South, especially students, injected a degree of radicalism into domestic movements in the North. Most importantly, struggles abroad served as an incredible source of inspiration, proving that revolutions were still possible, that people could still change the world.

The 1960s saw several revolutions in particular that inspired hope in the possibility of a new world. The Cuban Revolution, which seemed to hold the promise of a fresh path to socialism, distinct from the Soviet model. Young activists across the world looked to the Cuban example, with many traveling to the island to see the revolution firsthand. The Algerian Revolution, which led to independence in 1962, similarly captured the imagination, with Algeria styling itself as a kind of "mecca of revolution." Lastly, the "Great Proletarian Cultural Revolution" in China also seemed to present a new kind of socialist revolution. This perception was made possible in part because few people abroad had any deep familiarity with the events in China, and so could project their desires onto the revolution. But even still, specific ideas, images, and practices from China had great influence abroad. Maoism in particular emerged as a central reference point for activists in numerous countries, from the Black Panther Party in Oakland, California, which took to heart Mao Zedong's call to "serve the people," to student radicals in Paris, France, some of whom took up factory jobs to "become one with the people."

American imperialism was also a decisive factor in radicalizing people across the Global North. The United States emerged from the Second World War as the most powerful country on the planet, and took it upon itself to safeguard capitalism on a global scale, by whatever means necessary. This meant a string of assassinations, coups, and military incursions. The most important of these was the Vietnam War. Across the world, people condemned American aggression. What's more, antiwar activists often collaborated across borders, creating a new feeling of internationalism. For most people, especially in those capitalist countries formally allied with the United States, the Vietnam War was the central issue of the 1960s. Even in the "East," state-sanctioned antiwar demonstrations helped radicalize young people who would eventually use the opening to challenge their own governments for failing to live up to their emancipatory visions.

Solidarity with the Vietnamese, and the "Third World" more generally, was especially important for ethnic minorities in the Global North. In Canada, Québécois radicals drew inspiration from anti-imperialist movements abroad. In the United States, Black radicals argued that African Americans constituted an "internal colony" whose struggle for national liberation was an integral part of the anti-colonial revolutions. The Black struggle in turn inspired activists in Northern Ireland, who faced similar kinds of ethnic discrimination and state violence at home. Across territories known as Canada and Greenland, Indigenous peoples would forge "Fourth World" transnational solidarity.

In these years, the countries of the "West" and the "East" faced equally serious domestic crises. The unparalleled economic boom of the postwar period had rested on competing variants of "organized modernity," in which the—usually national—state took on a central economic role involving more or less formal arrangements with hierarchically organized interest groups, typically employers' federations and trade unions. The outcome, along with an unprecedented economic boom, was a broadly technocratic distributive politics, in which both direct financial gains and an indirect "social wage"—in education, health, housing, social welfare, and broader economic development—were available in particular to "insider groups" of various kinds.

Despite such unparalleled growth, affluence eluded outsiders. In the United States, African Americans were treated as second class citizens, often the last hired and the first fired. Despite strong welfare states across the Global North, and their lofty rhetoric of progress, poverty persisted, which led some to think twice about the welfare state as the privileged vehicle of emancipation.

Moreover, even those who enjoyed the fruits of the affluent society were often left with a bitter taste in their mouths. While there were more commodities on the shelves for those who could afford them, the economic boom did not give way to personal liberation: its rewards were narrowly redistributive—offering physical and economic security after the Great Depression and Second World War—but excluded questions of power and culture. Thus many people who lived through the 1960s recall everyday life in all these countries as constricting, repetitive, and conformist. Women could not wear jeans, men had to keep their hair short, premarital sex was taboo, students had to dress formally, strict standards governed interpersonal relationships. Many lacked a language to explain why they felt so bad amidst such plenty. But others diagnosed their society as boring, unfree, bereft of all adventure, and created rebellious subcultures in the late 1950s and early 1960s—the Mods, Rockers, Beats, Provos, Situationists, etc.

The rapidly expanding consumer culture played an ambiguous role in this regard. On the one hand, it provided those who were dissatisfied with the stifling mainstream culture the means to express their individuality. On the other hand, it left many others feeling empty. Increasingly, some people, especially the youth, felt the new consumer society was in fact amplifying the conformity of everyday life. Tormented by existential angst, they sought meaning, discovery, fulfilment, a sense of purpose. This feeling was most prevalent in wealthier capitalist countries, but anxiety over consumerism could even be felt in a country like the Socialist Federal Republic of Yugoslavia.

Dissatisfaction with the stuffiness of everyday life and concerns about consumerism were matched by disquiet over the political sphere. In most countries in the Global North, people felt the political process was blocked. In the East, a single Communist Party firmly controlled all political life. But variants of authoritarianism took root elsewhere, as single parties, almost always conservative, dominated politics in many countries throughout this period. In France, General Charles de Gaulle, who came to power in a coup of sorts, ruled in a semi-authoritarian manner from 1958 to 1969. In Japan, the conservative Liberal Democratic Party would govern continuously from 1955 to 1993. In Italy, the right-wing Christian Democrats would govern from 1946 to 1994. In Mexico, the Institutional Revolutionary Party held power uninterruptedly from 1929 until 2000. Even when ruling parties were challenged, they sometimes formed coalitions with the opposition in a way that foreclosed outside pressure. In West Germany, for example, in 1966 the ruling Christian Democratic Union simply entered into a Grand Coalition with the Social Democrats, giving them the vast majority of the seats in the legislature. For all the talk of democracy, many of these countries appeared profoundly undemocratic.

Even when the democratic process seemed open, mainstream parties often failed to deliver. In the United States, Canada, and Britain, liberal and social democratic parties promising change won elections in the early 1960s. In some cases, they did in fact put forward a progressive legislative agenda: the Great Society in the United States, or the reforms of the Labour Party in Britain and the Liberal Party in Canada. But while they raised expectations, these parties fell short. But while they raised expectations, these parties fell short, and their programs were littered with glaring contradictions, not least of which was the contrast between championing social uplift at home while pursuing, or actively supporting, imperialist war abroad.

In Czechoslovakia and Yugoslavia, the Party leadership initiated a series of reforms in the 1960s that liberalized life in these countries but either did not go far enough or created new problems. In Yugoslavia, liberalization of the economy was not only not paralleled by democratic liberalization, but contributed to growing wealth inequality. This points to one of the core dynamics of the period in all the countries surveyed here: the contradiction between the optimistic and triumphalist rhetoric of modernizing governments in the 1960s and the realities on the ground, a tension that generated significant discontent.

This reflected a broader crisis: Soviet-style communism and social democracy had both, in many countries, won power, and in others had achieved a substantial impact, with conservative states such as the United States or France forced to adopt substantial parts of the redistributive agenda. The results—in terms of poverty reduction, economic development, and other social benefits—were not negligible, but "actually-existing socialism," as the politics of Soviet-style states were often called, was no longer a utopia even for those who desperately wanted to move beyond actually-existing capitalism or actually-existing social democracy. The limitations—imperial and military entanglements abroad, continuing class inequalities, racism and patriarchy, various kinds of internal repression and stifling culture—increasingly undermined the credibility of both social-democratic and Stalinist political horizons.

Indeed, the state itself was starting to experience a wider crisis across the Global North as the repository for popular hopes for change. The nation-state as a central motor of economic development, and hence the privileged focus of strategies for radical social transformation, defined a particular historical period. By the late 1960s, with the economic ideologues whose neoliberalism would later justify a radical change of course sharpening their knives, these arrangements were starting to experience a slowing of growth and a blocking of employment opportunities in some sectors, with greater internationalization of trade and production. Although it was not visible directly at the time, the economic basis of these political orders was weakening, in what would later prove to be a terminal crisis.

Few countries possessed effective channels for capturing this new surge of discontent. Internationally, the Soviet Union, which seemed more concerned with achieving détente with the United States than fomenting world revolution, ceased to be a meaningful model for most radicals. In the "East," there were no legal alternatives. In North America, Western Europe, and Japan, ostensibly radical political forces like the Communist Parties appeared to accommodate themselves to the new postwar order. Two of the largest non-ruling Communist Parties in the Global North, the French and the Italian, both moderated their approach, prioritizing the electoral road to power. In most countries, trade union leaderships, some with radical pasts, worked to maintain the peace at all costs, even if it meant clamping down on worker militancy. In this context, the more institutionalized left, which had served as a kind of safety valve, became increasingly discredited.

To be sure, many leaders of the movements of the 1960s came from this organized left. Some had family who fought in earlier movements, such as the social movements of the 1930s or the anti-fascist resistance in or before the Second World War, and transmitted those radical experiences to new generations. Others belonged to union families, where activism and solidarity were a part of daily life. Still others had joined Communist youth groups, where they learned crucial skills. Yet the moderation, limits, even ossification, of what they would soon call the "Old Left" led many of these "red diaper babies" to take what they had learned and search for new alternatives.

A Diversity of Voices

Although activists from all backgrounds took to politics in the 1960s, the main drivers of protest were often the youth. In the years following the end of the Second World War, the birth rate skyrocketed across the Global North. In France, by 1967 one person in three was under 20 years old. Not only were there more young people, they saw themselves as a unique social group. They believed they lived in an entirely different world from their parents, and in many countries they used clothing, music, and language to accentuate that line of demarcation. Over the course of the 1960s, a distinct youth identity began to emerge—an identity, it should be noted, that was increasingly commodified by firms who suddenly had access to an unprecedented "youth market."

More children also meant more university students. In Italy, the student population increased from 268,000 in 1960 to over half a million in 1968. The problem, however, was that in many countries, universities were simply unprepared to absorb the flood of students. Dorm rooms were cramped, facilities obsolete, classrooms overcrowded. Students rarely interacted with their professors. The student to faculty ratio was abysmal. As a stopgap measure, universities hired assistants, who were often poorly trained, and made little money. The university system was highly archaic, effectively run along feudal lines. The curriculum was outdated. Professors droned on for hours on end. Students had almost no say in the curriculum, teaching methods, university operations, or disciplinary matters.

While more students were entering higher education, in many countries few actually finished. Examinations were incredibly difficult, students had little access to extra help, and the curriculum was designed to weed them out. The result was a staggering dropout rate. In France, 25 percent of university students would not even make it to the end of their first year. In Italy, in the mid-1960s, more than half of all university students would drop out.

University life was also extremely restrictive. In some countries, students were forbidden to move furniture or pin posters on walls. Men's and women's dormitories were often kept strictly separate, and students could be suspended for cohabitation. Students were often barred from engaging in political activities on campus.

State governments and university administrators recognized these problems, but their attempts at reform often made them worse. In Italy, educational reforms sought to fix overcrowding by simply limiting the number of students who could attend university in the first place. In France, the government tried to replace archaic curriculums with hypermodern ones geared toward producing technicians who could manage a modern economy. This only further infuriated students, who felt that the reforms would turn the university into a factory, training students to become cogs in a machine.

Paradoxically, the universities also gave students the very skills they used to critique not only the university, but society as a whole. We can see this most clearly with the spectacular rise of the humanities and social sciences. For example, in France, the percentage of students majoring in the humanities and social sciences increased from 32 percent in 1945 to 65 percent by 1962. They learned how to analyze texts, write clearly and convincingly, make arguments and debate, speak publicly, and to criticize social phenomena. In short, the university gave a whole generation of young, discontented people valuable, critical tools that would eventually be turned against mainstream society itself. Not coincidentally, many of the activist leaders in the countries surveyed here were humanities or social sciences majors or postgraduates.

Underpinning this critical energy was a Marxist revival. As people turned a critical eye toward society, they tried to understand the causes of the problems around them: war, poverty, racism, exploitation, existential malaise, persistent inequality, and, at the behest of women, sexism. Increasingly, they began to argue that these problems stemmed not from mistaken policies, or a few bad individuals, but from a larger "system." It was in their quest to understand this "system" that some activists turned to Marxism, which promised to not only explain the "system," but to help them change it. This was true not only in capitalist countries, but also those countries in the East, where activists couched their critique of the People's Democracies in the language of Marxism. It is precisely in this context that many countries saw an outpouring of innovative Marxist theoretical production that breathed new life into old ideas, broke ground on new problems, and reimagined Marxism itself in what soon became known as a "New Left."

It should be said that the majority of young people at this time were not students, and that student radicals themselves were an extreme minority in every country, sometimes less than one percent of the entire national student population. Nevertheless, they exercised influence beyond their numbers. Radical students made up for their small size with an almost fanatical devotion to the cause. They mobilized around issues, like poor university conditions, that resonated even with students who did not agree with their radical politics. Most importantly, they were assisted by administrative incompetence, or more likely, repression. In a classic cycle seen in many countries at this time, student radicals would stage an action, sometimes deliberately provocative; the university, or the police, would overreact; and then the repression would generate sympathy for the radicals. Because of police repression, those who were indifferent might become sympathetic, those who were sympathetic might join the activists the next time, and those who were already activists would grow even more radical. This cycle of provocation and repression expanded outward, in some cases drawing in other social forces. In this way, student struggles could help detonate larger struggles outside the university.

But students were by no means the only ones engaging in politics in the 1960s. What made this period so explosive was precisely the participation of other social forces. One of the most important of these groups was the workers. After the Second World War, many countries in the Global North codified some version of the Fordist compromise: the bosses pledged high wages, strong benefits, and good working conditions, while the unions promised to keep the working class in line. The result was relative peace in the 1950s. In Italy the number of working hours lost to strikes dropped from 64 million in 1948 to 22 million in 1958. But for a number of reasons, which varied from country to country, that compromise began to collapse over the course of the 1960s, resulting in a resurgence of working class militancy. In many of the countries surveyed here, sabotage, strikes, occupations, and violent battles with police became almost commonplace in the late 1960s and early 1970s. In some cases, class struggle reached serious proportions. In

May 1968, a general strike of around nine million workers crippled France. In the fall of 1969, over half a million workers went on strike in Italy. In 1970, about three million workers participated in nearly 6,000 strikes in the United States. In 1972, Britain experienced a similar strike wave, which became known as the Glorious Summer.

Even during the events of 1968 a myth emerged that all workers were acting spontaneously, breaking with their unions to take matters into their own hands. While it is no doubt true that many active workers were critical of their union leaderships, and that there was a surge in autonomous actions, militants with union experience, especially at the grassroots level, were often key instigators of actions. Indeed, the 1960s saw the emergence of progressive initiatives from within some of the very institutions that were seen as part of the problem. This is most clearly observed in countries like Czechoslovakia and Yugoslavia, where many of those calling for change were in fact card-carrying members of the Communist Party. The problem here was not perceived to be communism but rather the authorities' failure to deliver on the promises of communism.

Ethnic minorities, oppressed nationalities, Indigenous peoples, racialized peoples, and immigrants also played vital roles in the political ferment of the 1960s. None of the countries surveyed in this collection were socially homogeneous. All were home to minorities who faced discrimination of some kind, although that oppression took different forms. In some countries, like the United States and Northern Ireland, racial or ethnic discrimination was enshrined formally. In others, like Italy, internal migrants from the South were often racialized. In all countries, immigrants faced considerable obstacles, especially those who migrated not from other countries of the Global North, but came from the South, practiced different religions, and happened to have darker skin.

In colonial states, especially in North America, Indigenous peoples who had survived near-extermination continued to face oppression. In Canada, Indigenous peoples had not only lived through the sordid history of residential schools, which forcibly removed Indigenous children from their communities, but after World War II they experienced what was later called the "Sixties Scoop," or the accelerated adoption of Indigenous children into white, middle-class families in Canada and abroad, often involuntarily. Similarly, although on a much smaller scale, the Danish state had in 1951 sent a group of Greenlandic Inuit children to Denmark in order to make them into "little Danes" as part of an effort to modernize Greenland.

In response to these conditions, Indigenous people and other ethnic minorities formed new movements. For example, in Greenland, a part of the Danish Realm, Greenlanders called for "Development in Greenland on Greenlandic terms," and eventually won "home rule," but not full independence, in 1979. In fact, in a few countries, it was the struggles of minorities that kicked off the movements of the time. In the United States, the civil rights movement acted as a kind of "borning struggle" for other movements.[4] In Canada, revived nationalist sentiment in Québec radicalized activists. In Czechoslovakia, pressure from Slovaks helped initiate the "Action Program" of 1968. In Italy, migrant workers from the South launched some of the most militant early actions. These struggles all took different forms, and were in fact internally divided over tactics and goals. Some wanted better integration with the existing system. Others, especially in the East, sought federalization. Still others called for outright secession. Whatever their aims, these efforts all were informed by and contributed to the contestatory wave of the period.

The political explosions of the 1960s would have never happened, and never reached the levels they did, without women's activism. Women not only participated in every movement, they pushed the limits of activism by pointing to forms of oppression, like sexism, that were not only ignored by existing movements, but were in fact continually reproduced by them. Indeed, despite the little attention it received in most movements of the 1960s, sexism pervaded nearly all aspects of life in every country surveyed here.

The patriarchal impositions of marriage remained largely intact. In many countries, divorce was still not considered a basic right. In Italy, where the Catholic Church exerted great influence, divorce remained illegal until 1970. In those countries where it was legal, like Canada, it came with heavy restrictions, such as proof of cruelty or adultery. In very few places did women have the right to "no fault divorce," that is to say, the right to dissolve a marriage based on agreement, without having to show proof of wrongdoing. Women also enjoyed very little autonomy over their own bodies. In many countries, the contraceptive pill became legally available only over the course of the 1960s. Abortion was also illegal across most of North America and Western Europe. It would become legal in Great Britain only in 1967, in the United States in 1973, in France in 1975, and in West Germany in 1976, and even then, often came with strict conditions, like doctor's opinions, waiting periods, and so forth.

Women also faced considerable discrimination with regards to employment opportunities. After World War II, when women in many countries did work in large numbers outside the home, they were increasingly forced back into domestic roles. Depending on one's class, those who did work outside the home either found employment in manufacturing, especially textiles, or were relegated to so-called "feminine jobs," like teachers, nurses, typists,

---

4.   Bernice J. Reagon, "A Borning Struggle," *New Directions* 7, no. 3 (April 1980): 14.

housekeepers, or office assistants. Many occupations remained virtually closed off to women. In the United States, for example, although women represented one-third of the workforce in 1960, they only made up 3.5 percent of all lawyers, 6.8 percent of doctors, and 4.2 percent of physicists. And when men and women did work the same jobs, women consistently earned less than their male counterparts.

In addition, women had minimal formal political representation. Not a single country surveyed in this collection had a female head of government. Men dominated most cabinet positions, judicial appointments, and national legislatures. Even in the "East," which made greater strides toward women's equality, there were few women in positions of power in the government or the Communist Party.

Furthermore, women everywhere faced everyday sexism. Young girls were discouraged from playing certain sports. Schoolgirls in many countries were repeatedly told by their teachers not to pursue higher education, and especially in the sciences. Women were expected to speak a certain way, act a certain way, and look a certain way. Men rarely shared the household labor. On top of all this, women experienced sexual harassment, domestic violence, and rape, which were often tolerated by those in power. In the United States, most states did not include marital rape in their definitions of rape until the 1970s.

In those countries where consumerism was relatively developed, the new age of affluence actually contributed to women's oppression. In many cases, consumerism did not guarantee happiness, but created a generation of lonely, unfulfilled, and dehumanized women, a story most powerfully captured by Betty Friedan's famous 1963 book, *The Feminine Mystique.*

Many women, especially working-class women, lesbian women, and women of color, criticized this image of women's oppression, and the groups that upheld it, arguing that they only represented the travails of a small minority of wealthy, white women. Indeed, women's oppression and potential liberation was experienced very differently not only within the same country, but especially across different regions. For example, women's legal rights, such as the right to an abortion, were considerably more advanced in the People's Democracies of the "East." These states often provided childcare, instituted sex education in schools, and offered extra support for single mothers, widows, and divorcées. In Czechoslovakia, sexologists conducted extensive research into women's sexuality, particularly about the female orgasm, and publicly encouraged equality in the bedroom. Nevertheless, across the board, women were generally treated as second class citizens in the 1960s and 1970s.

What would launch the women's movement, however, was not only a reaction to pervasive sexism in contemporary society, but the fact that the very movements that emerged to challenge that society hypocritically reproduced this kind of sexism. Women were present in every movement, in every country. But they often did not feel entirely at home. The mundane tasks, or what some women later called "the shit work," seemed to always fall to them. Their proposals were frequently shot down by men. And they often faced casual sexism, and even sexual violence, in movement spaces. Women in almost every context surveyed here reported experiencing this anguishing contradiction. They came to realize that "frying the steak of a revolutionary took as much time as frying the steak of a reactionary."[5] It is from this tension that women's liberation would emerge. Fed up with "making tea for the revolution," they decided to make their own revolution within the revolution.

Other groups, like non-heterosexuals, also spoke out at this time. All the countries in this reader were deeply homophobic in the 1950s and 1960s. Lesbians, gays and other non-heterosexuals faced discrimination in housing, employment, and before the law. The age of consent, for example, was higher for gays than for heterosexuals in places like Britain and France. In other countries, like the United States, anti-sodomy laws in several states punished non-heterosexuals with fines, disenfranchisement, or even prison sentences. In a few, sexual acts between men was an outright criminal act. In West Germany, for example, nearly 50,000 gay men were sent to prison between 1945 and 1969. In this context, and taking inspiration from other movements unfolding at the time, activists in several countries launched robust gay liberation movements to challenge the existing state of things.

In short, the long 1968 proved so explosive in part because a range of related, but distinct struggles came together at roughly the same time. This was also a time when many activists, especially women, people of color, and gays and lesbians, tried to re-theorize the relationships between different kinds of oppressions in order to bring about more thorough revolutionary change. But while many activists passed through different movements, their movements shared similar reference points, and the struggles of the time often inspired one another, they were not always on the best of terms. Tensions abounded between, and often within various social groups. Unity was not a given, but had to be constructed. Failing to do so would mean that instead of creating a common wave of contestation, activists would be left with hundreds of isolated, dispersed currents. The single greatest question of the 1960s and 1970s was the following: how could activists build unity between these different struggles all while respecting their diverse origins, needs, and goals?

---

5. Jan-Werner Müller, *Contesting Democracy: Political Ideas in Twentieth-Century Europe* (New Haven: Yale University Press, 2011), 198.

Transnational Connections

As so many observers have commented, what made the 1960s and 1970s so remarkable was the fact that contestation was so widespread. The activism of the period took a global form not only because of shared structural factors, parallel developments, or even similar social forces in different countries, but because of a shared sense of unity across borders. Activists in these countries created a rich network of transnational connections that pulled these different movements onto the same imagined plane.

In fact, this period is almost unparalleled in the sheer density of international linkages, real and imagined. This was not only because common structural features made different societies intelligible to one another, but because all these countries were deeply embedded in larger international relations, fusing their fates to those of other countries. If activists could think so transnationally, it was because the international order had become so much more deeply interconnected.

The events of the long 1968 thus took place at a time when international exchange had been made easier than ever before. The 1960s was the decade in which the word "globalization" entered general dictionaries.[6] In the same decade, media theorist Marshall McLuhan coined the term "global village" in order to describe a world that was increasingly shrinking through new information and communication technologies. Indeed, 1968 has been described as "the first global rebellion."[7]

Transnational networks of sounds, images, objects, commodities, and people allowed activists in the 1960s to build a shared set of references. Music, for example, spread rapidly across borders. Electric guitars became coveted commodities, American and British records found their way into every country, and musicians adapted the new sound for their own needs, creating French blues, Mexican rock and roll, or Czech psychedelia. Fashion also served as a kind of glue, with blue jeans, for example, becoming an international signifier of youth culture.

Above all, images could capture an international audience. Che Guevara, for instance, could be spotted on political leaflets, dorm room walls, or in demonstrations everywhere, becoming a universal symbol of revolt. The well-known photo, taken by Cuban photographer Alberto Korda in 1960, was popularized by Italian leftist publisher Giangiacomo Feltrinelli in the

6. Paul James and Manfred B. Steger, "A Genealogy of 'Globalization': The Career of a Concept," *Globalizations* 11, no. 4 (2014): 418.
7. Wolfgang Kraushaar cited in Martin Klimke and Mary Nolan, "Introduction: The Globalization of the Sixties," *The Routledge Handbook of the Global Sixties: Between Protest and Nation-Building*, eds. Chen Jian et al. (New York: Routledge, 2018), 1.

context of Che's killing in Bolivia. Irish radical artist Jim Fitzpatrick created the famous two-tone print and distributed thousands free. By 1971 the image was so iconic that the British Gay Liberation Front, for example, could beautify Che with red lipstick and turquoise eye shadow on the cover of a December 1971 issue of *Ink* magazine.

Figure 0.1   Jim Fitzpatrick's classic Che Guevara
poster. 1968. By kind permission of Jim Fitzpatrick.

Then there was print culture. Periodicals and publishing houses like *New Left Review* in Britain and *Monthly Review* in the United States, or Wagenbach in West Germany, Maspero in France, and Feltrinelli in Italy, made radical ideas accessible to a new audience by resurrecting older texts, translating foreign works, or introducing new theories from the Global South. It is certainly an exaggeration to say everyone was reading the same texts, but activists did share common reference points. Few of these were more famous, or infamous, than Mao Zedong's *Little Red Book*, millions of copies of which flooded the Global North in the 1960s and early 1970s, in some cases creating shared political language.

In fact, while activists were linguistically divided over the course of the 1960s, many did adopt a kind of lingua franca: Marxism. Of course, not everyone was a Marxist, but many activists became familiar with core Marxist concepts. At a conference, not everyone could speak Japanese, or French, or German, but they knew what the capitalist mode of production, imperialism, or the working class were—or at least they thought they did. This perception of a shared language of revolution, despite the various dialects of Trotskyism, Maoism, and so forth, further contributed to this sense of internationalism.

Nearly instantaneous communication helped activists not only stay connected to current events, but to learn from one another. Tracts from one context were translated into another. Movements in one country, like Black Power in the United States, the student movement in Germany, the May events in France, or Prague Spring in Czechoslovakia, could become international sources of inspiration. In some cases, these technologies allowed activists to directly coordinate their actions. This is most commonly seen in the antiwar movement, where activists in different countries would deliberately synchronize their demonstrations. The famous October 21, 1967 antiwar march on the Pentagon, for example, was supported by massive demonstrations in over a dozen other countries on the same day.

Lastly, thanks to cheaper transportation, activists could meet one another face to face. In Western Europe, activists traveled extensively by car, bus, and train. In other contexts, they made good use of cheap airfare. In fact, the 1960s saw a boom in commercial air travel. In Japan, for example, the number of Japanese traveling overseas increased from just 120,000 in 1960 to nearly one million in 1970. This movement of bodies helped solidify transnational ties. Immigrant workers, students, and intellectuals brought their own political traditions with them, while bringing back home what they learned while abroad. Travel also made possible international conferences, like the famous Vietnam Conference in Berlin in February 1968, the International People's Conference against War and for Social Change in Tokyo in August 1968, the Congress of Black Writers in Montréal in October 1968, or the Indochinese Women's Conferences in Vancouver and Toronto in 1971, to name only a few.

All these linkages created a palpable sense of unity, a feeling that all the struggles were in some way connected. But this sentiment could be ambiguous. On the one hand, it kept activists informed about what was happening elsewhere, led to actual collaborations, and helped exemplary struggles proliferate. Activists from nearly all the major movements of the time—antiwar, student, workers', women's, to name only a few—not only took inspiration, but learned from one another, in some cases increasing their collective power. International antiwar activism played a significant if still debated role in constraining the options of the White House, while international outrage at Unionist violence in Northern Ireland made a

difference. Italian communists acted in solidarity with their Czechoslovak comrades, while French and German activists shared experiences and
debates. In some cases, activists even tried to merge their struggles. As a
poster from the Organization of Solidarity of the People of Asia, Africa and
Latin America (OSPAAAL) for the 1969 Day of International Solidarity
with the African-American People announced: "We Will Destroy Imperialism from the Outside. They Will Destroy it from the Inside."[8]

On the other hand, some activists had a tendency to project their desires
onto other struggles. In trying to translate examples from one context to
another, crucial differences were often collapsed, comparisons became
hyperbolic, and the hard work of building an organized, durable, and
functional unity of forces across borders often took the form of rhetorical
exclamations of support. As the Chicago police mercilessly beat protesters
outside the Democratic National Convention, for example, one activist
raised a sign that read, "Welcome to Prague," a reference to the Soviet
invasion of Czechoslovakia just a few days before. In both cases activists
were fighting against the forces of order, but Chicago 1968 was not Prague
1968. The problem was not just sloppy equivalences; exaggerated claims
of sameness could sometimes slide into orientalism—for example, when
antiwar radicals risked reducing living, breathing, dying Vietnamese into
one-dimensional symbols of their own visions. This kind of thinking made
it very hard to building the kind of unity that preserved, and respected, real
differences.

In short, the internationalism of the time was often contradictory. The
long 1968 showed that while imagined solidarities could lead to erasure,
appropriation, or self-glorification, they could also amplify struggles
globally. The struggles of the 1960s and 1970s raised huge questions about
whether there could be productive misreadings, whether exaggerations can
drive home a point, or if projections could enable more radical actions. At
the very least, they showed how awareness that a previously fixed social
structure had been challenged from below somewhere else was a powerful
source of hope and inspiration, not only between countries but within them.

The Movements of the 1960s and 1970s

The movements of the 1960s and 1970s were so heterogenous they defy any
simple categorization. Despite many parallels, differences between national
contexts could be stark. To take just one example, while student radicals
in Czechoslovakia fought for greater civil liberties, like the freedom of the
press, their peers in Japan sometimes decried these as a sham.

---

8. Cited in Chen Jian et al., eds., *The Routledge Handbook of the Global Sixties*, 13.

But even within the same country there were profound differences, between those committed to nonviolence and those advocating guerrilla war, between counterculturalists and hardened politicos, between anarchists and Marxist-Leninists. Even those adhering to the same broad traditions fought bitterly with each other, as the innumerable sectarian conflicts among Maoists or Trotskyist attest. For this reason, the 1960s and 1970s are often remembered in wildly contradictory ways. Depending on who you ask, this was the age of hippies or Maoists, students or workers, nonviolence or armed struggle, anti-imperialism or domestic reform, Stalinism or new social movements, or any combination of the above. There are, in other words, at least as many "1968s" as there were movements—and as many political projects evoking "1968" today.

Nevertheless, movements did share some core similarities, some of which were new. To begin with, to a degree unparalleled in earlier waves of contestation, the struggles of the 1960s and 1970s made visible oppressions that were often ignored by the organized left in many countries: in addition to exploitation at the workplace, for example, activists at the time pointed to racism, sexism, homophobia, or pollution. They pointed to different aspects of oppression, not just the legal, but the psychological. And activists, especially those in the women's and gay liberation movements, showed how oppression could exist in a variety of overlooked spaces, like the kitchen, the bedroom, or the doctor's office—indeed, *within* political organizations.

The struggles of the 1960s and 1970s are also unique because of the participation of so many diverse actors. All waves, all revolutions, require the coming together of different social forces, but in the past they have generally privileged some figures while excluding others. The same can be said about the 1960s, especially in the earlier years, but again, to a unique degree, the movements were blown wide open as new voices demanded to be heard. Of course, which social forces participated and when varied considerably from country to country—in some cases, for example, women's liberation came much later than others. But the condensation of so many distinct forces was a generally common feature of these movements.

The movements of the 1960s and 1970s also experimented with new organizational forms. While every country initially saw some of the same models—strict membership criteria, hierarchical organization, celebrity leaders, and so forth—activists soon set out to create more inclusive, flexible, dynamic groups. For many women in the women's liberation movement, doing politics meant not just going to meetings, but being part of a community, and feminist organizations tried to create a new kind of feminist sociability. For example, Danish Redstockings created "basis groups," safe spaces where women could not only organize, but forge genuine "sister solidarity."

Similarly, gay liberation groups, like the Homosexual Front for Revolutionary Action (FHAR) in France, eschewed the formalism of earlier movements, opting instead for a kind of anarchist principle of inclusion. As one FHAR text explained, "FHAR doesn't belong to anyone, it isn't anyone. It is only homosexuality on the march. All politically conscious homosexuals are FHAR: all discussion between two or three persons is FHAR. [...] Yes, we are a nebula of feelings and actions."[9] In Japan, the antiwar initiative Beheiren did not even see itself as a formal group, but a loose citizen's movement in which anyone could claim the name so long as they adhered to three slogans.

But organizational experimentation was not just limited to more libertarian or countercultural groups. Even some Marxist-Leninist or Maoist organizations began to shift their mode of operation, trying to fuse Leninist models with a kind of new social movement ethos. Consider, for example, how the Black Panther Party's concept of "survival pending revolution," combined a centralized organizational structure with a broad range of decentralized community initiatives, like the Free Breakfast for School Children Program.

Organizational experimentation went hand in hand with a kaleidoscopic variety of tactics. Activists in the long 1968 combined old tactics, like marches, sit-ins, occupations, sabotage, and strikes, with new ones, like teach-ins, consciousness raising, zapping, or experiments in communal living. Of special note was the emphasis on what has since been called "prefigurative politics," that is to say, the attempt to build the new world in the shell of the old.

Another common trend was the transformation of movements. In many countries, a self-conscious "New Left" displaced the Stalinist and Social Democratic "Old Left" in the 1960s. These New Left movements radicalized in the years leading up to 1968, and in the immediate aftermath of their defeats in the late 1960s, many of these New Left formations, like SDS in the United States, not only radicalized, but fractured, giving way to a frenzy of "Far Left" party-building in the late 1960s and early 1970s, in some ways creating new orthodoxies. As these "Far Left" groupuscules in turn declined, a host of new social movements, less radical and hierarchical, more focused on immediate needs or marginalized groups, grew. This is not to say that the same people went through all of these phases, or that each moment necessarily followed the other in linear fashion—in fact they often coexisted. Rather, there was a shifting center of gravity for activism as a whole, with different timings in different countries and regions. This complex situation

9.   Cited in Michael Sibalis, "Gay Liberation Comes to France: The Front Homosexuel d'Action Révolutionnaire (FHAR)," *French History and Civilization* 1 (2005): 274.

was an inevitable result both of how 1968 mobilized such large numbers, who were necessarily in different situations, and of the sometimes slower processes through which people learned to express previously silenced needs through struggle.

A final more or less common feature of struggles in the Global North at this time was a rethinking of the relationship to power, both within the state and within movements and organizations. Many countries had by this point seen a series of revolutions: national, liberal, democratic, anti-fascist, socialist—or taken elements of these agendas on board. The once-imagined "taking power" after which "everything would be different" was no longer, by 1968, a hypothetical future, but a known past or the familiar experience of another country—together with the dark sides of social-democratic imperialism, Soviet tanks, liberal hypocrisy on racism and poverty, the failure of parliamentary democracy to deliver popular rule,—and the patriarchal, heteronormative, ethnocentric and culturally conservative characteristics shared by all "actually-existing" post-revolutionary states.

While some activists still embraced a vision of "storming the Winter Palace," one of the most distinctive features of the period was the proportion of movements that explored alternatives to the intensely centralized focus on formal power within the nation-state as the goal of radical politics. Many activists now tried to theorize new ways of building power, new ways of doing politics at a distance from the state, new ways of uniting struggles inside and outside the state. As George Katsiaficas has noted, in the long 1968, "the meaning of revolution was enlarged to include questions of power in everyday life as well as questions of power won by past revolutions."[10]

Moving beyond the ideological intentions of the actors, it is notable that in none of the countries included in this book were those who sought a new "state-centric" left to replace the Old Lefts successful in simple numerical or organizational terms; with only a handful of exceptions, as the 1970s wore on, such parties became increasingly small sects, while, with the important exception of Northern Ireland, most military strategies also wound up increasingly isolated, not least by comparison with the movements of the Resistance that had preceded them by only a quarter of a century.

Equally important was the internal challenge to authoritarian power within one's own movement. Initially radical-democratic in emphasis, with elements from the Anglophone New Left and the continental resistance to fascism, this basic orientation proved immensely versatile, capable of being turned against the institutions of professorial power within the university, but also of male dominance within left organizations; against the tyranny of

---

10.   George Katsiaficas. *The Imagination of the New Left: A Global Analysis of 1968* (Cambridge, MA: South End Press, 1987), 4–5.

foremen and managers in the factory, but also of white or non-immigrant activists within the movement; against technocratic power in health, welfare or housing, but also against the power of intellectuals and organizational apparatchiks.

Because of the wider decline of mass organizations in this period, this challenge to established power was expressed as much by the split or the new movement as it was by radical models of internal democracy and diversity. But both were equally important. Never again, in many countries, could a single party dominate the radical movement field; less and less would any individual organization have the capacity to dominate a single movement. This did not mean that oligarchic tendencies disappeared—far from it. But no single oligarchy was hegemonic across movements, while the context and logic of organizing changed sharply by contrast with the movements of the previous generation.

This general tendency was of course not universal: for example, Northern Ireland's various republicanisms had a far more centralizing logic, tied to the centrality of the war. Less unusually, many of those who were radical in 1968 found themselves undertaking what Rudi Dutschke called a "long march through the institutions" of social democracy, the unions or the universities, the health service or the legal profession—a march in which they were often as strongly reshaped by these institutions as the reverse. Timings and modalities were very different not only as between different countries but also between different movements and social groups; the very move away from an unambiguously dominant focus on holding national state power within organized capitalism enabled a much greater diversity of pathways and outcomes.

Legacies

In their *Anti-Systemic Movements*, Giovanni Arrighi, Terence K. Hopkins and Immanuel Wallerstein wrote, "There have only been two *world* revolutions. One took place in 1848. The second took place in 1968. Both were historical failures. Both transformed the world."[11]

The revolutions that swept European cities in 1848 were tempestuous and enthusiastic affairs driven by liberal and parliamentary, sometimes democratic or nationalistic, occasionally working-class and socialist demands—and rapidly put down by the bayonets of older empires harking back to the *ancien régime*. Yet those eruptions proved the unsustainability of older modes of power, and within a couple of decades nearly

---

11.   Giovanni Arrighi, Terence K. Hopkins, and Immanuel Wallerstein, *Antisystemic Movements* (London: Verso, 1989), 97.

all European states felt pressured to adopt reforms, reconfigure state power, and restructure society itself.

So too did the struggles of the 1960s and 1970s end in defeat. Of course, the reasons vary from case to case, but some causes were common to movements everywhere. One must first point to the real internal limits of the movements themselves. Activists in every country ultimately failed to bring together a diversity of voices into an inclusive unity. In many cases the opposite happened, as intense frustration with widespread oppression within movements, coupled with combative rhetoric, ideological rigidity, and moralism led to factionalization.

Increasingly, movements divided over the course of the 1970s. Frustrated, some embraced essentialist conceptions of identity, others hardened into dogmatic sects that declared unwavering fidelity to some authoritarian nation-state, and still others converted to armed struggle, which in nearly every case actually isolated, delegitimized, and ultimately weakened radicals even further.

Additionally, movements had to contend with the great challenges of maintaining momentum over time, especially in the face of division, defeat, and repression. The founders grew older, leaders burned out, and many activists simply wanted to get on with their lives. Although a few, especially, and uncoincidentally, the movement celebrities, switched sides, the majority maintained their political convictions, but left their heady days of activism behind.

The international situation also contributed to decline. Just as the struggles of the Global South inspired activists in the Global North, so too did defeats abroad reverberate back home. To be sure, "Third World" struggles continued deep into the 1970s, but the old ideals of anti-imperialist unity began to break down. Movements were defeated, newly liberated states fell back into economic dependence, and some of what were once considered the guiding stars of the internationalist movement, like the People's Republic of China, betrayed the revolutionary project, effectively aligning with the United States on struggles in Chile, Angola, or Vietnam.

Most importantly, many of these movements faced ferocious state repression. States turned to the usual police violence, sometimes augmented by chemical weapons, firearms, armored vehicles, and helicopters. Some employed a range of more covert tactics to neutralize the movements, making use of surveillance, composing fake mail, spreading false information, raiding offices, destroying property, organizing counter demonstrations, collaborating with right-wing groups, infiltrating organizations, or arresting activists on trumped up charges.

A few states went even further, censoring radical publications, banning demonstrations, outlawing groups altogether, or rapidly expanding police powers. In France, the *Anti-Casseurs* law instituted the idea of collective responsibility: anyone who could be connected to any action in which property was damaged, or any representative of the state harmed, could be arrested for that action. In the United States, the Nixon administration unleashed the War on Drugs in large part as a cover for destroying student, antiwar, and especially Black political movements. As John Ehrlichman, Richard Nixon's aid, later explained, "We knew we couldn't make it illegal to be either against the war or black, but by getting the public to associate the hippies with marijuana and blacks with heroin, and then criminalizing both heavily, we could disrupt those communities. We could arrest their leaders. raid their homes, break up their meetings, and vilify them night after night on the evening news."[12]

At its worst, state repression could lead to assassination, outright murder, and mass executions—the murder of Black Panther Fred Hampton in the United States, the rampant violence in Italy that came to be known as the "years of lead," the deliberate massacre of unarmed demonstrators in Mexico, the Warsaw Pact invasion of Czechoslovakia, or the intensifying violence of loyalists, police, and British military in Northern Ireland. While it is true that most of these movements never came close to revolutions, it's worth recalling that at the time, the forces of order in many countries feared the worst, and acted accordingly.

For all these reasons, and many more, by the mid-1970s, the international wave of contestation that took shape in the 1960s was in crisis in most countries; by the late 1970s and early 1980s, it was over almost everywhere. In the countries explored here, the maximalist goals of nearly every movement were never realized, not a single government collapsed, and the old order swiftly reasserted itself.

Nevertheless, like the revolutions of 1848, these movements did force considerable change. Many of these societies became more open, as people won the freedom to dress as they liked, speak how they wished, or to live outside an early heterosexual marriage. Children gained a whole new level of autonomy. Some democratic air entered previously-closed institutions, not least education. Quite a few countries saw a host of legislative changes, such as educational reforms; lower voting ages; revocation of discriminatory laws; greater rights to contraceptives, divorce, or abortion; or major labor and social rights. New opportunities were opened for those who had been systematically excluded from politics, the professions, or academia. Indeed, it is worth remembering that much of what we now take for granted seemed unachievable at the time.

---

12. Quoted in Dan Baum, "Legalize It All: How to Win the War on Drugs," *Harper's Magazine*, April 2016, 22.

In addition, these movements expanded the field of the possible. They showed that mass engagement could win concrete freedoms. They showed that it was possible to fight for radical change even when history seemed frozen solid. At the same time, they radically expanded our very definitions of what politics could be. They identified new issues, introduced new ways of thinking about the relationship between different kinds of oppression, and created new forms of activism. Left politics, and in fact right politics as well, would never be the same.

As with the revolutions of 1848, the challenge these movements posed was so severe, it forced the ruling order to reinvent itself. The result was what we now call neoliberalism, whose hallmark has been not only the destruction of the conditions of possibility of the movements of the 1960s and 1970s, but the active recuperation of many of their elements into a new ruling order. Of course, no more than the states of the 1880s were democratic paradises was the "progressive neoliberalism" that selectively integrated the manageable features of 1968 a hippie commune.

Yet, from a longer historical perspective, cooptation has been perhaps the most obvious feature of the neoliberal order that consolidated itself in the 1990s and 2000s. To take only a few examples, the gay liberation movement's powerful critique of sexuality was transformed into a renewed emphasis on marriage as the only acceptable kind of amorous relationship; the long popular struggles in health and education, and around disability and mental health, gave way to the language of "consultation" and "participation"; the anti-racist struggles of people of color came to mean the slight diversification of the managerial and ruling classes; the quest for self-management gave way to a world where "flexibility," "autonomy," and "self-discovery" came at the expense of social benefits, job security, or rights to collective bargaining; the critique of capitalism led to the creation of environmentally-friendly, development-oriented, and socially-aware start-ups with a firmer grip on human social life than ever before; and the desire to live a meaningful life, to "do what you love," was transformed into a new kind of entrepreneurialism.

Part of what enabled this cooptation was the inability of most Old Lefts to reorient themselves in 1968 or afterwards, along with the weakening structural position of the organized working class in the Global North. Working-class demands, whether around redistribution or workplace power, would gradually lose ground in most contexts from some point in the 1980s, while the New Left attempts to build power around the coming together of movement struggles without a single, centralized, and authoritarian organization often saw some successes in subsequent decades, but foundered on the cooptation of some and the marginalization of others. In this sense it is probably fair to say that the *question* posed by the movements of the long

1968—how to bring together a variety of voices, demands, and goals, and how to democratize within one's own movements, in a context where the structural bases of Old Left models no longer apply—remains a live one, but one which thus far lacks a convincing answer.

Voices of 1968

This is a book about radical social movements. It is well-known that in nearly every country only a minority of people engaged in activist politics in the long 1968, and only a minority within that minority fought for some kind of radical change. Most people, then as now, went on with their lives, or if they were sympathetic, rarely converted their ideas to action. However, the radicals, although a minority everywhere, did have an enormous impact on society as a whole, sparking tremendous changes that affected even those who rejected their efforts. This is perhaps most clearly seen with women's liberation: relatively few women called themselves feminist activists, but even those who refused the title saw their lives transformed—more rights, greater opportunities, the freedom to dress, think, act differently.

In telling the history of these movements through primary sources, we were forced to make a series of difficult decisions about what to include. In general, we have attempted to show a wide range of movements, social contexts, and political traditions. In a handful of cases this has been less easy, whether because of the overwhelming centrality of a single conflict or the difficulty of mediating a specific context to general readers in another country. The Prague Spring in Czechoslovakia, the civil rights movement in Northern Ireland, and the student uprising in Yugoslavia are examples where we have opted for a deeper exploration of a single struggle.

We have consciously chosen voices from the movements themselves, not those coming "from above," which were typically hostile or uncomprehending. Rarely have we included commentary from "outsiders," just as no recent academic or journalistic interpretations have made their way into this book. We have also sought out documents of the time rather than later reflections and oral histories, which have their own different strengths and limitations. In addition, we have attempted to show a variety of forms of movement production, typically in movement-controlled media such as the poster, leaflet, or magazine, as well as a variety of genres, from reports to manifestos to theoretical essays, which were well within the reach of a broad range of actors at the time.

In order to include as many documents as possible, and to ensure accessibility, we have also chosen to include relatively short texts or excerpts from longer ones. Relatedly, to make room for a diversity of voices, and to create space for new texts, we have generally tried to prioritize previously untranslated texts while avoiding documents that are already well-known or widely available to Anglophone readers, such as the Black Panther Party's Ten Point Program.[13]

The texts included in this book are intended to show a diversity of voices not only within the individual country chapters, but across the book as a whole. For that reason, in selecting texts, we chose those that not only represent a given country's 1968, but contribute to the best possible representation of the long 1968 in the Global North as such. This ambition of double representation has likely led to some distortions in each. We also freely admit that a collection of primary sources is never neutral, but reflects the priorities and prejudices of its editors. We have inevitably been shaped by our current political, social, and intellectual climate, which has allowed us to see some things, but not others. Every history says just as much about the specific context in which it is written as the past it claims to present. Given all these factors, the collection is necessarily imperfect. However, we have tried to fail the best we could.

The value of compiling a documentary reader is to bring out the voices of the actors themselves, speaking to their comrades, enemies, and societies in a period of transformation. Reading a twenty-first-century historical or political account, we are necessarily presented with a secondhand synthesis of these movements, often skewed for specific purposes. Reading the actors' voices themselves, we are plunged into the richness, oddity, immediacy, and confusion of another time and place when everything might seem to be open to challenge and change. Primary sources not only allow us to more directly understand the motivations, desires, dreams, and goals of historical actors, but also their many limitations. Much can be learned by carefully reading for the silences, absences, and limits in older ways of thinking.

In that vein, as readers, we need to be aware of what the social historian and New Left figure E.P. Thompson, writing of another time, called "the enormous condescension of posterity":

Their hostility to the new industrialism may have been backward-looking. Their communitarian ideals may have been fantasies. Their insurrectionary conspiracies may have been foolhardy. But they lived through these times of acute social disturbance, and we did not. Their aspirations were

---

13. We have tried to remain as faithful as possible to the spirit of the original texts, but in some cases we were forced to make certain changes—such as providing descriptive titles for untitled texts; correcting spelling, punctuation, and grammatical errors in the original; or writing out abbreviations—in order to make these texts more accessible to readers.

valid in terms of their own experience; and, if they were casualties of history, they remain, condemned in their own lives, as casualties.[14]

In the texts included in this book, we may well find things that seem to us blindingly obvious, overly simplistic, or unbearably naive. Of course, part of what has happened since 1968 is the defeat of the movements' more radical goals. With that defeat comes the tendency even for radicals to internalize much of our own social order as natural, to narrow the scope of what can be changed. This challenge also faced the radicals of 1968: how to formulate a different way of seeing and to imagine a future which was radically changed in many dimensions at once.

Finally, we should remember that those who faced tanks, tear gas, dogs, baton charges, prison cells, loss of employment or education, social ostracism and exile in the attempt to change society, are still, in some cases, casualties in their own lives. By no means all have made an easy conversion to complacent upholders of the present day, or to celebrities who can pat themselves on the back for their radical youth. If in the Global North's 1968 comparatively few paid with their lives, many have spent their lives paying for the social change that they helped bring about. It is worth recognizing the price they paid and what we have gained even while—as entirely appropriate—we may disagree with many of their positions. This too, in many ways, is a gain of 1968: the recognition that a diversity of perspectives is a source of strength, and that meaningful change involves many different activists speaking from different places in different voices.

Further Reading

Álvarez, Alberto Martín, and Eduardo Rey Tristán. *Revolutionary Violence and the New Left: Transnational Perspectives*. New York: Routledge, 2017.

Arrighi, Giovanni, Terence K. Hopkins and Immanuel Wallerstein, *Anti-Systemic Movements*. London: Verso, 1989.

Bhambra, Gurminder K., and Ipek Demir, eds. *1968 in Retrospect: History, Theory, Alterity*. London: Palgrave Macmillan, 2009.

Bracke, Maud, and James Mark, eds. "Between Decolonisation and the Cold War: transnational activism and its limits in Europe, 1950s–1990s," special issue of the *Journal of Contemporary History* 50, no. 3 (July 2015).

Brown, Timothy, and Andrew Lison. *The Global Sixties in Sound and Vision: Media, Counterculture, Revolt*. New York: Palgrave, 2014.

Carey, Elaine. *Protests in the Streets: 1968 Across the Globe*. Indianapolis, IN: Hackett, 2016.

---

14. E. P. Thompson, *The Making of the English Working Class* (New York: Vintage, 1966), 13.

Caute, David. *The Year of the Barricades: A Journey Through 1968*. New York: Harper and Row, 1988.

Chaplin, Tamara, and Jadwiga E Pieper Mooney, eds. *The Global 1960s: Convention, Contest, Counterculture*. New York: Routledge, 2018.

Christiaens, Kim. "Europe at the Crossroads of Three Worlds: Alternative Histories and Connections of European Solidarity with the Third World, 1950s–80s." *European Review of History* 24, no. 6 (2017): 932-54.

Christiansen, Samantha, and Zachary A. Scarlett, eds. *The Third World in the Global 1960s*. New York: Berghahn, 2013.

Cook, Alexander C. *Mao's Little Red Book: A Global History*. Cambridge: Cambridge University Press, 2013.

Daniels, Robert V. *Year of the Heroic Guerrilla: World Revolution and Counterrevolution in 1968*. Cambridge, MA: Harvard University Press, 1996.

Davis, Belinda, Wilfried Mausbach, Martin Klimke, and Carla MacDougall, eds. *Changing the World, Changing Oneself: Political Protest and Collective Identities in West Germany and the U.S. in the 1960s and 1970s*. New York: Berghahn Books, 2012.

DeGroot, Gerard, J., ed. *Student Protest: The Sixties and After*. New York: Routledge, 2014.

Dubinsky, Karen, Catherine Krull, Susan Lord, Sean Mills, and Scott Rutherford, eds. *New World Coming: The Sixties and the Shaping of Global Consciousness*. Toronto: Between the Lines, 2009.

Fink, Carole, Philipp Gassert, and Detlef Junker, eds. *1968: The World Transformed*. Cambridge: Cambridge University Press, 1998.

Fraser, Ronald, ed. *1968: A Student Generation in Revolt: An International Oral History*. New York: Pantheon Books, 1988.

Frazier, Leslie Jo, and Deborah Cohen, eds. *Gender and Sexuality in 1968: Transformative Politics in the Cultural Imagination*. New York: Palgrave Macmillan, 2009.

Gassert, Philipp, and Martin Klimke, eds. *1968: On the Edge of World Revolution*. Chicago: The University of Chicago Press and Black Rose Books, 2018.

Gildea, Mark, James Mark, and Anette Warring. *Europe's 1968: Voices of Revolt*. Oxford: Oxford University Press, 2013.

Gorsuch, Anne E., and Diane P. Koenker, eds. *The Socialist Sixties: Crossing Borders in the Second World*. Bloomington, IN: University of Indiana Press, 2013.

Horn, Gerd-Rainer. *The Spirit of '68: Rebellion in Western Europe and North America, 1956–1976*. Oxford: Oxford University Press, 2007.

Jian, Chen, Martin Klimke, Masha Kirasirova, Mary Nolan, Marilyn Young, and Joanna Waley-Cohen, eds. *The Routledge Handbook of the Global Sixties: Between Protest and Nation-Building*. New York: Routledge, 2018.

Katsiaficas, George. *The Global Imagination of 1968: Revolution and Counterrevolution*. Oakland, CA: PM Press, 2018.

Klimke, Martin, and Scharloth, Joachim, eds. *1968 in Europe: A History of Protest and Activism, 1956–1977*. New York: Palgrave Macmillan, 2008.

Klimke, Martin, Jacco Pekelder, and Joachim Scharloth, eds. *Between Prague Spring and French May: Opposition and Revolt in Europe, 1960–1980*. New York: Berghahn Books, 2013.

Kornetis, Kostas. "'Everything links?:' Temporality, Territoriality and Cultural Transfer in the '68 Protest Movements." *Historien* 9 (2009): 34-45.

Kurlansky, Mark. *1968: The Year that Rocked the World*. New York: Ballantine Books, 2004.

Kutschke, Beate, and Barley Norton, eds. *Music and Protest in 1968*. Cambridge: Cambridge University Press, 2013.

Marwick, Arthur. *The Sixties: Cultural Revolution in Britain, France, Italy, and the United States, c. 1958–c. 1974*. Oxford: Oxford University Press, 1999.

Schildt, Axel, and Detlef Siegfried, eds. *Between Marx and Coca-Cola: Youth Cultures in Changing European Societies, 1960–1980*. New York. Berghahn Books, 2005.

Steen, Bart van der, Ask Katseff, and Leendert van Hoogenhuijze. *The City is Ours: Squatting and Autonomous Movements in Europe from the 1970s to the Present*. Oakland, CA: PM Press, 2014.

Suri, Jeremi. *Power and Protest: Global Revolution and the Rise of Detente*. Cambridge, MA: Harvard University Press, 2003.

Suri, Jeremi. *The Global Revolutions of 1968*. New York: W. W. Norton, 2007.

Toupin, Louise. *Wages for Housework: The History of an International Feminist Movement (1972–1977)*. London: Pluto Press, 2018.

Varon, Jeremy. *Bringing the War Home: The Weather Underground, the Red Army Faction, and Revolution Violence in the Sixties and Seventies*. Berkeley, CA: University of California Press, 2004.

Wainwright, Hilary. *Arguments for a New Left: Answering the Free-Market Right*. Oxford: Blackwell, 1994.

1
United States

Despite Cold War anxieties, the 1960s in the United States began with great optimism. The American economy was the strongest in the world, the United States had reached the height of its international powers, and faith in the government seemed stronger than ever. John F. Kennedy, the youngest American to be elected President in his country's history, ended his famous 1961 inaugural address with a rousing, patriotic call to action: "ask not what your country can do for you, ask what you can do for your country." While his assassination in 1963 came as a shock, his successor, Lyndon Johnson carried the torch forward with the "Great Society," a set of social programs designed to improve education, expand health care, and alleviate poverty.

Despite this idealism from above, discontent stirred below. While the government saw itself as the leader of the free world, American society was in fact profoundly unequal. Throughout the country, African Americans faced discrimination, disenfranchisement, segregation, and outright violence. In 1955, Emmett Till, a 14-year-old boy was lynched in Mississippi. In 1958, a poll found that 44 percent of whites said they would sell their homes if a Black family moved next door. Even after the landmark Brown v Board of Education ruling in 1954, many institutions in the South remained formally segregated, and interracial marriage remained illegal in some states until 1967.

African Americans had long organized against racial discrimination, and through the tireless efforts of groups like the Student Nonviolent Coordinating Committee (SNCC), eventually secured major gains, such as civic equality with the passage of the Civil Rights Act of 1964 and political inclusion with the Voting Rights Act of 1965. But Black struggles were by no means monolithic. While some fought for equitable access to the existing system, others, especially Black nationalists, called for a transformation of the system itself. Channeling the energy of Black urban rebellions exploding across the country, like Watts in 1965, they adopted a more combative politics. Looking to anti-colonial struggles abroad, they saw African Americans as an internal colony and understood their own struggle as part of a larger internationalist revolution. The most famous representative of this current was the Black Panther Party, formed in 1966.

Black struggles inspired white students across the country, many of whom first cut their teeth in the civil rights movement. By the 1960s, a student movement began to coalesce in the United States, led by the Students for a Democratic Society (SDS). In its founding manifesto, *The Port Huron Statement* of 1962, SDS articulated a sense of alienation from not only mainstream American society, but also what it considered to be the outdated ideas of the Old Left. Instead, they called for a New Left based on the idea of "participatory democracy." Born of the gap between the celebratory discourse of the country's leaders and the stark realities of American life, SDS soon took a radical turn, taking a leading role in opposing the Vietnam War, protesting the modern university, and fighting for a more equitable society. At its height in the late 1960s, the group claimed nearly a hundred thousand members.

At the same time, many young people began to search for an alternative to the mainstream culture of their parents. What would eventually become the counterculture arose from a paradox at the heart of American society: despite enjoying unprecedented affluence, many American youth felt a deep sense of emptiness, malaise, and meaninglessness. Rejecting the passionless world of routines, some sought to invent a new set of values through art, psychedelic music, underground newspapers, communal living, drugs, and sexual liberation. Although the "hippies" remained an extremely marginal phenomenon, countercultural sentiments spread widely, challenging many deeply-held mores.

The backdrop to this turmoil was the Vietnam War. In 1965, Lyndon Johnson escalated U.S. involvement in Vietnam, dispatching young Americans to fight in a country few could find on a map. Although most Americans initially supported their government, the war quickly became a deeply divisive issue. Young men burned draft cards, students occupied universities, and hundreds of thousands of Americans took to the streets. Despite growing opposition, at home and abroad, Johnson continued to escalate the war, driving many antiwar activists further to the left. Refusing to be complicit in their country's war abroad, some activists began to think seriously about opening a new front in the "belly of the beast."

Although the year 1968 did not culminate in a single explosion, as in France, the United States did experience a prolonged wave of activism that was no less transformative. The year began with the Tet Offensive, which gave the lie to imminent victory. The war, and the Offensive in particular, not only damaged Johnson's credibility, it threatened to tear the Democratic Party apart. Losing control over his party, Lyndon Johnson astounded the country by announcing on March 31 that he would not seek reelection. Less than a week later, Martin Luther King, Jr. was assassinated in Memphis, Tennessee, sparking urban rebellions across the country. Later in April, protesting students occupied academic buildings at Columbia University, signaling a new level of militancy in the student movement. In June, Americans witnessed yet another assassination when Robert F. Kennedy was gunned down after winning the California Democratic Primary. In October, Tommie Smith and John Carlos raised their fists at the Summer Olympics in Mexico City. In August, Chicago police mercilessly beat demonstrators outside the Democratic National Convention; inside, the Party fractured, as younger delegates tried to push the Democrats in a more leftist direction, while white Southerners began to rethink their party loyalties. In the end, Party insiders handed Vice President Hubert Humphrey the nomination, even though he never competed in a single primary, leaving many antiwar delegates disillusioned with the entire process. In the general election, Richard Nixon, who ran on a law and order platform, emerged victorious.

The extraordinary events of 1968 had a radicalizing effect. The majority of Americans now saw the war as a mistake. University occupations became more common. Student groups increasingly embraced the idea of revolution. Marxism, indeed Leninism, gained popularity. Workers' struggles grew in number and intensity. In fact, after having condemned the working class as bought off, many young activists firmly turned their attention to the class struggle, with some going so far as to find work in steel mills, auto plants, or mines to help organize the working class for revolution. Others, like the future Weather Underground, called for armed struggle. Although more committed than ever to revolutionary change, activists increasingly fell into sectarianism, a turn most powerfully symbolized by the collapse of SDS amidst a frenzy of factionalist in-fighting in 1969.

Nevertheless, the late 1960s also saw a diversification of emancipatory struggles. The Black Panther Party, which unveiled a range of "survival programs," such as free breakfast, medical clinics, dental programs, GED class, and research into sickle cell anemia, emerged as a model for other groups. Puerto Rican radicals formed the Young Lords Party, Mexican Americans created the Brown Berets, Asian Americans the Red Guards, poor whites the Young Patriots, and Native Americans the American Indian Movement. In some cases, these groups cooperated with one another. In Chicago, for example, the Panthers, Young Lords, Brown Berets, the Young Patriots, and others formed a multi-racial, anti-racist "Rainbow Coalition" for radical change.

Lastly, as in other countries, new social movements took shape in these years, such as women's liberation. Born in part as a reaction to the pervasive sexism within radical movements ostensibly fighting for radical change, women's liberation not only fought against sexism, winning important battles like the legal right to abortion, but redefined the meaning of politics.

Figure 1.1   The first issue of *Triple Jeopardy*, the paper
of the Third World Women's Alliance, a revolutionary
socialist organization of women of color. 1971.

Oppression, feminists argued, made itself apparent in hidden ways, in
gestures, comments, interpersonal relationships. Politics, therefore, was not
just something that happened at the ballot box or in the streets, but also
in seemingly private spaces. Alongside the women's movement emerged a
host of other new movements, such as gay liberation, a renewed interest in
environmentalism, or immigrant rights.

By the early 1970s, many of these leftist ideas, once confined to a
minority, won an even greater audience. Countercultural attitudes went
mainstream, strikes became even more frequent, and gay and women's
liberation overturned traditional ideas. At the same time, defeat in Vietnam
weakened American global hegemony, the decades-long economic boom
finally ended in recession, and Richard Nixon became the first President in
U.S. history to resign the office in 1974. The old order was deeply shaken,
opening the political space for alternatives. But the movements of the
left were in no position to take advantage of the crisis. By the mid-1970s,
intense repression, factionalization, burnout, and the changing international

context pushed many of these movements into terminal decline. One of the greatest challenges for activists in the American context was the question of diversity, and despite some attempts, activists failed to build lasting coalitions that could unite diverse social groups into an inclusive, unified force. In the end, it was not the left that mastered the crisis of the 1970s, but a resurgent right, in the form of Ronald Reagan.

THE INCREDIBLE WAR (1965)
Paul Potter

In March 1965, President Lyndon Johnson chose to escalate U.S. involvement in Vietnam by deploying marines to the Republic of Vietnam in the South and authorizing a massive bombing campaign against the Democratic Republic of Vietnam in the North. The following month, on April 17, 1965, Students for a Democratic Society (SDS) organized the first major national demonstration against the war. They expected a few thousand protesters. To their surprise, around 20,000 attended, making it the largest peace protest in American history to that date. One of the highlights of the day was the following speech by SDS President Paul Potter. Here he develops one of the core themes of the 1960s and 1970s: the need to focus not simply on reforms, but to change the larger "system" that makes war, inequality, and oppression possible in the first place.

*   *   *

Most of us grew up thinking that the United States was a strong but humble nation, that involved itself in world affairs only reluctantly, that respected the integrity of other nations and other systems, and that engaged in wars only as a last resort. This was a nation with no large standing army, with no design for external conquest, that sought primarily the opportunity to develop its own resources and its own mode of living. If at some point we began to hear vague and disturbing things about what this country had done in Latin America, or China, or Spain and other places, we remained somehow confident about the basic integrity of this nation's foreign policy. The Cold War with all of its neat categories and black and white descriptions did much to assure us that what we had been taught to believe was true.

But in recent years, the withdrawal from the hysteria of the Cold War and the development of a more aggressive, activist foreign policy have done much to force many of us to rethink attitudes that were deep and basic sentiments about our country. And now the incredible war in Vietnam has provided the razor, the terrifying sharp cutting edge that has finally severed the last vestiges of our illusion that morality and democracy are the guiding principles of American foreign policy. The saccharine self-righteous moralism that promises the Vietnamese a billion dollars while taking billions of dollars for economic and social destruction and political repression is rapidly losing what power it might ever have had to reassure us about the decency of our foreign policy. The further we explore the reality of what this country is doing and planning in Vietnam the more we are driven toward the conclusion of Senator Morse that the United States is rapidly becoming the greatest threat to world peace in the world today. This, this is a terrible and bitter insight for people who grew up as we did—and our revulsion at that insight, our refusal to accept it as inevitable or necessary, is one of the reasons that so many people have come today.

[...]

But the war goes on. The freedom to conduct that war depends on the dehumanization not only of Vietnamese people but of Americans as well; it depends on the construction of a system of premises and thinking that insulates the President and his advisors thoroughly and completely from the human consequences of their decisions. I do not believe that the President or Mr. McNamara or Mr. Rusk or even McGeorge Bundy are particularly evil men. If asked to throw napalm on the back of a ten-year-old child they would shrink in horror—but their decisions have led to mutilation and death of thousands and thousands of people.

What kind of a system is it that allows good men to make those kinds of decisions? What kind of a system is it that justifies the United States or any country in seizing the destinies of the Vietnamese people and using them callously for our own purpose? What kind of a system is it that disenfranchises people in the South, leaves millions upon millions of people throughout this country impoverished and excluded from the mainstream and promise of American society, that creates faceless and terrible bureaucracies and makes those places where people spend their lives and their work, that consistently puts material values above human values, and still persists in calling itself free? What place is there for ordinary men in that system and how are they to control it, and bend it to their will rather than them to its?

We must name that system. We must name it, describe it, analyze it, understand it, and then change it. For it is only when that system is brought under control that there can be any hope for stopping the forces that create a war in Vietnam today or a murder in the South tomorrow or all the incalculable, innumerable more subtle atrocities that are worked on people all over, all of the time.

How do you stop a war then? If the war has its roots deep in the institutions of American society, how do you stop it? Do you march to Washington?

Is that enough? Who will hear us here? How can you make the decision makers hear us, insulated as they are, if they cannot hear the screams of a girl burnt by napalm?

I believe that the administration is serious about expanding the war in Asia. The question, the question is whether the people who are here are as serious about ending that war. I wonder what it means for each of us to say we want to end the war in Vietnam—whether, if we accept the full meaning of that statement and the gravity of the situation, we can simply leave the march and go back to the routines of a society that acts as if it were not in crisis. [...]

There is no simple plan, there is no scheme or gimmick that can be proposed here. There is no simple way to attack something that is deeply rooted in the society. If the people of this country are to end the war in Vietnam, and to change the institutions which create it, then the people of this country must create a massive social movement, and if that can be built around the issue of Vietnam then that is what we must do.

By a social movement I mean more than petitions or letters of protest, or tacit support of dissident Congressmen; I mean people who are willing to change their lives, who are willing to challenge the system, to take the problem of change seriously. By a social movement I mean an effort that is powerful enough to make this country understand that our problems are not in Vietnam, or China, or Brazil, or outer space, or at the bottom of the ocean, but are here in the United States now. What we must begin to do is build a democratic and humane society in which Vietnams are unthinkable, in which human life and initiative is precious. The reason there are twenty thousand people here today and not a hundred or none at all is because five years ago in the South students began to build a social movement to change the system. The reason there are poor people here, Negroes and whites, housewives, faculty members, and many, many others is because the movement has grown and spread and changed and reached out as an expression of the broad concerns of people throughout this society. [...]

To build a movement rather than a protest or some series of protests, to break out of our insulations and accept the consequences of our decisions, in effect to change our lives, means that we open ourselves to the reactions of a society that believes that it is moral and just, and that we open ourselves to labeling and to persecution, and that we dare to be really seen as wrong in a society that doesn't tolerate fundamental challenges.

It means that we desert the security of our riches and reach out to people who are tied to the mythology of American power and make them part of our movement. It means that we reach out to people all over this country, whether they are workers or whether they are in churches—wherever they are and make them part of a movement to change the system.

It means that we will build a movement that works not simply in Washington but in communities and with the problems that face people throughout the society. That means that we build a movement that understands Vietnam in all of its horror as but a symptom of a deeper malaise, that we build a movement that makes possible the implementation of values that would have prevented the Vietnam, a movement based on the integrity of man and on a belief in man's capacity to determine his own life; a movement that does not exclude people because they are poor or have been held down; a movement that has the capacity to tolerate all the formulations of society that men may choose to strive for; a movement, a movement that is willing to take the forms of protest, such as the teach-in, which have begun to break out in this country and intensify them and expand them throughout the land; a movement that will support the increasing numbers of young men in this country who are unwilling and are now beginning to be ready to reduce the fight in the war in Vietnam; a movement, a movement that will not tolerate the escalation or prolongation of this war but will, if necessary, respond to the administration's war effort with massive civil disobedience all over the country, that will wrench this country into a confrontation with the issue of Vietnam; a movement that must of necessity reach out to all those people in Vietnam or elsewhere who are struggling to find decency and control of their lives.

For in a strange way and in a very unusual way that the people of Vietnam and the people on this demonstration are united in much more than a common concern that the war be ended. In both countries there are people struggling to build a movement that has the power to change their condition. The system that frustrates these movements is the same. All of our lives, our destinies, our very hopes to live, depend on our ability to overcome that system.

Republished on Voices of Democracy: The U.S. Oratory Project: voicesofdemocracy. umd.edu/potter-the-incredible-war-speech-text.

LETTER TO DRAFT BOARD 100, WAYNE COUNTY, DETROIT, MICHIGAN (1965)
General Gordon Baker, Jr.

Despite the palpable victories of the civil rights struggles, some Black activists grew dissatisfied with the mainstream movement. Critical of the established leadership, skeptical about nonviolence, insistent on Black autonomy, and committed to revolution, these activists pursed a different kind of politics, later captured by the slogan "Black Power." A leading figure of this current was General Gordon Baker,

*Jr.. who helped found UHURU, one of the many groups that made up the constel-
lation of Black radicalism in the early 1960s. Activists like Baker, Jr. adopted an
internationalist position, calling not for integration, but for systematic change on
a global scale. In 1964, he traveled to Cuba, which he later described as a "revolutionary laboratory." In September 1965, just weeks after the Watts rebellion,
Baker, Jr. submitted a letter to his draft board refusing to serve in Vietnam. Like
other Black radicals, he identified more with the Vietnamese than with the U.S.
government. As Soulbook, the journal that republished his letter, put it, the Black
community was "America's internal Vietnam." We reproduce his letter below.*

* * *

TO WHOM IT MAY CONCERN

Gentlemen:

This letter is in regards to a notice sent to me, General Gordon Baker,
Jr., requesting my appearance before an examining station to determine my
fitness for military service.

How could you have the NERVE knowing that I am a black man living
under the scope and influence of America's racist, decadent society??? You
did not ask me if I had any morals, principles, or basic human values by
which to live. Yet, you ask if I am qualified. QUALIFIED FOR WHAT, might
I ask? What does being "Qualified" mean: qualified to serve in the U.S.
Army? ...To be further brainwashed into the insidious notion of "defending
freedom"?

You stand before me with the dried blood of Patrice Lumumba on your
hands, the blood of defenseless Panamanian students, shot down by U.S.
marines; the blood of my black brothers in Angola and South Africa who
are being tortured by the Portuguese and South African whites (whom
you resolutely support) respectively; the dead people of Japan, Korea, and
now Vietnam, in Asia; the blood of Medgar Evers, six Birmingham babies,
the blood of one million Algerians slaughtered by the French (whom you
supported); the *fresh* blood of ten thousand Congolese patriots dead from
your ruthless rape and plunder of the Congo—the blood of defenseless
women and children burned in villages from Napalm jelly bombs ... With
all of this blood of my non-white brothers dripping from your fangs, you
have the damned AUDACITY to ask me if I am "qualified." White man;
listen to me for I am talking to you!

I AM A MAN OF PRINCIPLES AND VALUES: principles of justice and
national liberation, self-determination, and respect for national sovereignty.
Yet you ask me if I am "physically fit" to go to Asia, Africa, and Latin America
to fight my oppressed brothers (who are completely and resolutely within

their just rights to free their fatherland from foreign domination). You ask me if I am qualified to join an army of FOOLS, ASSASSINS, and MORAL DELINQUENTS who are not worthy of being called men! You want me to defend the riches reaped from the super-exploitation of the darker races of mankind by a few white, rich, super-monopolists who control the most vast empire that has ever existed in man's one million years of History—all in the name of "Freedom"!

Why, here in the heart of America, 22 million black people are suffering unsurmounted toil: exploited economically by every form of business—from monopolists to petty hustlers; completely suppressed politically; deprived of their social and cultural heritage.

But all men of principle are fighting men … MY FIGHT IS FOR FREEDOM: UHURU, LIBERTAD, HALAUGA, and HARAMBEE!

THEREFORE: when the call is made to free South Africa; when the call is made to liberate Latin America from the United Fruit Co., Kaiser and Alcoa Aluminum Co., and from Standard Oil; when the call is made to jail the exploiting Brahmins in India in order to destroy the Caste System; when the call is made to free the black delta areas of Mississippi, Alabama, South Carolina; when the call is made to free 12TH STREET HERE IN DETROIT!: when these calls are made, send for me, for these shall be Historical Struggles in which it shall be an honor to serve!

Venceremos!

Soulbook: The Quarterly Journal of Revolutionary Afroamerica 1, no. 2 (Spring 1965): 133–4.

TRIP WITHOUT A TICKET (1967)
The Diggers

In the 1960s, San Francisco emerged as one of the great countercultural centers of North America. Of the many groups that made up the West Coast scene, one of the most radical were the Diggers. Taking their name from a group of Protestant anarchists in the English Civil War, the Diggers not only imagined a world beyond private property, they advocated a kind of prefigurative politics. They hoped, in other words, to build the new world in the heart of the old. They distributed free food, organized festivals in the community, established a free medical clinic, and created free stores where anyone could give, or take, whatever they pleased. Below is an excerpt from a collection of Digger writings known as the "Digger Papers."

*   *   *

Our authorized sanities are so many Nembutals. "Normal" citizens with store-dummy smiles stand apart from each other like cotton-packed capsules in a bottle. Perpetual mental out-patients. Maddeningly sterile jobs for strait-jackets, love scrubbed into an insipid "functional personal relationship" and Art as a fantasy pacifier. Everyone is kept inside while the outside is shown through windows: advertising and manicured news. And we all know this.

[...]

But there is a real danger in suddenly waking a somnambulistic patient. And we all know this.

What if he is startled right out the window?

No one can control the single circuit-breaking moment that charges games with critical reality. If the glass is cut, if the cushioned distance of media is removed, the patients may never respond as normals again. They will become life-actors.

Theater is territory. A space for existing outside padded walls. Setting down a stage declares a universal pardon for imagination. But what happens next must mean more than sanctuary or preserve. [...]

Guerrilla theater intends to bring audiences to liberated territory to create life-actors. It remains light and exploitative of forms for the same reasons that it intends to remain free. It seeks audiences that are created by issues. It creates a cast of freed beings. It will become an issue itself.

This is theater of an underground that wants out. Its aim is to liberate ground held by consumer wardens and establish territory without walls. Its plays are glass cutters for empire windows.

Free store/property of the possessed

The Diggers are hip to property. Everything is free, do your own thing. Human beings are the means of exchange. Food, machines, clothing, materials, shelter and props are simply there. Stuff. A perfect dispenser would be an open Automat on the street. Locks are time-consuming. Combinations are clocks.

So a store of goods or clinic or restaurant that is free becomes a social art form. Ticketless theater. Out of money and control.

[...]

Diggers assume free stores to liberate human nature. First free the space, goods and services. Let theories of economics follow social facts. Once a free store is assumed, human wanting and giving, needing and taking, become wide open to improvization.

A sign: *If Someone Asks to See the Manager Tell Him He's the Manager.*

Someone asked how much a book cost. How much did he think it was worth? 75 cents. The money was taken and held out for anyone. "Who wants 75 cents?" A girl who had just walked in came over and took it.

A basket labeled *Free Money.*

No owner, no Manager, no employees and no cash-register. A salesman in a free store is a life-actor. Anyone who will assume an answer to a question or accept a problem as a turn-on.

[...]

Who's ready for the implications of a free store? Welfare mothers pile bags full of clothes for a few days and come back to hang up dresses. Kids case the joint wondering how to boost.

[...]

Where does the stuff come from? People, persons, beings. Isn't it obvious that objects are only transitory subjects of human value? An object released from one person's value may be destroyed, abandoned or made available to other people. The choice is anyone's.

The question of a free store is simply: What would you have?

[...]

Who paid for your trip?

Industrialization was a battle with nineteenth-century ecology to win breakfast at the cost of smog and insanity. Wars against ecology are suicidal. The U.S. standard of living is a bourgeois baby blanket for executives who scream in their sleep. No Pleistocene swamp could match the pestilential horror of modern urban sewage. No children of White Western Progress will escape the dues of peoples forced to haul their raw materials.

But the tools (that's all factories are) remain innocent and the ethics of greed aren't necessary. Computers render the principles of wage-labor obsolete by incorporating them. We are being freed from mechanistic consciousness. We could evacuate the factories, turn them over to androids, clean up our pollution. North Americans could give up self-righteousness to expand their being.

Our conflict is with job-wardens and consumer-keepers of a permissive looney-bin. Property, credit, interest, insurance, installments, profit are stupid concepts. Millions of have-nots and drop-outs in the U.S. are living on an overflow of technologically produced fat. They aren't fighting ecology, they're responding to it. Middle-class living rooms are funeral parlors and only undertakers will stay in them. Our fight is with those who would kill us through dumb work, insane wars, dull money morality.

Give up jobs, so computers can do them! Any important human occupation can be done free. Can it be given away?

Revolutions in Asia, Africa, South America are for humanistic industrialization. The technological resources of North America can be used throughout the world. Gratis. Not a patronizing gift, shared.

Our conflict begins with salaries and prices. The trip has been paid for at an incredible price in death, slavery, psychosis.

An event for the main business district of any U.S. city. Infiltrate the largest corporation office building with life-actors as nymphomaniacal secretaries, clumsy repairmen, berserk executives, sloppy security guards, clerks with animals in their clothes. Low key until the first coffee-break and then pour it on.

Secretaries unbutton their blouses and press shy clerks against the wall. Repairmen drop typewriters and knock over water coolers. Executives charge into private offices claiming their seniority. Guards produce booze bottles and playfully jam elevator doors. Clerks pull out goldfish, rabbits, pigeons, cats on leashes, loose dogs.

At noon 1000 freed beings singing and dancing appear outside to persuade employees to take off for the day. Banners roll down from office windows announcing liberation. Shills in business suits run out of the building, strip and dive in the fountain. Elevators are loaded with incense and a pie fight breaks out in the cafeteria. *Theater is fact/action*

Give up jobs. Be with people. Defend against property.

Republished in "The Digger Papers," *The Realist* 81, August 1968, 3.

TWO, THREE, MANY COLUMBIAS (1968)
Tom Hayden

One of the most dramatic student protests of the 1960s took place at Columbia University, in New York City. Students there criticized the university for weapons research, its strict disciplinary procedures, and for building a gym in a public park in Harlem. Although open to the community, Black residents would not only have limited access to the facilities, they would have to enter through a backdoor. On April 23, 1968, about 500 students, led by the Student Afro-American Society and the Students for a Democratic Society (SDS) tried to halt construction of the gym, sparking police repression. In retaliation, they occupied Hamilton Hall. Soon, however, Black students, insisting on their own autonomy, asked the whites to leave, which led to the occupation of even more buildings. On April

30, 1968, police cleared the buildings. Although the action ended in defeat, the university did scrap plans for the gym, Columbia terminated weapons research, and the occupation inspired students everywhere. Below we reprint a report on the occupation by Tom Hayden, one of the original leaders of SDS.

* * *

The goal written on the university walls was "Create two, three, many Columbias"; it meant expand the strike so that the U.S. must either change or send its troops to occupy American campuses.

[...]

The American student movement has continued to swell for nearly a decade: during the semi-peace of the early '60s as well as during Vietnam; during the token liberalism of John Kennedy as well as during the bankrupt racism of Lyndon Johnson. Students have responded most directly to the black movement of the '60s: from Mississippi Summer to the Free Speech Movement; from Black Power to Student Power; from the seizure of Howard University to the seizure of Hamilton Hall. As the racial crisis deepens so will the campus crisis. But the student protest is not just an offshoot of the black protest—it is based on authentic opposition to the middle-class world of manipulation, channeling and careerism. The students are in opposition to the fundamental institutions of society.

The students' protest constantly escalates by building on its achievements and legends. The issues being considered by 17-year-old freshmen at Columbia University would not have been within the imagination of most veteran student activists five years ago.

Columbia opened a new tactical stage in the resistance movement which began last fall: from the overnight occupation of buildings to permanent occupation; from mill-ins to the creation of revolutionary committees; from symbolic civil disobedience to barricaded resistance.

[...]

In the buildings occupied at Columbia, the students created what they called a new society or liberated area or commune, a society in which decent values would be lived out even though university officials might cut short the communes through use of police. The students had fun, they sang and danced and wisecracked, but there was continual tension. There was no question of their constant awareness of the seriousness of their acts. Though there were a few violent arguments about tactics, the discourse was more in the form of endless meetings convened to explore the outside political situation, defense tactics, maintenance and morale problems within the group. Debating and then determining what leaders should do were alternatives to the remote and authoritarian decision making of Columbia's trustees.

The Columbia strike represented more than a new tactical movement, however. There was a political message as well. The striking students were not holding onto a narrow conception of students as a privileged class asking for inclusion in the university as it now exists. [...] The Columbia students were instead taking an internationalist and revolutionary view of themselves in opposition to the imperialism of the very institutions in which they have been groomed and educated. They did not even want to be included in the decision-making circles of the military-industrial complex that runs Columbia: *they want to be included only if their inclusion is a step toward transforming the university.* They want a new and independent university standing against the mainstream of American society, or they want no university at all. They are, in Fidel Castro's words, "guerrillas in the field of culture."

[...] Columbia's problem is the American problem in miniature—the inability to provide answers to widespread social needs and the use of the military to protect the authorities against the people. This process can only lead to greater unity in the movement.

Support from outside the university communities can be counted on in many large cities. A crisis is foreseeable that would be too massive for police to handle. It can happen; whether or not it will be necessary is a question which only time will answer. What is certain is that we are moving toward power—the power to stop the machine if it cannot be made to serve humane ends.

American educators are fond of telling their students that barricades are a part of the romantic past, that social change today can only come about through the processes of negotiation. But the students at Columbia discovered that barricades are only the beginning of what they call bringing the war home.

Ramparts, June 15, 1968, 40.

REDSTOCKINGS MANIFESTO (1969)

Although they played an indispensable role in all the major movements of the time, many American women felt ignored, disrespected, and mistreated. In this context, activist women began to reflect on their experiences, hoping to develop a theory to explain what they were experiencing. Through consciousness-raising, they came to realize that what they assumed were personal issues were in fact shared, social problems. In the late 1960s, some women began to advocate for autonomous women's groups, giving rise to a constellation of feminist organizations that would make up women's liberation. Of course, women's liberation was by no means monolithic: women divided over questions of racism, heterosexuality, and capitalism. One wing of the movement, known as radical feminism, came to argue that the primary form of oppression in modern society was not capitalism, but patriarchy. One of the most famous early radical feminist organizations in the United States was Redstockings, formed in New York City in February 1969. Below, we reproduce the group's manifesto, from July 7, 1969.

* * *

1. After centuries of individual and preliminary political struggle, women are uniting to achieve their final liberation from male supremacy. Redstockings is dedicated to building this unity and winning our freedom.

2. Women are an oppressed class. Our oppression is total, affecting every facet of our lives. We are exploited as sex objects, breeders, domestic servants, and cheap labor. We are considered inferior beings, whose only purpose is to enhance men's lives. Our humanity is denied. Our prescribed behavior is enforced by the threat of physical violence.

    Because we have lived so intimately with our oppressors, in isolation from each other, we have been kept from seeing our personal suffering as a political condition. This creates the illusion that a woman's relationship with her man is a matter of interplay between two unique personalities, and can be worked out individually. In reality, every such relationship is a *class* relationship, and the conflicts between individual men and women are *political* conflicts that can only be solved collectively.

3. We identify the agents of our oppression as men. Male supremacy is the oldest, most basic form of domination. All other forms of exploitation and oppression (racism, capitalism, imperialism, etc.) are extensions of male supremacy: men dominate women, a few men dominate the rest. All power structures throughout history have been male-dominated and male-oriented. Men have controlled all political, economic and cultural institutions and backed up this control with physical force. They have used their power to keep women in an inferior position. *All men* receive economic, sexual, and psychological benefits from male supremacy. *All men* have oppressed women.

4. Attempts have been made to shift the burden of responsibility from men to institutions or to women themselves. We condemn these arguments as evasions. Institutions alone do not oppress; they are merely tools of the oppressor. To blame institutions implies that men and women are equally victimized, obscures the fact that men benefit from the subordination of women, and gives men the excuse that they are forced to be

oppressors. On the contrary, any man is free to renounce his superior position, provided that he is willing to be treated like a woman by other men.

We also reject the idea that women consent to or are to blame for their own oppression. Women's submission is not the result of brain-washing, stupidity or mental illness but of continual, daily pressure from men. We do not need to change ourselves, but to change men.

The most slanderous evasion of all is that women can oppress men. The basis for this illusion is the isolation of individual relationships from their political context and the tendency of men to see any legitimate challenge to their privileges as persecution.

5. We regard our personal experience, and our feelings about that experience, as the basis for an analysis of our common situation. We cannot rely on existing ideologies as they are all products of male supremacist culture. We question every generalization and accept none that are not confirmed by our experience.

Our chief task at present is to develop female class consciousness through sharing experience and publicly exposing the sexist foundation of all our institutions. Consciousness-raising is not "therapy," which implies the existence of individual solutions and falsely assumes that the male-female relationship is purely personal, but the only method by which we can ensure that our program for liberation is based on the concrete realities of our lives.

The first requirement for raising class consciousness is honesty, in private and in public, with ourselves and other women.

6. We identify with all women. We define our best interest as that of the poorest, most brutally exploited woman.

We repudiate all economic, racial, educational or status privileges that divide us from other women. We are determined to recognize and eliminate any prejudices we may hold against other women.

We are committed to achieving internal democracy. We will do whatever is necessary to ensure that every woman in our movement has an equal chance to participate, assume responsibility, and develop her political potential.

7. We call on all our sisters to unite with us in struggle.

We call on all men to give up their male privilege and support women's liberation in the interest of our humanity and their own. In fighting for our liberation we will always take the side of women against their oppressors. We will not ask what is "revolutionary" or "reformist," only what is good for women.

The time for individual skirmishes has passed. This time we are going all the way.

Republished in *Sisterhood is Powerful: An Anthology of Writings From the Liberation Movement*, ed. Robin Morgan (New York: Random House, 1970), 533–6.

RIGHT ON! (1969)
The Black Panther Party and Young Patriots Organization

Founded by Huey Newton and Bobby Seale in Oakland, California in October 1966, the Black Panther Party for Self-Defense was the most famous of the Black radical groups. As the name suggests, Newton and Seale initially created the group in response to police brutality. The best way to challenge police violence, Newton and Seale argued, was armed self-defense. Protecting their community, however, did not just mean taking up arms, but organizing a range of social welfare programs intended to "serve the people." Although focusing on the Black community, and remaining an all-Black group, the Panthers did not advocate separatism. In fact, in contrast to some cultural nationalists, the Panthers prioritized coalitions with other groups. One of the organizations the Panthers collaborated with was the Young Patriots Organization, a group of poor, white, Southern transplants. Below, we present the transcript of a meeting between the Panthers, Young Patriots, and white residents of Uptown, Chicago, captured in the 1969 film, American Revolution II.

* * *

Figure 1.2   A meeting between the Black Panther Party and the Young Patriots Organization. 1969.

Young Patriots organizer: […] I want to introduce us to a man, who come over tonight, from another part of town, but he's fighting for some of the same causes we're fighting for. And to start the meeting off, I'm going to introduce you to Bob Lee here. And I'm gonna let him rap a little while.

Bob Lee, Black Panther organizer: I'm a Black Panther. I'm a section leader of the Black Panthers. […] We met with Junebug and his brothers last Wednesday night in the Church of the Three Crosses where we both got a chance to rap, get together. The Panthers are here, are here. The Panthers are *here*. For Uptown. For anyone who lives in Uptown, whether he's brown, green, yellow, purple, or pink. When I say the Panthers are here, you have to tell us what we can do, and what we can do together. We come out here with our hearts open, you cats should supervise us, where we can be of help to you.

Junebug Boykin, Young Patriots organizer: One thing we have to do is put our heads together, and figure out how we can help Uptown, help the people of Uptown.

Young Patriots organizer: That's right.

Boykin: And the thing is that I want everybody who's got any questions at all to speak 'em up and say 'em now.

Lee: Who's here as concerned people? Who's here, wants to see this thing move? […] The first thing we are gonna talk about is how we organize, you know, where we gonna organize […] We gotta figure out what we want. What do we want? What do you want, man? What do you want, in your community? What do you want here?

Silence.

Lee: […] We not moving man. Are you afraid of the Panthers? Do you want us to take the berets off now? Or what?

Uptown Resident: Are you proposing doing a lot of marching and things like that?

Lee: No, sir. No, sir.

Uptown Resident: These marches seem to do more harm than good …

Lee: No, sir. No marches […] This is your community. This is *your* community. Let's move! You know, and we can't move without you. We can't move. We can't move without you people.

Uptown Resident: On the West Side, on the South Side, you have a basic unity to start with …

Lee: Skin color.

Uptown Resident: Right.

Lee: Ok, now, the thing we have to deal with is the concept of poverty, man. We gotta erase the color thing, see. I mean, the concept is the same

thing [...] there's welfare up here, people receive ADC [Aid to Families
with Dependent Children, a federal assistance program], there's police
brutality up here, there's rats and roaches, there's poverty up here. That's
the first thing that we can unite on. That's the common thing we have,
man. If we can unite on poverty, we can unite on the concept of poverty,
you know, everything becomes colorless, man.

Uptown Resident: Right on.

Uptown Resident: The building is not fit for dogs to live in but the humans
have to pay $144 a month for the thing [...] What we need is under-
standing among the people, coalition between the people, stick together,
and take them owners and put them in the lake somewhere.

Bobby Lee: Right on! Right on!

Clapping.

Lee: This man, the man right here, the things he's said, these are the things
to start working on, we're gonna start working on these very things.
Getting rid of the Urban Progress Center, if the cats gonna get themselves
together. Get rid of these little junkie employment agencies. These are the
things to start working from, man. These are things we can start working
from.

[...]

Uptown Resident: Call up the police when nothing's going on, the police
gonna come make it happen.

Uptown Resident: They try to put the words in your mouth, make you put
yourself in jail.

Uptown Resident: I want you people to stick together, and I'll stick with the
Black Panthers, if they stick with me. And I know they will.

Uptown Resident: We gotta do it our own way, and that's all there is to it.

Lee: Right on! Your own way.

Uptown Resident: I saw a Black Panthers movie last week. Their points are
real good, man. You gotta pick up the gun, that's all.

Lee: Right on!

Uptown Resident: I'm tired of it. I'm tired of them coming out of the street
and kicking my damn head in for nothing I ain't done.

Lee: Bobby Hutton gave his life, man. That cat was 18 years old. He gave his
life. And from that day on, the Panthers moved up [...] Panthers moved
up, cause Black communities knew, and felt, what Huey was saying. But
Huey, went out and did, for the people, what the people had wanted to
do for the last 15 to 20 years. He did to the pigs what Roger [previous
Uptown Resident] would like to do. We not saying "Go out and off the

Pigs," go out and start shooting the pigs. But that's the way Huey did it [...]

Uptown Resident [Roger]: But we gotta stop this shit one way or the other, if we have to fight with guns.

Lee: Before you can do that, gotta get some discipline [...] The first thing is discipline, man, gotta control the pig, before he off you. He off you, man. From here you start out going to community to community, know what you're doing. Cause see, if the pig off you, if he off you Roger, you be going to the funeral, you gonna get in the casket [...] You've got to have a community to back you. The pigs, the police, are protecting the landlords. If Roger runs out with a Molotov cocktail, to throw in one of these rat-infested buildings, they'll kill him. They kill him. They kill him. Someone answer, why does the man come down on us like that? Why?

Uptown Resident: It's what you're sayin', the police ain't about protecting people, they're about protecting property.

Lee: Right. You been to jail before, baby?

Uptown Resident: Yeah, twice.

Lee: Right on. [...] Once you realize, man, that your house is funky with rats and roaches, same as a Black dude's house is, once you realize that your brothers are getting brutalized by the cops, the same way the West Side and South Side is, once you realize that you are getting inadequate education in these high schools and junior high schools over here, same with the South Side and the West Side, once you realize you're paying taxes, taxes, for the cops to whoop your ass [...] You're paying 'em to whoop your ass. You're paying for them to come in and beat your children. You are paying for them to run you off the corner. And you're paying them to kill you. [...] The same thing is happening on the South Side and the West Side. If you can realize the concept of poverty, the concept of poverty, a revolution can begin [...]

Transcribed from *American Revolution II*, dir. Howard Alk, 1969.

13-POINT PROGRAM AND PLATFORM (1970)
Young Lords Party

The Young Lords began as a Puerto Rican street gang in 1960s Chicago. In 1968, the Young Lords took inspiration from the Black Panthers and reinvented themselves as a political organization, opening chapters in dozens of new cities, especially New York, home to the largest Puerto Rican community in the continental United States. Like the Panthers, the Young Lords aimed to serve the larger community by confronting police brutality, combating racial discrimination, and organizing a series of social welfare programs. Revolutionary internationalists, they not only called for Puerto Rican self-determination, but saw their struggle as deeply connected to the anti-imperialist movements unfolding across the globe in the 1960s and 1970s. The following is a revised version of their 13-point program.

* * *

THE YOUNG LORDS PARTY IS A REVOLUTIONARY POLITICAL PARTY FIGHTING FOR THE LIBERATION OF ALL OPPRESSED PEOPLE.

1. WE WANT SELF-DETERMINATION FOR PUERTO RICANS.
LIBERATION ON THE ISLAND AND INSIDE THE UNITED STATES.
For 500 years, first spain and then the united states have colonized our country. Billions of dollars in profits leave our country for the united states every year. In every way we are slaves of the gringo. We want liberation and the Power in the hands of the people, not Puerto Rican exploiters. QUE VIVA PUERTO RICO LIBRE!

2. WE WANT SELF-DETERMINATION FOR ALL LATINOS.
Our Latin Brothers and Sisters, inside and outside the united states, are oppressed by amerikkkan business. The Chicano people built the Southwest, and we support their right to control their lives and their land. The people of Santo Domingo continue to fight against gringo domination and its puppet generals. The armed liberation struggles in Latino America are part of the war of Latinos against imperialism. QUE VIVA LA RAZA!

3. WE WANT LIBERATION OF ALL THIRD WORLD PEOPLE.
Just as Latins first slaved under spain and the yanquis, Black people, Indians, and Asians slaved to build the wealth of this country. For 400 years they have fought for freedom and dignity against racist Babylon. Third World people have led the fight for freedom. All the colored and oppressed peoples of the world are one nation under oppression. NO PUERTO RICAN IS FREE UNTIL ALL PEOPLE ARE FREE!

4. WE ARE REVOLUTIONARY NATIONALISTS AND OPPOSE RACISM.
The Latin, Black, Indian and Asian people inside the u.s. are colonies fighting for liberation. We know that washington, wall street, and city hall will try to make our nationalism into racism; but Puerto Ricans are of all colors and we resist racism. Millions of poor white people are rising up to demand freedom and we support them. They are the ones in the u.s. that are stepped on by the rulers and the government. We each organize our people,

but our fights are the same against oppression and we will defeat it together. POWER TO ALL OPPRESSED PEOPLE!

5. WE WANT EQUALITY FOR WOMEN. DOWN WITH MACHISMO AND MALE CHAUVINISM.

Under capitalism, women have been oppressed by both society and our men. The doctrine of machismo has been used by men to take out their frustration on wives, sisters, mothers, and children. Men must fight along with sisters in the struggle for economic and social equality and must recognize that sisters make up over half of the revolutionary army; sisters and brothers are equal fighting for our people. FORWARD SISTERS IN THE STRUGGLE!

6. WE WANT COMMUNITY CONTROL OF OUR INSTITUTIONS AND LAND.

We want control of our communities by our people and programs to guarantee that all institutions serve the needs of our people. People's control of police, health services, churches, schools, housing, transportation and welfare are needed. We want an end to attacks on our land by urban renewal, highway destruction, universities and corporations. LAND BELONGS TO ALL THE PEOPLE!

7. WE WANT A TRUE EDUCATION OF OUR AFRO-INDIO CULTURE AND SPANISH LANGUAGE.

We must learn our long history of fighting against cultural, as well as economic genocide by the spaniards and now the yanquis. Revolutionary culture, culture of our people, is the only true teaching. JIBARO SI, YANQUI NO!

8. WE OPPOSE CAPITALISTS AND ALLIANCES WITH TRAITORS.

Puerto Rican rulers, or puppets of the oppressor, do not help our people. They are paid by the system to lead our people down blind alleys, just like the thousands of poverty pimps who keep our communities peaceful for business, or the street workers who keep gangs divided and blowing each other away. We want a society where the people socialistically control their labor. VENCEREMOS!

9. WE OPPOSE THE AMERIKKKAN MILITARY.

We demand immediate withdrawal of all u.s. military forces and bases from Puerto Rico, VietNam, and all oppressed communities inside and outside the u.s. No Puerto Rican should serve in the u.s. army against his Brothers and Sisters, for the only true army of oppressed people is the People's

Liberation Army to fight all rulers. U.S. OUT OF VIETNAM, FREE PUERTO RICO NOW!

10. WE WANT FREEDOM FOR ALL POLITICAL PRISONERS AND PRISONERS OF WAR.
No Puerto Rican should be in jail or prison, first because we are a nation, and amerikkka has no claims on us; second, because we have not been tried by our own people (peers). We also want all freedom fighters out of jail, since they are prisoners of the war for liberation. FREE ALL POLITICAL PRISONERS AND PRISONERS OF WAR!

11. WE ARE INTERNATIONALISTS.
Our people are brainwashed by television, radio, newspapers, schools, and books to oppose people in other countries fighting for their freedom. No longer will we believe these lies, because we have learned who the real enemy is and who our real friends are. We will defend our sisters and brothers around the world who fight for justice and are against the rulers of this country. QUE VIVA CHE GUEVARA!

12. WE BELIEVE ARMED SELF-DEFENSE AND ARMED STRUGGLE ARE THE ONLY MEANS TO LIBERATION.
We are opposed to violence—the violence of hungry children, illiterate adults, diseased old people, and the violence of poverty and profit. We have asked, petitioned, gone to courts, demonstrated peacefully, and voted for politicians full of empty promises. But we still ain't free. The time has come to defend the lives of our people against repression and for revolutionary war against the businessmen, politicians, and police. When a government oppresses the people, we have the right to abolish it and create a new one. ARM OURSELVES TO DEFEND OURSELVES!

13. WE WANT A SOCIALIST SOCIETY.
We want liberation, clothing, free food, education, health care, transportation, full employment and peace. We want a society where the needs of the people come first, and where we give solidarity and aid to the people of the world, not oppression and racism. HASTA LA VICTORIA SIEMPRE!

Palante 2, no. 15, November 20, 1970, 22.

Further Reading

Adam, Barry D. *The Rise of a Gay and Lesbian Movement*, Revised Edition. Farmington Hills, MI: Twayne Publishers, 1995.

Banks, Dennis, with Richard Erdoes. *Ojibwa Warrior: Dennis Banks and the Rise of the American Indian Movement*. Norman, OK: University of Oklahoma Press, 2004.

Brenner, Aaron, Robert Brenner, and Cal Winslow, eds. *Rebel Rank And File: Labor Militancy and Revolt from Below During the Long 1970s*. London: Verso, 2010.

Chávez, Ernesto. *My People First!: Nationalism, Identity, and Insurgency in the Chicano Movement in Los Angeles, 1966-1978*. Berkeley, CA: University of California Press, 2002.

Echols, Alice. *Daring to Be Bad: Radical Feminism in America, 1967–1975*. Minneapolis, MN: University of Minnesota Press, 1989.

Elbaum, Max. *Revolution in the Air: Sixties Radicals Turn to Lenin, Mao, and Che*. London: Verso, 2018.

Faber, David, ed. *The Sixties: From Memory to History*. Chapel Hill, NC: The University of North Carolina Press, 1994.

Georgakas, Dan, and Marvin Surkin. *Detroit, I Do Mind Dying: A Study in Urban Revolution*. Cambridge, MA: South End Press, 1998.

Halliwell, Martin, and Nick Witham, eds. *Reframing 1968: American Politics, Protest, and Identity*. Edinburgh: Edinburgh University Press, 2018.

Ishizuka, Karen L. *Serve the People: Making Asian America in the Long 1960s*. London: Verso, 2016.

Miller, James. *Democracy is in the Streets: From Port Huron to the Siege of Chicago*. Cambridge, MA: Harvard University Press, 2004.

Peniel, Joseph E. *Waiting 'Til the Midnight Hour: A Narrative History of Black Power in America*. New York: Henry Holt and Company, 2006.

Sonnie, Amy, and James Tracy. *Hillbilly Nationalists, Urban Race Rebels, and Black Power: Community Organizing in Radical Times*. Brooklyn, NY: Melville House Publishing, 2011.

Spencer, Robyn C. *The Revolution Has Come: Black Power, Gender, and the Black Panther Party in Oakland*. Durham, NC: Duke University Press, 2016.

Thompson, Heather. *Blood in the Water: The Attica Prison Uprising of 1971 and its Legacy*. New York: Pantheon Books, 2016.

Wells, Tom. *The War Within: America's Battle Over Vietnam*. Berkeley, CA: University of California Press, 1994.

Wu, Judy Tzu-Chun. *Radicals on the Road: Internationalism, Orientalism, and Feminism during the Vietnam War Era*. Ithaca, NY: Cornell University Press, 2013.

Young, Cynthia. *Soul Power: Culture, Radicalism, and the Making of a U.S. Third World Left*. Durham, NC: Duke University Press, 2006.

2
Canada

After the Second World War, Canada struggled to forge a national identity. The 1950s to 1960s was an important period in the full cultural and political separation of this former British colony from Great Britain. In practice, this meant realignment with the United States, as Canada not only allied with its southern neighbor in the Cold War, but emerged as the single most important national outlet for U.S. direct investment, provoking some anxiety among Canadians who feared American domination.

Domestically, the country remained divided. After the Second World War, Canada became a major destination for a new generation of migrants. Regional divisions also persisted, above all in Québec, where French Canadians complained of Anglophone political, cultural, and economic discrimination—in 1961, for example, the average income for Francophones was estimated at a full 35 percent less than their Anglophone counterparts. Most importantly, Canada remained haunted by its history as a settler colony, as Indigenous people remained second-class citizens in a land that had been systematically stolen from them.

In 1963, the Liberal Party came to power promising to enact social change, unify the country, and catapult Canada into the front rank of the advanced capitalist world. Over its years in power, this government decriminalized homosexuality, put a moratorium on capital punishment, legalized hormonal contraception, and introduced universal health care. In 1965, as if to symbolize the new Canada, the country adopted a new flag, the Maple Leaf.

At this time, Canada also experienced a massive economic boom, particularly in the province of Québec. Here, the "Quiet Revolution" secularized the government, established a robust welfare state, expanded education, and unleashed a period of unprecedented development. To showcase these changes to the world, in 1967, Canada's centennial, Montréal hosted Expo 67, the largest world fair to that date. Adopting the motto, "Man and His World," the Expo exemplified this almost boundless optimism in the progress of humanity. The following year, Pierre Trudeau, the mediagenic Québécois, became Prime Minister.

Yet despite all these signs of progress, dissatisfaction brewed across the country, sometimes in direct reaction to these developments. In the early 1960s, for example, Canada's realignment with the United States gave rise to a peace movement, especially when the U.S. government insisted that Canada field tactical nuclear weapons. The Combined Universities Campaign for Nuclear Disarmament (CUCND), which looked both to the Campaign for Nuclear Disarmament in Great Britain and the peace movements in the United States, introduced a whole generation to activism. When the CUCND began to decline in 1964, radical students formed the Student Union for Peace Action (SAPU) in December of that year. Inspired by American movements, particularly Students for a Democratic Society, SAPU organized a host of projects, from student syndicalism to community organizing, a school for social theory to actions in support of the civil rights movement in the United States.

As elsewhere, attention turned firmly to the Vietnam War after 1965. Although not a belligerent, Canada was involved in the war. Thousands of Canadians volunteered to serve in the U.S. armed forces; Canadian corporations sold war material to the United States; and although Canada was a member of the International Control Commission, and therefore tasked with trying to find peace, the government was strongly pro-American. The war also came home to Canada, as tens of thousands of Americans sought refuge up north. There, Americans worked with groups like SAPU, which helped them start new lives, and some, especially partners of draft dodgers, would play important roles in Canadian social movements, like women's liberation.

Figure 2.1 Poster sold by the Vancouver Women's Caucus to raise money for the Indochinese Women's Conference. 1971.

Although factional fighting and strategic dilemmas led to the dissolution of SAPU in the summer of 1967, radicalism quickly spread. Protests rocked campuses across the country. The Canadian Student Union took a militant turn. Young Canadians threw themselves into party building, forming dozens of radical organizations of all stripes. Feminists broke new ground, and in 1967 four SAPU women wrote, "Sisters, Brothers, Lovers ... Listen," one of the founding documents of women's liberation in Canada. Women's groups proliferated across the country, pushing the radical critique even further.

Discontent also took the form of competing nationalisms. By raising expectations, the Quiet Revolution helped shift the political terrain in Québec, creating space for more radical voices. Seeing Québec as a kind of internal colony, radical Québécois called for national liberation, taking inspiration from the decolonization struggles of the period. In 1963, some formed the Front de Libération du Québec (FLQ), which soon turned to armed struggle, carrying out over 150 attacks in the 1960s. In 1969, the FLQ bombed the Montréal Stock Exchange, and in 1970 kidnapped a British diplomat, leading Prime Minister Trudeau to invoke the War Measures Act during peacetime.

Ethnic minorities in Canada also took a stand. In Québec itself, Black Canadians, many of them Caribbean immigrants, fought to make their voices heard. In October 1968, Black students organized the Congress of Black Writers at McGill University. In 1969, after the administration dragged its feet over student accusations of discriminatory grading at Sir George Williams University, Black students took matters into their own hands, occupying the university's computer lab. Riot police were called, a fire broke out, and Canada's largest occupation ended with $2 million worth of property destroyed and 87 students under arrest.

At the same time, Indigenous peoples spoke out against discrimination, inadequate living conditions, unemployment, disproportionately lower wages, high rates of incarceration, and the long history of oppression and cultural effacement. Trudeau's government took notice, issuing a White Paper in 1969 that acknowledged the government's responsibility, but proposed a solution that many felt amounted to coercive assimilation. The paper's top-down approach further galvanized a wave of Red Power activism that was already taking shape in Canada, as in the United States further south. The Assembly of Indian Chiefs of Alberta, to name only one group, issued a thorough refutation of the federal government's proposal, called "Citizen's Plus," which became more commonly known as the "Red Paper."

This period was also marked by a crescendo of worker struggles. Although most of the attention went to the universities, the majority of young activists in Canada were not students. In fact, in 1965, only 11 percent of Canadians aged 18 to 24 were enrolled in university. Most youth, in other words, were workers, and they tended to live at home. Dissatisfied with authoritarian family life, anxious about future precarity, discontented with working conditions, and critical of moderate, bureaucratic, and often U.S.-dominated union leaderships, these young workers injected a new militancy into the labor movement. In the mid-1960s, wildcat strikes exploded throughout Canada, with nearly 7.5 million worker-days lost between 1963 and 1965. The mid-1960s conflagration initiated a wave of worker struggles that continued into the 1970s. In Québec, for example, unions came together in a "Common Front," which organized a major strike action in 1972 when public sector contracts came up for negotiation. In May of that year, 300,000 workers went on strike, workplaces were occupied, and even a radio station was seized.

Although sometimes overlooked, Canada's long 1968 was as dynamic as many of the other countries in this collection. The student movement was combative. Radical organizations were proportionally quite large, with one Maoist organization reaching around 5,000 members. Strikes were widespread, with rates similar to Italy. Armed struggle provoked a national crisis. Most importantly, many of the struggles were connected, with labor serving as a kind of anchor: students threw themselves into labor activism, feminists theorized the relationship between women's oppression and capitalism, abortion clinics were established in union offices, and strong links forged between labor and national struggles.

In fact, what made Canada's long 1968 so unique was the powerful articulation of layered national questions with a very high degree of class militancy. On the one side, the interplay of different forms of national oppression—Canada's dependence on the United States, Québec's subordination to the central government, ongoing racial discrimination, the plight of migrants, and the legacies of settler colonialism—generated intense political engagement. This context allowed for especially strong resonances with movements in the "Third World."

On the other side, the depth of labor mobilization was striking. From the start, students aligned with labor, building student unions, striking at vocational schools, and turning to deep labor activism. And like France and Italy, workers played a decisive role, as a variety of distinct sectors came together to build a vibrant labor movement. It was precisely the encounter of these two elements, activism around the volatile national questions and intense labor militancy, that propelled Canada's long 1968. This was most clearly seen in Québec, where economic exploitation and national oppression combined—many Québécois workers, for example, were forced to speak English at work because their Anglophone bosses did not want to learn French—to create an explosive situation where nationalism and class struggle super-charged each other, turning the province into a kind of epicenter of revolt.

The consequences of this wave of revolt were ambiguous. On the one hand, it generated lasting social benefits, improved labor rights, protection of the French language, a greater attentiveness to diversity. In some ways, much of Canada's "distinctiveness" with the United States was established in this period. On the other hand, these major concessions were limited— liberal multiculturalism instead of committed anti-racism, or the continuity of settler colonial relations instead of a radical break with the past—and some of these gains soon came under fire, such as wage and price controls in 1974, the beginning of what would be a counter-offensive against labor.

MESSAGE OF THE FLQ TO THE NATION (1963)
Front de Libération du Québec

The anti-colonial and anti-imperialist revolutions that broke out across the globe in the 1950s and early 1960s re-energized the Québec sovereignty movement. Inspired by the successes of struggles elsewhere, one wing of the movement turned to armed struggle. In 1963, these activists founded the Québec Liberation Front, a loose network of cells, and began a series of bombings. That year, the "Felquistes," as members of the group would be called, released their first manifesto, which surveyed the history of Québec, explained why they believed Québécois are an oppressed people, and outlined the FLQ's objectives. We reproduce this manifesto below.

* * *

Patriots:

Since the Second World War, the diverse dominated peoples of the world have broken their chains in order to acquire the freedom to which they have a right. The immense majority of these peoples have defeated the oppressor and today live freely.

After so many others, the Québécois people have had enough of submitting to the domination of Anglo-Saxon capitalism.

In Québec, as in all colonized countries, the oppressor furiously denies his imperialism, and is supported in this by our so-called national elite, which is more interested in serving its personal economic interests than in serving the vital interests of the Québécois nation. It persists in denying the evidence and works at creating multiple false problems, wanting to turn the subject people away from the only one that is essential: INDEPENDENCE.

Despite this, the workers' eyes every day open a little bit more concerning reality: Québec is a colony.

We are politically, socially, and economically colonized. Politically because we don't possess the political levers vital to our survival. The colonialist government in Ottawa in fact has all jurisdiction in the following domains: economy, foreign trade, defense, bank credit, immigration, criminal law, etc. In addition, any provincial law can be refused if Ottawa wills to do so.

The federal government, being totally owned by the interests of Anglo-Saxon imperialists, and who have an overwhelming constitutional and practical majority in it, serves to constantly maintain and accentuate Québécois inferiority. […] Politically, the people of Québec are thus a colonized people.

It is also so economically. One sentence alone is enough to prove it: more than 80% of our economy is controlled by foreign interests. We furnish the labor, they pocket the profits.

Even socially Québec is a colonized country. We are 80% of the population, yet the English language dominates in the most diverse domains. Little by little French is relegated to the rank of folklore, while English becomes the language of the workplace. The contempt of the Anglo-Saxons toward our people remains constant. The "Speak white, Stupid French Canadian," and other epithets of this kind, are very frequent. In Québec itself, thousands of cases of English unilingualism are arrogantly displayed. The colonialists consider us inferior beings, and let us know this without any shame.

[…]

The Québécois patriots have had enough of fighting for almost a century for things of no importance, of expending their vital energy in obtaining illusory profits that are always put in doubt.

It's enough to think of the hundreds of thousands of unemployed, of the wretched poverty of the fishermen of the Gaspe Peninsula, of the thousands of farmers across Québec whose revenue is barely more than $1,000 a year, of the thousands of young people who can't pursue their studies due to lack of funds, of the thousands of people who have no recourse to the most elementary medical care, of the poverty of our miners, of the general insecurity of all those who have a job: This is what colonialism has given us.

In Québec we also have the unjust and paradoxical situation that is exemplified in the comparison between the neighborhoods of St Henri and Westmount. On one side we find a mass typically Québécois, poor and miserable, while on the other side an English minority shows-off the most shameful of riches. Our progressive economic defeat, a foreign domination more and more complete, don't demand provisional and short-term solutions. The Patriots say NO TO COLONIALISM, NO TO EXPLOITATION.

But it's not enough to refuse a situation; it must be remedied. Our situation is one of national urgency. It is now that it must be remedied.

Let us acquire the vital political levers; let us take control of our economy; let us radically purify our social framework; let us tear off colonialist restraints; let's throw out the imperialists who live by the exploitation of the workers of Québec. The immense natural riches of Québec must belong to the Québécois!

In order to do this there is one solution and one solution alone: the national revolution in the midst of INDEPENDENCE. Otherwise the people of Québec cannot hope to live free.

But it's not enough to want independence, to work within the existing *independantiste* political parties. The colonialists will not so easily let go such a tasty morsel. The *independantiste* political parties can never have the power needed to defeat colonial political and economic power. What is more, independence alone will resolve nothing. It must at all costs be completed by the social revolution. The Québécois Patriots aren't fighting for a title, but for facts. The Revolution doesn't happen in salons. Only a total revolution can have the strength necessary to carry out the vital changes that will impose themselves in an independent Québec. The national revolution, in its essence, doesn't allow any compromise. There is only one way to defeat colonialism, and that's to be stronger than it! Only the most aberrant naïveté can lead one to believe the contrary. The time of slavery is over.

PATRIOTS OF QUÉBEC, TO ARMS! THE HOUR OF NATIONAL REVOLUTION HAS COME!

INDEPENDENCE OR DEATH!

Retrieved from Marxists Internet Archive: marxists.org/history/canada/quebec/flq/1963/message-nation.htm.

LETTER TO STOKELY CARMICHAEL (1968)
Charles Gagnon and Pierre Vallières

Some FLQ activists, like Charles Gagnon and Pierre Vallières, saw the Québécois struggle for national liberation as part of the larger wave of anti-imperialist revolutions. They drew particular inspiration from Black struggles in the United States. In fact, the analogy between French Québécois and Black Americans was so central that Vallières would later call French Québécois the "white niggers" of America. Gagnon and Vallières hoped to create a kind of coordinated network across North America to unify different movements. In the summer of 1966, they traveled to the United States, where they met radicals like Stokely Carmichael. After their own FLQ cell was infiltrated in Montréal, Gagnon and Vallières decided to stage a protest in front of the United Nations in September 1966, expecting their arrest to attract worldwide attention. While imprisoned they received a letter of support from Stokely Carmichael. On April 6, 1968, after Martin Luther King's assassination, they returned the gesture.

* * *

Brother and comrade, we are deeply indignant and revolted by the cowardly and racist attempt on Reverend King. The time has come for Black Americans and the white niggers of Québec and America to unite their forces to destroy the capitalist and imperialist Order which assassinates those who choose to break the chains of slavery and liberate humanity from oppression, exploitation and all forms of enslavement. We are uniting with you to avenge the heroic death of Reverend King, of Malcolm X, and all those who paid with their lives, their passion for justice, freedom, equality, brotherhood and peace. The only answer to capitalist and racist violence can be nothing but a liberating violence of the oppressed who together have the historic duty to free humanity from the old system's rottenness. We shall overcome brothers and sisters. Let's go forward.

Charles Gagnon
Pierre Vallières
Front de Libération du Québec
on behalf of the white niggers of Québec

Reprinted in Nicholas M. Regush, *Pierre Vallieres: The Revolutionary Process in Quebec* (New York: The Dial Press, 1973), 6.

BLACK WRITERS CONGRESS:
THE ORGANIZERS TALK ... (1968)
Keith Byrne, Rosie Douglas, and Elder Thébaud

In his attempt to theorize the experience of French-speaking Québécois, Pierre Vallières coined the phrase "white niggers." The oppression they faced at the hands of the Anglophones, he argued in his famous book from 1968, White Niggers of America, *was similar to that experienced by Blacks at the hands of whites in the United States. There were, however, tens of thousands of Blacks in Canada who rightly wondered where they fit into this schema. In fact, the 1960s saw the growth of vibrant Black communities across Canada, especially in Vallières' own province of Québec, where Blacks organized robust movements against racism. Among their many initiatives was the Montréal Congress of Black Writers, a four-day congress in October 1968 that brought together some of the leading Black thinkers on the planet, such as CLR James, Walter Rodney, and Stokely Carmichael. Here we reproduce an interview with the Congress organizers.*

* * *

The Review: Could you tell us something of the aims of the Congress, what you hope to achieve?

Keith Byrne: At the present moment, the struggle between oppressed and the oppressors is bordering on total racial war. Black people are becoming really fed up with being pushed about and it is necessary now, especially with what has been happening in the States—spontaneous outbursts of violence—to take some sort of perspective as to where we go, what the problem really is, who we are, where we come from, and where we are going. This is the purpose: to trace the whole history of black literature. That is why the program is called, "The dynamics of black liberation."

The conference in itself is an analysis, a diagnosis—for instance you have cancer: in order to find the cure for cancer, you must first find the cause of cancer. This conference is designed, and the purpose of it really is, to analyze the problem, to diagnose the problem, to find the cause of the problem, and then to cure it.

The Review: Can you tell us something about the people, or groups, who are organizing the Congress?

Rosie Douglas: Well, originally, we started with a group of people who were interested in trying to organize a conference which would bring to light the very crucial problems which the black community in Montreal and those all over the world are facing. [...]

[...]

No associations were involved in the early stages—it was based more on individual interest. But something happened which probably will stand out as a landmark of this Congress, in that for the first time we were able to bring together English and French-speaking black people to unite and join this very serious effort. This I think will be the primary achievement of the Congress, not to mention the fact that there were brothers and sisters from Africa, Canada, the United States, Latin America, and the Caribbean.

The Review: Do you see a relation between the struggle for black liberation and the student movement, the idea that students, white and black, in North America and in world university campuses are oppressed in a certain fashion? Do you think there can be, as the Panthers have said in their manifesto, a principled coalition between the oppressed blacks and the oppressed whites, or do you think that students are an oppressed class at all?

Keith Byrne: This is a very tricky question, the participation of white students in black liberation. Of course, they are in some way related. But I do not think you can compare them because they are two separate issues. Students and student movements did not at any time experience the type of decerebration and deculturation, dehumanization, that black people have encountered or experienced; so in this respect, I think that one has to draw very clear lines as to what you meant by that.

[...]

Rosie Douglas: At this particular point, I think that it is absolutely necessary despite the similarities, which obviously exist between the two different groups, for whites to organize themselves and work on their level while blacks work on theirs. We might be working towards a similar goal, but the time for a coalition—I don't think we have arrived at that stage yet. The SNCC started in that way, with the white students participating in voter registration. And many of them made a valuable contribution.

Poussaint will probably be dealing with that in his talk. He drew a pretty clear line on this particular point when he said that the years of slavery and the years of the struggle have formed or created a certain atmosphere or environment in which it is almost impossible for a white man to really understand the problems of a black man. And working together is almost meaningless—there is no respect.

Elder Thébaud: Distrust between the communities is too deep. Some white people think that there is good reason to support, for example, black power, because to have a white teacher teaching black children is a kind of psychological trauma that should be avoided at this moment. It seems that it is better if white and black people work separately and if white people try to educate their own communities. And here I'm not speaking about separatism as such.

[...]

The Review: Elder, would you care to expand on what Rosie said about the significance of both French and English speaking people taking part in the Congress?

Elder Thébaud: First, I would say that Québec is a bilingual province, but this is only secondary. In fact, what's important is that blacks of different languages have realized that they have a community of interest, that they were subjected to slavery in the same way that their English-speaking brothers, or their brothers in Brazil, who speak Portuguese, were. They have finally realized that the black liberation movement has to be internationalized.

[...]

The Review: What do you hope will happen as a consequence of the conference having taken place?

Rosie Douglas: [...] [W]e do hope that the Congress will generate interest among white and black people in this community. [...] We hope that this will be only the beginning of the continuing development of a new level of consciousness among black people in Montreal. The problems of black people in Canada are very severe, and difficult because they are covered up, not as open as they are in the U.S. [...]

[...]

The Review, McGill Daily Supplement, October 11, 1968, 2, 4–5, 7.

EIGHT-POINT PROGRAM (1969)
Native Alliance for Red Power

Several centuries of settler colonialism destroyed most of the Indigenous population in what came to be known as Canada. Those who survived were forcibly integrated into Canada's nation-building process, expelled from the land, sent to residential schools, and saw their ways of life eradicated. Assimilation was deliberately uneven, as Indigenous peoples were integrated not as equals, but as marginalized subjects. Nowhere was the contradiction between the rhetoric of the postwar decades and the realities on the ground more glaring. In general, Indigenous peoples saw little of the "just society," and by some metrics, their situation worsened in the 1960s. But they drew on older traditions, as well as new movements, like Black Power, to fight back. Founded in 1967, the Native Alliance for Red Power (NARP) emerged as one of Canada's earliest Red Power groups. Below, we reproduce the group's program, first published in the January–February 1969 issue of their newsletter.

* * *

Figure 2.2 Cover of the *NARP Newsletter*. June/
July, 1969.

1. We will not be free until we are able to determine our own destiny.
   Therefore, we want power to determine the destiny of our reservations

and communities. Gaining power in our reservations and communities, and power over our lives will entail the abolishment of the "Indian Act," and the destruction of the colonial office (Indian Affairs Branch).

2. This racist government has robbed, cheated and brutalized us, and is responsible for the deaths of untold numbers of our people. We feel under no obligation to support this government in the form of taxation. Therefore, we want an end to the collection of money from us in the form of taxes.

3. The history of Canada was written by the oppressors, the invaders of this land. Their lies are perpetrated in the educational system of today. By failing to expose the true history of this decadent Canadian society, the schools facilitate our continued oppression. Therefore, we want an education that teaches us our true history and exposes the racist values of this society.

4. In this country, Indian and Métis represent three percent of the population, yet we constitute approximately 60 percent of the inmates in prisons and jails. Therefore, we want an immediate end to the unjust arrests and harassment of our people by the racist police.

5. When brought before the courts of this country, the red man cannot hope to get a fair hearing from white judges, jurors and court officials. Therefore, we want natives to be tried by a jury of people chosen from native communities or people of their racial heritage. Also, we want freedom for those of our brothers and sisters now being unjustly held in the prisons of this country.

6. The treaties pertaining to fishing, hunting, trapping and property rights and special privileges have been broken by this government. In some cases, our people did not engage in treaties with the government and have not been compensated for their loss of land. Therefore, for those of our people we want fair compensation. Also, we want the government to honor the statutes, as laid down in these treaties, as being supreme and not to be infringed upon by any legislation whatsoever.

7. The large industrial companies and corporations that have raped the natural resources of this country are responsible, along with their government, for the extermination of the resources upon which we depend for food, clothing and shelter. Therefore, we want an immediate end to this exploitation, and compensation from these thieves. We want the government to give foreign aid to the areas comprising the Indian Nation, so that we can start desperately needed programs concerning housing, agricultural and industrial cooperatives. We want to develop our remaining resources in the interests of the red man, not in the interests of the white corporate elite.

8. The white power structure has used every possible method to destroy our spirit, and the will to resist. They have divided us into status and nonstatus, American and Canadian, Métis and Indian. We are fully aware of their "divide and rule" tactic, and its effect on our people.

RED POWER IS THE SPIRIT TO RESIST.
RED POWER IS PRIDE IN WHAT WE ARE.
RED POWER IS LOVE FOR OUR PEOPLE.
RED POWER IS OUR COMING TOGETHER TO FIGHT FOR LIBERATION.
RED POWER IS NOW!

NARP Newsletter, June–July 1969, 4.

SALT OF THE EARTH … TWO FOR THE PRICE OF ONE (1971)
Workers' Unity

As in other countries, Canada witnessed the rise of a women's liberation movement. Many of its founders emerged from the New Left, often in reaction to the sexism they faced within the larger movement. From the start, feminism in Canada was heavily inspired by women's liberation in the United States. An important difference, however, was the relative strength of socialist feminism in Canada. In fact, Canadian women produced a plethora of sophisticated analyses that attempted to theorize the relationship between capitalism and the oppression of women. Margaret Benston's "The Political Economy of Women's Liberation" and Peggy Morton's "Women's Work is Never Done," are only two of the most famous examples. Below, we reprint an article from Workers' Unity, *a paper produced by rank-and-file workers in the United Auto Workers (UAW) in Windsor, Ontario, which synthesizes some core socialist feminist ideas of the period.*

* * *

Very few of us think of work that is done in the home as work for the company. It is hard to believe that preparing meals, washing and mending clothes, or mopping floors has anything to do with auto production. Yet, in a very real way, the work that is done by housewives is essential to every corporation in this society. Perhaps we can best understand this if we look at the work done inside the plant in the area of maintenance. First of all, there are various types of repairmen whose job it is to keep the machines in working order; then there are janitors who keep the plants clean. None of these men are directly involved in the actual production of cars, but without them, the plants would soon cease operation.

Just as the company cannot get along without its internal maintenance, so it cannot get along without its *external* maintenance—housewives who work in the home. In each working family, the woman has the job of maintaining the workers so that they can go on working—and making more profits for the company. We are responsible for preparing meals, washing clothes, and keeping the house clean and livable. We do not mind doing these jobs for our families, but we do resent the fact that our labor allows the company to exploit our men even more. Without our services, the workforce would not be able to carry on. That is one of the reasons why every corporation prefers to hire married men. Every time we load those dirty, oily work clothes into the washer, for example, we should remember that the basic reason why the company does not provide and maintain protective clothing for its workers is because we women do that—for nothing! And not only do we keep the present workforce going; we also feed, care for, and educate our children who are the workers of the future.

As women, we know how important our work in the home is, but in a very real way our labor is not considered "real work" at all. We've all had the experience of having our husbands come home, sit down to dinner in a nice clean kitchen, and say "Now, dear, what did you do all day?" Of course, this attitude is not his fault; our last article talked about the way in which men are so cut off from the lives of their families that they do not know what goes on all day. In another way, though, such a comment reveals a great deal about what is regarded as "real work" in society. Our economic system considers that the only "real work" involves the production of things to be sold.

Because housewives do not *produce* anything, their labor has no "exchange value" (an economist's term for labor which produces goods to be sold) and, in the eyes of this system, it is not "real work."

This may seem like a silly word game until we look at what it means for us in our everyday lives. It is estimated that a woman with one or more children works at least 60 to 80 hours per week at housework and childcare. At the same time her husband works 40 hours a week in auto production and receives about $4 per hour. Yet, in paying the man's wage, the company actually buys the labor of *two* people—it gets 100 hours (40 plus 60) for the price of 40. And if the man is killed or seriously injured on the job, the woman is left with nothing beyond a meager pension, or, more often, the humiliating handouts of the welfare system. Her labor is vitally necessary to the society, but under the present economic system, she has no assurance of secure financial support.

Even if all goes well and the man is able to keep his job, it is very difficult to make ends meet. More and more families are finding it necessary to have a second wage—the woman's—so that they can afford the things they need. Yet even on the labor market, a woman is not treated fairly. Usually her place of work is not unionized and her wages are ⅓ to ½ that of men doing similar work. If she is in the union—like UAW—her needs as a woman are overlooked by the union bureaucracy. The union seldom, if ever, demands that the company provide some sort of care for her children, for example, so that the woman must pay for a babysitter out of her wages. As well, she is now expected to hold down two jobs, since working in the factory does not mean that she can forget about the work at home. If anything, her work in the factory is considered secondary to her primary job of housewife and mother, even though she may have to work because her husband does not make enough to support the family! Very few women take jobs in a factory because they *like* it!

We recognize, of course, that the work women do, at home or outside, is done because we love our families and want to provide the best we can for them. This does not mean, however, that women should accept silently the treatment we receive. We can find solutions to the problems we face by first understanding clearly where the cause of these problems lie, and then by working together to solve them. At the most basic level, the fault lies with the corporations who control our lives and not the individual husband. This paper is the beginning of an attempt to understand that control and to find an alternative to it. When we talk about Workers' Unity, then, we must talk about the unity of men *and women*, whether they work in the factory or at home.

Republished in *Women Unite!: An Anthology of the Canadian Women's Movement* (Toronto: Canadian Women's Educational Press, 1972), 149–50.

PHASE ONE (1971)
Corporation des Enseignants du Québec

The early 1970s witnessed a sharp rise in working-class militancy across Canada. In Québec, rank-and-file workers pushed the unions to not only adopt a more radical stance, but to form a "Common Front" between the province's three largest unions, the Confédération des Syndicats Nationaux (CSN), the Fédération des Travailleurs du Québec (FTQ), and the Corporation des Enseignants du Québec (CEQ), the federation representing Québec's 70,000 French-speaking teachers. Together, these unions, which represented 210,000 out of 250,000 public sector workers in the province, called for higher wages, better conditions, a greater say in the workplace, and an end to discrimination. As a sign of the new radical turn, committees within each of the unions proposed manifestoes to chart a more militant path forward. Below we reproduce excerpts from the foreword of the CEQ's manifesto, "Phase One."

* * *

[...]

The most upsetting thing about actual trade-union work is that everything is reduced to collective bargaining. As important as that may be, it ignores too many of the problems which confront us in everyday life.

If salaried workers like us accept this situation and forget all about the rights which we have obtained through the many struggles of the working-class movement in general and the trade unions in particular, it means we accept a situation of dependency. In other words, freedom means deciding how much money you can bargain for. Is everybody to let his liberty be defined by the will of the bosses? Wages make the worker's life depend on his job and his boss, in the same way as the umbilical cord makes the foetus's life depend on its mother. Separate the two and the dependent one dies. No men or women who call themselves free can accept such a situation.

The only people who produce wealth in capitalist societies are the wage-earning classes, but their only access to that wealth is through wages. This means that real freedom is impossible for everybody, because the instruments that create wealth are concentrated in the hands of a small minority who alone decide how to use it.

Despite periods of inactivity, it's clear from an examination of trade unionism that a desire for profound change has always been at the roots of the movement.

Unionized teachers have tended not to consider themselves involved in this process of radical change. However, since the beginning of the century, they've begun to see things in a new light. Their situation has evolved with the increasing organization of an urban industrial society and the unpredictable changes brought about by technology, changes concerned with the economic, social, and political relations between teachers, their employers, and the rest of the society. We now see that teachers are forced to compete on the labor market, and are at the mercy of mass communication. There are reasons for this. We will come back to them.

What we've got to stress is that the teacher has become, as far as work conditions are concerned, a wage earner like any other. This worker has a boss who gives him a job to do, telling him "what" to do and "how" to do it. That boss controls the worker-teacher through his wages, as any employer controls "his employee."

We needn't pretend the teacher produces commodities that make the capitalist richer through the accumulation of "surplus value." The teacher is a producer of ideology. His production permits the existing setup to reproduce itself through the educational system as a whole, to perpetuate the status quo. So the teacher has an eminently political role. In the existing system, he's given the job of reinforcing the attitudes and behavior of young people in accordance with the dominant ideology. For that the teacher is paid a salary. So the teacher is a wage earner like all the others who feel themselves forced to serve as the mouthpiece for the traditional values of society. (In the jargon of the sociologists: they are given the task of production in the ideological sphere.)

It's the fact that he's a wage earner that has made the teacher opt for unionism. The teacher sensed that somebody else was making his decisions for him. He understood that social planning was carried out with no regard for his interests and those of others like himself, "who had to sell their brains to live." He saw that he had no say in how much money he could make and how this limited his means of social action. Taking all this into consideration, he came to understand that he should fight for his fundamental rights of free speech and action, his right, along with those who have the same needs and the same interests, to build a democratic, free and equitable society.

Teachers, along with other workers, know that it is over economic issues that the battle must be fought, because it is here that we can act effectively. But it is becoming clearer and clearer that in order to win the battle on the economic front, the union movement must make its mark in the social and political spheres. These three facets must be considered together when it comes to building a democratic society, that is, a society which allows every individual to have access to the collective wealth, each according to his needs. That means that a small class of individuals can no longer appropriate the means of production and use them according to their individual whim.

It is well to remember that the labor movement and the C.E.Q. have carried out hard-fought struggles. It is inevitable that others will follow, because unionism, despite its shortcomings, has been aware of these strategic necessities. Viewed in this light, teachers, because of their work, training, and intellectual skills, constitute an extremely important part of the union movement, provided that they accept their proper role in building a democratic society.

[…]

Republished in *Quebec: Only the Beginning: The Manifestos of the Common Front*, ed. Daniel Drache (Toronto: New Press, 1972), 101–3. Translated by John Chambers.

LESBIANS BELONG IN THE WOMEN'S MOVEMENT (1972)
Vancouver Women's Caucus

In 1968, women in the student movement at Simon Fraser University formed what would eventually become the Vancouver Women's Caucus. The Caucus published a newspaper, fought for abortion rights, and organized for free childcare, among other campaigns. In 1971, the Caucus also helped organize the Indochinese Women's Conference, which brought together feminists from Canada, the United States, Vietnam, and Laos. Around the same time, the group opened a discussion about lesbianism, thanks in large part to Doreen-Jean O'Donnell. At this time, the relationship between straight feminists and lesbians was far from uncomplicated, not only in Canada, but across North America and Western Europe. In the United States, Betty Friedan, the first President of the National Organization for Women, saw lesbians as a threat to the movement, calling them the "lavender menace." This text, originally unsigned, calls for a more inclusive women's liberation movement.

*   *   *

There are a lot of lesbians in women's liberation in Vancouver and other cities in Canada. There are a lot more lesbians (thousands more) who are not a part of the movement, some who have never been in contact with women's liberation, others who have chosen not to come to the movement because "they will give it a bad name," or will not be accepted. That's right! [...]

Most are alone and isolated, having made an individual rebellion which puts them in for all kinds of shit. Psychological and social guilt which male dominated religions heap on lesbians, and which gets us even if we're not believers. And fear. Fear of losing jobs, fear of being found out by family, not just because of rejection but because parents agonize and mutilate themselves trying find out where they failed. Because even if we don't feel guilty, they do.

And friends. The experience of being cut off from them. Friendship turned to pity and fear. The assumption that because you are a lesbian you are going to exploit other women sexually. That, of course, comes from straight women's experience that sexuality usually means exploitation. But that assumption lays a male role on lesbians, denying us our humanity.

To the degree that the fucked-up roles of "butch" and "femme" really exist among lesbians, it is because the only models of sexual relationships lesbians see are the dominant-submissive, aggressive-passive, dick-jane ones that stifle all women's, and for that matter all men's, human growth. A growing number of lesbians both in and out of the movement are struggling with and are rejecting those sex roles. We are building relationships in which those polarities, those limitations are broken.

Feminism has much to give us as lesbians, as we have much to give our sisters in the women's movement.

Because lesbian relationships have almost no validity "in the world" and no institutional reinforcements, lesbians have had to spend a lot of time trying to understand what female sexuality and what personal relationships are all about—and what they can be.

[…]

[…] As we all know, the first impact of the so-called "sexual revolution" of the '60s was to increase the sexual demands men made of women, which on one level, at least, actually increases women's sense of oppression. The women's movement in part grew in response to that oppression, and with it grew recognition that the sexuality that is so "free" is in fact a male sexual power trip. And on a gut level lesbians have always known that—but only as individuals.

There is no lesbian community. The gay bars are almost the only place where lesbians meet each other as a group and they are painfully alienating places.

As lesbians we have to begin to find alternatives to the bar, and to build a common understanding of our lives and our oppression. For women to love other women is a powerful, personal, political rebellion. It is an assertion that we can change our lives to meet our needs, our survival.

[…]

Asserting our lesbianism doesn't mean that women who are in relationships with men are not really committed to the feminist struggle or that lesbians are the vanguard of the women's liberation movement. As the experience of the male left should make clear, for any one person or any small group of people to claim to be leading the Canadian revolution is arrogant, self-destructive and absurd.

Women's liberation has to include all women. Male supremacy affects all of us in different ways. It is the sharing of those differences that can help us all to survive and struggle.

Republished in *Women Unite!: An Anthology of the Canadian Women's Movement* (Toronto: Canadian Women's Educational Press, 1972), 171–3.

Further Reading

Adamson, Nancy. "Feminists, Libbers, Lefties, and Radicals: The Emergence of the Women's Liberation Movement." In *A Diversity of Women: Ontario, 1945–1980*, edited by Joy Parr, 252–80. Toronto: University of Toronto Press, 1995.

Austin, David. *Fear of a Black Nation: Race, Sex, and Security in Sixties Montreal.* Toronto: Between the Lines, 2013.

Austin, David. *Moving Against the System: The 1968 Congress of Black Writers and the Shaping of Global Consciousness.* London: Pluto Press, 2018.

Cleveland, John W. "New Left, Not New Liberal: 1960s Movements in English Canada and Quebec." *Canadian Review of Sociology and Anthropology* 41, no. 1 (February 2004): 67–84.

Fournier, Louis. *FLQ: The Anatomy of an Underground Movement.* Toronto: NC Press, 1984.

Henderson, Stuart. *Making the Scene: Yorkville and Hip Toronto in the 1960s.* Toronto: University of Toronto Press, 2011.

Jenson, Jane, and Martin Papillon. "Challenging the Citizenship Regime: The James Bay Cree and Transnational Action." *Politics & Society* 28, no. 2 (2000): 245–64.

Kostash, Myrna. *Long Way from Home: The Story of the Sixties Generation in Canada.* Toronto: Lorimer, 1980.

McKay, Ian. *Rebels, Reds, and Radicals: Rethinking Canada's Left History.* Toronto: Between the Lines, 2005.

Milligan, Ian. *Rebel Youth: 1960s Labour Unrest, Young Workers, and New Leftists in English Canada.* Vancouver: University of British Columbia Press, 2015.

Mills, Sean. *A Place in the Sun: Haiti, Haitians, and the Remaking of Quebec.* Montreal: McGill-Queen's University Press, 2016.

Mills, Sean. *Empire Within: Postcolonial Thought and Political Activism in Sixties Montreal.* Montreal: McGill-Queen's University Press, 2014.

Palaeologu, M. Athena ed. *The Sixties in Canada: A Turbulent and Creative Decade.* Montreal: Black and Rose, 2009.

Palmer, Bryan D. *Canada's 1960s: The Ironies of Identity in a Rebellious Era.* Toronto: Toronto University Press, 2009.

Squires, Jessica. *Building Sanctuary: The Movement to Support Vietnam War Resisters in Canada, 1965–73.* Vancouver: University of British Columbia Press, 2013.

3
Mexico

Mexico highlights the complexities of 1968 in post-colonial societies. By 1968 the Mexican Revolution was fifty years in the past and the ruling party called itself the Institutional Revolutionary Party (PRI). The language of revolution was thus associated with the regime's empty rhetoric, but activists could claim to pursue the original visions of the Revolution. The state's routine co-option of radical and intellectual voices enabled by its revolutionary claims pushed the movements of 1968 to organize in participatory ways that made it harder to buy off individuals—or repress them.

With one foot in the Global North and another in the Global South, twentieth-century Mexico condensed many contradictions: a representative democracy, but also a single-party authoritarian state; an advanced economy within a land of persistent underdevelopment; an American ally with pretensions to independence; a discourse of national unity papering over intense regional and ethnic differences.

The enormous transformations of the 1940s and 1950s heightened these tensions. The PRI would hold power uninterruptedly from 1929 to 2000, winning 98 per cent of all mayoral and congressional elections between 1946 and 1973. Under PRI rule, Mexico experienced massive population growth, industrialization, and urbanization. Riding an economic boom, the "Mexican Miracle," the government undertook major construction projects, building new highways, dams, airports, and the Ciudad Universitaria, home of the National Autonomous University of Mexico (UNAM) in Mexico City.

But such development exacerbated existing regional variations, highlighted the lack of genuine democracy, sharpened domestic social differences, and increased dependence on the United States, which financed much of this growth. Although the wealthy saw their incomes grow spectacularly, real wages declined and the cost of living increased. The 1950s was therefore also a decade of social discontent. Workers complained about corrupt union bosses. Women, who only won the right to vote in 1953, demanded greater opportunities. And in 1956 tens of thousands of students launched a strike at the Polytechnic Institute in Mexico City, going beyond university demands to take on larger political issues, like American imperialism and government corruption. The PRI responded with force, sending in the army to arrest students and occupy the university.

The years after 1956 saw the rise of a kind of Mexican New Left, and later a coherent student movement. PRI power, however, had deep roots. Repression remained a core instrument, as when the government crushed the railway strike of 1958–9. But the PRI also built consent through more subtle means, such as wage increases, land redistribution, popular reforms, co-opting moderates, stage-managing elections, and installing agent provocateurs in oppositional movements. Clientelism—the selective distribution of material benefits to supporters—represented a central mechanism. This characteristically post-colonial form of rule would shape the course of contestation in the long 1968.

Despite the government's best efforts, the universities remained hotbeds of dissent. Between 1943 and 1966, the student population in Mexico City had quadrupled. Students were also more radical, not least because of the international context. They were especially attentive to developments abroad, especially the Cuban Revolution; it was from Mexico that Fidel Castro had set sail for Cuba.

Dozens of new radical student organizations emerged across the country. In 1963, some students sought to unify the movement in a common front, creating the National Confederation of Democratic Students (CNED). Reaching perhaps 100,000 members, CNED voiced some of the key demands of the 1960s, most famously in the "Declaration of Morelia." But as elsewhere, the movement began to factionalize, as some students took a more radical direction. Others turned to the counterculture, inspired by foreign influences like rock and roll, but also by hippies from the United States, Canada, and Western Europe who traveled to Mexico in search of "authentic" Indigenous cultures. This appropriation of native cultures was in turn copied by urban Mexican youths. Thus Mexicans created a uniquely syncretic counterculture, mixing foreign elements and imagined native ones.

Meanwhile, the PRI sought to prove Mexico's progress to the world—economically competitive with Europe, more stable than its Latin American neighbors, an independent "peacemaker" internationally, a unifier of internal divisions, and a model for the Third World. With that goal in mind, President Adolfo López Mateo (1958–64) fought an aggressive campaign to win the Olympic bid. In 1968, Mexico became the first "developing nation" to host the Olympic Games, symbolizing its quest to join the club of advanced nations.

Students, however, criticized the financial priorities represented by the Games and the cost to ordinary Mexicans, as well as highlighting state authoritarianism, undermining Mexico's claim to be a modern democracy.

Olympic images were widely reworked; for example, the rings of the games reimagined as the wheels of a tank. Students used international attention to amplify their calls for more democracy. The impending opening of the Games on October 12 and fear of political embarrassment would play a role in Mexican authorities' move toward mass murder.

Figure 3.1   Protest Poster. 1968. Reprinted in United
States Committee for Justice to Latin American
Political Prisoners, *Mexico '68: The Students Speak*, 12.

In 1968, state repression backfired. A fight between rival secondary schools was broken up by the riot police in July, followed by attacks on student gatherings and invasions of secondary schools; famously, police used a bazooka to blow open one school's ancient doors. Secondary and university students protested, and state violence escalated, including the use of the military. Students "disappeared," were killed, injured, and imprisoned. In response, they developed on-the-ground organizations for building defense, communications, and legal support. This upsurge of participation and shared opposition to repression enabled collaboration spanning academic and vocational schools, rival universities, and different left factions. A general student strike followed in August.

The PRI's absolute dominance over the state and media created specific problems for activists, who had to create alternative channels to communicate their politics, forcing wider connections with popular groups. The movement's pre-existing decentralization was formalized with struggle committees in different institutions directing political brigades of about ten people each. Some organized the printing and distribution of leaflets and posters, painting wall slogans and giving street-corner speeches to bring the movement's message directly to different neighborhoods, on buses and trams, at the marketplace, on street walls, and at workplace entrances. Different groups collected donations, organized street theater "happenings" drawing on international models to thematize activism and repression, or held small protests that vanished before the police or military could appear.

These intensely participatory strategies helped the strike spread socially, geographically and politically. On August 1 the UNAM's Rector led a protest against repression. Teachers brought 200,000 people to a demonstration on August 13. Some locals of the PRI-controlled trade union federation CTM supported the strike, as did railway workers and electricians, the Confederation of Independent Peasants (CCI), informal workers like taxi drivers and peddlers, and the movement spread far beyond Mexico City. On August 27, perhaps 400–500,000 people joined a national demonstration. Repression continued: in the second half of September the university was occupied by the military, followed by the Polytechnic; over a dozen people were killed in the latter invasion.

In this context, several thousand people demonstrated on October 2 at the Plaza of the Three Cultures, in the new housing project of Tlatelolco. The Plaza was shortly surrounded by a large military force including armored vehicles and helicopters. Soldiers opened fire on the trapped crowd with rifles and machine guns, followed by mass arrests with summary executions. Perhaps two or three hundred people were killed, with over 1,000 arrests.

Tlatelolco was a turning point: the trauma of the events left the movement increasingly incapable of acting coherently. Together with increased factionalism and the difficulty of finding activists willing to step into front-line positions, the movement called a truce and then called off the strike. However, this level of violence, and the state's support for it, marked an irreversible loss of legitimacy and shaped new generations of social movements. The killings also sparked a major international outcry as activists everywhere mobilized against the massacre.

Activism continued after Tlatelolco, but changed shape. Some registered their discontent by abstaining from official politics. Others channeled their discontent into the counterculture. Still others turned to armed struggle: on the first anniversary of the massacre, revolutionary groups set off bombs in government and newspaper buildings in Mexico City. Armed struggle was strongest in the countryside, where rural groups had been resisting state violence well before 1968. The state responded by disappearing, torturing, and executing activists in what would become known as Mexico's "Dirty War."

The 1970s also saw the rise of new movements led by marginalized sectors of Mexican society, such as peasants, Indigenous peoples, women, and gays and lesbians. Women's mobilization in 1968, to take just one example, fed into the birth of second-wave feminism in Mexico. The 1975 conference for the United Nations' International Women's Year, held in Mexico, showed the impact of the movement in the PRI's anxiety to co-opt it. The feminist counter-conference led to the formation of the Coalition of Feminist Women, which united feminist groups around three demands: voluntary maternity (abortion rights, sexual education, access to contraception), freedom from sexual violence, and freedom of sexual choice (lesbian and gay rights).

The memory of Tlatelolco would continue to shape Mexican society. The contrast between official state and media cover-ups and blaming of protesters and the popular memory of deliberate, targeted mass killing created a space which the political left and radical intellectuals filled with research and critical analysis and with literary and artistic representations. This politics of memory enabled a permanent reproach to the PRI's broader modernizing project.

LIST OF DEMANDS (1968)
National Strike Council

The National Strike Council (CNH) was the newly-formed organization of the student strike declared on August 5. The CNH initially contained 250 representatives from 128 different schools and universities, with a rotating directorate intended not only to exemplify themes of direct democracy but also to prevent the formation of an identifiable leadership that could be targeted by the state. Its demands were consciously moderate, bridging wide differences in perspectives and enabling outreach to substantial sections of the population. Demands 1 and 4 had particular implications: they directly targeted the Mexican state's claim to be a parliamentary democracy respecting human rights and the freedom of opinion, and were understood as including the release of Valentín Campa and Demetrio Vallejo, leaders of the 1958–9 railway strikes. In demand 2, Cueto and Mendiolea were the chief and second-in-command of the Mexico City police.

* * *

1. Freedom for all political detainees.
2. The dismissal of General Luis Cueto Ramírez and General Raúl Mendiolea, as well as Lieutenant-Colonel Armando Frías.

3. The dissolution of the Grenadier Corps [riot police] as a direct instrument of repression. Not to be replaced by similar bodies.

4. The repeal of articles 145 and 145bis of the Federal Criminal Code (the offense of "social dissolution"), as the legal instruments of repression.

5. Compensation for the families of the dead and for the wounded victims of repression from Friday 26 July onwards.

6. Establish responsibility for acts of repression and destruction carried out by authorities in the police, riot police, and army.

Republished on In Defence of Marxism: marxist.com and elsewhere. Translated by Laurence Cox and Simon Jones.

FOR A WORKER/PEASANT/STUDENT ALLIANCE (1968)
National Strike Council

This text was released the day before the "silent march" in Mexico City, which drew tens of thousands of people, many with their mouths taped to highlight censorship and repression. The march was organized to counter official accusations that violence and disruption was coming from the students, and to recall similar marches in the 1950s and 1960s. Protestors were discouraged from carrying images of Che or Ho Chi Minh and asked to bring images of Mexican revolutionary heroes. The march also saw a public shift in gender relations, with Roberta Avendaño addressing the crowd. It was remembered as a highpoint of the movement for its strength and discipline, and for the widespread popular support. This program below grew out of developing links with other, long-standing popular struggles; flyers for the march targeted specific groups while committees from neighborhoods occupied by the police and military had made contact directly with student activists.

*   *   *

Our struggle has laid bare not only the repressive character of our government, but also the structure of injustice and exploitation on which it rests.

The support that we have received from the popular sectors obliges us to discuss this structure and to let the popular masses know about our point of view on how to transform it, as well as the line of action that students, workers, peasants—in a word, the people as a whole—must take in order to banish from our country once and for all exploitation, poverty, abuse and repression.

Much has been said about the prosperity the country is enjoying. But it has not been pointed out that it is only the prosperity of a privileged minority, which increases its wealth at the expense of the working people. The worker, the peasant, wage earners in general, see how the cost of living increases while wages and income stay fixed or rise more slowly than the prices. Furthermore, increasing numbers of workers are being deprived of the opportunity to work because all of the innovation in industry, in agricultural machinery, etc. are for the benefit of the bosses alone. Through generalized repression the government has turned the organizations (such as the parties and trade unions) of the people into new means of subjugation and exploitation. The independent trade unions have practically disappeared; the peasants' organizations do not defend the interests of the agricultural workers but are instruments of political control in the hands of the corrupt leaders of the official party. Finally, more and more workers have been forced to work in unproductive and underpaid jobs as their only recourse for obtaining enough income to survive.

The government is not the government of all Mexicans; rather its resources are mainly devoted to increasing the privileges of the big bourgeoisie, consisting of the large industrialists, the large merchants and landowners, the bankers and the corrupt politicians of the "revolutionary family."

The PRI is a political apparatus which forces the masses to act and vote for its candidates by means of deceit, threats and blackmail. A long time ago it stopped representing any of the popular sectors, which it forces to remain within its ranks for the benefit of the big bourgeoisie.

With the repressions of 1959, those trade unions which used to be controlled by leaders representing the workers ceased being representative in any sense and have become gangs at the service of the bosses and their government.

As time passes, the number of Mexicans who lack education, housing, jobs, etc. increases while, at the same time, part of the national resources are delivered to foreign interests, especially those of the U.S.

The peasants are subjected to more arbitrariness every day. They are exploited not only by the landowner, the money lender, state and private banks, but also by the *ejido* [government farm cooperative] commissariat, trade unions, transportation companies, middle-men, and a whole gamut of corrupt politicians.

These circumstances, and many others too numerous to mention, have led us to the conclusion that we cannot wait any longer. We must begin a general struggle, together with all the workers, in order to demand a minimum of rights that will place us on the road to the final liberation of the Mexican people. The people are our country, not the professional politicians whose only ties with the country are exploitation, treason and crime.

Defense and Improvement of the Standard of Living Through Immediate Wage Increases and Successive Increases Corresponding to Price Rises.
The working masses who, by their labor, produce goods and move the machinery that creates all of the wealth, must begin to partake of these riches. For this reason our first issue is an *increase in wages* to a level that would let all workers and their families live decently. But we all know that wage rises are nullified by the rise of prices. Therefore, as an issue complementing the one mentioned above, we propose that a clause should be introduced in workers' contracts that would oblige employers to raise wages in accordance with increases in the cost of living.

Stop Unemployment by Reducing the Hours of Work.
It is by exploiting the workers that the employers have become rich and can replace their old equipment with machinery which increases productivity. Therefore, the working people cannot tolerate being thrown on the ash-heap of unemployment once they have been squeezed dry. In order to avoid this, workers must fight so that each technological advance results in *a shorter working day without a reduction of wages.*

Workers' Control to Insure a Just Distribution of Profits.
Workers are entitled, by law, to profit-sharing. However, employers dodge this responsibility by fraudulent accounting. The only way to avoid this is by workers' control of production and accounts.

Win Independent and Democratic Trade Unions, Organize Committees of Struggle Elected Directly by the Workers.
The employers and the government are using gangster-like groups in charge of the trade unions to control the workers politically and to prevent them from fighting for better conditions of living and work. Therefore, we propose that workers fight for *independent and democratic trade unions through Committees of Struggle.* This struggle must side-step the legal trap which forces all the workers' organizations to be recognized by the government. The Committee of Struggle must actually represent the workers, must decide upon strikes, stoppages and all other actions for the defense of workers' rights. Workers do not need the approval of the government to stop production in factories and on farms, for the simple reason that it is not the government that gets production going. Naturally, the first steps in this direction must be taken before the bosses, the government and their spies catch on. The committees can only come into the open when they are strong and they can fight a decisive battle against their enemies.

For a Workers' Federation Based on the Committees of Struggle.

If the gangs now in power in the trade unions can maneuver so easily, this is due to the fact that, besides having the support of the bosses and the government, they are well organized. The workers must oppose this organization with a revolutionary organization, based upon the Struggle Committees. The strategic objective in this direction is the creation of a revolutionary federation of workers, that is to say, an organization for the workers equivalent to the students' National Strike Council.

We have already said that the creation of workers' Committees of Struggle cannot exist in the open at the beginning like the student Committees did. However, their objectives are similar: unite and organize the workers apart from the puppet organization as a means of defending their interests.

The way in which the Committees of Struggle must act during the period in which they cannot operate in the open is by presenting the general points expressed in this program, and others that they favor, to each section of the factory, branch of industry, etc., where they are active. For this purpose the publication of leaflets and newspapers that would reach all the workers is of the greatest importance.

For the Organization of Peasants' Committees of Struggle.

In the countryside, it is also necessary to organize militant committees with basic elements of leadership; however, it is necessary to distinguish between salaried workers and those who own or rent a small piece of land, or belong to an *ejido*. For the former, the same points are valid as for the factory workers, with slight alterations, such as introducing social security for all, etc.

For Easy and Low-Interest Farm Loans.

The policy of the government toward the countryside has two basic defects—the funds dedicated to giving credit to the peasants are scarce; in addition, they are distributed very badly: most of the funds disappear through corruption, bribery and chicanery. The small landowners must declare war on those evils. The first demand in this direction is that *state agricultural banks must be managed by the peasants themselves or their representatives, subject to recall when necessary. More funds for the countryside.*
[...]

Eliminate the Middle-Men, Creating Struggle Committees of Peasants and Workers to Perform Their Services.

One of the most frequent forms of exploitation is that of the middle-men, who buy produce below the guaranteed or market prices. This is often done because these brokers are the only ones who can transport the produce to the shopping centers, for they own the means of transport. The peasants must organize Committees of Struggle together with the workers to take care of services; the strategic objective of these committees should be the elimination of the middle-men through expropriation of the means which they use to exploit the peasants, and the use of those means for the benefit of the workers and peasants themselves.

Fight to Get Back the Lands That Were Taken Away from the Peasants for Water Works and Other Reforms by the Government.

It is well known that many politicians and capitalists, clued in on programs for the building of dams, etc., have become rich by buying land fraudulently—with threats, deceit, etc. This land must be rescued for the benefit of the deceived peasants and workers in general. For this reason we propose that *all the lands wrongly acquired should be expropriated with all the installations on them for the benefit of peasants and workers.*

Project

This is the program which we propose to workers and peasants as a starting point toward a nation-wide, long-term, joint struggle. Obviously, it is not the last word and doubtless it must undergo modification that will enrich it with the participation of the workers. However, it can show that our interests have been enlarged in this fight through the contact we have had with the masses of the people and that we are willing to fight in order to fulfill the obligations that we have contracted in the struggle.

We know that the classes in power will scream to high heaven and accuse us of all kinds of things. We don't care. If the government, if the bosses, if those who call themselves patriots and good Christians, truly want to serve the country—that is, the large majority of the Mexican people—let them adopt this program in real life, not in speeches.

For our part, this is our answer, on the one hand, to the angry threats of the government and, on the other hand, to the support the people have given us, not only in this movement, but also by giving us the opportunity to study.

If one day our schools are occupied by military force, we will leave for the national battlefield, brandishing this program; and we will not stop under any circumstances, whoever falls and whatever happens.

University City, Mexico
September 12, 1968

United States Committee for Justice to Latin American Political Prisoners, *Mexico '68: The Students Speak* (New York: self-published, 1968), 25–7. Translation modified.

EYEWITNESS ACCOUNTS (1971)
Gilberto Guevara Niebla, Ana Ignacia Rodríguez, and María Alice Martínez Medrano

Elena Poniatowska's Massacre in Mexico, *subtitled* Testimonies from oral history, *challenged the official version of the events of October 2 by weaving together eyewitness accounts, many collected in prison, photographs, official documents and her own commentary into an immensely powerful narrative. The book highlights the scale and violence of the massacre as well as the attempts to rewrite or deny what had happened. Gilberto Guevara Niebla was one of the student leaders, who was imprisoned for three years and spent time in exile. Ana Ignacia Rodríguez had already been in jail after the army's attack on UNAM; she fled the city after the massacre but was captured and tortured. María Alicia Martínez Medrano was involved in dramatic "happenings" and would become a leading figure in Indigenous theater. The "Olimpia" battalion were a paramilitary group set up for the Olympic Games, wearing civilian clothes with white armbands to distinguish them.*

* * *

The Army units approached from all directions and encircled the crowd in a pincers movement, and in just a few moments all the exits were blocked off. From up there on the fourth floor of the Chihuahua building, where the speakers' platform had been set up, we couldn't see what the Army was up to and we couldn't understand why the crowd was panicking. The two helicopters that had been hovering over the Plaza almost from the very beginning of the meeting had suddenly started making very hostile maneuvers, flying lower and lower in tighter and tighter circles just above the heads of the crowd, and then they had launched two flares, a green one first and then a red one; when the second one went off the panic started, and we members of the Committee did our best to stop it: none of us there on the speakers' stand could see that the Army troops below us were advancing across the Plaza. When they found themselves confronted by a wall of bayonets, the crowd halted and immediately drew back; then we saw a great wave of people start running toward the other side of the Plaza; but there were Army troops on the other side of the Plaza too; and as we stood watching from up there on the speakers' stand, we saw the whole crowd head in another direction. That was the last thing we saw down below, for at that moment the fourth floor was taken over by the Olimpia Battalion. Even though we had no idea why the crowd had panicked and was running first in one direction and then in another, those of us who had remained there at the microphone till the very last found ourselves looking down the barrels of machine guns when we turned around. The balcony had been occupied by the Olimpia Battalion and we were ordered to put our hands up and face the wall, and given strict orders not to turn around in the direction of the Plaza; if we so much as moved a muscle, they hit us over the head or in the ribs with their rifle butts. Once the trap they had set snapped shut, the collective murder began.

Gilberto Guevara Niebla, of the CNH

[...]

I left the University with a group of comrades. We arrived at the Plaza de las Tres Culturas, and it started to rain. We all assembled in our various groups, and I was carrying a banner that read, THE LAW SCHOOL REPRESENTED HERE TODAY. There were other banners, one for instance that said, "The blood of our brothers will not have been shed in vain." I was sitting on the steps in front of the Chihuahua building when suddenly I saw the flares go off, and a few seconds later I heard what I found out later were machine guns firing on the crowd. Our comrade on the speakers' stand shouted, "Don't move, anybody! Keep calm! Sit down!" So I sat down, holding onto my banner. I had no idea what was happening, or rather, I didn't realize how serious the situation was, so I just sat there clutching my banner till a comrade shouted to me, "Get rid of that thing!" because I was a perfect target sitting there with my banner. I threw it down and started running with Tita. We ran to where the flags were flying, the flagpoles in the Plaza de las Tres Culturas, over to one side of Vocational 7, and Tita and I tried to get under cover. Then I heard a girl begging for help: "Oh, God, please help me!" I also heard voices shouting things like "My purse, my purse, where's my purse?" At one point we leaped over those pre-Hispanic walls there and fell into a sort of ditch. I lay there on the ground, and other people started falling on top of me. We heard shouts and groans and cries of pain, and I realized then that the gunfire was getting heavier and heavier. Tita and I crawled out of there and ran toward the Calle Manuel González, and the soldiers yelled to us, "Get the hell out as fast as you can!" As we ran out of the Plaza, a white Volkswagen full of students drove by, and they shouted to us, "Come on! Climb in!" I can't remember if they called us by name: "Come on, Nacha, Tita, get in!" and one of the funny things about the whole bit is that I don't remember how we managed to pile into that car that was already crammed full of a whole bunch of students. We lit out down the Paseo de la Reforma to the Avenida de la República de Cuba, and then Tita climbed out because everybody knew her by sight and she would have been recognized instantly. We all said as much. "You're so big they'd spot you half a mile away," we told her. I went back in that same car with two Movement people from Theoretical Physics at Poli—I don't know who they were—to see if we could find a couple of comrades we had no idea what had happened to. The boys stopped the car somewhere near the Secretariat of Foreign Relations—I don't know the name of the street because I'm not from Mexico City, I'm from Taxco, in the state of Guerrero. They got out and said to me, "Stay here in the car," and I stayed there in the car waiting for them all by myself, but as the minutes ticked by, I got more and more nervous; the shooting still hadn't stopped, it was worse in fact, and ambulances were drawing up with their sirens screeching, more and more soldiers were going by, tanks and convoys of troops armed to the teeth. An ambulance drew up right in front of me, and the attendants put a student in it: his head was all bloody; he was dripping blood from head to foot. I was sitting there in the car no more than ten or twelve feet away, and seeing that student in that shape turned my stomach. Then a whole bunch of people ran by shouting, "They've set fire to the Chihuahua building!" I looked up and saw smoke. A high-tension wire fell down then, and everyone running past that Volkswagen I was in was screaming. I was suddenly frightened and scrambled out of the car in a panic and started running. I must have run for a much longer time than I realized, because I suddenly found myself at Sanborn's, on Lafragua. An acquaintance of mine stopped me there on the street. "What's the matter?" he asked me. I realized then that I'd been crying and my mascara was running down my cheeks. I felt as though I didn't have one ounce of strength left—I was really in terrible shape. Some kids went into Sanborn's and brought me out some coffee because I was trembling so. "Take it easy, take it easy," they kept saying. Then some more kids came to the door. The only thing I could blurt out was, "They're killing the students!" These same kids then took me to an apartment on the Avenida de Coyoacán, where I was living with Tita and another girl friend.

Ana Ignacia Rodríguez (Nacha), of the Action Committee, UNAM

[...]

There was nothing we could do but keep running. They were firing at us from all directions. We ran six or eight feet, keeping under cover, and then ten or twelve feet out in the open. Rifle fire sounds very much like a jet taking off. There was nothing to do but keep running. We heard the display windows of the shops on the ground floor of the Chihuahua building shatter, and we suddenly decided we ought to make a run for the stairway. As I stood down there, babbling all sorts of nonsense, I also suddenly remembered all my many friends and comrades at the meeting and got terrible cramps in my stomach. I remembered names, faces. As I reached this stairway that the people from the CNH who were going to speak had been going up and down all during the afternoon, I met Margarita and Meche, who said to me in the most despairing tone of voice, "María Alicia, our children are up there on the fourth floor!"

For the first time I had the feeling I might be able to do something useful amid all this confusion and suffering, despite my sense of utter helplessness, and I said to them, "I'll go up there with you."

The youngster who had saved my life—by leaping on me and throwing me to the floor there on the speakers' stand when they first started shooting at us—went upstairs with us: he was my armor, my cape, my shield. I have no idea who he was. I have a photographic memory, but I can't remember his face at all ... The three of us started up the stairs, and on the first landing we met another youngster. I had seen him on the speakers' stand there on the fourth floor of the Chihuahua building, too, talking with various Movement people as though he knew them very well. I remember him particularly because he'd apparently been wounded in the right wrist and had a white handkerchief wrapped around his hand.

"Don't leave, *señora*, it'll all be over soon," he said to me.

I was about to go downstairs again, because I'd spied some girl friends of mine down on the esplanade. But the boy took me by the arm and very solicitously helped me up the stairs. I was touched by this courageous behavior on the part of yet another student hero, and went upstairs with him.

Then Mercedes shouted, "*Señor*, my children are there upstairs!"

Margarita shouted that her children were up there too, and I stopped there on the stairs and looked at the youngster escorting me, thinking that the courage of those kids is really incredible sometimes. Many hours later, I discovered that my escort was one of the assassins guarding the stairway so that none of the CNH people would escape. He took us back downstairs then, and I remember that we were caught up in a whole crowd of people and shoved to the corner of the Chihuahua building, and that meanwhile there was a steady hail of bullets from the building.

A girl came by shouting, "You murderers, you murderers!" I took her in my arms and tried to calm her down, but she kept screaming, louder and louder, until finally the youngster behind me grabbed hold of her and started shaking her. I noticed then that her ear had been shot off and her head was bleeding. The people in the crowd kept piling one on top of another, seeking shelter from the rain of bullets; we were all right on each other's necks, and I felt as though I were caught in the middle of a riot or squeezed in a sardine can.

I stood there staring at the tips of the coffee-colored shoes of some woman. Several rounds of machine-gun bullets suddenly raked the spot where we were standing, and I saw one bullet land just a few inches from that woman's shoe. All she said was, "Oh, my goodness!" and another voice answered, "Make a run for it. If you stay here you'll be even worse off; you're sure to get hurt here." We all started running again and just then I spied a red Datsun with a young girl at the wheel. She'd been shot, and I saw her collapse on top of the steering wheel; the horn kept blowing and blowing … The youngster kept saying, "Don't look, don't look." We ran on toward one of the buildings behind Chihuahua …

María Alicia Martínez Medrano, nursery-school director

Elena Poniatowska, *Massacre in Mexico* (Columbia, MO: University of Missouri Press, 1975), 213–21. Translated by Helen R. Lane.

TLATELOLCO, 68 (1972)
Jaime Sabines

The events of Tlatelolco would become a point of reference for popular memory and culture just as much as for social movements and more explicitly documentary material. Indeed, an extensive "Tlatelolco literature" appeared, including poems and novels, films and music. In the context of official denials and misrepresentation, this literature served to present and keep alive an alternative, popular understanding of the events and critique of those responsible. Sabines' poem addresses this explicitly: "Let us trust in the people's poor memory," at the same time as it criticizes the general drive toward forgetting and silence, parading "in glorious unity/to construct the country of our dreams." The "little man" is Mexican president Gustavo Díaz Ordaz. Rio Blanco and Cananea mark the killing of strikers in 1907 and 1906 respectively under the reviled dictator Porfirio Díaz.

I

No one knows the exact number of dead,
not even the assassins,
not even the criminal.
(Most assuredly, this little man, every part of him
is history now,
incapable of anything, save malice.)

Tlatelolco will be mentioned in years to come
like the way we talk today about Rio Blanco and Cananea,
but this was worse,

here they have killed the citizens:
they weren't workers out on strike,
they were mothers and children, students,
teenagers of fifteen years,
a girl on her way to the cinema,
a foetus in its mother's womb,
all swept up, unmistakenly gunned down
by the machine gun for Order and Social Justice.

After three days, the army was the victim of the wicked,
and the town was joyously getting ready
to celebrate the Olympics, which would have brought glory to Mexico.

2
The crime is there,
covered by the sheets of newspapers,
by televisions, radios, Olympic flags.
The thick air, stagnating,
the terror, ignominious.
Around the voices, the traffic, the life.
And the crime is there.

3
They must have washed not only the floor, but the memory.
They must have plucked out our eyes for what we had seen,
and have assassinated the mourners too,
so that nobody could cry, that there be no more witnesses.
But the blood puts down its roots
and grows like a tree in time.
The blood in the cement, the walls,
in the ivy: splashing on us,
drenching us in shame, shame, shame.

The mouths of the dead spit on us
the hushed perpetual blood.

4
Let us trust in the people's poor memory,
put order in the rest,
forgive the survivors,
set free the prisoners,
let us be generous, magnanimous, and prudent.

The exotic ideas invade us like an enema,
but we restored the peace,
consolidated the institutions;
the businessmen are with us,
the bankers, the true Mexican politicians,
the private schools,
the respectable people.

We have destroyed the conjurer,
shored up our power:
now we are not going to fall from our beds
because we will have sweet dreams.

We have Secretaries of State capable
of transforming shit into aromatic essences,
alchemist deputies and senators,
ineffable leaders, the flashiest,
a troop of spiritual whores
gallantly hoisting our flag.

Nothing has happened here.
Now begins our new reign.

5
The cadavers are on slabs in the police stations.
Half-naked, cold, pierced,
some wearing a death masque.
The people gather outside, impatient
hoping not to find their own:
"Oh go look somewhere else."

6
Youth is the theme
of the revolution.
The Government supports its heroes.
The Mexican peso is stable
and the country's development is on the rise.
The comic strips and TV villains go on unchanged.
We have demonstrated to the world that we are able,
respectable, hospitable, sensible.

(How marvelous are the Olympics!)
and now we shall continue "The Metro"
because nothing can stop the wheels of progress.

Women, in pink,
men, in sky blue,
Mexicans parade in glorious unity
to construct the country of our dreams.

The River Is Wide/El Río Es Ancho: Twenty Mexican Poets, a Bilingual Anthology,
ed. Marlon L. Fick (Albuquerque: University of New Mexico Press, 2005), 324–5.
Translated by Marlon L. Fick.

FIRST PRINCIPLES
Party of the Poor (1972)

Although armed groups had already emerged earlier in the 1960s, they grew significantly after the Tlatelolco Massacre. One of the most important of these was the Party of the Poor (PDLP), a rural guerrilla group from Guerrero, a mostly impoverished state in southwestern Mexico along the Pacific coastline. After years of watching the PRI crush local social movements, some activists, like the schoolteacher Lucio Cabañas, created the PDLP to not only defend local communities, but to spark a general uprising of what they called the "poor class" against the "rich class." Unlike many other armed groups in the Global North in this period, the PDLP won considerable popular support from peasants in the region. Below, we publish a document co-signed by the PDLP and its armed wing, which provides a glimpse into the rural discontent that led to peasant support for the guerrillas.

* * *

1. Defeat the government of the rich class. That a government be formed of workers and *campesinos*, technicians and professionals, and other revolutionary workers.
2. That the new government of the poor class create laws that protect and assert the interests and rights of the working people. That it enforce the right to paid work, the right to strike, the right to assemble and to express opinions publicly and in private, the right to form unions, political parties, and other associations, the right to choose and vote for candidates and governors.
3. That to enforce their laws and protect their interests, workers form their own juries or tribunals, name their judges, and are given weapons to defend themselves.

4. Expropriate the factories, buildings, machines, means of transportation, and the plantations from the large landowners, national and foreign millionaires. That the properties are given to the workers.

5. To assert poor people's rights to their produce with justice, and that security be given to workers and their families in case of illnesses, accidental loss of products, sickness, disability or death on the job.

6. That laws be created to ensure that workers can benefit from their work through capital, machines and tools, water, electricity and fuel, seeds and fertilizers, technicians and scientists, workers' organizations, and everything necessary to improve production.

7. Bring the poor class out of its ignorance, out of sickness and vices through truthful information, guidance, and teachings that serve the working people. That workers control all the means of communication.

8. Ensure the right of workers and their families to have a house, education and culture, good hygiene, health care, and rest without having to pay.

9. Liberate women by asserting their equal rights with men. Mainly enforcing the right to work with equal pay for equal capacity, the rights to free association and speech, the right to higher education and culture. Protect children, ensuring the rights that belong to them, such as sufficient food and clothing, care homes, and education.

10. Protect the elderly and disabled through special homes and care, free food and clothing, sufficient work, and education and culture. Ensure the rights of people who suffer or suffered imprisonment for crimes caused by poverty, ignorance, or disease, through appropriate systems to improve their living conditions. Enforce the right to protection against mistreatment, torture, and [false] charges, the right to expression, the right to paid work, the right to hygiene and health care, and the right to return to society as a free man and worker after paying the penalties [for one's actions].

11. Ensure the right of students to education at all levels, through systems of scientific teaching that serve the working people to improve their culture and improve the well-being of the body and the spirit, that allow them to create and apply their knowledge in jobs paid equally according to their capacity.

12. Enforce the rights of technicians and professionals to improve their living conditions, to improve their professional capacity, and to create and apply appropriate systems of work that serve the working people. Ensure the rights of writers, artists, and intellectuals to maintain the product of their works with dignity, the right to advance their spirit of creation, and the right to create and apply the appropriate methods to the spiritual progress of all the working people.

13. Enforce the right of the *campesinos*, who the rich class calls "Indians," and who have lived in the mountains since Spanish domination expelled them from [their] lands, to be treated as equals to all Mexicans. Unite all in the struggle against racial discrimination in the world, principally with Blacks, Mexicans, Chicanos, and other racial minorities in the United States.

14. Make Mexico completely economically independent, make it politically independent against the new colonial system of the United States of North America and other foreign countries. Unite with the poor peoples of the world in the struggle against the same foreign domination that sustains the rich classes.

Sierra de Guerrero, March 1972

Archivo General de la Nación, Dirección Federal de Seguridad, 100-10-16-4, Legajo 6, 230–23. Translated by Liz Mason-Deese.

RESOLUTIONS (1974)
First Indigenous Congress

Mexico's large Indigenous population suffered racial oppression as well as economic exploitation, and was particularly vulnerable to violence by the state and large landowners. Fueled by pre-existing traditions of resistance, a new generation of bilingual leaders, Catholic religious figures influenced by liberation theology, and left organizations, a wave of Indigenous militancy took shape in the 1970s. After a series of local and regional meetings, authorities responded by sponsoring a 1974 conference in San Cristóbal. They invited Bishop Samuel Ruiz to help organize the event, but he ended up turning the agenda over to Indigenous peoples themselves. The result was the First Indigenous Congress, which united 1,230 delegates from 327 communities, bridging ethnic differences. The Congress would be remembered as a decisive moment in the history of Indigenous peoples in Mexico, and the demands issued there would inform future activists, like those who went on to form the Zapatista Army of National Liberation (EZLN).

* * *

[...]

Accords: Land
The Land Belongs to He Who Works It

1. We all want to solve the problems of land, but we are divided, each for himself, and so we feel we have no strength. We are looking to organize

each group so that it will have strength, because union makes strength
[...]

2. We demand that the communal lands taken away from our fathers be returned to us.

3. That the employees of the Agrarian Department effectively resolve pending administrative questions. We demand an end to extortion by engineers and zone chiefs and forestry officers.

4. That there be an Agrarian Department branch office in San Cristóbal for the administrative business of our agrarian affairs. And above all that it have complete authority to resolve our agrarian problems.

5. That the problem of the Tuliljá dam be justly resolved, and that they take us into account.

6. That the minimum wage be paid to Indians who work on fincas and in cities, and that they receive all the benefits that the law provides.

7. That taxes not be imposed on sterile land. That taxes be fair.

8. We demand that to settle our problems the government not send in the army. That problems be settled with the community, not with the army.

Figure 3.2 Governor Manuel Velasco Suárez inaugurates the First Indigenous Congress. San Cristóbal de las Casas, Chiapas, 1974. Photo by Rogelio Cuéllar.

Accords: Commerce
Equality and Justice in Prices

1. We want an Indian market, that is, that we ourselves be the ones who buy and sell, that this be organized in each municipality, starting with hamlets, colonies, and settlements, concentrating produce in our warehouses, so that among ourselves, Tzeltals, Tzotzils, Tojolabals, and Chols, we can sell each other our various products [...]

2. We want to organize ourselves into cooperatives for selling and producing, to defend ourselves from monopolizers and so that profits do not leave the community.

3. We demand that Inmecafe [the federal coffee-purchasing agency] not sell itself out to monopolizers, that it buy [from us] at guaranteed prices through the representative elected by the community.
4. We want to study well and in groups the matter of alcoholic drinks, knowing that liquor is bad when it becomes a means of exploitation. Because of liquor they have despoiled and ruined our health [...]

Accords: Education
To Renew the Education of Our Children

1. We want Indian teachers to be trained who will teach in our language and our custom, and that they also teach Spanish. We do not want teachers who do not know our language and customs.
2. We want teachers who will respect the communities and their customs. We want them to teach us our rights as citizens. We want the community to be taught its rights.
3. We do not want them to be merchants.
4. We do not want them to get drunk.
5. We do not want them to set bad examples.
6. We do not want them to ask for a fine when a girl over 15 who is in school gets married.
7. We do not want them to be lazy.
8. We want them to commit themselves to the service of the community.
9. We want our communities to organize themselves better, that there be a committee independent of the teachers, elected by the community, to watch over the teacher's work.
10. Education and teaching are very necessary, but they should help us to improve our human conditions and respond to the needs of the community, in land and animals, social integration, cultivation, tailoring, bricklaying.
11. That there be an Indian newspaper in our four languages [Chol, Tzotzil, Tzetzal, Tojolabal]. That the paper be the Indians' and that it serve for our own communication.

Accords: Health
Health is Life

1. We need to organize our community so that we can take care of our health.
2. We want the old medicine not to be lost. It is necessary to know the medicinal plants in order to use them for the good of us all.

3. We ask that there be clinics in the big Indian villages and that they serve the smaller communities with Indian nurses who know both medicines, that of pills and that of plants. This way medicine will get to us all.

4. That the sale of medicine by merchants be prohibited, because they trick people a lot on prices and medicine past its expiration date.

5. In many of our zones there is tuberculosis. We ask for an effective campaign against tuberculosis.

6. That there be education on health to prevent diseases, and for hygiene, so that the two medicines are not mixed up […]

John Womack, Jr. ed., *Rebellion in Chiapas: An Historical Reader*, ed. John Womack, Jr. (New York: New Press, 1999), 159–61. Translated by John Womack, Jr.

EDITORIAL (1976)
La Revuelta

Activism in the 1960s shook up traditional gender roles, as women became public speakers, brought political activism within the family sphere, and forced men to treat them as political actors, not simply auxiliaries. In the immediate aftermath of the Tlatelolco massacre, the mothers of those killed, imprisoned, or "disappeared" organized widely, initially around repression but increasingly around other issues. The 1971 formation of Women Acting in Solidarity (MAS) and its Mother's Day protest are often seen as one of the beginnings of second-wave feminism in Mexico, which included consciousness-raising, women's activism within left parties, and the development of feminist media, such as the publications Fem, Cihuat, *and* La Revuelta. *Below, we reproduce the editorial from the first issue of* La Revuelta.

* * *

With this publication, the Women's Liberation movement in Mexico seeks to create an organ for the dissemination of feminism in our country. However, given the diversity of schools and focuses that feminism has had and still has, we find ourselves needing to specify what we mean by feminism. For us, it represents women's struggles against their *specific* oppression and exploitation—we underscore the word specific to indicate, in this way, that the goal of feminism is not only to highlight and struggle against the oppression and exploitation that women suffer in our society because of the division of classes—but that we suffer for the "simple fact" of being women. We maintain that the waged woman is doubly exploited: a woman worker is not only exploited by the boss, but she is also oppressed and exploited as a housewife. Without losing sight of society's class divide, we propose to struggle against *sexism*, that is, against the division of society according to sexes, which discriminates against us as people at all levels: in school, at home, in the street, at work.

Based on a feminist conception of our world, the Women's Liberation movement proposes, on the one hand, to fight for a series of partial achievements or demands that can be obtained within the system in which we live, with the goal of conquering rights that we still do not have today: We want to obtain the right to free and accessible abortion. We want to be the owners of our own bodies! We need day care in order to stop being slaves to our children. We demand the equitable distribution of domestic work between men and women.

Women must learn to think of themselves as independent, autonomous human beings, and not as subordinate or inferior. Only when women have their own concept of themselves, of the society in which men have dominated up until now, of history which is men's history, will there be a real base for solidarity, for common struggle between men and women. Women must liberate themselves from the narrow role of mother-wife that has been imposed on them for centuries.

On the other hand, the ultimate objective for which we fight is impossible to achieve within this system, since it would imply the dissolution of the patriarchal family, the complete socialization of domestic work, of education … etc. and the *true* liberation of women and of all men.

The movement arose in Mexico, as in many other places, from a need for unity. From the disenchantment, the dissatisfaction, the frustration that we, as women, experience in the isolation of everyday life, emerges the need to unite with other women, at first perhaps as pure instinct. The need for communication, the desire to know the reason for all these feelings, is the first common denominator for women.

Through communication, the exchange of ideas about experiences lived individually, women become aware that it's not only about individual problems, that our problems are also the problems of other women, and that they are, at the end of the day, *social* problems.

Consciousness raising necessarily leads us to act outwards and to seek forms of organization that allow us to carry out the struggle so that women's consciousness of women increases day by day.

Our struggle, for the moment, requires autonomy in respect to men. In all the mixed-gender organizations or political parties—those that support change, to say nothing of the other organizations—women continue to be kept in their traditional role. In addition, the issue of women's oppression is considered a secondary, subordinate problem that "will be resolved after social change."

For us women, there will be no real social change if we do not participate with our own demands and if we do not struggle from now on to obtain women's liberation.

Based on this autonomy and given the infinite difficulties that we face in disseminating our ideas and expressing ourselves in the existing organs of dissemination, we have decided to put out our own newspaper. We no longer want others to write about us. Now women will write about and for ourselves.

We think that a feminist newspaper represents another weapon for raising consciousness. With this first issue, we seek to initiate discussion, the exchange of ideas, and communication among women. Furthermore, we want to learn something that we have traditionally been denied: to express ourselves in multiple ways.

WOMEN SEIZE THE WORD

La Revuelta, September 1976, 1. Translated by Liz Mason-Deese.

Further Reading

Aviña, Alexander. *Specters of Revolution: Peasant Guerrillas in the Cold War Mexican Countryside.* Oxford: Oxford University Press, 2014.

Calderón, Fernando Herrera, and Adela Cedillo, eds. *Challenging Authoritarianism in Mexico: Revolutionary Struggles and the Dirty War, 1964–1982.* New York: Routledge, 2012.

Carey, Elaine. *Plaza of Sacrifices: Gender, Power, and Terror in 1968 Mexico.* Albuquerque, NY: University of New Mexico Press, 2005.

Draper, Susana. *1968 Mexico: Constellations of Freedom and Democracy.* Durham, NC: Duke University Press, 2018.

Flaherty, George. *Hotel Mexico: Dwelling on the '68 Movement.* Berkeley, CA: University of California Press, 2016.

Muñoz, María L. O. *Stand Up and Fight: Participatory Indigenismo, Populism, and Mobilization in Mexico, 1970-1984.* Tucson, AZ: The University of Arizona Press, 2016.

Olcott, Jocelyn. *International Women's Year: The Greatest Consciousness-Raising Event in History.* Oxford: Oxford University Press, 2017.

Paz, Octavio. *The Other Mexico: Critique of the Pyramid.* New York: Grove Press, 1972.

Pensado, Jaime M. *Rebel Mexico: Student Unrest and Authoritarian Political Culture During the Long Sixties.* Palo Alto, CA: Stanford University Press, 2013.

Pensado, Jaime M., and Enrique C. Ochoa, eds. *México Beyond 1968: Revolutionaries, Radicals, and Repression During the Global Sixties and Subversive Seventies.* Tucson, AZ: University of Arizona Press, 2018.

Zolov, Eric. *Refried Elvis: The Rise of the Mexican Counterculture.* Berkeley, CA: University of California Press, 1999.

Zolov, Eric. *The Last Good Neighbor: Mexico in the Global Sixties.* Durham, NC: Duke University Press, forthcoming.

4
Japan

After accepting the terms of unconditional surrender in September 1945, Japan fell to Allied occupation. The United States, the leading force of the occupation, moved quickly to restructure Japan's state and society, going so far as to rewrite the country's constitution.

As the Cold War took shape, U.S. priorities shifted from democratizing Japan to transforming the country into a bulwark against the spread of communism. This intense anti-communist turn triggered dissent in Japan, such as opposition to Japan's support of U.S. involvement in the Korean War, which in turn elicited massive repression, especially of the organized left.

Although the occupation formally ended in 1952, the American presence continued. Okinawa remained under the control of the U.S. military and through the Treaty of Mutual Cooperation and Security Between the United States and Japan, or Anpō, the United States maintained its right to keep bases on Japanese territory, which troubled many in Japan.

In the 1955 elections, conservative forces, soon organized as the Liberal Democratic Party (LDP), took control over the government, holding power continuously for the next thirty-eight years. Under the LDP, Japan would experience a series of extreme, and sudden, postwar transformations. To begin with, the population skyrocketed. Between 1945 and 1955, the population increased by 18.6 million. Not only was Japan's population growing, it was becoming more urbanized. In fact, the country's urban population rose from 38 percent in 1950 to 75 percent by 1975.

Under the military protection of the United States, Japan also experienced an unprecedented economic boom, initially fueled by the Korean War. From 1950 to 1973, the economy expanded at an astonishing average rate of more than 10 percent. New buildings were constructed, roads were paved, and railways connected the country together like never before. With economic growth also came a robust consumer society, surpassing even the affluence seen in many Western European countries. By 1963, for example, about four out of five households owned a television set. Japan's remarkable transformation, from ground zero in 1945 to one of the most successful capitalist economies in the world in the 1960s, was showcased to the world in the 1964 Summer Olympics.

Figure 4.1   Anti-War Day Demonstration. October 21,
1970. Mizoguchi, Akiyo, Saeki Yōko, and Miki Sōko, eds.
Shiryō Nihon Ūman ribu shi (Kyoto: Shōkado Shoten, three
volumes, 1992–95). Photo credit: Matsumoto Michiko.

Although Japan stood as a model of capitalist development, the high costs,
from pollution to alienation, continually disrupted the dominant image of
seamless modernization. In fact, postwar prosperity went hand in hand with
a rippling tide of continuous protest. In the 1950s, students, labor unions,
peace movements, and women's organizations all raised important questions
about the legacies of Japan's imperial past, the country's special relationship
to the United States, and the uneven effects of rapid postwar change.

These streams of protest came together most powerfully in the summer
of 1960, when LDP Prime Minister Kishi Nobusuke, a former Class A
war criminal, rammed through a revised Treaty of Mutual Cooperation and
Security in the face of widespread opposition. In response, workers went on
strike, tens of thousands took to the streets, and nearly ten million signed
petitions against the treaty. On June 15, 1960, activists stormed the Diet,
and the police responded with violence, leaving hundreds injured, and one,
Kanba Michiko, a 22-year-old student at the University of Tokyo, dead.
While the Anpō protests forced Kishi's resignation, no revolution took
place, the anti-treaty coalition dispersed, and radical forces diminished.

After a brief lull, however, a new cycle of struggle emerged in the mid-1960s. As in other countries, this later cycle certainly built on these earlier experiences, but because it responded to the changing conditions of the 1960s, it necessarily assumed a different shape. While this subsequent round of activism in many ways never reached the amplitude of the 1960 Anpō protests, it did strike out in new directions.

One of the key causes of this new cycle of contestation was growing student dissatisfaction. The years after the Anpō protests saw a massive spike in university enrollments. Between 1960 and 1975, the college matriculation rate in Japan rose from 10.3 percent to 37.8 percent. Despite the relative affluence of the time, many students protested university conditions. Classes were too large, instructors too few, amenities lacking, and academic competition fierce. Many students felt increasingly anxious about job prospects after graduation.

Rapid development in the 1960s led to feelings of anxiety, loneliness, and emptiness. Some students felt guilty about the country's newfound wealth. Others rejected the consumer society around them. Still others feared the loss of traditional ways of life. They began to search for some sort of meaning. As in other countries, these impulses would give rise to a kind of counterculture.

This dissatisfaction translated into a rejection of existing political parties. Many youth became independent voters, or turned to extra-parliamentary politics altogether. Here, they found an array of radical formations called Zengakuren. Zengakuren, or the All-Japan League of Student Associations, was not actually a single organization, but rather a collection of competing factions. Although one faction, Minsei, was controlled by the Japanese Communist Party (JCP), the others, though leftist and even pro-communist, were critical of the JCP, which they found moderate, undemocratic, and bureaucratic. The Zengakuren factions experienced a surge of growth as discontented students and young workers searched for political alternatives in the 1960s. This formation helped catalyze what would later be referred to as the Japanese New Left.

Students threw themselves behind many issues at this time, but one of the most urgent was the Vietnam War. As one of the United States' closest allies, Japan played an enormous role in the war effort. Japan sub-contracted for the U.S. military, housed thousands of American military personnel, and sent aid to prop up the Republic of Vietnam, while Okinawa served as a pivotal base of operations. Without the crucial support of Japan, it is very unlikely the United States could have waged the war it did. In this way, Japanese citizens had a much more complicated relationship to the war than other advanced capitalist countries: subjects of American imperialism, yet also accomplices in the war abroad.

One of the most important antiwar initiatives in Japan was called the Citizen's League for Peace in Vietnam (Beheiren). Less of a formal organization than a kind of catch-all civic movement, Beheiren called for peace in Vietnam, Vietnamese self-determination, and an end to Japanese involvement in the war. The group, which had close ties to the American left, promoted nonviolence, decentralization, and flexible tactics. But Beheiren was by no means the only force in the struggle against the Vietnam War. The various Zengakuren factions also took part, but unlike Beheiren, they were very hierarchical, constantly fought amongst themselves, encouraged violent confrontation, and called for revolution.

In October 1967, activists from several Zengakuren factions tried to prevent Prime Minister Satō Eisaku from leaving Haneda Airport for Saigon. On November 12, 1967, tens of thousands of activists marched on Haneda Airport once again, this time to stop Satō from departing for the United States to meet with President Lyndon Johnson. Another ferocious battle ensued, as 5,000 police fought back with fury. A turning point came in January 1968, when tens of thousands of demonstrators descended on Sasebo to protest the arrival of nuclear-powered aircraft carrier, the USS *Enterprise*. Police hurled concussion grenades, blasted tear gas into the crowd, and showered protesters with water cannons spiked with eye irritant. Many bystanders found themselves caught in the melee, and police overreaction elicited sympathy for the protesters, just as it did in other parts of the world, such as France in May 1968.

Unrest became generalized in 1968. Students at the University of Tokyo, arguably Japan's most prestigious university, formed Zenkyōtō,

Figure 4.2   Flag of the women's liberation group, "Scarlet Letter." The image is a visual pun, meant to depict both a vagina and a sea shell, while evoking the *ama* pearl divers, who were sexualized and marginalized by mainstream society. March 3, 1974.

the All-Campus Joint Struggle Councils. Independent from the factions, Zenkyōtō activists occupied the university, declaring it a liberated zone. The example spread across Japan, engulfing hundreds of high schools and universities. In fact, students occupied over 195 campuses across Japan that year. Like Beheiren, Zenkyōtō was a loose network of student activists, many of whom had grown tired of the sects. Instead, Zenkyōtō stressed autonomy, flexibility, mass democracy, and a focus on the local and everyday.

But the state fought back. The LDP passed new legislation in 1969 to increase state power, police found ways to effectively counter student offensives, and radical activists lost public support, as evidenced by the LDPs massive electoral victory in December 1969. Symbolically, the Security Treaty was renewed again in 1970 despite massive opposition. Facing serious repression, engulfed in intersect violence, finding itself isolated from the broader public, and unable to develop alternatives to break the impasse, the organized New Left largely collapsed in the early 1970s.

Nevertheless, radical activism continued well into the 1970s, although it changed form. Some activists adopted armed struggle, while others embraced electoralism, winning a string of grassroots campaigns in small towns and cities in the 1970s. This period also saw the rise of new social movements, like environmentalism, the disabled citizen's movement, women's movement (known as *ūman ribu*), and movements of ethnic minorities, such as Koreans, Okinawans, Ainu, and Burakumin. In some cases, their concerns overlapped with one another, for example, when *ribu* women targeted Japanese men and women's complicity in the exploitation of Korean sex workers, not only in the past, but in the present. Taken together, many of these new social movements not only challenged the core assumptions of Japanese political life, but presented a new model of politics altogether, generating new ideas about subjectivity, non-hierarchical organizations, and inclusive coalitions.

TO THE FIGHTING STUDENTS AND WORKERS OF ALL JAPAN AND THE WHOLE WORLD (1967)

Akiyama Katsuyuki

In 1948, student activists decided to unite the various self-governing student associations across Japanese universities into a league, the Zengakuren. The Zengakuren would play an important role in student politics throughout the postwar period, especially the 1960 Anpō protests. By this point, many student radicals had turned against the Japanese Communist Party (JCP), which they considered too reformist. In this context, three anti-JCP Zengakuren factions united as a Three Faction Alliance in the hopes of building a revived left. One of their biggest actions took place on October 8, 1968, when students, armed with color-coded helmets and staves, marched on Haneda Airport to prevent the Prime

Minister from flying to South Vietnam. When the dust settled, over 50 activists were arrested, hundreds injured, and one, Yamazaki Hiroaki, killed. Below, we reproduce a report from the leader of the Three Faction Alliance on what came to be called the First Haneda Incident.

* * *

I want to send my most heartfelt greetings and passionate solidarity to the fighting students and workers of all Japan and the whole world. We protest Yamazaki's murder, and proclaim the following to all the fighting students and people who are trying to overcome his death and move forward: that the Zengakuren will surely avenge this death, expose the real culprit of this murder, and fight on till we shatter.

Almost ten days have passed since the Haneda demonstration, the raw memory of which lingers in our minds. But all of Japan remains under the taut anxiety that Zengakuren tossed over them during the battle at Haneda. And with the passage of time, it will be possible to judge ever more clearly who in Haneda was on the side of the righteous, and who the criminals were. It is becoming obvious that the fierce struggle of Zengakuren, which exhausted all its efforts, is the force that most seriously met and attempted to stop Prime Minister Satō's visit to Vietnam, and also that these desperate efforts pose a serious question to all citizens of this nation.

[...]

It is obvious to the point of being overwhelming that the Zengakuren have exhausted every last effort to overcome all obstacles, to fight the violence of the riot police, those savage watchdogs of state power, and to carry out the interests and objectives of all the people. Zengakuren's opposition is so clear that state power seeks to prevent its development by desperately trying to lay blame on Zengakuren. The state's array of false propaganda such as "Some students are out of control" and "Students have killed other students" grows stronger, and they attempt to find their way out through unreasonable and unjust crackdowns.

[...]

It is not only the bourgeoisie, but also the Japanese Communist Party that flings hate-filled words at the Haneda demonstration, chastising it as "unforgivable violence by a faction of the extreme left." What on earth were they doing on October 8? Didn't they only hold what they call a "Red Flag Festival" to sabotage the struggle, but also betray us by opposing us fully? The Japanese Communist Party opposes the Haneda demonstration and also Zengakuren; it therefore provides Prime Minister Satō with consummate rearguard support. We must not countenance the reactionary apostasy of these Stalinists, but resolutely protect Zengakuren's able actions, and further refine our position for the sake of victory.

[...]

The Haneda battle of October 8 released and freed every single repressed struggle; it has clearly raised up a new revolutionary banner to replace all the movements for peace and society that have lost their pre-existing vitality. Zengakuren's struggle has broken through the boundaries of the pre-established, officially recognized leadership and begun a struggle against Japanese imperialism that is new, sharp, and uncompromising, one which will stretch out over the long term until the day it is victorious. The battle of October 8 inherited the Anpō struggles of seven years ago; it stands at the forefront of Zengakuren's struggles, which advance like a raging wave, forming a vital beacon for the resistance and struggles of the Japanese people.

[...]

Satō's visit to Vietnam has unmistakably spurred the infinite evil of Japanese imperialism to turn frenzied and reactionary. Echoes are rising of the former "Greater East Asia Co-Prosperity Sphere," aiming to once again rule and invade developing countries in Southeast Asia and semi-colonial countries, while plans are being laid for revising the U.S.-Japan Security Treaty in 1970.

[...]

Zengakuren's struggle is by no means isolated. At Haneda on the 8, did we not have companions, like the workers of the Japanese National Railways and the progressive workers of the Anti-War Youth Committee, who fought alongside us till the end? A force several times more advanced than the Anpō struggles of the 1960s surrounds Zengakuren. Nay, the real fire is being lit by the struggle of the main units of workers. Shall we not shatter all barriers by the firm union of the workers led by the Anti-War Youth Council and Zengakuren?

At precisely this present time, when the turbulent waves of the Haneda demonstration on October 8 have yet to recede, the next battle is looming.

[...]

Reprinted in *Shinsayoku Riron Zenshi: 1957–1975*, eds. Kōji Takazawa and Kazunari Kurata (Tokyo: Shinsensha, 1984), 352–6. Translated by Shi-Lin Loh.

WITHOUT WARNING, RIOT POLICE BEAT CITIZENS AS WELL: DISPATCH FROM OUR REPORTER INSIDE THE MAELSTROM (1968)
Iwadare Hiroshi

In 1966 Japanese citizens learned that they should expect a visit from the USS Enterprise, a nuclear-powered, American aircraft carrier. The details of the visit were hazy, but the carrier was to arrive at Sasebo from the United States, then head to the Gulf of Tonkin as part of the American war effort. The news met widespread opposition, stoking anxiety about nuclear power, and sparking anger at Japan's involvement in the Vietnam War. But the government continued as planned, with the carrier expected to land on January 18, 1968. Antiwar forces resolved to show their opposition. The result was a colossal showdown between protesters and police. The intense state repression at Sasebo, along with reports of police intentionally beating innocent bystanders, generated greater sympathy for the protesters. In this article, a reporter from the newspaper, Asahi Shimbun *reports on the police violence.*

* * *

Sasebo. It was completely out of the blue. Dozens of riot police, clubs raised, appeared in front of the citizens and the on-the-scene press who were watching the collision of the students and the police forces from the slightly elevated lawn of the Sasebo Citizens' Hospital. There was no warning, no "we will use force" or "students will be rounded up." There was not even the "Dear citizens, please take shelter" that up until now has always preceded such incidents. Because of this, these citizens by the hospital were completely taken by surprise and fled in confusion.

Before they knew it, a mass of riot police were right in front of them like a black tsunami.

It is too late to flee forward. One group of citizens attempting to flee rush into the entrance of the Citizens' Hospital. Police batons fall on those citizens last to run. Rising to flee, they are again battered. Because they are but ordinary citizens, they have neither helmets nor staves. They cringe, shielding their heads with both hands. They are beaten. Kicked with boots. With no way to escape, they press against the wall of the hospital. Again and again they receive heavy blows. Truncheon blows fall even upon the motionless and cowering.

I shouted "I'm an *Asahi* reporter!" Whether or not they heard, the rain of blows did not abate. My reporter's helmet flew off. I covered my head with both hands. "I'm probably going to die," I thought amid glancing blows. I recall as many as four or five blows to my scalp. Diving through the legs of a riot policeman, I attempted to escape, but was again beaten and kicked.

At last I escaped, struggling my way into the Citizens' Hospital, where injured students were receiving medical treatment in what might have been a wartime treatment unit. The "Asahi Newspaper" armband on my sleeve was drenched with blood. My slacks were in tatters. My head, with three stitches, and both hands hurt intensely.

Asahi Shinbun, Tokyo evening edition, January 17, 1968, 9. Translated by William Marotti.

DECLARATION OF WAR (1969)
Council on Armed Revolution, Red Army Faction, Communist League

On January 18, 1969, over 8,000 riot police put an end to the occupations at the University of Tokyo. Students threw Molotov cocktails, built barricades, and declared a liberated zone. But the police triumphed, sending a symbolic message across the country. Although the violence and repression, which continued to escalate over the course of 1969, led some to abandon activism, it radicalized others. Looking to events at home and abroad, one of these radicals, Shiomi Takaya, argued that the world situation was now marked by a transition from imperialism to socialism, with the masses in the imperialist powers ready to embrace socialist alternatives, and the weakened imperialist powers fighting back. Inspired by other movements, Shiomi advocated unified international armed struggle. In the summer of 1969, his faction, soon labeled the Red Army Faction, announced its existence with the following "Declaration of War."

* * *

Declaration of War

Members of the bourgeoisie!

In order to drive you into revolutionary wars across the world and wipe you out, here we openly make a declaration of war.

Members of the bourgeoisie!

You may attempt a general mobilization of the U.S. Army, NATO troops, UN forces, the Allied military in Vietnam, or other police forces around the globe; you may even try to mobilize the troops of the Soviet Warsaw Pact countries, which you have rendered boneless and degenerate, but we warn you that we will gather the strength of all the world's proletariat into a global party—a global Red Army—a global revolutionary front guaranteed to knock you down.

We know all too well the historical record of your crimes. Your history is stained with blood. In the First World War as well as the Second World War, for the sake of these global and predatory conflicts amongst your kind, you deceived our comrades into fighting for you, you made them fight amongst themselves, and out of all this, you profited massively.

You killed our comrades for the sake of plundering colonies. You incited them to colonial plunder by promising them a share of the loot, and so made them kill their comrades in underdeveloped countries for your ends. And this is not all. In the same way you incited more of our comrades to mutual slaughter, dragging them into the rapacious conflicts you fought with your own kind over the colonies you plundered.

Members of the bourgeoisie in our own Japan! You too will not be allowed to deny any of this. Under the slogan of "enrich the state and strengthen the military," have you not carried out rapacious conflicts in the Sino-Japanese War, the Russo-Japanese War, as well as the First and Second World Wars?

We will no longer be incited or deceived. Nay, it is not only that we refuse to suffer further temptation or deceit. We will curse you with our past resentments, and furthermore, to counter your actions, this time our side is prepared.

If you have the right to kill our Vietnamese comrades as you please, then we too have the right to kill you as we please.

If you have the right to murder our Black Panther comrades and crush ghettoes with tanks, then we too have the right to kill Nixon, Satō, Kiesinger, or de Gaulle, and the right to use bombs to destroy the Pentagon, [Japan's] Defense Agency, the National Police Agency, as well as your homes.

If you have the right to pierce our Okinawan comrades with bayonets, then we too have the right to pierce you with our bayonets.

In order to make another war in Korea, you multiply the Self-Defense Forces, conduct Operations Focus Retina and Mitsuya, and in order to re-elect the Park dictatorship to a third term, you arrest our comrade Im for his opposition and sentence him to death; if you have the right to do such things, we too have the right to build our Red Army, raise a revolutionary front, arrest you and sentence you to death.

Members of the American bourgeoisie!

After the Second World War, you have unceasingly killed our comrades in Korea, the Congo, and Vietnam.

Members of the Japanese bourgeoisie!

You continue to increase the Self-Defense Forces and the riot police; even now you collaborate in Vietnam, and seek the future deployment of troops to Korea.

Members of the West German bourgeoisie!

We may well ask what you intend by fortifying your national defense troops and restraining France, and why you keep your eyes on Czechoslovakia, Eastern Europe, as well as the Middle and Near East.

Members of the bourgeoisie!

It is a huge mistake for you to think that things will always go your way. In the past, we were agricultural slaves bound like livestock to the prison of our master's land under feudalism. You tore apart the bounds of this status, and to make us free, you fought with the nobility under the slogan of "liberty, equality, fraternity." But now we firmly and clearly declare that we refuse to be manipulated by you. Your time is done. We will fight through to the bitter end for the final war that will end class warfare on this earth; that is, we will fight for victory in the global revolutionary war, and to eradicate you from this world.

We will openly point our guns at the Self-Defense Forces, the riot police, and the U.S. troops. Those alarmed at the prospect of being killed, turn those guns around! Turn them to point at those who instigate you—the bourgeoisie who control you from behind.

We will surely and mercilessly eradicate those who interfere with the labor of liberating the world's proletariat, no matter who they are, in the midst of our revolutionary war.

Proletarians of all countries, unite!

We hereby issue this declaration of global revolutionary war.

Preliminary Armed Insurrection—Victory in the Global Revolutionary War!

Members of the proletariat!

At present the class struggle taking place in Japan and the world has attained the phase of openly declaring war on the bourgeoisie. This is because the global class struggle that appeared all over the world in 1968 has now embarked on a new spurt of progress. Is there not a new note sounding in the prelude to global revolutionary war? China and the U.S.S.R. carry out violence at their state boundaries, and rebellion arises in Czechoslovakia. In Ireland the Catholics and Protestants wage religious war, which English troops interfere with.

After the Second World War, there has been of late an entirely new state of affairs destroying the world, arising in diverse forms. The 17th Parallel in Vietnam; the war of liberation in the South, anti-communism in America; the continuous emergence of antiwar struggles, the virtual inability of the Chinese Communist Party to complete its own dismantling and sublation, which is being incorporated and carried out by Red Guards, farmers and other groups. The waves of exaltation after October 8 exceeded the Molotov cocktail battles conducted by the Self-Defense Troops of the Japan Communist League's Chūkaku-ha. The waves of consolidated resistance movements in France and Italy surging to surpass their Communist Parties. The revolutions in Latin America (Guevara), the Liberation Front in Palestine, the guerrillas of the Middle and Near East and to the south of the 38th Parallel in Korea, the differentiation of Okinawa's struggles with and its confrontation of the bayonets pointed at it by the dual imperialisms of Japan and the U.S. that have operated after the Second World War.

In the midst of all this, something is emerging, something which seeks not only to overcome, but to conquer the very nature of growth in those movements it has overcome.

It is being birthed amidst the havoc (class crisis) surrounding the question of how to break through the limits of revolution, for victory in the global revolutionary war as a mere extension of spontaneous growth in armed self-defense action committees is impossible. We may see this phenomenon when we look broadly at a bloc which consists of the Red Army, which emerged from in-faction struggles within the Japanese Bund, the Students for a Democratic Society in America, the Black Panther Party, and the Chinese Communist Party. [...]

[This] bloc has begun the work of determining the nature of a global Party—a global Red Army—a global revolutionary front through war. The way of Guevara in Latin America, the Near and Middle East, Africa. America's BPP. China. Asia, via Vietnam, is almost attempting to determine the same. Only in Japan and Western Europe were such efforts lacking. But the entry of Japan's Red Army onto this stage, and its influence in Germany and Italy, shows that the war at last involves the whole world. The global class struggle has begun to turn toward an age of fighting for its establishment and development.

This is what we mean by the sounding of a new note.

Behold America!

They too have issued a declaration of war.

"Bring the War Home! All Power to the People!" So SDS proclaimed in Chicago on October 11.

The growth of the international proletariat is now attempting to walk the road of fundamental global sublation; it seeks the conversion of the armed proletariat from the revolutionary subject of a transitional world into a full-fledged movement; it does this, at precisely this moment, in a time when the enemy bourgeois class is attempting a piecemeal rebuilding of fascism's power.

The "Bring the War Home" movement in United States is significant because it comes from that same America which carried out anti-revolutionary wars of invasion and oppression in Korea and Vietnam. Even though this antiwar struggle only developed after the Vietnam War began, and failed to take place during Korea, it nonetheless carries the decisive meaning that America is poised to make a great leap forward from "antiwar" toward "war!" U.S. imperialism plays the world's savior, fighting wars for peace, calling itself the defender of the free world, and making peace through the balance of power.

The material basis that enables us to make such judgements is to be found in the process through which imperialism is waging war to divide the world again for the third time in history. At the same time, modern imperialism, as piecemeal fascism, is disposing of excess financial capital through endless wars (which of course transform into endless wars of class struggle). These processes are sufficiently transformative to fundamentally change this material basis into world revolt, but they are not the reasons why antiwar struggles and revolutionary wars are taking place. It is not that antiwar struggle happens because imperialism causes war; there is another meaning to antiwar struggle, and when we understand this other—nay, this true—meaning, that is when the transformative leap from antiwar to revolutionary war will take place.

Indeed, the other true meaning of antiwar struggle lies in how this third historical war of division, which has changed this material basis, and the transformation of imperialism's excess financial capital into class struggle, have been enough to connote radical global revolution by fundamentally changing the world after the Second World War. Consequently, it is precisely here that the true meaning of the antiwar struggle lies. Japan's October 8 and France's May 1968, the invasion of Czechoslovakia, the internal repressions in China and the U.S.S.R.: the profound depths of this true meaning must be clarified by seeing how all these mysteries stem from the chaos of the entire transitional world order fundamentally turning toward sublation, as well as how fundamentalism, spontaneous growth, and other things are turning into intermingled phenomena. From that understanding we will achieve the triple unification of a global party, a global Red Army, and a global revolutionary front, and with this we will oppose the enemy's third historical war of division, led by anti-revolutionary U.S. imperialism. We will smash participation in the wars of invasion and oppression that take place through anti-revolutionary war in Japan and West Germany, which also represent the piecemeal rebuilding of fascist power, and so give birth to the tactics and strategy that will lead us to victory in a preliminary armed insurrection and a global revolutionary war.

Members of the proletariat!

Be victorious in the preliminary armed insurrection of the global revolutionary war!

Reprinted in *Sekigun Dokyumento*, ed. Sashō Henshū Iinkai (Tokyo: Shinsensha, 1975), 59–64. Translated by Shi-Lin Loh.

AMPO INTERVIEWS MAKOTO ODA (1969)

Although most U.S. allies did not send troops to Vietnam, they did offer support in other ways. This was especially true of Japan, which in some respects played the role

*of quartermaster. While some Japanese profited handsomely from this arrange-
ment, others felt it amounted to collaboration. The response was the Japanese peace
movement. Of the many groups that participated, arguably the most important
was Beheiren, formed in 1965. A kind of decentralized citizen's initiative,
Beheiren broke with the hierarchical structures of existing groups. Anyone could
claim the group's title so long as they agreed with its three core slogans: "Peace in
Vietnam," "Vietnam for the Vietnamese," and "Stop the Government of Japan
from Cooperating in the Vietnam War." One of Beheiren's most visible figures
was the famed novelist, Oda Makoto. In this interview, conducted in English,
Oda shares his thoughts about the antiwar movement in Japan.*

*   *   *

AMPO: What do you think that Beheiren has introduced into Japanese
politics that's new?
[…]
ODA: The peace movement, or the antiwar movement, was built primarily
from the standpoint of the victims. From that position you can just make the
general statement that war is there and we as its victims must oppose it. In
particular in Japan, with regard to the Pacific War, the Second World War,
I think this has been a good thing in a sense. On the whole the Japanese
people were victims in World War II. And so the Japanese movement after
the war began from the position that we never again want to be the victims.
[…] [A]nd this was the time of the Cold War, and if a nuclear war did occur,
there was absolutely nothing we could do, we would be completely in the
position of victims. Therefore it was quite natural that we began from the
viewpoint of victims.
[…]
[…] But in the process of the movement itself we began to realize that
we felt our position to be different from that of the old peace movement.
We began to realize that the Japanese state had become powerful enough
to be in the position of the oppressor. And as this became increasingly clear,
we began to think about the actual basis of the peace movement. We saw
that we had to fundamentally reexamine the basis of the movement. Our
position is typified by that of the Japanese workers on an Okinawan air base.
Whenever they try to strike they find themselves facing a bayonet, and from
this point of view they are entirely in the position of victims; but at the same
time if you ask what they are actually doing, you find that they are loading
bombs on B52s. […]
[…]
[W]e are quite rigid about ourselves, but at the same time we have a
kind of tolerance about what others are doing. This kind of tolerance is

another of the characteristics of Beheiren. And one of the defects of radical movements all over the world is that such movements lack tolerance. [...] [O]ne of the main principles of Beheiren is that we do not want to make a criticism without our own *doing*. [...] When you want to do something, you have to do it, and without making any stupid complaints about what others are doing. [...]

[...]

And so there are many kinds of actions at the same time inside of Beheiren. [...] I think that such kind of actions at the same time are quite necessary.

Now I think the [...] progressive movement in Japan, and all over the world maybe, has two kinds of extremes. One extreme is to want to have military uprisings, to resort to military weapons, to violence, direct violence, and they want to have a kind of revolutionary war or something like that. This is one extreme. And another extreme we might have is the situation created by the Socialist Party or the Communist Party or Sohyo ... too much belief in the parliamentary system, or in elections. When they conduct a demonstration, it's a kind of ritual. [...] It doesn't have any kind of political influence on the government or on the people. They just make a march; I went down to Sasebo and found that they are making a very glamorous march, without doing anything. Just a march. So we have *this* extreme, and we have *this* extreme, but as true human beings we think we are standing in between [...]

AMPO: To change the subject: you're planning to go to America ... if you have permission to go, what will you do in America? Where are you going?

ODA: In the first place, I want to mobilize the people [...] to make a *demonstration* against the coming of Satō ... my dear Satō. And also after that, I will participate in some kind of speaking tour, maybe, where I can explain the situation of the Japanese peace movement, or the antiwar movement, or the radical movement, to the American people [...]. And also I would like to explain how dangerous, morally and physically and spiritually the Security Treaty is ... for both nations, you see.

[...]

AMPO: What kind of thing could the American radicals do now ... what kind of thing would you like to see them do, as far as the Security Treaty is concerned?

ODA: [...] I think that when we make a movement against the Security Treaty, of course we are making one now, at the same time [the Americans] can make many kinds of demonstrations, sit-ins, against the State Department, and also against the White House [...]. But at the same time they can put the pressure on the feeling of the American people, and if they can be successful in making the feeling of the American people change, a little bit, about the foreign policy, especially in Asia, in Japan too […] [T]he American people don't know anything about the situation in Asia, the Japanese situation, and including the situation of Korea, and the situation of Okinawa […] I think they are quite naïve. [I]f the American movement can have some strong movement, directly against the Security Treaty and the Okinawa problem, for example, when Mr. Satō comes to the United States, if they can have a very strong demonstration against the coming of Satō.

[…]

AMPO: Isn't it true that the Security Treaty can probably never be smashed without a strong movement against it also in America?

ODA: I think so … without a very strong movement in America the security treaty cannot be smashed at all. We need the cooperation of the American movement […] And also our movement is needed, I think, by the American movement too, for the future of the United States.

[…]

AMPO: A Report From the Japanese New Left 1, November 1969, 2, 10–11.

LIBERATION FROM THE TOILET (1970)
Tanaka Mitsu

In 1970, a new kind of women's liberation movement, ūman ribu, arose across Japan, adding to the cacophony of voices revolting against patriarchal authority around the world. These Japanese activists reappropriated and reworked Marxist and Black Power concepts to politicize sexuality and sex-based power relations akin to other radical feminists of the Global North. The manifesto excerpted below became one of the most iconic texts of the Japanese radical women's liberation movement. It was authored by Tanaka Mitsu, a leading figure of the movement and a member of a cell called Group of Fighting Women (Gurūpu Tatakau Onna). This Tokyo-based group served as one of the key organizing and communication centers for a nationwide movement that denounced the patriarchal structure of Japanese society and the masculinist culture of the Japanese left.

* * *

Introduction

In our class society, every woman is born possessing one property. That property is virginity. If she can deal with it skillfully and sell it at a high price, her life is set.

However, virginity is ranked according to a woman's inherent and acquired characteristics. In other words, depending on a woman's family status, wealth, her appearance, her level of education, her virginity's market value can vary significantly. Strangely enough, it actually doesn't matter that much whether or not she is really a virgin.

What is important is if she *acts like a virgin.* [...] Now, whether or not one acts like a virgin is the dividing road as to whether one is going to declare one's rebellion toward men and society. Women's liberation means that we reject this "virgin-like" performance [...] and we will develop our struggle as women by presenting our true selves against this society and the men who try to measure our worth as women by this criteria of virgin-likeness.

[...]

"Women's Liberation Movement" – Why it Sounds So Lame

[...]

For women who have had the belief, "marriage is a woman's happiness" seep into the marrow of their bones, this society has the imperative to shape women as such, based on this system of private property, which has as its highest order to maintain purity of blood to ensure the preservation and succession of property; regarding children, for men their existence is such that they have to believe that children originated from them. Accordingly, those women who are not satisfied with marriage, men, and society, who dare to revolt, are bashed and made into bad examples. As a method of maintaining this system, first, on the one hand, men are told not to choose this kind of woman, and the consciousness of these kind of men is precisely the mind of the dominant class. On the other hand, the family and schools are made as places that function to produce women who flatter and prostrate themselves before such men in order to reproduce this discriminatory structure of masculinity and femininity. [...]

[...]

[...] When we consider how in previous times women were under a multitude of oppressions [...] when the emphasis in the struggle was placed on women to gain their economic independence, to earn fundamental human rights such as the freedom to divorce, universal suffrage, the freedom to choose one's employment—in the midst of this struggle to acquire the rights equal to men, as human rather than as cattle, these women who manned the movement had to hack away and discard their own sexuality [...]

[...]

[...] As for our struggle, which aims toward human liberation, as we continue to interrogate women's sexuality and reproduction, what kind of undesirableness will be ours as we develop our movement? But before we think about this, we would like to consider how sex is used to control men and women, how the one-husband-one-wife system is maintained through the way that women and men relate to each other and in total, how sex has been used as a fundamental means to make humans into a slave-like class.

Servile Consciousness is Produced

This economic system that aims at the preservation and the inheritance of property binds women's sexual desire to men and the patriarchal family in order to guarantee the purity of blood. Thus, the rule of the one-husband-one-wife system only applies to women. [...] Insofar as the one-husband-one-wife system has been essentially made to limit and confine women's economic independence and women's sexual desire, the structure of consciousness that despises sex is even more oppressive toward women's sexuality.

[...]

Authoritarianism [...], which is the basis of the ideology that exercises class domination, is reproduced through patriarchal marriage, in other words, in the day to day relations between men and women in the family. [...]

I'm the Toilet and You're the Excrement ... Our Miserable Sex

[...] What does it mean that the structure of consciousness that denies sex is even more oppressive to women? This structure, which uses sex as a fundamental means to subjugate humans is mediated by a male consciousness, which in turn, regulates male sexuality by oppressing female sexuality. In addition to the fact that women's sex is endowed with reproduction, women's sex is much more powerful, with essentially anarchistic potential. This is likely the reason for the production of this structure.

[...]

For men, women are either Mother, maternal tenderness, or Toilet, the vessel to dispose of sexual urges; women's image is divided into these two. Male consciousness abstracts the holistic figure of woman into two sides—Mother (tenderness) and the Other (SEX)—and assigns antithetical emotions to each. Within the context of human history, where the marriage system existed alongside prostitution and slavery, the one-husband-one-wife system has despised sex and supported this structure of consciousness that separates sexuality and spirituality. [...]

Whether you are a man's mother or a man's toilet, this consciousness is expressed by whether in actuality you are being targeted for marriage or simply an object for a man to fool around with. And in order to be seen as an object to marry, and not to be selected as a sexual playmate, a woman has to act as though she sees nothing, hears nothing, and says nothing about sex, just like an innocent cute little girl, and in doing so woman oppresses herself by betraying her totality that possesses both tenderness and her natural sexual desire.

Woman, who possesses both the tenderness and sexual desire as a whole, has been divided by man's split consciousness, which has been produced according to the demands of the ruling class, and she is coerced to only live as a part of herself. But man, who only allows woman to live as a part of herself, is also oppressing himself because he too is also allowing himself to only live a part of himself. [...]

[...]

Women are oppressed by this male consciousness that divides women between a toilet and a mother, which amounts to a virginism that is meant to maintain the purity of bloodlines.

Nowadays, if you do not behave virgin-like as the object of marriage, you have to be resigned to suffer a variety of losses, and given the fact that most women expect the possibility of finding happiness in material comforts and in social status, these women act in such a way to keep up the display of this virgin-likeness, rather than living their own *true self*. [...]

The Women's New Attitude and Struggle

[...]

[...] This male consciousness that divides women between mother and toilet comes from the structure of consciousness that denies sex and this is the root of whether you are seen as an object of sex to play with, or as an object to marry.

Whether you are a mother or a toilet, they are both raccoons in the same den. When, regardless of which one you are seen as, you realize that they both essentially amount to the same thing, women start to challenge authoritarian male dominant society. [...]

[...]

Since we will achieve the liberation of women as a part of the proletariat liberation, we must develop our struggle against authority toward world revolution. For this struggle against authority must have totality due to its inherent globality and universality, and our relations with men constitute a part of this struggle [...]. Without continually questioning our personal relationship with men, children, and the family, and the contradictions inherent to these relations, in the tense struggle against authority, we will not be able to grasp the means to universalize what it means to be human [...].

[...] We can understand that the mistake of the women's struggle thus far lies in the fact that is has departed from a place which only grasped women's existence, in the past, present, and future terms, through the terminology of Marxism. While the perspective of class conflict is fundamental, to only take this perspective to understand women completely misses so many crucial points. By taking care of men who are worn down through the survival of the fittest, and caring for them by creating a comfortable, relaxing home, in order to send them out again into the market as a commodified labor force, women also execute the task of slave dealers.

[...]

[...] Our struggle does not begin with what in Marxist terms would be a pure revolutionary woman, who in fact exists nowhere, but it begins with me, here and now, with all the contradictions that defy reason. It is through casting back our grudges against men and the powers that be that we can begin as women to construct our theory of liberation for women. [...]

[...]

Women Give Birth, Men Don't

The future of the world will depend on which side can integrate women—the side that is for the system or against it. If women's strength of stability is mobilized, it can become a truly radical power, but if it is used as a conservative force, it can serve as a basis of the dominant system. [...]

[...]

Virgin-Likeness Sustains Aggression and Anti-Revolutionary Forces

[...]

[...] The human foundation of this class society is based on the one-husband-one-wife system which oppresses women's sexual desire; it denies women's sexuality and makes it taboo. By treating women who don't act *virgin-like* below those who *act virgin-like*, and debasing their value as a toilet, this male dominant society has thus punished them and thereby thoroughly confined and regulated women's sexual desires. [...]

[...]

[...] For women, the ruling authority's strategy regarding sex materializes through the toiletization of their sex. Thus, women return to their virgin-likeness as a reactionary facade that coincides with toiletization of their sex. It is this structure of consciousness that denies sex that makes the extreme opposites of the chastity of the wives of the military nation versus the comfort women's vaginas defiled by semen! The aggression of the ruling powers and counter-revolution are sustained through the oppositional pairing of chaste women and comfort women.

The Truth Spoken by Sex Organs is All the More the Truth

Even in movements that aim toward human liberation, women drop out from the frontlines because there is no theory of struggle that addresses male and female sexuality, and given our servile dispositions, the struggle for liberation becomes thoroughly masculinist and male-centered [...].

[...] Marx's various theories regarding the slave-like relationship between capitalists and workers fail to recognize how profoundly these relations are mutually mediated through sex. Thus, the liberation of the proletariat wears out [...]. Women are at a loss for their own words in the face of the structures of male logic who distinguish women from humans, and without any question talk about solidarity, proletarian internationalism, and unified will.

[...]

Women's worship of men renders male logic the absolute truth. [...] Why has this ridiculous discriminatory structure that has divided women comrades been allowed to continue until now! Now is the time for women to assert that the non-logic of the *here-existing woman* is fine and beautiful.

Needless to say, this does not mean that women's logic is superior to men's logic. Rather our outcry for the restoration of women's logic is the necessary antithesis to the fact that until now patriarchal society's male exclusivism has only approved men's logic as good and legitimate. As African-Americans have asserted that "Black is beautiful," we must claim that "Women's (il)logic is beautiful." Since our struggle is based on women's historical burden, which cannot be easily expressed by words, based on our anger and resentment toward men and society, we must assert, "Our irrationality is beautiful" in the face of our male colleagues who continue to try to evaluate our struggle for its effectiveness and productivity.

[...]

We declare the liberation of women as a liberation of sex.

We declare it is a self-liberation from the structure of consciousness that denies sex. [...]

From woman to woman, from Toilet to Toilet!

Unity Empowers Women!

So we gonna go for it?

Translated from the revised October 1970 version, republished in Tanaka Mitsu, *Doko ni iyou to riburian: Tanaka Mitsu hyōgenshū* (Tokyo: Shakai Hyōron Sha, 1983), 265–80. Translation and introduction by Setsu Shigematsu.

POLLUTION AND RESIDENTS STRUGGLE (1974)
Ui Jun

In the 1970s, activists began to argue that the breakneck development of the postwar period, which many Japanese had regarded as an unmitigated success, had in fact caused major environmental degradation. In 1972, Ui Jun, an engineer turned activist, declared that Japan likely had "the worst environmental pollution problems of any country in the world." For Ui and other activists, environmental pollution, or kōgai, referred to the totality of problems, including contaminants in the air, mercury in water, arsenic in food, factory noise, congestion, and diseases. Victims of these many different forms of pollution soon organized grassroots movements, sometimes called residents struggles, to not only introduce safer standards, but to push the public into rethinking some core assumptions about the value of rapid industrial growth. Below, we reproduce Ui's reflections on the environmental movement.

* * *

If anything at all can prevent our country from experiencing the world's greatest pollution, it is the residents movement. In the past (and unfortunately for some time in the future), minimizing or preventing pollution has occurred not as a result of institutional means such as laws or regulations, but only as a result of protest movements by residents of polluted areas. We have to face this fact squarely.

It is impossible, however, to embrace all such movements with a single term. Some last more than ten years, while others disappear after a single action. Some are powerful and others weak. They take all different forms of organization. Even the number of residents movements in Japan is impossible to calculate. When asked about their number, I once answered that, judging from my limited experience, at least 3,000 must exist. However, this is at best a rough measure for movements which daily rise and dissolve. It pretends to no accuracy.

From the viewpoint of those accustomed to formal organization, this seems fragile and unreliable indeed. In fact I have heard such comments from people related to political parties and labor organizations. Many of those in government [...] understand residents movement organizations only as [...] citizens committees formally organized on the municipal level. [...] However, now that relations are developing among various movements throughout the country, this lack of formula for residents protest seems to me to have the merit of elasticity, multiplicity and variety. When a movement is limited by no fixed formula, it provides no clues to its adversaries for its annihilation. What cannot be grasped cannot be crushed.

Many such examples have a relatively long history and their results are known to the world, as Minamata Disease, Kanemi Rice Oil Disease (Yusho), Itai-Itai Disease, and Morinaga Arsenic Milk Case. But since I have been associated with only a few of these movements I feel hardly qualified to discuss them all. I have nevertheless decided to write about them in the hope that my limited experience might be of some use for exchange of views. As the experiences gathered here all evince, study is the only weapon of the residents movement, and exchange of information their major method. [...]

Difficulties Facing Residents Movements

Residents movements face great difficulties. First, in many cases they must confront powerful enterprises which have no morality. It is often hardly possible to expect so much as a shred of human morality from management. In fact, high-speed growth and expansion of enterprise scale were commonly made possible by ignoring morality. Today's enterprises have been able to rise to power because they have been freely allowed to drain wastewater and gas because residents protests have been ignored. It takes great courage even to complain about this very lack of morality. Only last year, not once upon a time, employees at Chisso Company's Goi nitrogen factory not only beat up some Minamata Disease victims but also complained to the authorities. [...] Many participants in residents movements have experienced the threat of physical violence from enterprises.

The enterprises employ various other more subtle pressures such as interfering with a resident's business, jeopardizing his job, and causing him to be discriminated against in the community. [...]
[...]

The Walls of Administration

Government, especially pollution control departments of the municipal government, not only supports the enterprises' tyranny, but in many cases it actively confronts the residents movement [...]
[...]
In many cases, the residents movement has to break through the futile agreements about ppms [parts per millions]. [...] In safety bulletins concerning fish pollution, the kinds of fish with clearly high mercury and PCB content were excluded from the start of the investigation. [...] In Chiba prefecture, it was discovered that the head of the prefectural pollution control department had given advance warning to the factories prior to the

inspection of the prefectural congress. [...] In the face of this, the residents movement has no means but to arm itself with the force of facts, clarifying one by one unshakable truths. [...] In the Kuise Apartments in Amagasaki, residents kept a pollution diary, and their awareness of air pollution proved far more precise than expensive meters. [...]

[...]

Scientists Must Rise

The time seems finally passed when, as 10 years ago, established leading authorities all stood on the side of business and when even mild criticism could cost a scientist his career. Right now studies of pollution are the fashion, and if one gives his work a plausible title, one can expect as large a research grant as one wishes. Nevertheless, or rather precisely for this reason, few scientists can be trusted by the residents movement, for they are preoccupied with their own research and are unable to respond to new problems. [...]

[...] [A]s yet very few scientists stand by the residents. We constantly hear residents movement people in various places say that they wish they could have ten more, or even one more, trustworthy scientist.

[...]

Another method is to associate with students. This certainly involves considerable trouble. They are querulous and their language is incomprehensible. They purposely wear bizarre clothes, and injure each other, even those in the same group [...] Some movement people make it a rule to have nothing to do with students for fear of being looked upon as radicals. [...] However, students at least have spirit and energy. Their disproportionate emphasis on knowledge, ignoring reality, indefatigable factionalism, and impatience commonly regarded as their defects, should rather be recognized as a result of today's education. [...] What we have felt to be the fault of education, we must realize, was in fact the very purpose of education designed to serve business.

Students however feel insecure in this conveyor belt society, and begin to doubt whether it is right. This is of course just: pollution means eating what should be left for the future, and precipitating unreasonable environmental changes for which later generations are not responsible. [...] Youth led brilliant anti-pollution movements in the Taisho period [1912–25]. If youth will again begin to do so, the residents movement will enter a new phase. Also, to transmit to the next generation the experience of the middle-aged group which support the present movement, we must actively encourage the participation of youth.

[...]

The Place of Lawsuits

From my experience [...] in pollution problems, a lawsuit should not absorb more than 50% of the energy of the movement. [...]
[...]
Anti-pollution suits in the past had no precedents to rely on. Since they had to build theories from the first step, the lawyers' efforts were great. In the future, the suits will to some extent follow a fixed pattern and it will be possible to estimate what kind of case can be won by what effort. [...]
[...] [I]n the field of administrative law, many tend to face pollution with the same parasitic attitude toward power with which they have been producing theories. Such people never try to tackle the reality of pollution and then deduce theories from it. Rather they share the bureaucratic viewpoint which handles pollution within the framework of established legal interpretations [...] Therefore, there is absolutely no possibility that they can produce a study favorable to pollution victims. [...]

The Future of the Residents Movement

[...]
First, ten years ago, few residents movements won victories. Particularly in big pollution cases, the victims' movements all ended in defeat. At present we have several examples of complete victory. [...]
Second, some movement tactics have been established on the basis of experience. Since the success of the protest movement in 1964 against the Mishima Numazu petrochemical complex, the importance of residents standing on their feet and making things clear by themselves has been proved. [...]
Third, the environment of pollution movements is changing for the better. [...] Mass media, like newspapers and TV, despite strong management control, at present are treating the residents movement favorably. [...]
[...]
Finally, anticipating an often repeated discussion, I would like to consider an international comparison of the residents movement. [...] The environmental movement in the West so far has been a movement centering on the upper middle class. It has had no strength to cope with the development policy advanced under the catchphrase of raising poor people's income. The movement in the U.S. is quite varied, and has the quality of a youth movement. However, it has not reached the point of organizing Blacks. [...] The Japanese residents movement organizes, with no self interest, peasants who refuse development itself. In addition it includes lower middle class people like school teachers and civil servants. This is a phenomenon unpar-

alleled anywhere in the world. The Japanese residents movement has not yet been systematically introduced overseas, but were it to be it would evoke great response.

[...]

Kogai: The Newsletter from Polluted Japan 4, Summer 1974, 1–14.

Further Reading

Ando, Takemasa. *Japan's New Left Movements: Legacies for Civil Society*. New York: Routledge, 2014.

Avenell, Simon Andrew. *Making Japanese Citizens: Civil Society and the Mythology of the Shimin in Postwar Japan*. Berkeley, CA: University of California Press, 2010.

Eiji, Oguma. "Japan's 1968: A Collective Reaction to Rapid Economic Growth in an Age of Turmoil." Translated by Nick Kapur with Samuel Malissa and Stephen Poland. *The Asia-Pacific Journal* 13, issue 12, no. 1 (2015): 1–27.

Havens, Thomas R. *Fire Across the Sea: The Vietnam War and Japan, 1965–1975*. Princeton: Princeton University Press, 1987.

Kapur, Nick. *Japan at the Crossroads: Conflict and Compromise After ANPO*. Cambridge, MA: Harvard University Press, 2018.

Koda, Naoko. "Challenging the Empires From Within: The Transpacific Anti-Vietnam War Movement in Japan," *The Sixties* 10, no. 2 (2017): 182–95.

Marotti, William. "Japan 1968: The Performance of Violence and the Theater of Protest." *American Historical Review* 114, no. 1 (2009): 97–135.

Sasaki-Uemura, Wesley. *Organizing the Spontaneous: Citizens Protest in Postwar Japan*. Honolulu: Hawaii University Press, 2001.

Shigematsu, Setsu. *Scream from the Shadows: The Women's Liberation Movement in Japan*. Minneapolis, MN: University of Minneapolis Press, 2012.

Steinhoff, Patricia. "Memories of New Left Protest." *Contemporary Japan* 25, no. 2 (2013): 127–65.

Walker, Gavin, ed. *The Japanese '68: Theory, Politics, Aesthetics*. London: Verso, 2018.

5
West Germany

West Germany in the mid-1960s was a deeply closed and conservative society. Constitutional rights coexisted with narrow limits on political action, cultural difference, and strongly authoritarian relationships within most social institutions. Here the long 1968 would express itself as a dramatic refusal of this condition, involving sharp theoretical critique, radical opposition, and attempts at institutional transformation.

In the postwar settlement, the Western occupation zones were formed into the Federal Republic of Germany, opposing the German Democratic Republic in the East. Cold War and membership of NATO combined with the Soviet repression of the 1953 workers' uprising in East Germany and the 1961 Berlin Wall to cement a situation where the state was defined by loyalty to U.S. leadership globally and the liberal-capitalist model. "Totalitarianism," associated with "social movements," was ascribed equally to the Nazi past and the Soviet present, delegitimizing internal opposition. In practice, however, purges of Nazis had been curtailed quickly as the Cold War developed, meaning that much of the state apparatus was staffed by ex-party members and collaborators: in 1968 the prime minister, Kurt Georg Kiesinger, was an ex-Nazi and the president, Heinrich Lübke, had used concentration camp prisoners as forced laborers during the war.

Within families and communities, too, the shadow of the past was a long one. Many in older generations had been party members, had been involved in the Holocaust or committed atrocities. This helps to explain why radical writing from the period has a particular edge: behind the curtains of postwar respectability and prosperity lay mass murder. Patriarchal family relationships were ubiquitous and deep-rooted; the postwar emphasis on hard work and "achievement" offered acceptable goals at the cost of a narrowing of personal and cultural horizons.

Meanwhile, the long tradition of status groups marking external respectability was translated into a new politics of consumption in the postwar "economic miracle," creating narrow cultural options albeit differentiated by class and region. The physical destruction of Germany's Jews, Sinti and Roma, and others created an ethnically closed society in which the Turkish, Kurdish, and southern European immigrants needed to staff an expanding industry were formally treated as "guest workers," expected to return "home" once no longer needed.

In this context, the right-wing Christian Democrats (CDU-CSU) dominated postwar politics, often in alliance with the secular right-wing Free Democratic Party (FDP). The firmly anti-communist Social Democratic Party (SPD) constituted an extremely loyal opposition, supporting capitalism and NATO. This tendency became official in 1966 as the SPD joined the CDU in a "grand coalition," combining virtually all parliamentarians. Meanwhile, the Communist Party (KPD) had been banned in 1956. Radical movements thus constituted an "extra-parliamentary opposition."

This lack of space for dissent also rested on corporatist workplace arrangements. The SPD-associated German Trade Union Confederation (DGB) had achieved a system of collective bargaining with employers' federations whose outcomes were backed by the state. This went together with works councils and co-determination in industry, and a wider "social wage" in social insurance, education, health, pensions, housing, and other benefits to mean that West German workers gained significantly from capitalist development, in return for accepting the "social market economy" as a political framework. The net result was to reduce conflict to technocratic questions of management.

However, the dynamism of West German capitalism tended to undermine political and cultural closure. Modernization meant a further shift away from farming, the decline of villages, the growth of the great cities, internationalization, and especially the extension of education to build the new technocracies and staff the welfare state. The crisis struck first in the universities.

Figure 5.1   "Under the Ruffs—The Dust of a Thousand Years." Protest at the inauguration of Hamburg University's new rector. November 9, 1967. The "thousand years" pointed not just to the medieval dress of the professorial caste but also its extensive collaboration with the "Thousand-Year Reich." Courtesy of the Staatsarchiv Hamburg.

Student activism had been radicalising for some time by the late 1960s: the Socialist German Student League (SDS), once the youth wing of the SPD, was expelled in 1961 because of its opposition to NATO and West German rearmament. SDS developed as a key organization of the extra-parliamentary opposition, influenced by the international New Left and cultural radicals such as the Situationists and the Dutch Provos. The movement was polycentric, with a presence in regional centers (Frankfurt, Hamburg, Munich) and smaller university towns (Heidelberg, Tübingen, Erlangen). West Berlin, physically isolated and no longer the capital, formed a particularly important locus of activism.

One key issue was opposition to NATO and the government's unconditional support of U.S. foreign policy, particularly in relation to the war in Vietnam. Already in February 1966 police and mob violence against antiwar protesters in Berlin showed the symbolic resonance of this issue and raised the wider question of whether "democracy" West German style, had space for radical opposition. In later years this orientation would produce strong Third Worldist tendencies, according to which struggles at home, in the "belly of the beast," were secondary to those taking place in the Global South.

A second aspect, particularly as Old Left groups lost ground within SDS, was the struggle to democratize relationships within the education system. In 1967–8 nearly a dozen "critical universities" were founded across the country, building on a wider wave of critiques of authoritarian pedagogy and of a narrow focus on training for the labor market, along with many internal struggles and symbolic challenges to academic power. This co-existed with a more countercultural critique of consumerism and the political passivity of much of the wider society.

In many ways the West German student movement was particularly isolated, notably from the working class which it was often theoretically oriented toward—the contrast with Italy or France is striking. The integration of social democracy, corporatist decision-making, and consumerist popular culture contributed strongly to this. Frankfurt School theories, which highlighted the difficulty of independent working-class thought and action and the pacifying role of the culture industry, were therefore particularly attractive to German radicals. Class differences in education also played a role: early stratification in secondary school meant that few experiences or personal connections linked university students and young workers.

The dominant Springer press, particularly the tabloid *Bild-Zeitung*, brought these themes together. Springer media routinely attacked protesters in a period of police and informal violence. On June 2, 1967, student Benno Ohnesorg was killed by police at a demonstration against the Shah's visit to West Berlin. A year later, on April 11, 1968, a right-winger shot student leader Rudi Dutschke, severely wounding him. The demand "Expropriate Springer!" and associated actions followed, along with the development of an extensive alternative press to speak from and for the movements, which would grow well into the 1970s.

It was in this charged context that the grand coalition used its massive majority to pass the "Emergency Laws" in May 1968, enabling the suspension of a range of basic rights in emergency situations, including "internal emergencies." This was met with strong resistance from the extra-parliamentary opposition, which saw it in line with the increasingly aggressive police response to protests; some feared a general suspension of democracy.

Protests in West Germany never reached the high points seen elsewhere, and state power was never seriously threatened, meaning that activists faced increasing costs from repression and burn-out and fundamental strategic questions about the way forward for radical movements. A tiny minority responded by moving toward armed struggle strategies; despite its small numbers their actions produced a significant spectacle, particularly in tandem with the repression which followed. Larger numbers moved from New Left to far left activism, whether orthodox communist, Maoist, Trotskyist, or "Sponti" (spontaneous).

Considerably more powerful in the years that followed was the rise of a new generation of feminism which took the extra-parliamentary opposition's critique of authority and cultural norms and the theoretical and organising skills developed in struggle and turned them against the patriarchal relations within and then beyond the movement. Similar paths were followed by the developing lesbian and gay movements.

In the 1970s, these movements joined with the wider emancipatory impulses from 1968 to transform many spheres of West German society and sections of the population which had remained unaffected or hostile to the movements of that year. These strategies could mean either a "long march through the institutions," as Dutschke proposed, or the creation of counter-institutions. In education, for example, egalitarian, democratic, and feminist struggles, from kindergartens to universities, were paralleled by the construction of alternative educational institutions. Similar logics could be found in health, welfare, media, and publishing among others, leading to the creation of archipelagos of alternative institutions as well as radical networks and associations of professionals.

So too, ecological struggles would involve farming and small-town populations in opposition to nuclear power and other projects, often with extensive direct action and aggressive police involvement; these connected to the development of alternative lifestyles (including organic farming, communal living, and new religious movements) in rural areas; meanwhile urban areas saw the development of a squatting movement which would grow massively by the later 1970s. The 1980s would see mass activism against nuclear weapons and the radical direct action of the Autonomen and Antifa. If 1968 never had a chance of winning in West Germany, it nonetheless reshaped much of wider society.

MURDER (1967)

Students' Trade Union Working Group, SDS Munich, Liberal Students Association Munich, Social Democratic Higher Education Association Munich

In the summer of 1967, Mohammad Reza Pahlavi, the Iranian dictator who came to power after a CIA coup in 1953, toured West Germany with his wife. The Shah's secret police was one of the most vicious in the world, and Iranian students worked with local groups to protest the Shah's visit. One demonstration, on June 2, 1967, turned particularly violent, as the Shah's supporters beat the protesters, while the police joined in with tear gas, baton charges, and water cannon. While observing police attacking fleeing protesters, a student named Benno Ohnesorg was shot in the back of the head. Protests took place across the Federal Republic, marking a generalized loss of police legitimacy in the eyes of students. This flyer—signed not only by the local SDS group, but the student wings of the SPD (in government) and the liberal FDP—shows the impact of the murder.

* * *

MURDER
or manslaughter or grievous bodily harm causing death? The legal profession may argue about this.

During the protests against the Persian dictator's visit, in front of the Opera House in West Berlin on June 2, 1967, the 26-year-old student of German and Romance languages and literature at the "Free University"
BENNO OHNESORG
was *shot by the police* (DPA).

According to witness statements Ohnesorg, who was taking part in a demonstration for the first time, was on his own, surrounded by about eight police officers at the point when the fatal shot took place. According to the autopsy results the shot must have hit him from behind. The bullet was found and secured in Ohnesorg's head in the Institute for Forensic Medicine.

THE PERSIAN DICTATOR'S VISIT DEMANDED A HUMAN LIFE.

The Federal Government invited the Shah and felt it had to protect him from any possible assassination attempt. As might have been expected, nothing happened to the Shah.

BUT THE WEST GERMAN AND WEST BERLIN "SECURITY SERVICES"'
PROTECTION OF THE HATED REPRESENTATIVE OF A REGIME OF
TERROR TURNED INTO TERROR ITSELF!

We call all Munich citizens to protest with us on *Monday, June 5 at 7 pm
at the University (Amalien Street).*

Archive of the Institut für Zeitgeschichte, Munich: ED 328/1. Translated by
Laurence Cox and Órfhlaith Tuohy.

SELF-DENIAL REQUIRES A GUERRILLA MINDSET (1967)
Rudi Dutschke and Hans-Jürgen Krahl

*In September 1967, radical theorist Hans-Jürgen Krahl joined the creative and
provocative activist leader Rudi Dutschke in presenting an influential position
paper to SDS' Frankfurt conference. The two had met at Benno Ohnesorg's funeral
and agreed on the need for a new strategy. The success of their arguments led to the
"anti-authoritarian wing," committed to direct action, grassroots organizing, and
the challenge to mainstream culture, taking the lead in SDS, and the marginalization of the Old Left faction. Krahl and Dutschke argued that capitalism had
reached a new stage where the masses had internalized an all-encompassing power
structure, and that radical action and messages were needed to break through
this. A "guerrilla mindset" and a transformed way of living and organizing were
part of a new revolutionary strategy, opposed to the fundamentally bureaucratic
strategy previously pursued by SDS. The text's extensive structural analysis acts to
legitimate the practical political conclusions drawn by the authors.*

*   *   *

The two central political events which this organization's political activity
polarized around since its last delegate conference were the formation of the
grand coalition and the political murder in Berlin on June 2. For the first
time since the split from the SPD, the organizational question became a live
one internally. Depending on which of these events was seen as more politically significant, there were different tendencies toward forming fractions,
distinguished by their objective intention to concretize theoretical opinions
as practical political struggles over direction.

Their possible organizational implications were described by the federal
leadership—from the point of view of the protest movements, particularly
young people's—in vague and content-free ways as an organization which
would be loose in form, united in substance, and working publicly. In Berlin
this was discussed in terms of counter-university and [academic] department
associations, while for other groups the formation of the Grand Coalition

offered possibilities for a renewed attempt to bring socialist groups and groupuscules together in a single movement.

Moreover, the organizational question became much more urgent for some SDS groups after June 2 as they were forced to experience their organizational incapacity in practice. The SDS' inherited organizational structure, still oriented toward the SPD, was not up to the unprecedented spread of anti-authoritarian protest after June 2. The movement's spontaneity threatened to paralyze the largest groups organizationally. Their political behavior thus appeared largely forced on them in a reactive way, and attempts to take political initiatives were mostly helpless.

[...]

3. In a still-pluralist society, the dead weight of interest groups within the system of interest-based democracy could not simply be dismantled, but at the end of the [postwar] reconstruction had to be brought under control. Thus concepts of rationalization, of construction, and finally of "concerted action" appeared. The various attempts to "reform" the system in the present period are to be understood as capital's attempts to adapt itself to the changed conditions in terms of power and profit.

4. The most striking development in the present period of economic formation is the growth of state interventions into the real production process as a unity of production and circulation. This total complex of the economic regulation of state and society forms a system of integral statism. Unlike state capitalism, this suspends the laws of capitalist competition on the basis of the maintenance of private ownership of the means of production, and organizes the once organically arising equalization of the rate of profit via a distribution of the total social surplus value which is geared toward state and society.

To the extent that the state becomes the total social capitalist via a symbiosis of state and industrial bureaucracies, society becomes a total state barracks and employment within the firm becomes employment within society. Integral statism is the highest stage of monopoly capital.

Extra-economic coercive power achieves an immediate economic significance within integral statism. It thus plays a role for contemporary capitalist social formation which has not been seen since the days of primitive accumulation. If in that phase it accomplished the bloody process of expropriating the popular masses, which first brought about the division between wage labor and capital, according to Marx it is hardly used any more within established competitive capitalism. For the objective self-movement of the concept of the commodity form, its value, becomes one of the laws of capitalist development to the extent to which economic violence is internalized within the consciousness of the immediate producer. The internalization of economic violence permits a tendential liberalization of state and political rule, of moral and legal rule.

The naturally produced crisis context of capitalist development in today's crisis makes the internalization of economic violence problematic. According to a materialist interpretation, two solutions are available for this. On the one hand, the crisis creates the potential for proletarian class consciousness and its organization as a material counter-power, in the autonomous action of the working class as it emancipates itself. On the other hand, it objectively forces the bourgeoisie, in the interests of their economic power, to draw on the state's physical, terrorist, and coercive violence.

Capitalism's escape route from the world economic crisis of 1929 relied on the fix offered by the terrorist power structure of the fascist state. After 1945, this extra-economic coercive violence was in no way dismantled, but rather manifested on a psychological level of totalitarian dimensions.

This internalization entails doing without an overt suppression inwards and was constitutive of surface liberalism and surface parliamentarism, albeit at the price of the anti-communist projection of an absolute external enemy. [...]

These hypotheses have fundamental implications for the strategy of revolutionary action. The global one-dimensionalization of all economic and social differences means that the (once practically justified and in Marxist terms correct) critique of anarchism as voluntaristic subjectivism—that Bakunin relied on revolutionary will alone and ignored economic necessity—is now obsolete.

If the structure of integral statism appears as a gigantic system of manipulation in all its institutional mediations, it now gives a new quality to the suffering of the masses, who are no longer independently capable of outrage. The self-organization of their interests, needs, and wishes has thus become historically impossible. Now they can only grasp social reality through the categories of the power system which they have internalized. The possibility of qualitative political experience has been reduced to a minimum. The revolutionary consciousness groups can generate alternative messages, enabling some degree of enlightenment through empirically visible action based on their specific position in the institutional structure. They use a form of political struggle which distinguishes them fundamentally from the traditional forms of political conflict.

Agitating through action, and the sensory experience of the individual organized fighter in their encounter with the state's executive violence, form the mobilizing factors in spreading the radical opposition. They tend to enable a process of consciousness development for active minorities within the passive and suffering masses, to whom the system's abstract violence can come to sensory awareness through visible, irregular actions. "Armed

propaganda"(Che) in the "Third World" must be completed by a "propaganda
of the deed" in the metropolis, which historically enables the urbanization
of rural guerrilla activity. The urban guerrilla organizes absolute irregularity,
as the destruction of the system of repressive institutions.

The university forms their secure zone, or more exactly their social basis,
in which and from which the guerrilla organizes the struggle against the
institutions, the struggle over the canteen fees and over state power.

Does all of this have anything to do with the SDS? We know very well
that there are many comrades in the association who are no longer prepared
to accept an abstract socialism which has nothing to do with their own
life activity as a political perspective. The personal conditions are present
for a different organizational form of working together in SDS groups.
Self-denial in one's own institutional milieus requires a guerrilla mindset, if
integration and cynicism are not to be the next stop.

The SDS structure to date was oriented toward the revisionist model of
the bourgeois membership parties. The leadership bureaucratically captures
its paying members, who must make an abstract profession of faith in the

Figure 5.2   "Everyone's Talking About the Weather. We're
Not." This SDS poster subverted a German railway
slogan—and helped fund protesters' legal fees. 1968. Image
from Papiertiger—Archiv für soziale Bewegungen Berlin.

goals of their organization. On the other hand, the SDS could not fully take over the ideal administrative function of the revisionist membership parties, as it is only a partially bureaucratized association, an organizational her-maphrodite. By contrast, the problem of organization presents itself today as the problem of revolutionary existence.

Republished on glasnost.de. Translated by Laurence Cox and Órfhlaith Tuohy.

CONSUMER, WHY ARE YOU BURNING? (1967)
Kommune I

Since the late 1950s artists and activists influenced by Situationism and the Frankfurt School had explored ways to challenge a narrow mainstream culture. In 1967, together with SDS members, some of these activists founded "Kommune I" in West Berlin, the numeral indicating a self-understanding as pioneers. Members attempted to live in ways that broke with the bourgeois family, including nudity and transgressive clothing, psychological and drug experiments. Public provoca-tions were a key part of their political activity, leading to media hostility and police intervention, for example around the plan to "pie" U.S. Vice President Hubert Humphrey. On May 22, 1967 a Brussels department store caught fire, with 251 deaths. The fire, at the start of an "American fortnight," was mistakenly ascribed to protestors. Kommune I took up this theme and distributed a series of leaflets satirising media reactions; two of its members were tried for incitement to arson but found innocent.

* * *

2nd edition
NEW! UNCONVENTIONAL! NEW! UNCONVENTIONAL! NEW!
NEW! TAKES YOUR BREATH AWAY! NEW! TAKES YOUR BREATH
AWAY!
As we all know, American industry's productive capacity is exceeded only by American advertising's wealth of inspiration. Fascinating and exciting achievements like Coca-Cola and Hiroshima, the German economic miracle and the Vietnam War, the Free University of Berlin and the University of Tehran are the world-famous quality marks of the American drive to action and spirit of discovery. On both sides of the Wall, barbed wire and Iron Curtain they're sewing "freedom and democracy."

Now, an American week in Brussels has opened with a gimmick which is new in the wide-ranging history of American advertising methods. An unusual spectacle was presented to the inhabitants of the Belgian metropolis on Monday:

For the first time in a European city, a burning department store with burning human beings offered that authentic crackling Vietnam experience (the sense of being there and burning together), which we haven't yet been able to enjoy in Berlin.

Skeptics might caution that "the customer is king" and we shouldn't simply burn the consumer, the consumer who is so courted and unambiguously privileged in our society.

Pessimists might see our oh-so-complicated and hard to guide advanced economy in danger.

Of course we share the pain of those bereaved in Brussels. Yet despite the human tragedy, those of us who are open to the New cannot hide our admiration (within reason) for the daring and unconventional approach of the Brussels department store fire.

Nor should we be misled by the attempt to ascribe these fireworks to anti-Vietnam demonstrators. We know these unworldly young people, who always carry yesterday's (placards), and we know that despite all their abstract book-learning and romantic dreams, our dynamic American reality has always passed them by.

"APO und soziale Bewegungen" collection of the Free University of Berlin archive, file K1, L4-5-67. Translated by Laurence Cox and Órfhlaith Tuohy.

OBSERVATIONS ON THE TACTICS AND DEPLOYMENT OF WEST BERLIN'S FASCISTOID PRESS (1967)

H. Heinemann

The West German mainstream media, particularly the Springer press and its mass-market Bild-Zeitung, *were bitterly hostile to protest beyond very narrow limits. This fed into violence by the police and right-wing groups against social movements, creating the climate for the shooting of Benno Ohnesorg (and later Rudi Dutschke). This text uses the tools of literary analysis to criticize the ideologies of media discourses and their close relationship to state power, linking the process to the movement toward the Emergency Laws which would be passed the following year. The text also criticizes Kommune I's provocations around the Brussels warehouse fire, seen as isolating radicals from the wider population: cultural and social radicalism are understood as mutually exclusive. Indicative of the movement's isolation, however, this text's critique of the failures of the student movement to appeal to the working class is not complemented by any indication of actual organizing efforts.*

* * *

If it is against democracy, peace, and freedom, Springer's newspapers and the "volunteer Springer rags" are always involved.

As early as December 1966, the *Berliner Morgenpost* delivered this ultimatum in relation to a demonstration on the Kurfürstendamm: "Eradicate the troublemakers!" Five and a half months later, a West Berlin student was "eradicated" in front of the German Opera House. Admittedly, the flaw in the beauty of this bloody Friday was that Benno Ohnesorg had not belonged to any political college group and thus could not be dismissed under the usual heading of "hotheads."

Despite this, the next day the Springer yellow press and most other newspapers were stirring up the West Berlin population against the students after the dress rehearsal for a state of emergency had been carried out with extreme brutality; the subtext was a recommendation to use violence. The *Berliner Morgenpost* considered that the demonstration against the Shah's visit to West Berlin was the work of "hysterical troops of academic yobs, trained communist street fighters, and amused slackers" and demanded that "these rioting radicals be driven out of the temple." "We have had enough. The patience of the Berlin population is exhausted." In line with this paper for the middle and petty bourgeoisie, the *BZ* told the workers what they had to do: "The city belongs to the decent folk. Only to them." Having been brought onto the right track, outside Schöneberg City Hall West Berliners demanded "concentration camps and gas chambers for the students" (according to *FU-Spiegel* 58).

However, the same *BZ* came to the conclusion on June 9 that "We want to live with the students and not against them. But they also have to finally learn to live with the population. As part of them and not a plague on them," and spoke with a touch of self-criticism of an "avalanche, in whose dreadful guilt we were ultimately all involved." The relationship to the Springer house's usual trivialization of fascist rule is clear.

What had happened? The previous method of presenting the "radical minority at the FU" [Free University] as "troublemakers, loudmouths, academic strike forces, hooligan brothers" (*Morgenpost*), "hotheads, radicalinskis, a corps of twerps" (*Bild-Berlin*), "radicals who present a public danger, neurotic know-alls" (*BZ*) as well as "fools and wolves" (*Telegraf*), had certainly affected the Governing Mayor's discourse ("Hooligan brothers, ruffians, lunatics and malicious people"), but it brought FU students— still fresh from the impression made by rubber batons, boots to the head, and pistol shots—closer together. Now, while some students restricted themselves in discussions on the Kurfürstendamm to the question of whether throwing stones was justified, others went outside factories and firms, distributed leaflets there and gave the discussions a political content. They made it clear that if students are the victims today, tomorrow it will be striking workers, and that there is a straight line from eliminating the democratically minded student body to abolishing trade union rights and thus giving free rein to any arbitrary actions of the employers. In this context, West Berlin's precarious economic situation was also discussed.

These actions had no discernible success, because the working class had been ignored for years by the students and the latter were only now remembering them once again as a potential ally.

Nonetheless, this sort of education had to be prevented at all costs by the media that serve state and entrepreneurs. That there was a real fear of student influence on the workers can be shown by a certain Herr Sickert's immediate reaction; among many other things, he is the regional chairman of the West Berlin DGB. His warning "not to be harnessed by an anarchist minority" was rushed into print and correspondingly cannibalized in most West German and West Berlin newspapers. The political demands, and the student organizations' analyses, were as usual consistently ignored. However, as Mr Kurras' shot [killing Ohnesorg] had received greater publicity than desired, the background to this action could not be entirely repressed. Thus a new tactic was adopted.

As if at a word of command, the West Berlin press switched to a "soft approach" on June 6, 1967, after the lies and misinformation of the Holy Trinity of Senate, police, and press had been unmasked. The new version, of the "isolated excesses of over-zealous police officers," went public at the Springer house. Typical of this attempt to distract was and is, for example, the demand to "employ a police psychologist."

All the papers were gripped by "regret for the unfortunate events." Indications of the state of emergency drill (planned and carried out in detail) were generally suppressed, although e.g. Permanent Secretary Prill had already declared months earlier, "Let them come, then they'll get a baton to the head. That would be a good practice ground for our police"; although a West Berlin newspaper had written as late as the morning of Bloody Friday "This will be a hard day for our police"; and though the bloody traces of the Shah's visit could be followed across West Germany.

This state of emergency, "which is euphemistically described as not a drill" (*Andere Zeitung*), had meant lengthy house arrests, occupants being driven out of their houses and giant closures of public routes. For the "front-line city press," however, only "any infringements by individual members of the security forces" and "regrettable individual incidents" could be mentioned.

(It was however a certain and unassailable fact that the police had been provoked by stone-throwing.)

[...]

A few words about the so-called Kommune I. It is absolutely no surprise that their lordships produced arguments for the reactionary press. The damage caused by these "agents provocateurs" (*Berliner Extrablatt*) to the student left and thus indirectly to the workers can be measured in discussions with progressive West Berliners. In the West German press, this group's activities produce some grotesque fruits. I can mention a probably intentionally malicious commentary of the *Stuttgarter Zeitung* from June 9, 1967, which discusses the call to "set fire to department stores," while on inhabited Berlin streets fires blaze, passers-by are molested, cars are destroyed, and counter-demonstrators struck down.

Kommune I's leaflet about the department store fire in Brussels alone could justify the conclusion that batoning policemen, the "front-line city's" yellow press, and Kommune I belong indissolubly together. To avoid misunderstandings: these comments are not about actions which unmask West Berlin's pseudo-democracy, but about leaflets which give the ruling class the chance to distract people from the students' demands.

Look at this city! See a Governing Mayor who is outraged that a Persian potentate was insulted, and who couldn't find a word of sympathy for the slain man's widow until several hours later; a press which misdirects popular anger against the student minority; a DGB chairman who incites workers against the students highlighting the dangers of the emergency laws; and a senate which tries out the state of emergency for the employers. Truly, "an abyss of dirty opinion tricks is opening up" (*BZ*).

It must be possible to wake the class consciousness of the working class. That is our only chance. The first signs are showing since June 2, 1967.

berliner manuskripte 2, July 1967, 12. Translated by Laurence Cox and Órfhlaith Tuohy.

SPEECH TO THE TWENTY-THIRD
SDS DELEGATE CONFERENCE (1968)
Women's Liberation Action Council/Helke Sander

Women within SDS had been organizing since 1967, with a variety of initiatives like Kinderläden *(anti-authoritarian kindergartens) in universities and elsewhere, leading to the formation of the Women's Liberation Action Council. By September 1968 the movement was strong enough to be able to speak at the*

SDS conference despite some opposition. This speech, highlighting the feminist challenge to the organization's internal patriarchy and criticizing both the anti-authoritarian and orthodox communist wings, is often seen as the start of the new West German women's movement. Its symbolic power was marked at the end by a feminist activist who threw tomatoes at the SDS leaders, much as student activists had challenged university authorities. The speech rightly notes the exhaustion (political as well as personal) of SDS activism by late 1968; the move to grassroots and needs-oriented organizing would become widespread in many movements over the following years. Alternative education, feminist and anti-authoritarian childrearing and family practices, and the struggle for reproductive choice were hugely influential in the 1970s.

*   *   *

Dear comrades,

I am speaking on behalf of the Women's Liberation Action Council. The Berlin regional association of SDS gave me a delegate position, although only a few of us are members of the association. We are speaking here because we know that we can only do our work together with other progressive organizations; and today in our opinion the SDS is the only such body.

However, the precondition for cooperation is that the organization understands women's specific problematic, which means nothing more than finally articulating within the organization conflicts which have been suppressed for years. Thus we broaden the conflict between the anti-authoritarians and the communist party fraction, and stand against both camps at once, because both camps are *practically* against us, whatever their theoretical claims. We will attempt to clarify our position, and we demand that the substance of our problematic is discussed here. We will no longer be satisfied with women occasionally being allowed to say something that gets listened to because one is an anti-authoritarian, before going back to the agenda items.

We register that in its internal organization SDS is a mirror image of broader social conditions. Efforts are then made to avoid everything that could help articulate this conflict between claims and reality, because that would mean reorienting SDS politics. This articulation is easily avoided: by dividing off a given sphere of life from society and stigmatising it by calling it private life. In this stigmatization, the SDS is in no way different from the trade unions and the existing parties.

Because of this stigmatization the specific relationship of exploitation which women are subject to is obscured, thus ensuring that men need not yet give up the old identity they won through patriarchy. Of course women are given freedom of speech, but the reasons why they struggle to succeed, why they are passive, why they are able to help implement the association's policies but not to decide them, are not explored. (On the first day of the delegate conference only one woman spoke.) This suppression is complete when we are shown the women who have achieved a certain position within the organization where they can be active. What is not asked is what they had to deny to gain this. The fact that this is only possible through adaptation to a performance principle which men also suffer under and whose abolition is the point of their activity, is also overlooked. Emancipation of this kind only seeks equality in injustice, through the means of competitive struggle and the performance principle which we reject.

[...]

Women seek their own identity. They cannot arrive at it through participating in campaigns which do not directly affect their own conflicts; that would be a false emancipation. They can only arrive at it if the social conflicts which have been forced into private life are articulated so that women can enter into solidarity with one another and politicize themselves. Most women are unpolitical because politics has previously always been defined in a one-sided way which never included their needs. They therefore clung to authoritarian voices within the state, because they were unable to recognize how their demands represented social contradictions which could not be contained within the system.

The groups who are most easily politicized are women with children. The frustrations are strongest here and there is least loss of voice. Those women who can now study can thank not so much the bourgeois emancipation movement but rather economic necessity. If these relatively privileged women have children, they are thrown back on ways of behaving which they thought they had already overcome thanks to their emancipation. They break off or delay their studies, their personal development is stuck or limited by the demands of their husband and child.

[...]

The conclusion which the Women's Liberation Action Council drew from this is as follows: We cannot resolve women's social oppression individually. We cannot wait for the time after the revolution, because a revolution which is only political and economic will not overcome the suppression of private life, as has been shown in all socialist countries.

We seek living conditions which overturn the competitive relationship between men and women. This can only happen through transforming the relations of production and hence power relationships to create a democratic society.

As the openness to solidarity and politicization is strongest among women with children, because they feel the pressure most strongly, we have concentrated our practical work up to now on their conflicts. This does not mean that we do not take the conflicts of women students without children seriously, or that despite the common characteristics of all women in oppression we ignore class-specific mechanisms of oppression. It simply means that we want to carry out the most effective work possible and we must create a starting point which allows us to approach the problematic systematically and rationally.

[…]

The helplessness and arrogance that we have to appear with here is not particularly enjoyable. We are helpless because we really expect that progressive men should realize how explosive our conflict is. We are arrogant because we can see the blinkers you are wearing that mean you can't see that suddenly people are organizing without your involvement, people you have never thought about—and in such numbers that if they were workers you would think the red dawn had come.

Comrades, your events are unbearable. You are full of inhibitions which you act out as aggression against comrades who say something stupid or something you already know. These frustrations are only partly due to political insight into the other side's stupidity. Why not finally come out and say that you are exhausted after the last year, that you don't know how you can cope any longer with the stress of wearing yourselves out physically and intellectually in political actions without gaining any pleasure from it? Why not, before you plan new campaigns, discuss how on earth they are to be carried out? […] Why do you talk about class struggle here and about difficulties with orgasms at home? Is that not an issue for the SDS?

We no longer want to be part of this suppression.

In our self-imposed isolation we therefore concentrated our work on women with children, because they are worst off. Women with children can only think about themselves again if their children are not constantly reminding them of the failings of society. Since political women have an interest precisely in no longer bringing up their children according to the performance principle, the result was that we took society's requirement that women must bring up children seriously for the first time: in the sense that we refuse to continue to bring up our children according to the principles of competitive struggle and performance, knowing that the precondition for the existence of the capitalist system overall depends on their maintenance.

We want to attempt to develop models of a utopian society within the existing one. However, our own needs must finally be recognized in this counter-society. Thus concentrating on bringing up children is not a substitute for our own suppressed emancipation but a precondition for resolving our own conflicts productively. The main challenge is not to bring our children up in a vacuum removed from any social reality, but rather to give children the strength to resist by supporting their own emancipatory efforts, so that they can resolve their own conflicts with reality in the direction of changing reality.

At the moment five of these *Kinderläden* are already in operation. Four more are being organized and others are in a pre-organizational stage. We are working on a model for the FU kindergarten and are organizing kindergarten teachers or helping them to organize themselves. Theoretically, we are trying to critique the bourgeois principle of reason and the patriarchal concept of science.

There is such a huge interest that we can barely manage it organizationally.

[...]

The work on *Kinderläden* creates further tasks, which are closely connected. The children who are now in our *Kinderläden* will no longer fit into normal schools. Their parents will no longer accept the existing schools. Through the broad basis we are trying to give these *Kinderläden*, we are trying to create a wide basis for conflict within the mainstream school system. This conflict will have effects in children and parents who did not go through our *Kinderläden*. We have to prevent children being educated only in what a capitalist society allows them to learn.

[...]

If the SDS understands itself as an organization that wants to set emancipatory processes in train within existing society, in order to make revolution possible at all, it must draw the implications from our work for its politics.

[...]

Comrades, if you are not ready for this discussion, which has to be one of substance, we will certainly have to conclude that the SDS is only a collapsed, counterrevolutionary cake with a soggy bottom!

Women comrades will then know what conclusions to draw.

Republished on 1000dokumente.de. Translated by Laurence Cox and Órfhlaith Tuohy.

STATEMENT OF ACCOUNTS (1968)
Wimmin's Council of the Frankfurt Group

Following Helke Sander's speech, women activists were prevented from distributing leaflets at the SDS' celebration of the fiftieth anniversary of women's suffrage. At the next conference, a meeting sharing women's experiences within the movement led eight SDS women's groups to support the distribution of this leaflet. In the text, the Stammtisch *is the regular's table in an inn, a common German location of male bonding. The key to the list of trophies in the graphic includes leading male figures of 1968, academics and key figures of the left. The emphasis on "penis envy" is connected to Freud's significance both for the Frankfurt School and masculine theories of sexual liberation. The decapitalization in the original marks attempts to dethrone official language; feminists would develop their own ways of writing German to challenge gender norms. The wimmin's council (Weiberrat) did not last long, but the ripples from the feminist critique of the SDS would spread throughout social movement organizing.*

* * *

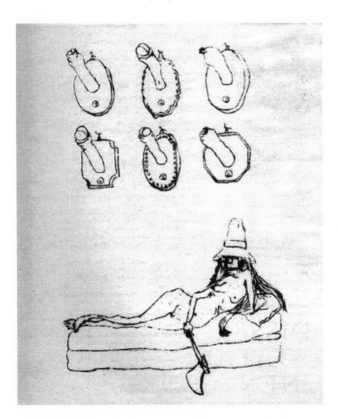

Figure 5.3
[Key:]
1) schauer 4) krahl
2) gäng 5) rabehl
3) kunzelmann 6) reiche

7. schmitz-bender 8. wölf(f)e 1-3 9. offe 10. habermas 11. schmierer 12. neusüß 13. noth 14. giese 15. dutschke 16. cohn-bendit 17. salvatore 18. geulen 19. freud 20. schaterberg 21. bärmann 22. adorno 23. bechmann 24. wetzaf 25. lefèvre 26. riechmann 27. roth 28. semmler 29. deppe 30. neusüß 31. teufel 32. oberlercher 33. mangold 34. ... 35. lederer 36. mao 37. petermann 38. lukasjk 39. richter 40. dabrowski 41. amendt 42. amendt 43. taubes 44. marx 45. enzensberger 46. lauermann 47. lenin 48. leithäuser 49 + more to follow!

dickless—dickless—dickless—dickless

We're not able to open our mouths! If we do open them, nothing comes out! If we keep them open, we get gagged: with petty bourgeois dicks, socialist pressure to fuck, socialist kids, love, socialist thrownness, pontificating, potent socialist horniness, intellectual socialist pathos, socialist counselling, revolutionary groping, sexual-rational arguments, total social orgasm, socialist emancipation claptrap—DRIVEL!

If something does emerge, what follows will be socialist pats on the shoulder, fatherly fussing over us. Then we get taken seriously, then we're wonderful, amazing; we get approval, and then we can join the *Stammtisch*, then we are one of the boys. Then we type, distribute leaflets, paste up wall newspapers, lick stamps; we get turned on theoretically!

Let's vomit it up publicly. Are we: suffering from penis envy, frustrated, hysterical, uptight, asexual, lesbian, frigid, losers, irrational, suffering from penis envy, anti-desire, hard, masculine, spiky, bitchy, compensating, over-compensating, suffering from penis envy, penis envy, penis envy, penis envy, penis envy.

Women are *different!*

LIBERATE THE SOCIALIST EMINENCES FROM THEIR BOURGEOIS DICKS!!!!!!!!!!!!!!!

Politikon-extra 1, no. 1, December 1968, 4. Translated by Laurence Cox and Órfhlaith Tuohy.

BUILD THE RED ARMY (1970)
Red Army Faction

The Red Army Faction (RAF) was one of West Germany's small armed struggle groups. Andreas Baader, Gudrun Ensslin, and others felt that Kommune I's leaflets about the Brussels fire missed the point—and were sentenced in 1968 for setting fire to two Frankfurt stores. In 1970, the radical journalist Ulrike Meinhof joined others in freeing Baader; the ensuing shootout injured one person. The action and this communiqué announced the formation of the RAF. Its tone reflects the RAF's relative isolation and reliance on moral pressure, and the attempt to make links with the working class: the places mentioned highlight the geography and institutions of working-class West Berlin. 883 is the radical periodical where this statement appeared. Westmoreland was the U.S. army chief of staff; Neubauer the Mayor and Interior Minister of West Berlin. FRG was by this point a pejorative abbreviation for "Federal Republic of Germany." The cycle of RAF and state violence would keep escalating up to the "German Autumn" of 1977.

*　　*　　*

Comrades from *883*—there is no point trying to explain the right thing to the wrong people. We have done that long enough. We do not need to explain the Baader liberation action to the intellectual gasbags, the chickens, the know-alls, but to the potentially revolutionary elements of the people. That means those who can immediately grasp the act, because they are prisoners themselves. Who cannot respond to the verbiage of the "Left," because it means nothing and no action follows. Who have had enough!

You need to explain the Baader liberation action to young people in the Märkisches Viertel, the girls in the Eichenhof home, in Ollenhauer, in Heiligensee, the boys in the home, in the youth services center, in the Green House, in the Kieferngrund juvenile jail. The families with lots of children, the young workers and apprentices, the lower secondary school students, the families in the areas marked for slum clearance, the workers at Siemens and AEG-Telefunken, SEL and Osram, the married women workers who still have to take on piecework to cover children and household—fuck it!

You have to communicate the action to those whose exploitation is not compensated by their standard of living, consumption, building loan contract, mini-loans, or middle-class car. Who can't afford all that crap, who aren't attached to it. Those who have seen through all the lies about the future promised by their kindergarten teachers, schoolteachers, building super, carer, supervisor, foreman, trade union bureaucrat, and the local mayor and now are only afraid of the police. Tell them—not the petty-bourgeois intellectuals—that we've had enough, that it's kicking off now, that Baader's liberation is just the start! That we can foresee an end to rule by cop! It is them you have to tell that we are building the Red Army—it is their army. It is them you have to tell that it's kicking off now. They won't be asking stupid questions, "why precisely now?" They have already walked a thousand times to officials and offices, the courtroom dance, waiting times and waiting rooms, the date when it will certainly work and when nothing worked. And the conversation with the nice teacher, who then didn't prevent the transfer to the special school, or with the helpless kindergarten teacher, when there wasn't a place in the end. They won't ask you why precisely now, fuck it.

Of course they won't believe a word of it if you can't even distribute the paper before it is confiscated. Because it's not the leftist ass-lickers you're trying to organize here but the people who are objectively on the left, you have to build up a distribution network that the bastards can't get at. Don't bullshit that it's too hard. The Baader liberation action wasn't a ballroom dance.

[...]

What does it mean to bring the conflict to a head? It means: not letting yourself be butchered. This is why we're building the Red Army up. Behind the parents are the teachers, the youth services, the police. Behind the supervisor is the foreman, the personnel office, the firm's security, the welfare office, the police. Behind the janitor is the building manager, the landlord, the bailiff, the eviction notice, the police. Whatever the bastards can achieve with grades, letting people go, termination notices, bailiff's notices, and clubs, they'll get that way. Of course they will use their service pistols, or tear gas, hand grenades, and machine pistols, of course they will escalate the means if they can't achieve their goals any other way. Of course GIs in Vietnam are being trained in guerrilla tactics and Green Berets are being sent on torture courses. So what? Of course sentences are being increased for political crimes. You have to make it clear that it is all social-democratic shit to claim that imperialism, together with all the Neubauers and West-morelands, Bonn, the Senate, the regional youth services and local offices, the whole fucking crap could be undermined, tricked, caught out, intimi-dated, abolished without a struggle. Make it clear that the revolution won't be a walk in the park. That the bastards will obviously escalate the means as far as they can—and no further. We're building the Red Army up to bring the conflict to a head.

Unless we build the Red Army up at the same time, every conflict, all political work in the workplace, in Wedding, in the Märkisches Viertel, in the Plötze [prison], and in the courtroom will degenerate into reformism. I.e.: you will only bring about better means of discipline, better methods of intimidation, better methods of exploitation. That will just break the people; it won't break what breaks the people! Without building up the Red Army, the bastards can keep on going: locking people up, firing them, distraining, stealing children, intimidating, shooting, ruling. Bringing the conflicts to a head means: that they can no longer do what they want, but have to do what we want.

You have to make this clear to those who gain nothing from the exploita-tion of the Third World, from Persian oil, Bolivia's bananas, South Africa's gold—who have no reason to identify with the exploiters. They can understand that what is kicking off here has already kicked off in Vietnam, Palestine, Guatemala, Oakland and Watts, Cuba and China, Angola, and New York. They will understand it if you explain that the Baader liberation action isn't isolated, never was, just the first one of this kind in the FRG. Fuck it.

Don't sit around on the sofa after they've searched the house to count your oh-so-dear and petty shopkeepers' souls. Build up the right distribu-tion network. Leave those who are shitting themselves, the red cabbage eaters, the social workers, that useless mob who are just sucking up. Find out where the homes are, the families with too many children, the subproletariat and the proletarian women who are just waiting for the right person to hit in the face. They will take over the leadership. Don't let yourselves be caught, and learn from them how not to let yourselves be caught—they know more about it than you.

Develop the class struggles.
Organize the proletariat.
Start armed resistance!
BUILD THE RED ARMY!

Agit 883, June 5, 1970, socialhistoryportal.org. Translated by Laurence Cox and Órfhlaith Tuohy.

WATCH ON THE RHINE (1974)
Walter Mossmann

*"Watch on the Rhine" (*Die Wacht am Rhein*) is a well-known nationalist anti-French song. This rewrite highlights the collaboration between German, French, and Swiss environmentalists against the Marckolsheim chemical plant and the planned Wyhl nuclear power station, in Alsace (France) and Baden (Germany) respectively. Its style is typical of radical reworkings of traditional regional culture. This movement grew out of 21 local citizens' initiatives (*Bürgerini-tiativen*). Dr Rosenthal was managing director of CWM, the firm behind the Marckolsheim plant. Sicurani had been a colonial official in French Polynesia. Stolberg and Norderham had experienced lead pollution; the insecticide DDT had been highlighted in Rachel Carson's* Silent Spring *and Contergan was the trade name for thalidomide. References to the parish house, the use of tractors, commuter activism, and so on highlight how environmentalism could involve much wider social groups while keeping a grassroots organizing style and use of direct action. Opposition to nuclear power in particular would become a central issue in West German movements.*

* * *

1 In Alsace and in Baden
We used to be so poor
We shot each other
For our lords in the war
Now we're fighting for ourselves
In Wyhl and Marckolsheim
Together we're keeping
A different watch on the Rhine.
Which side are you on?
Hey! We're occupying here

We're protecting ourselves from the crap
Not tomorrow, but TODAY!

2 Herr Rosenthal has a plan
We don't like it at all.
Herr Rosenthal doesn't care
It's just the money he sees.
But we care about
The river, the wood, the field
And our health —
Nobody can buy that from us.

3 Who wants lead-polluted wine,
Lead milk, lead pike, lead eel?
Who eats beef steak with lead?
Maybe Herr Rosenthal?
But no, he keeps himself very healthy,
Clean and elegant
It's just his CWM rubbish bin
That he puts in our homeland.

4 In Strasbourg on the battlement
The good prefect lives
He's licked the big money
From the chemical industry.
Sicurani, Sicurani
You've conned us!
But watch out:
You haven't colonized Alsace.

5 The 20th of September
It was already high time
We spread ourselves out
On CWM's land.
And when he stopped us,
That goblin Sicurani,
We quickly closed
The border on the bridges.

6 At Limberg-over-Sasbach
A red wine grows
It tastes quite good, we like it so

And it should stay that way.
First there were three awake
Now the whole place is up
They'll push every Rosenthal
Away from here with tractors.

[…]

8 In Weisweil in the parish hall
The struggle did begin
People aren't just praying
They're also doing things.
And in the "Fisher Island" inn
TWENTY ONE OF US fit in
There we decided:
NUCLEAR POWER AND LEAD PLANT: NO WAY!

9 Some people sleep very badly
In the town of Wyhl, of Wyhl,
Because the mayor there
Took us for a ride.
Now he's sitting with his gun
In his Judas house
And thinking "I wish I hadn't done it,
Soon it's all up for me!"

[…]

11 Many people drive to Riegel
Across the Rhine to work
And say "If the lead plant comes,
I'll be the first to fall.
What use is such a workplace
If I die a dismal death?
Herr Rosenthal, you sod, sod off,
Get lost with your crap!"

12 And the public prosecutor comes
And the blue police
They come in the early dawn—
It's all the same to us.
For we agree with each other

And daily we are more
And if we stand together
There'll be more and more of us!

13 And if they tell us
The citizen's first duty
Is peace in good faith,
We don't believe them.
Faith didn't help us
In Stolberg and Nordenham,
We haven't forgotten
DDT and CONTERGAN.

14 In Alsace and in Baden... (as above)

Republished on bund-rvso.de. Translated by Laurence Cox and Órfhlaith Tuohy.

Further Reading

Brown, Timothy. *West Germany and the Global Sixties: The Anti-Authoritarian Revolt, 1962–1978*. Cambridge: Cambridge University Press, 2015.

Cornils, Ingo. *Writing the Revolution: the Construction of "1968."* Rochester, NY: Camden House, 2016.

Davies, Meredid. *Writing and the West German Protest Movements: the Textual Revolution*. London: Institute for Modern Language Research, 2015.

Geronimo. *Fire and Flames: A History of the German Autonomist Movement*. Oakland, CA: PM Press, 2012.

Häberlen, Joachim. *The Emotional Politics of the New Left: West Germany, 1968–1984*. Cambridge: Cambridge University Press, 2018.

Karcher, Katharina. *Sisters in Arms: Militant Feminisms in the Federal Republic of Germany since 1968*. New York: Berghahn, 2017.

Klimke, Martin. *The Other Alliance: Student Protest in West Germany and the United States in the Global Sixties*. Princeton: Princeton University Press, 2010.

Milder, Stephen. *Greening Democracy: the Anti-Nuclear Movement and Political Environmentalism in West Germany and Beyond, 1968–1983*. Cambridge: Cambridge University Press.

Sedlmaier, Alexander. *Consumption and Violence: Radical Protest in Cold-War West Germany*. Ann Arbor: University of Michigan Press, 2014.

Thomas, Nick. *Protest Movements in 1960s West Germany: a Social History of Dissent and Democracy*. Oxford: Berg, 2003.

Tompkins, Andrew. *Better Active than Radioactive: Anti-Nuclear Protest in 1970s France and West Germany*. Oxford: Oxford University Press, 2016.

6
Denmark

The postwar years radically transformed Danish society. A small country in Northern Europe, Denmark's population suddenly soared after World War II. By the early 1950s, nearly a quarter of all Danes were children. Population growth went hand in hand with massive internal migration and urbanization, while cities like Copenhagen grew outwards as suburbs expanded.

Socially, the country had to reckon with its wartime past. During the war, the Danish Protectorate Government collaborated with the occupying Nazi forces. Immediately after World War II, Danish leaders promised to never again align with an outside force, with the Prime Minister declaring, "We shouldn't place our country in any bloc at all." But with the onset of the Cold War, memories of occupation resurfaced, and the country's leaders decided to join NATO. This created a major fault line within Danish politics, and would later prompt the formation of activist groups like the Campaign Against Nuclear Weapons.

Politically, the Social Democrats held the premiership continuously from 1953 to 1968. To their left, the local Communist Party had lost the momentum it had gained during World War II. The Soviet invasion of Hungary in 1956 triggered internal conflict, which led to a split. In early 1959, former Communist leader Aksel Larsen formed a new party, the Socialist People's Party (SPP), which scored a surprising 6.1 percent of the vote in the 1960 general election, while the Communist Party failed to win enough votes to secure parliamentary representation. This was the first parliamentary sign of a New Left in Denmark.

Perhaps the most significant postwar transformation, however, was the economic boom. From 1958 to 1961, industrial production grew by 30 percent, while industrial employment grew by 20 percent. Exports soared. Women entered the labor market en masse. By 1970 one in two women would be a salaried employee. Unemployment was virtually nonexistent, which put an already highly organized labor force in a favorable position. Demand for white-collar labor also exploded in industry, in the service sector, and in government. The number of public employees, for example, almost doubled from 1950 to 1970.

The Social Democrats drew on this unprecedented growth to build one of the most robust social welfare states in Europe. Significantly, they prioritized wage increases from increased productivity and output over the redistribution of wealth. Indeed, real wages would almost double during the 1950s and 1960s, while the working week dropped from 48 hours before 1958 to only 40 hours in 1976. To be sure, while economic inequality remained small compared to other countries, it nevertheless persisted, especially between men and women and between skilled and unskilled labor.

The result of the economic boom was the rise of a new middle class. Fueled by wage increases, job security, tax reforms, and mortgage credit, middle-class families moved from inner-city apartments to single-family homes in the suburbs. In general, this increase in wealth went hand in hand with new patterns of consumption. Demand for television sets, cars, country cabins, and all-inclusive charter tourism grew, as would time and money spent on home and leisure in general.

But the generation born in the mid-1940s, later known as the "baby boomers," were not at all impressed by their parents' life choices. For them, the age of affluence into which they had been born came with the hefty price tag of blind consumerism, consensus, and conformity. They dreaded what would be known as "privet fascism"—supposedly self-sufficient isolation behind privet hedges in the suburbs. Undergirding this new conformity, they felt, was a profound authoritarianism in all the core institutions of Danish society, from the family to the school. In response, young people tried to fashion a distinct anti-authoritarian youth culture. As in many other countries, this took the form of a kind of counterculture, carried forward by a new generation of musicians. In 1967, poet and singer Eik Skaløe, who had "returned from a crazy trip to the Middle East," released the seminal rock album *Hip* with his band Steppeulvene (named after Herman Hesse's novel *Steppenwolf*). The Danish counterculture climaxed that year, complete with flower power, love-ins, hippies, and mind-altering drugs, like hash and LSD.

1968 saw the explosion of the student movement. The postwar population boom and the welfare state's strong support for expanded education to match the needs of the economy led to a surge in university enrollments. In fact, the number of students in higher education almost quadrupled over the course of the 1950s and 1960s. Yet problems within the university triggered a wave of student unrest that would come to define 1968 in Denmark. One of the most spectacular actions of the year was a week-long university occupation by psychology students at the University of Copenhagen. Student activism not only continued into the 1970s, it became increasingly radical. It was also in these years, precisely as students were looking for a radical alternative, that many of Karl Marx's writings appeared in Danish for the first time. But as the movement grew more radical, it also tended to fissure, as

Figure 6.1 "Break the Rule by Professors. Participation in Decision Making Now!!" "Academic Freedom! Also for Students." Psychology students at the University of Copenhagen demonstrate. March 22, 1968. Finn Ejnar Madsen's collection. Courtesy of Jens Berthelsen.

activists began building an array of rival revolutionary organizations. One of the most notorious was the "Blekingegade Gang," which robbed banks to support the Popular Front for the Liberation of Palestine.

These years also saw the formation of a Danish women's liberation movement, which emerged as a reaction to sexism not only in Denmark, but also *within* the countercultural groups, social movements, and far left organizations in which many women had played so great a role. One of the most famous of the Danish groups was called the Redstockings. As in the United States, which also boasted its own Redstockings group, the Danish organization rallied around the idea that the private and the personal were political. Yet some women in the Danish Redstockings were also socialists. As their slogan put it, "No women's struggle without class struggle and no class struggle without women's struggle."

But women's liberation in Denmark, as elsewhere, was far from coherent. In fact, Redstockings would soon fracture under the weight of internal differences, with new groups breaking off to go their own way, like the Socialist Women's Group, founded in 1972. Other feminists turned their attention to the burgeoning gay liberation movement. As with the women's movement, the 1970s saw a sharp division between the more moderate gay organizations, like Danish Association of Homophiles, finally recognized by the state in 1969, and more radical gay activists, who would go on to form the Gay Liberation Front (GLF) in 1971. GLF activists saw the Association's emphasis on respectability politics as not only bourgeois, but guilty of perpetuating a kind of self-oppression.

Another movement with particularly strong roots in Denmark's capital, Copenhagen, was squatting. Sharp population growth, urbanization, and rent increases all led to a major housing shortage in the decades following World War II. In response, some activists, soon to be known as the "Slum Stormers," occupied vacant buildings in Copenhagen. But to squatters and counterculturalists, housing did not simply mean a roof over their heads; the struggle over housing was about creating community spaces where people could experiment with new forms of living that challenged the nuclear family. Relatedly, Denmark became home to a vibrant network of counter-cultural communes. In Northern Jutland, activists founded the Thy Camp, a commune inspired by countercultural festivals abroad. In Copenhagen, the Slum Stormers turned an abandoned military site into the "Freetown Christiania."

Environmentalism also grew in popularity in the 1970s. Inspired by the general student uprising of 1968, many science students at the University of Copenhagen became environmental activists. Ecology and organic food production became big issues, not least because of the many new communes with environmentally conscious consumer demands. In line with the general trend of the time, the ecological movement also split, giving way to two factions, the "carrot freaks," who focused on ecology, and the "rubber boot socialists," who were more interested in co-ownership.

A final aspect of Denmark's long 1968 was the country's changing relationship to its massive colony, Greenland. Although the 1953 Constitution legally changed Greenland's status from a colony to a county, Denmark embarked on an ambitious modernization project, with dramatic consequences for the native Inuit population. In the 1970s, a new generation of Greenlanders grew critical of this "post"-colonial situation, with some demanding recognition and equality, while others wanted to separate outright. Greenland finally won home rule in 1979; although this did not mean formal independence, home rule gave Greenland increased autonomy within the Danish Realm (Denmark, the Faroe Islands, Greenland).

EMIGRATE (1968)
Ole Grünbaum

Ole Grünbaum was among the most original and prolific writers of the Danish youth uprising. Having spent time in Amsterdam, he was a self-declared "provo" known for his "happenings." The son of a Social Democratic Finance Minister, Grünbaum critiqued the authoritarian structures embedded in politics, the family and his parents' generation in general. His writings combined a humanist critique with a social one; he would later describe himself as having had one foot—the biggest—in the hippie year of 1967 and one foot in 1968, the year of the student uprisings and Vietnam War opposition. The following excerpt from the title essay of his early 1968 collection touches on the shift from consciousness-raising to practical experiments. The tendency for young people to "emigrate" from "hierarchical structures" that he identifies in his essay would be further deepened in the months and years that followed.

* * *

If a power structure doesn't adapt to how society changes, it will become increasingly isolated until it's left empty and reactive. This means that you will get a period of empty institutions—but these are only empty in terms of ideas, while they are stuffed full of people who will defend them—because this means defending their own position.

They are defending their position against those who have the right to power, and against those who have the best ideas (which here means especially the most socially relevant ones), i.e. their defense becomes an attack on initiatives and new ways of doing things. The power structure becomes a brake on further development.

[...]

The so-called youth uprisings and youth cultures are the first phases of a long-term struggle for new structures. The first phase, *the consciousness of a need for a new culture*, is coming to an end. The other, *the time of experiments and utopias*, is starting to develop. Since the structure of authority prevents the realization of these new possibilities, the talents involved will aim at other directions: they are becoming independent of the ruling power structure.

[...]

[...] [I]f we want radical changes, we will have to begin with our own lives. When we meet obstacles, we will have to fight—but it is possible to carry out far-reaching experiments in Denmark without the authorities intervening.

It's possible to emigrate from oppression [...] and settle in the land of freedom. Not only is it possible, it's increasingly necessary for many people.

The authoritarian structure is a principle whose effects are felt everywhere in society. For this reason, whole new kinds of institutions have to be created. This initiative can only come from outside the existing ones. The fundamental work is being done in the new land of freedom.

[...]

It will be especially young people who move, as they have quite specific reasons to be against the family, the school and educational system, the system of work, bureaucracy, politics, the system of money, and the nation-state principle.

The family is an indispensable link in the ruling structure. The small child is shaped here in decisive ways. It is here that leisure time unfolds. And here, woman is kept outside society.

The family means isolation, lack of space and little change in your social contacts. The family means the preservation of the ruling system of gender roles and the adult-child system. The family means economic selfishness.

School is coercion, both having to go there and while you are there. It is isolated from the rest of life; it doesn't value choosing the life you want or learning how to choose the life you want.

School takes the initiative away from children and teaches them how to conform to the opinions of others around them. Furthermore, it points backwards. Precisely because of its hierarchical structure, news ideas only penetrate slowly. This is very unfortunate as it is, after all, mostly children who are exposed to them.

Higher education is constraining. It aims at quite narrow jobs and doesn't give the individual any possibility of creating new jobs through their education.

The universities are the most hierarchical system in our society. Here formal gerontocracy still dominates, meaning that it is a single big pyramid where new ideas struggle to enter.

Work is constraining if it is to give returns in the form of money. (Virtually) all workplaces are governed by conditions which can only be described as dictatorship. Work itself is mostly far from workers' interests. It is often downright inhuman, and it is always impersonal.

Bureaucracy knows more about rules than about human beings. It is an impersonal hierarchy, which is inefficient because it follows general principles rather than deciding from one case to the next. One's experience of bureaucratic power increases with age. For this reason alone, bureaucracy is reactionary.

Politics has become a professional activity for a collection of people who all have an interest in preserving society as it is. Politics has become ossified around certain economic issues, which there isn't even any real disagreement about. Political roles are traditional and hierarchical. Politics takes away initiative and is therefore conservative. Through the politicians' professional position, everyone on top of power in society is in the same boat. For this reason, political life is not at all suited (as intended in the constitution) as a means for the people to control the administration. And since more and more top politicians are recruited from the civil service, this will not become better with time.

Politics is exclusively an old men's activity. No young people have any career chances.

Politics is problem-solving within an outdated national structure. Youth is internationally oriented in its whole culture. Politicians' international visions are things like a United States of Europe, where national structures are preserved but an imperial superstructure is placed on top.

The nation-state does not match the development of industry. The international market is a reality; so are the international corporations. All young people speak English. More and more young people travel for a long time. Youth cultures are communicated internationally at the speed of light. Preserving the nation-state is important to politicians, who think nationally and hardly speak any foreign language or inform themselves about international events. For this reason, the core of many youth rebellions has been international politics: the American student movements, the West Berlin unrest after the Persian Shah's visit, the Vietnam movements in general (that one can even speak of such a thing!).

Hierarchy

The family, the school and educational system, work, bureaucracy, politics, and the nation-state—all of this is built on a fundamental pattern, which can vary in many ways that refresh it (without ever renewing it). The hierarchical idea that there always have to be some people who are and have more than others works through almost every single process of change—and the fate of the so-called youth cultures stands or falls on exactly this point. Is it possible to *emigrate from hierarchical culture?* Or is it so deeply human that fleeing it can only lead to degeneration?
[...]
Nothing can be more wrong than believing that the various new youth movements will put up with having leaders. If too much unrest happens in Denmark, the police may very well negotiate with a lot of "provos" or "hippies" about keeping the peace, but the outcomes will not be binding in the slightest for anyone other than those who take part in the negotiations.

The question "is it possible to emigrate from the hierarchical structures?" can thus be answered by saying that by now there are a few people trying to create all kinds of things, and that at least these don't look like the old hierarchy.

Ole Grünbaum, *Emigrér: Lærestykker om det tiltagende kaos* (Copenhagen: Hans Reitzels Forlag, 1968), 18–24. Translated by Bjarke Skærlund Risager and Laurence Cox.

DEMOCRACY OR STUDENT RULE? (1968)
Erland Kolding Nielsen

The student uprising, particularly at the University of Copenhagen, was the most significant event of Denmark's 1968. In late March, psychology students began to demonstrate against what they called "rule by professors," and demanded the right to participate in the decision-making process and to discuss the form and content of the curriculum. Key demands included 50 percent student representation on the university's administrative bodies and an educational wage. The uprising culminated in April with a five-day occupation and a large demonstration. The following text was written by history student Erland Kolding Nielsen. It was published as an op-ed in a local newspaper in Aarhus, where students were also attempting to bring about change to their university. The text offers a narrative account as well as a political analysis of the most intense period of the uprising in Copenhagen.

* * *

THE UNREST at the University of Copenhagen culminated with the big demonstration on Frue Square (April 23), with the actions for an educational wage and, finally, with the psychologists' barricades up under the roof in the Psychological Laboratory.

[...]

What is happening and what has happened is not a coherent, left-wing action aimed at overthrowing democracy. There is certainly an action movement, and extensive left-wing elements. However, firstly, this volume of actions can be more clearly analyzed and divided up according to their different aims, which certainly don't have any political shape overall beyond what they may have got through their methods. Secondly, the left-wing elements do not dominate in any way, so that the overall character of the movement cannot be credited to them.

[...]

The first action was started by the psychologists on March 21. Its aim was to achieve influence and a right to participate in decision making within their own discipline. [...] As the negotiations about solutions for these problems collapsed, students were robbed of the only legal possibility of participation, that is, through the form of negotiation. Their only legal means to achieve acceptable conditions had been blocked. What happens in the labor market in such circumstances? One side threatens a strike, the other a lockout. The students don't have these forms of sanction and pressure. Both strike and lockout would harm the students more than furthering the democracy which these means are recognized as legal ways to achieve. The barricades, which thus became the outcome of this situation, are not recognized as a democratic means. The reason for this can only be that there is no such democracy which this means can be used to maintain and secure. A small group hold power and it is considered illegal to overthrow the power of this group—even despite the fact that you want to replace it with a democracy.

The whole time, the psychologists' action has been an internal, disciplinary action, methods which cannot be regarded as characterizing the rest of the actions. These have been revolutionary—as must always be the case when the aim is to overthrow an existing, well-established, autocratic system and replace it with a democratic one. They can only be described as illegal when legality is defined as identical to the existing relations of power in any given system. That the law equals power is, after all, not a new experience.

This action can really be said to have come to an end now, as they have been successful in gaining really positive results; they have got a study committee with equal representation for teachers and students. [...]

The other action—the main action for the right to participate in decision making—started a week later, and even though it was inspired by the psychologists, it wasn't dominated by them, nor should it be. Being cross-disciplinary and cross-political is characteristic for this general action movement. All the important disciplines are involved, all political shades from the reddest Maoists to the conservatives stand together and form a united front against the archaic conditions in the university as a whole, which, both from teachers' and students' point of view are highly inacceptable. [...] Its aim is to create a university democracy, neither more nor less. [...]

There is thus no question at all of a student dictatorship. Nor is this about mob rule. It is about establishing proper and formal cooperation at all levels within the structure of the university.

[...]

In order to bring about this cooperation at lower levels within the individual disciplines, so that a group of teachers can no longer block this on a whim, students must have the right to participate at 50 percent in decision making within the Senate, the highest organ of the university. This will become a revolution in the history of the university. It will perhaps break the hearts of many old, conservative university people, but we cannot take the past into consideration: this concerns the future and future cooperation. Everywhere in society, youth is given more responsibility and more influence. If this development is not followed up at the university—where in many ways young people have the best conditions and the greatest will to work with these problems if they are given the opportunity to do so—the consequence will be that the university environment, which has always been the most fertile soil for new currents, for advance and progress, will stagnate and be left standing as a hopeless, archaic monument of a period in our society's history when democracy only began for the individual when they were older than 25–26 years.

[...] On Frue Square, [the University's Rector, Professor] Mogens Fog stood in complete solidarity with the students on their demand to participate in decision making. But he added that "taking the law into one's own hands (i.e. the psychologists' occupation of the Psychological Laboratory) does not have anything to do with democracy." The statement was unfortunate, not so much in and of itself, but because of the use that has been made of it. It has been highlighted as nothing short of the main theme of his speech and made into a catchphrase in polemics against the students with no consideration of its place in the speech as a whole. Therefore this isolated statement has to be refuted by the students.

Democracy presupposes in principle the right to vote. If all the various groups living in a given system do not have the right to vote, then the system is not democratic. Students don't have the right to vote today. In a democratic system, negotiations take place between equal negotiating partners. Students are not equal to the professors as a negotiating partner. [...]

[...] We have worked to get our views across using democratic means in an authoritarian and unified system. We have cried out in order to be heard, but they have chosen to turn a deaf ear.

We will no longer accept this autocracy. Nor do we want to replace it by a student dictatorship or a mob rule. We don't want to subject anyone to diktats. What we do want is a democratic cooperation between all partners, in which the joy of work rules and where this unreasonableness has been replaced with fairness and agreement.

But in order to get this democracy in the university, autocracy has to be broken down—if necessary by undemocratic means. It is a paradox, but if democracy wants to come to power, this can only happen using the ruling system's own methods!!

Aarhus Stiftstidende, May 23, 1968, 14–15. Translated by Bjarke Skærlund Risager and Laurence Cox.

SOMETHING IS HAPPENING, BUT YOU DON'T KNOW WHAT IT IS, DO YOU, MR. JONES? (1970)
Lisbeth Dehn Holgersen, Åse Lading, Ninon Schloss and Marie-Louise Svane

In the early 1970s Denmark saw the emergence of its own Redstockings. Distancing themselves from liberal wings of the Women's Liberation Movement, the Redstockings identified capitalism as the root of patriarchy. The following text, originally published as an op-ed, is often seen as the Redstockings' first manifesto. The title was taken from Bob Dylan's 1965 song, "Ballad of a Thin Man"—a song about a "Mr. Jones" who finds himself unable to become part of the counterculture. With the manifesto, however, the Redstockings did not just take aim at the bourgeois bystander who doesn't know what's happening, but also at the male-dominated counterculture and left organizations. In the years that followed, the Redstockings would become an important group, particularly known for their annual all-women camp, taking place on the small Danish island of Femø, where both the "natural" body and equal pay was on the agenda.

* * *

Figure 6.2 "Freedom, Equality, Sisterhood." Restockings Ninon Schloss (second from the left), Åse Lading (holding sign in front of the truck), and others at a march. Copenhagen, April 8, 1970. Photo by Per Lading.

[...]

WHAT is a redstocking? If we go by the press, it is a silly girl who makes fun of the guard and tears up and down the high street with balloons in her bra. "What the hell do these girls want?" Mr. Jones might well ask, because he has never ever really been told. Nor will he be this time round, but we will do our best at least to "attune" him to a little part of the problem.

[...]

The members of the first redstockings group belong to a generation who have really shaken things up. Our aim is to shake things up both inside and outside of our own generation, since the pattern of gender roles is almost the same in both places. We are going to put a bomb under the holier-than-thou leftists and the hippies as well as under the lost right-wingers. Nobody should feel safe because nobody is safe.

Within our own circles, we have been accused of creating false divisions because we claim that men and women have contradictory interests. Of course we believe that there shouldn't be any, but the actual conditions show that there are. If you define human beings based on what they do, then the person who makes tea for the revolution can't have the same interests as the person who makes the revolution. The same contradictory interests between men and women exist in all other groups in society as well. For this reason, we believe that before we can properly form an opinion about whether we want a revolution or not, women have to make a revolution across all social classes—and then we can begin to talk about things as one human being to another. [...]

[...]

Mona Lisa on her ass

THE MAIN point of attack is not discrimination against women as such but capitalism with all of its consequences: consumerism, militarism, racism, sexism, etc. We refuse to see women's issues as isolated: this is an atomization that only serves the existing society. Talking about "the disastrous war in Vietnam," saying "history" has treated women unfairly—these are diversions, from the root of what is wrong to its results. The war and discrimination are not natural disasters but logical consequences of the system.

It is no use to hold forth with dry numbers and facts proving that women are exposed to discrimination—around wages, educationally, sexually, psychologically, politically. The Danish Women's Society has tried this for 50 years. Women must act, organize, act in solidarity, expand their own self-awareness, and develop a new collective consciousness about their common situation. We—the pretty bourgeois daughters—are indoctrinated into accepting a socio-economic system that assigns women a subordinate position. Passive, inferior, dependent, isolated, and the most exposed of all: the housewife working in the home.

The isolation of the individual woman is a precondition for male supremacy. Since we were little, we have been told by our mothers how we should be: gentle and compliant. Even if you weren't, you should act like it: that's what would get you furthest, our mothers said. This is when you began to learn the concept of the power of the vagina. If you can't reach your goal by going the direct way, then try the back way. And, by the way, even if you could reach it going the direct way, take the back way instead, because men like this better. It gives them the feeling of being someone. Then you can wrap them around your little finger and make them do everything—afterwards.

General education for girls emphasizes the service professions: cooking, typewriting, language. We are steered into low-income groups and become unable to maintain a standard of living equivalent to men's. Thus we are forced to get a provider if we want similar economic conditions. The means for this is internal competition, the goal is high social status.

[…]

[…] A hostile orientation to the enemy is a healthy sign. But if you say: "Isn't the capitalist a victim of capitalism and the man of male society? And isn't the real enemy the system, then?" The answer is no. The capitalist can give up the system and the man his role. The white capitalist man is no victim. He preserves a system that may give him certain inconveniences but still more privileges, and for this reason the struggle must be fought against him. For capitalism, gender discrimination doesn't exist as a Platonic idea independent from the existence of human beings. Capitalism presupposes the capitalist and male supremacy the man. To hate a system isn't at all dangerous for the system. We must go as far as daring to hate the Lord, the Lord who preserves these unworthy conditions. The passivity of our masochistic self-hatred must be transformed into an outward-oriented emotional activity.

In the next phase, we will be able to upbraid ourselves for having put up with it for 6,000 years. All this liberated self-hatred, united with so much sisterly solidarity, is the fuse we light under the technocratic-bureaucratic-capitalist white male society.

[…]

Mona Lisa on the left front

THEN THERE is the left front with all its kind progressive boys who sit on the panels and tell us all the right things. Because girls don't sit on the panels, we sit down there and have all the right opinions.

[…]

We sit, among other things, and our opinion is that bourgeois gender roles are ridiculous and useless. The panel boys also analyze the phenomenon now and again, and present bourgeois gender morality, in private-capitalist terms. Of course we understand this immensely well; we have also disregarded bourgeois roles, bourgeois morality and all the other shit. We are liberated. Finally we have become free from simulating being chaste and precious; finally we dare to admit that we want to have sex. Actually, we no longer dare to admit that once in while, exceptionally, maybe we *don't* really want to have sex. If, for example, we would prefer to talk to him rather than having anything at all to do with his dick. But we would prefer anything to being misunderstood and perceived as straitlaced, unfree, and (the left front's nastiest smear word) frustrated. We put all our efforts into holding onto our position as the left front's lovely liberated ladies, and the panel boys love us because we want to when they can.

Freedom? Bullshit, dear friends. Men's freedom. Our indoctrinated liberation. The men have solved the problems together in panels and high-handedly liberated both themselves and us. Yet again it is the men who have "done" something to the women. We have been made "free" to be at the disposal of his sexual liberation. We have still not *taken* our sexual freedom *ourselves*. For we are being used to prove *his* non-bourgeois character, not ours—when we actually don't want to, when we actually don't want him, but still say yes because we know it is good form.

And, so help us, we believe it ourselves. We believe that we too are proving our own liberation—because for years now the men have sat and propagandized for themselves in the panels. They have defined freedom and liberation on the premises of men themselves—so long that we now inadvertently perceive them (the premises) as our own. Hence our false consciousness, hence our false liberation.—But this is the old story once again: we *have to* manifest ourselves somewhere and when it can't be on the panel, it has to be, now as for the last 6,000 years, in bed.

[...]

Mona Lisa's acid smile

[...]

WE HAVE to distinguish between fake and real hippies. Today, there are an incredible number of fake hippies running around with all the outer attributes of hippies, but whose behavior is more petty bourgeois than "high." This time round, we are going to disregard the fake hippies, who belong on the right, and concentrate on the real hippies.

You become a hippie because you loathe the alienated world you find yourself in. All around you, you see that it is about power and money, everything from human relations to pins are measured in money—and then you say no, you jump off the carousel and fumblingly try to realize what it really means to be a human being. You go about your existence in a new way, no longer saying "I'll really start living when ..., when ..., when ..." and saying instead "I'll really start living right now." These "high" experiences of the now, though, are a necessary but not a sufficient condition for a world that will look different, because they are just as important for the inner revolution as they are unimportant for the outer revolution. This implies that we need a dialectical relationship between these two forms of revolutionary activity.

Just like all other social groups, men dominate the hippie group as well. True, these men look androgynous, but you shouldn't be fooled by that. They are just as much men as wolves in sheep's clothing are wolves. It is still the man who is the head and the woman who is the body. It is still the man who speaks and the woman who listens. It is still the man who comes and the woman who waits. Still the man who strives to transcend himself and the woman who doesn't strive further than to the man.

[...]

WHEN YOU begin your career as a hippie girl, you do it from the same basis as the hippie guys, but you'll quickly discover that you can't step into a group in the same way that a guy with long hair and a chillum can. The hippie groups are male groups that you as a girl can fuck yourself into and out of, and in this way these groups are just as reactionary as the society they claim to be an alternative to.

Here, as anywhere else, it is, of course, the girls' own fault that they put up with their own passivity and apparently love it. But one day the scales must fall from their eyes and they will have to see that their own existence contains the same possibilities as the men's—and that it is just a matter of taking advantage of these possibilities instead of continuing to belong to the group of those who never do anything themselves but only admire that others bother to, dare to, have the talent to, etc. It will be a beautiful day when it will be just as natural for girls to form a beat group, a commune, or take a trip to the Himalayas as it is for men do these things.

[…]

Information, May 6, 1970, 4. Translated by Bjarke Skærlund Risager and Laurence Cox.

THE MILITARY'S "FORBIDDEN CITY" ON CHRISTIANSHAVN WAS QUIETLY TAKEN BY ORDINARY CIVILIANS (1971)

Jacob Ludvigsen

On September 26, 1971, six activists climbed over the fence into an 84 acre military area in the Inner City of Copenhagen. Previously home of the Båds-mandsstræde Barracks, the area had been abandoned by the military earlier that year, there were no official plans to reuse it, and the country was in between governments. One of the "invaders" was Jacob Ludvigsen, the author of the following account of the "happening," which would appear about a week later in the countercultural weekly Hovedbladet. *Soon after, hippies, artists, and social outcasts would "settle" "Freetown Christiania." The founding of Christiania was part of a wider squatters' movement known as the Slum Stormers. Despite government attempts to "normalize" this valuable piece of land and "clear" its "Pusher Street," notorious for its open cannabis transactions, Christiania remains in existence to this day.*

* * *

A Sunday on Amager: or, emigrate on the number 8
Report on a walk in the "forbidden city" that can warm the hearts of born pioneers

It caused us no difficulties to enter the area. A couple of members of our six-man invasion army were a little uneasy, but we had barely made it into the natural beauty by a shortcut when we found ourselves at the foot of the

Figure 6.3   The "invasion" of
Christiania. Jacob Ludvigsen
presents his press pass.
Copenhagen, September 26,
1971. Courtesy of Gudrun
Forchhammer and Elizabeth
Løvegal.

ex-military pear tree and were eating the fruits that, for the first time in
many years, can fall to the ground without being ashamed of being touched
by war. Whether pears otherwise have such thoughts...

And now house after house appeared. Big sturdy buildings which are now
empty, hollow shells crying out for content. We were in the new country,
Christiania.

Was it exaggerated to play at being victors in a conquered city? While we
were waving our banners and feeling militant, ready to respond to challenges
as they presented themselves, the visions took a hold of us to such an extent
that we could already imagine a society where a whole other folklore and
culture blossomed.

We took a rest up on the ramparts. The necessary equipment we had
brought along was put aside and the thermos flask was opened. While we
swore that the revolution isn't a tea party, we felt thrown into another world
and agreed that if elves live in the immediate vicinity of Copenhagen, then
their home is in Christiania.

The barbed-wire entanglements that had been laid out proved to be
relatively easy to force and almost without knowing it we found ourselves in
the grounds of the special military laboratory. It is surrounded by a barbed-
wire fence and it is the only one in the big city which is still in use.

Here, we civilians were challenged! A friendly watchman asked us
to document our business and we responded by asking for the exit. We

chuckled at the thought that the big military lets a common, civilian watchman protect its property. But actually, this is just nice and proves that the military has written off its privileges in this place. The laboratory should, in our opinion, have a reasonable phasing out period and should just be gone around January 1.

Christiania is the pioneers' country. It is the biggest chance yet to build a society from the ground up—but still to some extent on the remains of the existing one.

Its own power station. Its own bathhouse. A giant building for gymnastics where everyone seeking peace could have their big meditation and yoga center. Halls that can have rotary presses for newspaper printing. Halls where theater groups can feel at home. Houses that can accommodate stoners who are too paranoid and weakened to take part in the rat race. You can fill in the rest yourself.

And you could set up a funny little steam railway, sail along the ramparts, and visit Rabbit Island out in the moat.

And there should also be space for older people who don't want to move into a nursing home. Many collective arrangements like cheap places to eat together. Parties, happiness. The city where the harp plays once more.

Certainly, for those who feel a pioneer's heart beating within them, there can be no doubt about what Christiania should be used for. It is a part of the city that has hitherto been kept secret from us—that's over with now.

Emigrating to the new, free town will be easy: Just take Line 8 to Prinsessegade. Travel expenses: one token.

Hovedbladet 1, no. 39, October 2–3, 1971, 10–11. Translated by Bjarke Skærlund Risager and Laurence Cox.

WILL WE BE SQUEEZED TO DEATH IN YOUR BOSOM, MOTHER DENMARK: THE FOURTH WORLD AND THE "RABID" GREENLANDERS (1975)

Aqqaluk Lynge

The success of independence movements in the "Third World" inspired liberation struggles for Indigenous minority populations who began using the term "Fourth World" in the early 1970s. This was the case for a new generation of Inuits in Greenland critical of Danish colonialism. In 1973, Copenhagen hosted an Arctic Peoples' Conference for Indigenous minorities which passed a resolution on their common demand for recognition and equality. The Young Greenlanders' Council

174 VOICES OF 1968

(YGC) was one of the participating groups from Denmark. Consisting of Green-landic students at the University of Copenhagen, YGC had emerged as the most radical element in the de-colonial struggle in the Danish Realm (Denmark, the Faroe Islands, Greenland). Below we reproduce an op-ed written by YGC's Aqqaluk Lynge on September 10, 1975. A few years later, Lynge would become the first leader of the socialist separatist party Inuit Ataqatigiit.

* * *

Did the Queen come across any rabid Greenlanders during her trip this summer?

No, she said.

Did she come across any rabid Danes?

No, she would say. What else.

Let's make it clear that if rabid Greenlanders exist at all, they exist among those of Greenlandic descent, whom the Queen has spoken with. These rabid Greenlanders have for centuries, for generations, supported Danish state power to force all the Greenlandic people into a political development which has been more destructive than any change to nature, which time and again forced the Eskimo people to find other ways to subsist.

There are also plenty of rabid Danes in Greenland, half-racist arrogant people, who have been telling Greenlanders for generations that they were not good for anything, that time was so valuable that they couldn't even be used as unskilled labor.

[...]

To be rabid is normally understood as someone who demands things beyond what they have a right to.

Danes have for centuries demanded things to which they have no right—morally, politically, and legally. They have demanded that we should become like them. That we should begin to compete with each other, where community used to be given pride of place. You have demanded that we should change our way of life. That we should become civilized, meaning that we should learn to make distinctions between people. That it was natural for some to have big houses and plenty of food, while others should have less. You have demanded that our skin, our soul, must be changed entirely so that they can now adapt to today's demand for efficiency.

A completely efficient death came from this. So that it was no longer possible to find a rabid Greenlander.

If anyone has ever been rabid, it is you and only you!

The actions and engagement that we, Greenlandic youth living in Denmark, are creating are forced through out of indignation that our society is being driven away in a truck and tipped out over the Atlantic.

That we are forced, through manipulation over generations, to go to Europe to learn how to live in Europe and not in the Arctic societies.

It is not rabid to demand national integrity, to try to rediscover ways of cultivating the self-respect which political violations over generations have driven away. It is a human right which should be universal and natural.

We live here in Europe and lose our personal integrity day by day. Europeans have lost it with such a force that it is no longer natural to them to respect the human being as a being. "Europe where they are never done talking of the Human Being, yet murder human beings everywhere they find them, at the corner of every one of their own streets, in all the corners of the globe," as Frantz Fanon says. Murder doesn't necessarily have to be carried out with machine guns. Murder can also be committed through a self-proclaimed humane orientation, a know-all attitude and good intentions.

This is rabid. This is what is called colonialism, also called imperialism. [...] The way I look at it, the nature of imperialism is many-sided, and it doesn't necessarily have to mean that a country is exploited economically.

[...]

[...] Greenlanders' attitude toward Danes have shifted tremendously and the Greenlanders' permanent demand is clarification. Clarification as to what it is exactly that the Danes want with us. What their intentions are.

For generations, we have bid you welcome in our own country. Because in those parts, there's a tradition for hospitality. It came as a festive gift. And naively, we believed that you would be only visiting, just like the Dutch whalers did, and then it would be over when the summer ended. But, by god, the Danes stayed. Soon, the Danish flag waved all along the coast, just as it did at the Gold Coast, in the West Indies and even in East Asia!

And then we asked what you wanted with us. There is no wealth for you to collect, since seal meat can only be eaten by the barbarous "Esquimaux." You then answered that you really only wanted to help. With what?

So that we could survive all the diseases that you infected us with! It appeared that you wanted to prepare us for life in your capitalist society. That you changed our society so that you would be able to live in it and let time pass until the oil sprung down from Davis Strait, where we normally fish. You prepared us for the Canadian "Black Angel Project" (Profit) which was about to start. That the hunters, to their great surprise, should see their ice hunting grounds sailed through and destroyed for all game, since an icebreaker had to sail to the mine. In April, when Northern Greenlanders were busy shooting seals, whose furs the Royal Greenlandic Trading Department would sell to a Europe that was hungry to be covered up by fur!

When you excuse yourself for being present in the country of another people on the plea that you want to help them, then something is wrong. To my ears, you have always protested too much that we were in need of help.

[...]

This letter is not an expression of hatred. Before it's too late, I will declare my happiness at coming across good, nice, and inspiring Danes in their own country. I love the people, even on a very personal level, which I won't go into further here.

What I want to do with this letter is to try to make the Danes understand that I want to be recognized as a Greenlander, neither more nor less. That I have my nationality, which I want to protect, and that I have the will to defend it against any attempts on it. The Greenlandic people has to be recognized as ONE people living under the same polity. The Danes must see Greenland and Greenlanders as in themselves having a political status, a political integrity. Greenland is political. Extraordinarily important globally—strategically.

[...]

A single demand for respect.

Is that rabid?

[...]

Greenland still in many ways has its own intact legal and political system. This is the case, for example, when it comes to the right of using the land. We have not known anything of the right to own land. The hunting grounds were and are property of everyone, and something that everyone has the right to and responsibility for. Now the outsiders come and want to take these hunting grounds as possessions, just as happened with the lead and zinc mine in Maarmorilik in Northern Greenland. Just as it is now happening with oil, which of course has been found. The question now is just about finding the right place to drill.

You can talk until next summer and assure us of the fellow-feeling between these two nations in the form of an economic system, which you call capitalist with a common Danish word. What matters here is our personal and national integrity. Something which, of course, also concerns you as you are entering the failed bosom of Big Europe.

[...]

It's not a cliche, it's not romantic to talk about Denmark being imperialist. Right now, we have every right to talk about it: now, that the resources have finally been found, now, where the eternal gold diggers finally want to try to brave the cold and loosen the riches that you have elsewhere started to move away from because of political instability. Greenland is a stable area whose 45,000 people will hardly have the possibility to get up from the sickbed built by the Danes. We won't see any Algerian Wars, no Vietnam.

But our annihilation as a troublesome element in the Kingdom of Denmark.

We are on the threshold of a development where exploitation and the ruthless hunt for our natural riches will damage a society, which we are trying to rebuild after the Danes' depredation.

It's now that we need the support from that part of the Danish population which send declarations of solidarity and support at both the right and wrong moments. What became of those?

Are there too few Greenlanders to have a claim on support and protection? Are they too few even to be included in a scientific analysis of our political situation.

An international conference has been planned in Canada, where the fourth world, that is, the indians, the eskimos and all the other minorities who have seen their lands taken over by the Europeans, will discuss these matters and form an organization. In a global context, it has to figure out how we best protect ourselves against further denial of our rights.

[...]

Historically, we are on the threshold of the third world freeing itself completely from other national powers. It is only a question of time. Then the third world will at least have gotten its national independence, even if of course there is still a long road ahead to human and economic freedom.

In the coming generations, the struggle for the next decades will take the form of a rejection of the European way of life. Meanwhile, the continuous demand from the economic powers will be to integrate minorities and annihilate the national and cultural differences which are assumed to be sources of political instability and [dis]harmony for capital.

The third world has awoken.

The fourth world is rising and claiming self-respect—respect for the individual human being. The fourth world has always received guests out of hospitality and humility. It will no longer do that, since the guest takes all the food before it's even served. This is against the nature of hospitality, against its faith in the human being as human being. The concept of guest has disappeared. They even want to eat us alive. We will no longer submit to this. The only weapon we have, against all assumptions and theories, are words and an attitude to life that cannot be defeated.

And in a historical perspective, as have we experienced, this is after all not enough.

[…]

Originally published in Politiken, 1975, reprinted in Aqqaluk Lynge, *Isuma: ukiuni 25-ni taalliat, oqalugiaatit allaaserisallu. Synspunkt: digte, taler og artikler gennem 25 år* (Nuuk: Forlaget Atuagkat, 1997), 296–303. Translated by Bjarke Skærlund Risager and Laurence Cox.

Further Reading

Bjerregaard, Karen Steller. "Guerillas and Grassroots: Danish Solidarity with the Third World in the 1960s and 1970s." In *Between Prague Spring and French May: Opposition and Revolt in Europe, 1960–1980*, edited by Martin Klimke, Jacco Pekelder, and Joachim Scharloth, 213–32. New York: Berghahn Books, 2013.

Dahl, Jens. "Greenland: Political Structure of Self-Government." *Arctic Anthropology* 23, nos. 1–2 (1986): 315–24.

Dahlerup, Drude. "Three Waves of Feminism in Denmark." In *Thinking Differently. A Reader in European Women's Studies*, edited by Gabriele Griffin and Rosi Braidotti, 341–50. London: Zed Books.

Førland, Tor Egil, ed. "Special Issue on 1968," *Scandinavian Journal of History* 33, no. 4 (2008).

Gade, Rune. "Art, Sexuality and Images: The Legalization of Pornography in Denmark." *Performance Research* 15, no. 2 (2010): 23–8.

Jensen, Helle Strandgaard. "TV as Children's Spokesman: Conflicting notions of Children and Childhood in Danish Children's Television around 1968." *The Journal of the History of Childhood and Youth* 6, no. 1 (Winter 2013): 105–28.

Jørgensen, Thomas Ekman. "Scandinavia." In *1968 in Europe: A History of Protest and Activism, 1956–1977*, edited by Martin Klimke and Joachim Scharloth, 239–52. New York: Palgrave Macmillan, 2008.

Jørgensen, Thomas Ekman. *Transformations and Crises: The Left and the Nation in Denmark and Sweden, 1956–1980*. New York: Berghahn Books, 2008.

Karpantschof, René, and Flemming Mikkelsen. "Youth, Space, and Autonomy in Copenhagen, 1965–2010." In *The City is Ours: Squatting and Autonomous Movements in Europe From the 1970s to the Present*, edited by Bert van der Steen, Ask Katzeff, and Leender van Hoogenhuijze, 178–205. Oakland, CA: PM Press, 2014.

Kleivan, Inge. "The Arctic Peoples' Conference in Copenhagen, November 22–25, 1973." *Études/Inuit/Studies* 16, nos. 1–2 (1992): 227–36.

Kuhn, Gabriel, ed. *Turning Money into Rebellion: The Unlikely Story of Denmark's Revolutionary Bank Robbers*. Oakland, CA: PM Press, 2014.

Stadager, Anne. "The Spiritual '1968.'" In *Rebellion and Resistance*, edited by Henrik Jensen, 151–65. Pisa: Edizioni Plus, 2009. Available at ehlee.humnet.unipi.it/books4/2/11.pdf.

Thörn, Håkan, Cathrin Wasshede, and Tomas Nilson, eds. *Space for Urban Alternatives? CHRISTIANIA 1971–2011*. Möklinta: Gidlunds Förlag, 2011. Available at gupea.ub.gu.se/handle/2077/26558.

7
France

The 1960s in France began with decolonization. National liberation movements plunged Europe's second largest empire into crisis in the 1950s and 1960s. The most serious challenge came from Algeria, France's largest colony, and the home of nearly a million French settlers. Inspired by the crushing victory of the Viet Minh at Dien Bien Phu in French Indochina, the Algerian Front de Libération Nationale launched a ferocious struggle for independence in 1954.

The war that ensued was not only one of the bloodiest decolonization struggles of the period, it ultimately brought down the French government in Paris. Desperate to fend off a coup from recalcitrant settlers and the military, the government agreed to hand power over to General Charles de Gaulle, who promptly rewrote the constitution in 1958, inaugurating the Fifth Republic. De Gaulle oversaw a booming consumer economy, reasserted France's role as an independent global force, and clung to power for over a decade. Despite boasting the second largest Communist Party in Western Europe, and a vibrant leftist culture, France was firmly governed by the right during these years.

Nevertheless, in the late 1950s and early 1960s, cultural criticism made itself heard through the writings of avant-garde groups like the Situationist International (SI). Decrying consumerism, conformity, and alienation, the SI called for the rediscovery of authentic desires and a revolution in everyday life. The SI's turn to revolution exemplified a general trend: the 1960s witnessed a genuine renaissance of Marxism in France. This was a time of extraordinary intellectual experimentation, with various currents of Marxism competing with one another: humanism, anti-humanism, Maoism, Trotskyism, Left Communism, and Guevarism, to name only a few.

At the same time, a younger generation of activists began to take their distance from the French Communist Party (PCF). The PCF leadership, they charged, seemed more committed to accumulating votes than organizing the revolution. Moreover, the Party's undemocratic structure made course corrections exceedingly difficult. As a result, younger activists began to search for radical alternatives outside the Party.

Figure 7.1 Poster depicting an immigrant and a native-born French worker overcoming the boss' attempts to divide them. 1968.

This growing radicalization coincided with the rise of student protest. The unprecedented postwar population boom simply overwhelmed the existing university infrastructure. Between 1950 and 1964, the student population in France grew more rapidly than any other major European country. Students complained about crowded classrooms, inadequate curriculum, and a lack of real autonomy. On some campuses, like Nanterre, built in the outskirts of Paris, students challenged the administration. Of course, only a little over one percent of Nanterre students actually belonged to any kind of revolutionary organization in 1967, but radicals learned that they could exercise influence far in excess of their numbers.

Around this time, workers challenged the technocratic postwar compromise, signaling the return of militant class struggle in France. In 1967, a strike at the Rhodiacéta plant in Besançon soon spread to the entire region. In January 1968, a strike at the Saviem factory in Caen devolved into running battles between workers and riot police. The strong participation of the working class was one of the main reasons why the long 1968 would be so explosive in France.

Given the country's deep colonial past, the international situation was especially decisive in France. Anti-colonial and anti-imperialist struggles served as a powerful source of inspiration for French activists. Many had been radicalized during the Algerian War, looked to Cuba or China for new models of socialism, and made opposition to the Vietnam War one of their primary axes of struggle. Antiwar activism in particular radicalized

French youth, helped them to bypass the Communist Party, and allowed them to gain crucial organizing experiences that would play a tremendous role during the May events.

Although in retrospect France was a tinderbox waiting to ignite, to contemporaries, the dramatic events of 1968 came as a surprise. In fact, compared to events elsewhere, France seemed placid in the 1960s. When young radicals looked across the Global North, they were likely to draw inspiration from the United States, Italy, or West Germany, not France. In an editorial published in the pages of *Le Monde* on March 15, journalist Pierre Viansson-Ponte went so far as to write, "what defines our public life at the present time is boredom." French students, he continued, are not taking part in the "great upheavals shaking the world."

Yet it was here that the struggles of the 1960s erupted most spectacularly. The year 1968 began with a particularly militant antiwar action in Paris. Then in March, six antiwar activists were arrested for attacking the offices of an American Express office in Paris. In response, their comrades at Nanterre occupied an academic building, forming the March 22 Movement. Their activities soon led to the closure of the university, and on May 3 the students congregated instead at the Sorbonne (University of Paris). The Dean panicked and called the police, who ran amok. Hundreds were arrested, including bystanders. Demonstrations to free the arrested students soon led to a week of street fighting. Protests climaxed on May 10, 1968. Activists build barricades, set fires to halt police advances, and unleashed salvos of cobblestones. When the plumes of tear gas finally cleared, around 200 cars lay in ruins, hundreds were injured, and over 400 arrested. Remarkably, despite the violence, polls showed that most Parisians supported the students.

While they may not have entirely agreed with the students, many Parisians felt the police had gone too far. To protest police repression, show support for the students, and to take advantage of the government's moment of weakness, major trade unions called a one-day strike for the following Monday. But experienced workers took matters into their own hands, pushing the unions in a more radical direction. What began as a one-day action spiralled into a general strike wave of nearly ten million workers. At the same time, political unrest spread across the country. For a month, all of France was in turmoil.

But activists did not wish to simply bring down the existing order; they wanted to build a new one in its place. Guided by the idea of "autogestion," or self-management, students and young workers took over the Latin Quarter, creating not only an alternative university, but what they hoped would be the embryo of a different world, free from individualism, fixed social roles, and rigid hierarchies. It should be said, though, that some

Figure 7.2   Barricade. Rue Paul-Bert, Bordeaux, May 1968.

divisions persisted, above all those between men and women. As in other countries, women found themselves relegated to preparing food, making beds, minding the children, and typing up tracts. It was this contradiction that would contribute to the rise of women's liberation.

Hoping to end the strike, de Gaulle's government tried to buy off the workers. To their shock, the striking workers rejected the offer. The country ground to a virtual halt, as garbage piled up in the streets, gasoline ran low, and workers refused to go back to work. With the future uncertain, de Gaulle left the country on May 29 to confer with his generals in West Germany. Despite the unexpected opening, the left proved unable to organize a viable alternative. The radical elements that helped detonate the crisis were too marginal, and the established left was too concerned with simple electoral victory. As for the Communist Party, its leadership not only opposed any kind of revolution, but actively positioned itself as the guardian of order. Taking advantage of the confusion, and the PCF's refusal to escalate the strike, de Gaulle returned to France to end the revolt. He called his supporters into the streets, restored order, dissolved parliament, forced workers back to work, and banned radical organizations.

While the May events did not catalyze a revolution, and the right would continue to govern for another decade, May substantially altered the political horizon not only in France, but across the Global North. May 68 led to a host of concrete gains, such as increased wages, university reform, and a lowered voting age. But even more importantly, it opened the space for other struggles, many of which lasted well into the 1970s. Movements proliferated, radicals built new organizations, and workers continued to revolt in the factories. In fact, the number of strikes increased in the 1970s.

In some places, such as the Lip watch factory, workers simply took over the workplace and managed it themselves.

May also ushered in a new a conception of politics. People now wanted a change in their quality of life, a greater say in their society, a radical transformation in interpersonal relations. Personal liberation alongside social change was the order of the day. All spheres of life had to be revolutionized.

Relatedly, May 68 allowed the voiceless to make their voices heard. It gave tens of thousands an opportunity to break out of the normal routines of everyday life, to think of themselves as historical actors instead of passive objects. With the opening of May, a range of social groups organized their own movements in the late 1960s and 1970s: women's liberation, gay liberation, regional autonomy, immigrant rights, to name only a few.

Lastly, the May events seemed to prove that revolution might still be possible in the advanced capitalist world. At a time when many had given up on major change in the Global North, projecting all their desires on the "Third World," May 68 showed that young people could act as catalyzers, that the working classes did wield enormous power, and that radical change could happen in the core as well as the peripheries. In this way, May inspired radicals across the world.

FEBRUARY 21: A TRIBUTE TO VIETNAMESE HEROISM (1968)

La Jeunesse Communiste Révolutionnaire

On February 17, 1968, thousands of antiwar radicals from across Europe traveled to West Berlin for a conference on the Vietnam War. There, they made contacts, learned from one another, and promised to escalate their efforts, with some even calling for a "second front" in Europe. Encouraged by the Tet Offensive, and inspired by Che Guevara's call to create "two, three, many Vietnams," antiwar militants resolved to bring Vietnam home to the heart of imperialism. The conference strongly influenced the French contingent, which returned to France committed to radicalizing the antiwar movement. The occasion was a demonstration organized by the leading radical antiwar formation in France, the Comité Vietnam National (CVN), for anti-imperialist day, February 21, 1968. Below, we reproduce a report on the events of that day.

* * *

Wednesday, February 21, 1968. At 11:50 a.m. six CVN militants were nimbly maneuvering on the roofs of the Sorbonne. At precisely noon, the flags of the NFL [National Liberation Front] and the DRV [Democratic Republic of Vietnam] were waving in the breeze on the end of two lightning rods. But the action of the fire department, called in by the Rector, proved to be ineffectual; after the firemen had left, new flags replaced the old ones, and remained there all afternoon.

This was the opening volley of anti-imperialist day, on February 21, 1968. The CVN had been making plans for this day for nearly a month. On this occasion, it decided to inaugurate a new kind of political demonstration, which would no doubt break with the routine nonchalant procession to which the "great democratic worker organizations" had accustomed us. Following its initiative, the UNEF [National Union of Students of France] and SNESUP [National Union of Higher Education] called for a demonstration about 6:30 p.m. on the Boulevard St. Michel. This was not a matter of organizing one slipshod demonstration. The idea was to occupy the heart of the Latin Quarter for a good two hours in order to turn it into "Heroic Vietnam Quarter."

HEROIC VIETNAM QUARTER

All afternoon groups of militants walked up and down the Quarter distributing thousands of leaflets, the *Vietnam Courier*, and various pamphlets.

About 5 p.m., certain of those groups had a violent confrontation with an "Occident" commando.

At 6:15, militants acting as marshalls held up traffic on the Place St. Michel, to allow the demonstration to start. To turn the Latin Quarter into "Heroic Vietnam Quarter" is not a simple operation, and requires thorough participation. In addition to the 150 marshals, who were particularly "well seasoned" since Berlin, the poster brigades fell into line here and there in the procession. Finally came the "special intervention groups," who were carrying "propaganda materials," including two magnificent papier-mâché figures representing Lyndon Johnson.

By 6:30 p.m. there were several thousand demonstrators on the Place St. Michel. The militants from the "intervention groups" climbed on the statue of St. Michel slaying the Dragon, and hung an effigy of the U.S. President from its avenging finger, pointing heavenward. Numerous NLF flags were held up in front of the fountain, while Johnson was being soaked with gasoline. At 6:35 p.m. the President of the United States burst into flames to the approval of all the onlookers. When he had been reduced to ashes the demonstration started up again to cries of "NLF will win," "NLF in Saigon ..." The procession marched back up the Boulevard St. Michel, while perfect order was maintained by its marshals. When it reached the Boulevard St. Germain, the demo stopped, holding up traffic.

A militant speaker announced that the Boulevard St. Michel would henceforth be called "Heroic Vietnam Boulevard." While he was shouting his explanations into a loudspeaker, an immense banner started to unfurl above the heads of the marches. Members of the "intervention groups," perched in trees, let the huge streamer slowly fall down until it reached the middle of the boulevard, while the demonstrators cheered. Written on it in red letters was: "Heroic Vietnam Boulevard." The crowd then sang the *Internationale* and started marching again while the poster-pasters covered street signs, which would henceforth beat the name of "Heroic Vietnam Boulevard." The demonstration stopped when it reached the Lycée St. Louis, against the façade of which an "intervention group" set a ladder in order to hang an NLF flag from the principal's window. The Lycée St. Louis would henceforth be called "Lycée Nguyen Van Troi," which was the name that now appeared over the entrance. The procession started up once more, then stopped in front of the Luxembourg where the slogan "NLF will win" appeared in letters of fire. Finally it branched off toward the Senate, under the protection of a heavy police force. In order to cut short any tendencies to obstruct the street, the marshals quickened the pace to the rhythm of "Ho-Ho-Ho-Chi-Minh" and "Che-Che-Guevara," both imported from Berlin. We next turned into the Rue Tournon headed for the Boulevard St. Germain. All along the way the poster-pasters had been covering the street signs with our imitation signs marked "Heroic Vietnam." They also pasted CVN posters proclaiming the recent Front victories on all the walls and billboards. When the demonstration reached the Place Maubert it was met by Comrade Boulte from the national board of the CVN, who said that the Paris American Embassy would follow (which did not necessarily mean that it would be the next target).

The dynamic, militant nature of this occupation of the Latin Quarter presented a contrast with the apathy of traditional demonstrations. The CVN, which had given proof of its influence on the masses on February 3 and 13, showed on the 21 that it knew how to adjust its political actions to the new demands of the present situation in Vietnam, marked by the general offensive of the Front and increased risks of escalation. We can be sure that it will know how to carry on and progress in this direction.

[...]

For an NLF Victory
Against Police Repression of Demonstrators
A United Front of Anti-Imperialist Militants

Republished in *The French Student Uprising, November 1967–June 1968: An Analytical Record*, eds. Alain Schnapp and Pierre Vidal-Naquet (Boston: Beacon Press, 1971), 70–72. Translated by Maria Jolas. Translation modified.

WHY WE ARE FIGHTING (1968)
Action

In late 1967 and early 1968, the French student movement grew stronger and more militant. In March, students formed the March 22 Movement. By early May, their actions led to the closure of not only Nanterre, but the Sorbonne. The motivating issues of the movement were broad, covering everything from the critique of the university to protesting police repression. Soon, however, protesting students recognized that they had to communicate with each other, popularize their ideas, and explain their actions. With most media outlets blocked, or openly hostile, activists decided to launch their own publications to spread their message. One of the most successful of these movement papers was Action, *which soon emerged as a kind of mouthpiece for the action committees that began to sprout up across Paris. Here, we reproduce an article from the paper's inaugural issue explaining why French students were taking to the streets.*

* * *

The Reasons for the Revolt

It is not with pleasure that students are confronting the gardes-mobiles helmeted and armed to the teeth. It is not with pleasure that, at the period of examinations, students are responding to police violence.

It is never out of pleasure that one fights someone stronger than oneself.

For years students have been protesting the authoritarian methods that the government wanted to force upon them. Calmly, they *protested* against the Fouchet Reform, then against the Peyrefitte measures. For years, calmly, but also in an atmosphere of general indifference, the government ignored their protest just as it ignored the workers' protests. For years these protests remained in vain and without response.

Today, the students are *resisting*.

Their only crime is to reject a University whose sole goal is to train future bosses and domiciled tools for the economy. Their only crime is to reject an authoritarian and hierarchical social system which rejects any radical opposition; this means refusing to be the servants of this system.

For this crime alone, they are being rewarded by blackjacks and prison sentences.

University and lycée students have rallied and faced repression, because they want to *defend* themselves against police repression and the bourgeois government; the students are in a state of *legitimate defense*.

What you are also being led to believe is that this is merely a matter of the released inhibitions of a handful of isolated agitators who, of course, come from Nanterre, the source of all evil. Recourse to "nanterrorism" explains nothing. The government is easily reassured: the Nanterre "trouble makers" are not and never have been isolated. If this were not true, how may we explain the fact that students all over Europe are demonstrating? Where there is general unrest there are general causes.

All over Europe

To stop the student revolt, beheading Nanterre would not be enough: the revolt that has now started in Paris has no boundaries; in Berlin, thousands of students have checkmated a strong reactionary governmental authority. The SDS too was only a small handful of agitators; today it represents the only large movement opposed to growing fascism in Western Germany. In Italy, thousands of students have enforced the right to question the social system. They have responded to violent repression through demonstrations there even more violent than those of last Friday. In Spain, England, Brazil; in Louvain, throughout Europe and the world, students have taken to the streets to confront the forces of bourgeois "order." Everywhere, even in Paris, the violence of the repression has shown that governments are afraid of these movements, apparently so weak, but which nevertheless have begun to upset the existing order. However, press campaigns have tried to isolate and discredit the movements: it is not thanks to any particular love on the part of journalists that student revolts have made the front page of the newspapers. On the contrary, their only aim is to proportion the hate campaign to the potential danger to the social order.

The Same Combat

In Paris and in Nanterre they are not fighting alone; they are not fighting only for themselves. In Germany, on May first, tens of thousands of students and workers were *together*, on the initiative of the SDS, in the first anti-capitalist demonstration that has taken place in Berlin since Nazism. The "handful of agitators" became a mass movement. Those who are combating the capitalist University stood shoulder to shoulder with those who are combating capitalist exploitation.

In France we also know that our fight has only begun; we know that youth is sensitive to the capitalist crisis and to the crisis of imperialism oppressing people in Vietnam, and Latin America, everywhere in the Third World. In Redon, in Caen, young workers are revolting violently, more violently than we are. On that subject the press, which is attacking us today, has remained silent. In spite of the government, in spite of the silence and the manipulations of the servile press, our struggle and theirs will converge.

Today students are becoming aware of what they are being trained for: to be managers for the existing economic system, paid to make it function the best possible way. Their fight concerns all workers because it is also the workers' fight: they refused to become professors in the service of an educational system that chooses the sons of the bourgeoisie and eliminates the others; sociologists who manufacture slogans for governmental election campaigns; psychologists responsible for making "worker teams" function in the best interest of the employers; managers responsible for applying against the workers a system to which they themselves are subjected.

Young people in the high schools, universities, and from the working class reject the future offered them by today's society; they reject unemployment, which is becoming a growing threat; they reject today's University, which gives them only worthless, ultra-specialized training in which, under the pretext of "selection," reserves know-how for sons of the bourgeoisie, and is but a tool for repression of all nonconformist ideas in the interests of the ruling class.

When young people resort to violent revolt, they are conscious of making this rejection stand out more clearly; they are conscious that the fight can give results only if the workers understand its meaning and make it their own. This is why today we are continuing the fight; this is why we appeal to you.

Republished in *The French Student Uprising, November 1967–June 1968: An Analytical Record*, eds. Alain Schnapp and Pierre Vidal-Naquet (Boston: Beacon Press, 1971), 365–8. Translated by Maria Jolas. Translation modified.

LIBERATED CENSIER: A REVOLUTIONARY BASE (1968)
Fredy Perlman

After the Night of the Barricades on May 10, students turned to occupations. The first Parisian university building occupied was Censier, the Sorbonne's annex, in the afternoon of Saturday, May 11. Inspired by this first example, about 500 students occupied the Sorbonne the following Monday, May 13. In these occupied buildings, radical students set about creating an alternative way of life, one based in the ideals of communalism, self-management, and the transcendence of social roles. Students not only discussed the new world, they created institutions to keep the occupations going, such as day-care centers, infirmaries, and communal dormitories. Below, we reproduce an analysis of the Censier occupation by Fredy Perlman, an American who taught in Italy in early 1968, traveled to Paris during the May events, and ended up participating in the Censier occupation.

* * *

[...]

The explosion of May–June 1968 is a sudden break with the regularities of French society, and it cannot be explained in terms of those regularities. The social conditions, the consciousness of students and workers, the strategies of "revolutionary" sects, had all existed before May 1968, and had not given rise to a student revolt, a general strike, or a mass movement determined to destroy capitalism. Something new appeared in May, an element which was not regular but unique, an element which transformed the "normal" consciousness of students and workers, an element which represented a radical break with what was known before May 1968.

The new element, the spark which set off the explosion, was "a handful of madmen" who did not consider themselves either a revolutionary party or a vanguard. The story of the student movement which began in Nanterre with a demonstration to end the war in Vietnam has been told elsewhere. The actions of this student movement were "exemplary actions"; they set off a process of continuous escalation, each step involving a larger sector of the population.

One of the steps in this process of escalation was the occupation of Censier, annex of the University of Paris Faculty of Letters (Sorbonne). Not as publicized as the actions or personalities of the Nanterre student movement, the activity which developed at Censier during the last two weeks in May parallels and supplements that of the March 22 Movement. This essay will try to describe the steps in the process of escalation as they were experienced and interpreted by the occupants of Censier.

What happened in Censier cannot be explained in terms of French everyday life. The occupants of Censier suddenly cease to be unconscious, passive *objects* shaped by particular combinations of social forces; they become conscious, active *subjects* who begin to shape their own social activity.

The occupants of Censier aim at the destruction of capitalist social relations, but they do not define themselves as the historical subject who will overthrow capitalism. Their actions, like those of the March 22 Movement, are exemplary actions. Their task is to communicate the example to a larger subject: the workers. To make the example overflow from the university to the working population, the Censier occupants create a new social form: worker-student action committees.

Each action is designed to go beyond itself. The aim of the occupants of Censier is not to create a self-governing commune in that building, but to set off the occupation of factories. The occupation of Censier is a break with continuity; the occupants' aim is to create other breaks.

The occupants do not proceed on the basis of what is "normal," but on the basis of what is *possible*. Radical breaks with everyday life are not normal, but they are possible. A movement with the slogan "anything is possible" proceeds on the basis of the *potential*, not the usual.

The task of these revolutionaries is not to define the conditions which make revolution impossible, but to create the conditions which make revolution possible. This orientation is probably the most radical break of March 22 and Censier with the traditional Western Left, which begins by pointing to the "objective conditions" (for example, the apathy, self-interest and dependence of workers) which make revolution impossible. The French movement begins by pushing beyond the "objective limits," an orientation which it shares with a handful of Cuban revolutionaries and Vietnamese revolutionaries who began struggling at a time when any analysis of "objective conditions" would have led to a prediction of certain defeat. The French revolutionaries broke out of the psychology of defeat, the outlook of the loser, and began struggling. Their struggle, like that of the Cubans and the Vietnamese, was exemplary: the example overflowed to sectors of the population who are far stronger and more numerous than the initial revolutionaries.

[...]

"On Saturday, May 11, at 6 in the evening, militants of the May 3 Action Committees occupy the annex to the Faculty of Letters, the Censier Center. All night long and on the days that follow, the atmosphere is similar to that of the 'night of the barricades,' not in terms of violence, but in terms of the self-organization, the initiative, the discussion."[1] The university ceases to be a place for the "transmission of a cultural heritage," a place for training managers, experts and trainers, a place for brainwashing brainwashers.

The capitalist university comes to an end. The ex-university, or rather the building, becomes a place for collective expression. The first step of this transformation is the physical occupation of the building. The second step is discussion, the expression of ideas, information, projects, the creative self-expression of the occupants. "In the large auditoriums the discussion is continuous. Students participate, and also professors, assistants, people from the neighborhood, high schoolers, young workers."[2] Expression is contagious. People who have never expressed ideas before, who have never spoken in front of professors and students, become confident in their ability. It is the example of others speaking, analyzing, expressing ideas, suggesting projects, which gives people confidence in their own ability. "The food service," for example, "is represented at the meetings by a young comrade: he's thirteen, maybe fourteen. He organizes, discusses, takes part in the auditoriums. He

1. "L'Occupation," *Action*, May 13, 1968, 7.
2. Ibid.

was behind the barricades. His action and his behavior are the only answer
to the drivel about high-schoolers being irresponsible brats."[3]

What begins at this point is a process of collective learning; the
"university," perhaps for the first time, becomes a place for learning. People
do not only learn the information, the ideas, the projects of others; they
also learn from the example of others that they have specific information to
contribute, that they are able to express ideas, that they can initiate projects.
There are no longer specialists or experts; the division between thinkers
and doers, between students and workers, breaks down. At this point all are
students. When an expert, a professor of law, tells the occupants that the
occupation of a university is illegal, a student tells him that it is no longer
legal for an expert to define what is illegal, that the days when a legal expert
defines what people can and cannot do are over. The professor can either
stay and join the process of collective learning, or else he can leave and join
the police to re-impose his legality.

Within the occupied university, expression becomes action; the awareness
of one's ability to think, to initiate, to decide, is in fact an awareness of
one's ability to act. The occupants of the university become conscious of
their collective power: "we've decided to make ourselves the masters."[4] The
occupants no longer follow orders, they no longer obey, they no longer serve.
They express themselves in a general assembly, and the decisions of the
assembly are the expression of the will of all its members. No other decisions
are valid; no other authority is recognized. [...] This awareness of the ability
to express oneself, this consciousness of collective power, is itself an act of
de-alienation: "You can no longer sleep quietly once you've suddenly opened
your eyes."[5] People are no longer the playthings of external forces; they're
no longer objects; they've suddenly become conscious subjects. And once
their eyes are open, people are not about to close them again: their passivity
and dependence are negated, annihilated, and nothing but a force which
breaks their will can reimpose the passivity and dependence.

The general assembly does not only reject former masters, former
authority; it also refuses to create new masters, new authority. The occupants
conscious of their power refuse to alienate that power to any force whatever,
whether it is externally imposed or created by the general assembly itself.
No external force, neither the university administration nor the state, can
make decisions for the occupants of the university, and no internally created
force can speak, decide, negotiate, or act for the general assembly. There are

---

3.   Ibid.
4.   "Travailleurs de chez Rhône Poulenc," Comité d'Action Ouvriers-Étudiants, Centre
Censier, May 14 , 1968.
5.   Sign on a Censier wall, quoted in *Action*, May 13, 1968, 7.

neither leaders nor representatives. No special group, neither union functionaries, nor a "coordinating committee," nor a "revolutionary party," has the power to negotiate for the university occupants, to speak for them, to sell them out. And there's nothing to negotiate about: the occupants have taken over; they speak for themselves, make their own decisions, and run their own activities. The State and the capitalist press try to set up leaders, spokesmen, representatives with whom to negotiate the evacuation of the university; but none of the "leaders" are accepted: their usurped power is illegitimate; they speak for no one. In the face of this appearance of direct democracy, of grass-roots control (the Capitalist and Communist press call it "anarchy and chaos"), the State has only one resort; physical violence.

Consciousness of collective power is the first step toward the appropriation of social power (but only the first step, as will be shown below). Conscious of their collective power, the university occupants, workers and students, begin to appropriate the power to decide, they begin to learn to run their own social activities. The process of political de-alienation begins; the university is de-institutionalized; the building is transformed into a place which is run by its occupants. There are no "specialists" or "responsibles." The community is collectively responsible for what takes place, and for what doesn't take place, within the occupied building. Formerly specialized social activities are integrated into the lives of all members of the community. Social tasks are no longer performed either because of direct coercion or because of the indirect coercion of the market (i.e. the threat of poverty and starvation). As a result, some social activities, like hair dressing and manicuring, are no longer performed at all. Other tasks, like cooking, sweeping the rooms, cleaning the toilets—tasks performed by people who have no other choice in a coercive system—are left undone for several days. The occupation shows signs of degeneration: the food is bad, the rooms are filthy, the toilets are unusable. These activities become the order of the day of the general assembly: everyone is interested in their efficient performance, and no one is institutionally coerced to perform these tasks. The general assembly is responsible for their performance, which means everyone is responsible. Committees of volunteers are formed. A Kitchen Committee improves the quality of the meals; the food is free: it is provided by neighborhood committees and by peasants. A service of order charges itself with maintaining clean toilets stocked with toilet paper. Each action committee sweeps its own room. The tasks are performed by professors, students and workers. At this point all of the occupants of Censier are workers. There are no longer upper and lower class jobs; there are no longer intellectual and manual tasks, qualified labor and unqualified labor; there are only socially necessary activities.

[…] Townspeople—observers and potential participants—stream into Censier constantly and are unable to find their way around the complex social system which has started to develop within the building: an information window is maintained at the entrance and information offices are maintained on each floor to orient the visitors. Many militants live far from Censier: a dormitory is organized.

Censier, formerly a capitalist university, is transformed into a complex system of self-organized activities and social relations. However, Censier is not a self-sufficient Commune removed from the rest of society. The police are on the order of the day of every general assembly. The occupants of Censier are acutely aware that their self-organized social activities are threatened so long as the State and its repressive apparatus are not destroyed. And they know that their own force, or even the force of all students and some workers, is not sufficient to destroy the State's potential for violence.

The only force which can put the Censier occupants back to sleep is a force which is physically strong enough to break their will: the police and the national army still represent such a force.

The means of violence produced by a highly developed industry are still controlled by the capitalist State. And the Censier occupants are aware that the power of the State will not be broken until control over these industrial activities passes to the producers: they "are convinced that the struggle cannot be concluded without the massive participation of the workers."[6] The armed power of the State, the power which negates and threatens to annihilate the power of collective creation and self-organization manifested in Censier, can only be destroyed by the armed power of society. But before the population can be armed, before the workers can take control of the means of production, they must become aware of their ability to do so, they must become conscious of their collective power. And this consciousness of collective power is precisely what the students and workers acquired after they occupied Censier and transformed it into a place for collective expression. Consequently, the occupation of Censier is an exemplary action, and the central task of the militants in Censier becomes to communicate the example. All the self-organized activities revolve around this central task. […]

[…]

Censier exists as a place and as an example. Workers, students, professors, townspeople come to the place to learn, to express themselves, to become conscious of themselves as subjects, and they prepare to communicate the example to other sections of the population and to other parts of the world. Foreign students organize a general assembly to "join the struggle of their

6.   "Travailleurs R.A.T.P.," Les Comités d'Action, Censier, May 15, 1968.

French comrades and give them their unconditional support." Realizing that "the struggle of their French comrades is only an aspect of the international struggle against capitalist society and against imperialism," the foreign students prepare to spread the example abroad.[7] Eastern European students express their solidarity and send the news to their comrades at home. A U.S. group forms an Action Committee of the American Left, and they "plan to establish a news link-up with the U.S.A."[8]

Most important of all, Censier's main contribution to the revolutionary movement, the worker-student action committees, are formed. "Workers … to destroy this repressive system which oppresses all of us, we must fight together. Some worker-student action committees have been created for this purpose."[9] [...]

Worker-Student Action Committees, eds. Fredy Perlman and Roger Gregoire (Kalamazoo: self-published, 1969), 36–8, 40–47.

SLOGANS (1968)

The May events triggered an outpouring of creative expression as those who had been marginalized for so long made their voices heard. The desire to seize the power of speech took many forms, from the boisterous general assemblies to the posters crafted at the occupied École des Beaux Arts. The same energy animated the political graffiti that adorned the many buildings, walls, and bridges of the country's capital during those heady weeks. In some cases inspired by the Situationists, much of this graffiti combined politics with poetry, condensing some of the major animating ideas of the May events into pithy slogans. Below, we reproduce a selection of these slogans, many of which began as graffiti scrawled across Paris.

*   *   *

Be realistic: demand the impossible.
The barricade blocks the street but opens the way.
We refuse to dialogue with those who club us.
Beneath the paving stones—the beach!

---

7.   "Assemblée Générale des Étudiants Étrangers," Centre Censier, May 20, 1968.
8.   "Permanence Americaine," Centre Censier, April 17, 1968. In this leaflet, the American students also mention that they are willing to inform their French comrades of "attempts of students to organize workers" in the U.S. The Americans found very few action committee militants who were interested.
9.   "Travailleurs," Comité d'Action Étudiants-Travailleurs, Censier, May 16, 1968.

We don't want a world where the certainty of not dying from hunger is traded for the risk of dying from boredom.

We will claim nothing, we will ask for nothing. We will take, we will occupy.

Since 1936 I have fought for wage increases. My father before me fought for wage increases. Now I have a TV, a fridge and a Volkswagen. But my whole life I've been taken for a fool. Don't negotiate with the bosses: abolish them.

It is forbidden to forbid.

In a society that has abolished all adventures, the only adventure left is to abolish society.

The emancipation of humanity will be total or it will not be.

Run, comrade, the old world is behind you!

A single nonrevolutionary weekend is infinitely more bloody than a month of permanent revolution.

The more I make love, the more I want to make revolution.

The more I make revolution, the more I want to make love.

Poetry is in the street.

Don't liberate me: I'll do it myself.

I love you!—Oh, say it with cobblestones!

Workers of the world, have fun!

All power to the Imagination.

The economy is suffering—let it die.

Republished on libcom.org. Translations modified.

ALSTHOM WORKERS ON SELF-MANAGEMENT (1968)

On May 27, the government, employers' organizations, and the unions reached an agreement, informally called the Grenelle Accords. Workers would receive salary hikes, a progressive reduction of the work week, an increase in the minimum wage, and union rights, while employers won the right to recover lost working hours. The same morning, union leaders presented the Accords to 10,000 striking workers at the Renault factory in Billancourt, a bellwether of the balance of forces between capital and labor in the country. To the surprise of the union leaders, workers responded with a resounding "no." This did not mean that the French working class wanted revolution instead. In fact, in most workplaces, the movement remained firmly under the control of the unions. The refusal did indicate, however, that some workers wanted more than just a raise. Below, we reproduce a text by radical workers at Alsthom, an electricity plant, which called for something different: self-management.

* * *

The workers at Alsthom-RSC-SIG, without meaning to neglect immediate demands, hope that the benefits they won as a result of their struggle will not quickly become illusory. Consequently, they consider that the real problem posed in business is the problem of *power*, and therefore of *management*.

In fact the power of the workers, which implies participation of each one of them in management of the company and organization of the work, is the only thing that will permit development of the company and economic expansion in the best interests of the workers.

For this reasons, the workers claim responsibilities in management that they will only really be able to assume if they own the tools of production; the latter, which are very often the property of distant stockholders, are in fact the property of the workers because they are the ones who use them.

It is therefore necessary, in order for workers' power to be expressed on all levels, to set up *management committees whose duty it will be to check the hierarchy's application of the objectives defined by the workers' general assembly.*

The workers will freely determine how the proceeds of the business shall be used, especially:

—remuneration of capital, which is a means of production placed at the disposal of the company;

—investments;

—remuneration of personnel

These objectives can be completely attained only through the solidarity and action of all workers, and especially those in businesses having economic contacts with the firm under consideration, that is to say, essentially: banks, customers, and suppliers.

The workers of Alsthom-RSC-SIG have decided to give maximum publicity to their position, among other workers, and ask for the support of this priority objective by all the union organizations.

Republished in *The French Student Uprising, November 1967–June 1968: An Analytical Record*, eds. Alain Schnapp and Pierre Vidal-Naquet (Boston: Beacon Press, 1971), 553–4. Translated by Maria Jolas. Translation modified.

MANIFESTO (1971)
Le Groupe d'Information sur les Prisons

After May 68, activists faced a wave of state repression. Raymond Marcellin, the Minister of the Interior, tightened censorship laws, increased police powers, arrested activists, and banned leftist organizations like the Maoist Gauche Pro-létarienne (GP). In the face of this repression, the prisons flooded with radical militants from all currents. In response, radicals, especially those from the now illegal GP, reexamined their strategies. They built alliances with moderates, rallied around the defense of civil liberties, and organized in the prisons. One of the initiatives to come out of this new turn, was the Groupe d'Information sur les Prisons (GIP), a partnership between the ex-GP and a number of leftist intellectuals, such as Michel Foucault, Gilles Deleuze, and Jean Genet. Below, we reproduce the group's statement, issued on February 8, 1971.

* * *

None of us is sure to escape prison. Today less than ever. Police control over day-to-day life is tightening: in city streets and roads; over foreigners and young people; it is once more an offense to express opinions; anti-drug measures increase arbitrarily. We live in the shadow of "police custody." They tell us that the system of justice is overwhelmed. We can see that. But what if it is the police that have overwhelmed it? They tell us that prisons are over-populated. But what if it was the population that was being over-imprisoned? Little information is published on prisons. It is one of the hidden regions of our social system, one of the dark zones of our life. We have the right to know; we want to know. This is why, with magistrates, lawyers, journalists, doctors, psychologists, we have formed a Groupe d'Information sur les Prisons.

We propose to make known what the prison is: who goes there, how and why they go there, what happens there, and what the life of the prisoners is, and that, equally, of the surveillance personnel; what the buildings, the food, and hygiene are like; how the internal regulations, medical control, and the workshops function; how one gets out and what it is to be, in our society, one of those who came out.

This information is not in the official reports that we have found. We will ask those who, for some reason, have an experience of the prison or a relation to it. We ask them to contact us and tell us what they know. A questionnaire has been compiled which can be requested from us. As soon as we have sufficient responses, the results will be published.

It is not for us to suggest reform. We merely wish to know the reality. And to make it known almost immediately, almost overnight, because time is short. This is to inform opinion and to keep it informed. We will try to use all means of information: daily newspapers, weeklies, monthlies. We therefore appeal to all possible platforms.

Finally, it is good to know what threatens us, but knowledge is also good to defend oneself. One of our first tasks will be to publish a small *Manuel du parfait arrêté* [Complete Arrest Guide], paired of course as an *Avis aux arrêteurs* [Note for Arrestors].

All those who want to inform us, be informed or participate in the work can write to the GIP at 285, rue de Vaugirard, Paris-XVe.

On behalf of the Groupe d'Information,
Jean-Marie DOMENACH,
Michel FOUCAULT,
Pierre VIDAL-NAQUET

Esprit, March 1971, 531–2. Translated by Stuart Elden. Translation modified.

MANIFESTO OF THE 343 WOMEN (1971)

As in other countries, feminist collectives began to take shape in France in the 1960s. May 1968 played a catalyzing role, as did the example of women's liberation in the United States. By 1970, one could speak of a coherent women's liberation movement (Mouvement de Liberation des Femmes, MLF). On August 26, MLF activists held a protest at the Tomb of the Unknown Soldier, at the base of the Arc de Triomphe, one of France's national symbols. They laid a wreath for the wife of the unknown soldier, whom they argued was even more unknown than him. Notably, they timed their action to coincide with the fiftieth anniversary of the adoption of the twentieth Amendment, which gave women in the United States the right to vote, signaling the profound internationalism of the women's movement in the long 1968. MLF took on a range of causes, but one of the most important was legal abortion. On April 5, 1971, feminists published a manifesto calling for the right to bodily autonomy, which was signed by 343 women who admitted to having an illegal abortion.

* * *

One million women in France have abortions every year.

Condemned to secrecy, they do so in dangerous conditions, even though this procedure, under medical supervision, is one of the simplest.

We are silencing these millions of women.

I declare that I am one of them. I declare that I have had an abortion.

Just as we demand free access to contraception, we demand the freedom to have an abortion.

[...]

The list of signatures [...] is a first act of revolt. For the first time, women have decided to lift the taboo weighing down on their wombs: women of the Mouvement de Libération des Femmes, the Mouvement pour la Liberté de l'Avortement, women who work, women who stay at home.

At the Mouvement de Libération des Femmes we are neither a party, nor an organization, nor an association, and even less so their women's subsidiary. This is an historic movement which not only brings together women who come to MLF, this is the movement for all women, wherever they live, wherever they work, who have decided to take their lives and their freedom into their own hands. Fighting against our oppression means shattering all of society's structures, especially the most routine ones. We do not want any part or any place in this society which has been built without us and at our expense.

When womankind, the sector of humanity that has been lurking in the shadows, takes its destiny into its own hands, that's when we can start talking about a revolution.

[...]

Abortion

A word which seems to express and define the feminist fight once and for all. To be a feminist is to fight for free abortion on demand.

Abortion

It's a women's thing, like cooking, diapers, something dirty. The fight to obtain free abortion on demand feels somehow ridiculous or petty. It can't shake the smell of hospitals or food, or of poo behind women's backs.

The complexity of the emotions linked to the fight for abortion precisely indicates our difficulty in being, the pain that we have in persuading ourselves that it is worth the trouble of fighting for ourselves. It goes without saying that we do not have the right to choose what we want to do with our bodies, as other human beings do. Our wombs, however, belong to us.

Free abortion on demand is not the ultimate goal of women's plight. On the contrary, it is but the most basic necessity, without which the political fight cannot even begin. It is out of vital necessity that women should win back control and reintegrate their bodies. They hold a unique status in history: human beings who, in modern societies, do not have unfettered control over their own bodies. Up until today it was only slaves who held this status.

The scandal continues. Each year 1,500,000 women live in shame and despair. 5,000 of us die. But the moral order remains steadfast. We want to scream.

Free abortion on demand is:

- immediately ceasing to be ashamed of your body, being free and proud in your body just as everyone up until now who has had full use of it;
- no longer being ashamed of being a woman. An ego broken into tiny fucking pieces, that's what all women who have to undergo a clandestine abortion experience;

- just being yourself all the time, no longer having that ignoble fear of being "taken," taken into a trap, being double and powerless with a sort of tumor in your belly;
- a thrilling fight, insofar as if I win I only begin to belong to myself and no longer to the State, to a family, to a child I do not want;
- a step along the path to reaching full control over the production of children. Women, like all other producers, have in fact the absolute right to control all of their production. This control implies a radical change in women's mental configuration, and a no less radical change in social structures.

1. I will have a child if I want one, and no moral pressure, institution, or economic imperative will compel me to do so. This is my political power. As any kind of producer, I can, while waiting for improvement, put pressure on society through my production (child strike).
2. I will have a child if I want one and if the society I will be bringing it into is suitable for me, if it will not make me a slave to that child, its nurse, its maid, its punching bag.
3. I will have a child if I want one, if society is suitable for both me and it, I am responsible for it, if there is no risk of war, and if I control my work rhythm.

[...]

Le Nouvel Observateur 334, April 5, 1971, 5–6. Retrieved from 343sluts.wordpress. com. Translated by Rachel C. Translation modified.

"EVERY TIME WE ADVANCE THE LIBERATION OF THE ARAB PEOPLE, WE ALSO ADVANCE THE FRENCH REVOLUTION" (1971)

Moktar

As in many countries, the postwar economic boom was made possible by cheap immigrant labor. Between 1954 and 1974 several million immigrants arrived in France, many of them taking on the most difficult, exhausting jobs. They received low wages, faced regular discrimination, and experienced poor living conditions—in 1966, around 75,000 immigrants lived in shanty towns on the outskirts of Paris and other cities in France. Although most immigrants arrived from elsewhere in Europe, many came from the Global South, especially North Africa. In the 1960s and early 1970s, immigrants began to mobilize, although legal restrictions made activism very difficult. In some cases, they made alliances of sorts with the various radical groups in France. One of these was the Gauche Prolétarienne, the most dynamic Maoist group of the period. Below, we reproduce an excerpt from an interview with a 24-year-old Moroccan worker who describes his turn to Maoism.

* * *

[...]
    We were lodged in the immigrant hostels. The managing company said the hostel is for the good of the workers, that it doesn't make a profit, but in looking closely, one sees that the company makes very substantial profits. They rent the rooms for 15,000 francs. There is a bed to lie down on, but that's it. And this hostel isn't the most disgusting. There are often ten to a room. We don't have the right to have visitors, to make noise, to come home late, really a prison. So I said to myself: "It's clear this isn't good, so I will do what everyone does, I will resist." [...] I go to the factory, the work is hard, the bosses scream, the pace drives me crazy, the pay is terrible. I return home, the manager yells, I don't have time to cook ... So as soon as the contract ended—it was a six month contract—we all quit Chausson. We said we'd go work somewhere else. We talked then about Renault.
    [...]
    Working at Renault-Flins, that's where I started to see pamphlets, to hear that there were Maoists. About China, I knew it was good. I never heard someone say China was bad. I understood that it was a progressive country, but different from the others since no one said anything bad about China, unlike Russia. The fact that China wasn't in the United Nations, that was great, too. And I even explained to people why China was good; China knows that the other governments are all bastards, so it doesn't go to the UN. I saw pamphlets signed by "the Maoists" that were distributed at Flins. I read them and saw the difference with the other tracts distributed by the CFTC [French Confederation of Christian Workers] and all the other unions. If there's a despicable boss, the Maoists' tracts explained what to do about it. For the pace at work, here's what to do about it. For the CGT [General Confederation of Labor], one saw a heap of figures for the what-you-call-it coefficients and everything, I didn't understand. Finally I realized that didn't interest anyone. That workers have a higher or lower wage scale, that's not going to slow down the pace of the line. They were also the only pamphlets that defended the immigrants, that said there isn't a difference between French and immigrants, that we all have the same rights, and that we all have to unite. [...] But the CGT wasn't interested in immigrants.
    Before meeting the Maoist friends to organize struggles, I did stuff mainly in the hostel. That's not to say there were victories, I didn't know how to

do it. But there was a worker arguing with the manager about the rent …
it was loud. I worked at night, I was still in pajamas, I opened the window
and I saw everyone at the windows trying to see what was happening below.
So I went down and heard the manager tell the worker, "You don't have the
right to speak because you don't know how to read. […]" I yelled, "Is that it,
you think that because he doesn't know how to read he's a brute, an animal?"
And I told the other workers, "You have to come down." All the workers
came down, but I didn't know what to do. […]

[…]

It was after that that I started to meet the Maoist friends. Before, I bought
La Cause du peuple, I was happy because it was straightforward. What they
said was true. Meeting the Maoists changed my perspectives because I saw
that it was necessary to organize […]

[…] To be Maoist, for me, means that here, in France, the workers and
especially the immigrant workers will raise their heads. […]

About unity with the French, before, I thought that there were some
French who weren't racist, but in general they were all racist. I did not
think that one day the French could unite like brothers to fight a battle
where the risks and the goals are the same, like we do now. I told myself,
there may be exceptions like when, during the Algerian War, there were
some French who got involved, but I thought there were many racist ideas
among the French. Now I don't think so anymore, and I see we've made
great strides toward unity between immigrants and French. […] It's much
easier with the younger generation of French workers. Young people didn't
have the experiences the old French workers did. I've talked with quite a few
French workers. The level of consciousness of the old workers is very clear
on the question of bosses, but on the question of immigrants, it's tough.
The language barrier is not the main issue because immigrants, as soon as
they arrive in France, make great effort to speak French. Literacy is a good
thing for comprehension between workers, but the question of unity will be
learned in the struggle in the factory, by multiplying the struggles here and
by supporting the struggles of the Arab peoples. […]

The questions of the French Revolution and the Arab Revolution are
closely linked. […]

Michèle Manceau, *Les maos en France* (Paris: Éditions Gallimard, 1972), 170–76.
Translated by Salar Mohandesi.

Further Reading

Abidor, Mitchell, ed. *May Made Me: An Oral History of the 1968 Uprising in France.*
London: Pluto Press, 2018.

Bourg, Julian. *From Revolution to Ethics: May 1968 and Contemporary French Thought.* Montreal and Kingston: McGill-Queen's University Press, 2007.

Davey, Eleanor. *Idealism Beyond Borders: The French Revolutionary Left and the Rise of Humanitarianism, 1954–1988.* Cambridge: Cambridge University Press, 2015.

Duchen, Claire. *Feminism in France: From May '68 to Mitterand.* London: Routledge, 1986.

Feenberg, Andrew, and Jim Freedman. *When Poetry Ruled the Streets: The French May Events of 1968.* Albany, NY: State University of New York Press, 2001.

Gordon, Daniel. *Immigrants & Intellectuals: May '68 & and the Rise of Anti-racism in France.* Pontypool, Wales: Merlin Press, 2012.

Katler, Christoph. *The Discovery of the Third World: Decolonization and the Rise of the New Left in France, c. 1950–1976.* Translated by Thomas Dunlap. Cambridge: Cambridge University Press, 2016.

Jackson, Julian, Anna-Louise Milne, and James S. Williams, eds. *May 68: Rethinking France's Last Revolution.* Basingstoke: Palgrave Macmillan, 2011.

Martel, Frédéric. *The Pink and the Black: Homosexuals in France since 1968.* Translated by Jane Marie Todd. Palo Alto, CA: Stanford University Press, 2000.

Quattrocchi, Angelo, and Tom Nairn. *The Beginning of the End: France, May 1968.* London: Verso, 1998.

Reid, Donald. *Opening the Gates: The Lip Affair, 1968–1981.* London: Verso, 2018.

Reid, Donald, and Daniel Sherman, eds. "May '68: New Approaches, New Perspectives," special issue of *French Historical Studies* 41, no. 2 (April 2018), (with contributions from Françoise Blum, Salar Mohandesi, Bethany S. Keenan, Ludivine Battigny and Boris Gobille, Tony Comé, and Sandrine Sanos).

Reynolds, Chris. *Memories of May '68: France's Convenient Consensus.* Cardiff: University of Wales Press, 2011.

Ross, Kristin. *May '68 and its Afterlives.* Chicago: University of Chicago Press, 2008.

Seidman, Michael. *Imaginary Revolution: Parisian Students and Workers in 1968.* New York: Berghahn Books, 2006.

8
Italy

Italy's 1968 was both longer and further reaching than any other West European experience, and produced a rich intellectual legacy. In part this comes from the speed of social change in this period, in part from the deep contradictions of Italian society.

One aspect of this complexity is the quasi-colonial relationship constructed during unification, in effect annexing the "South and islands" (Sicily, Sardinia) to the North and brushing aside the popular struggles of cities like Naples. From the later nineteenth century on, Northern industrial capitalism boomed while quasi-feudal relationships persisted in much of the rural South, with bandits resisting the new state's taxes and laws and a constant stream of emigration from the South to the North and the New World.

Up to the near-revolution of 1919–20, the main organizations of northern workers as well as much working-class culture saw the state as representing modernity and enlightenment against a South seen as clerical, ignorant, and racially inferior. Conversely, the rural Southern poor had little independent organizing capacity outside of the clientelist relationships constructed by landowners, priests, and other notables. These different histories cast long shadows in a society with many different local political centers and cultural traditions.

Cutting across these regional and ethnic contrasts were class and political differences. Postwar Italy was "pillarized"; different subcultures each had their own institutions, including mass media, trade unions, political parties, leisure associations, festivals and so on. On the right, the Catholic subculture (including much of the upper class, some rural areas and much of the petty bourgeoisie) had largely supported fascism up to 1943, when the Italian state joined the Western Allies against Benito Mussolini's puppet republic of Salò and the Wehrmacht. After the war, it largely supported the Christian Democrat party, which dominated all governments until the 1990s in arrangements marked by clientelism and corruption. With anti-fascist purges only of the most senior officials, this tradition was deeply conservative and strongly entrenched not only in the church, health, and education, but also in the military, police, and carabinieri and Italy's often semi-independent secret services. Meanwhile a secular-liberal tradition, particularly among the educated classes, sought to stake out an independent position for a modernizing state within a capitalist and NATO framework.

The Italian left was large and complex, rooted in the urban working classes and in strong regional traditions of peasant and small-town radicalism in much of the North. It had dominated resistance to fascism before and after 1943: one of Western Europe's strongest resistances fighting an effective guerrilla war, backed up with strikes, food riots, and an underground press. The orthodox Italian Communist Party (PCI) and its associated trade unions was the largest force here, followed by socialists, anarchists, and smaller numbers of radical democrats and others. Permanently excluded from government, the PCI's acceptance of the Yalta allocation of Italy to the U.S.' sphere of influence and decision not to fight on for a more revolutionary outcome was contested among sections of the working class.

This history left a fundamental problem of legitimacy for a state which claimed its genesis in anti-fascist resistance but was in practice run from the right, often by the same individuals who had administered the fascist state. In 1960, the post-fascist party, Italian Social Movement (MSI), had come close to government and met with a powerful and successful working-class response.

In the 1960s the ground was also shifting under these historical formations of region and culture, not least due to economic development: between 1950 and 1970 per capita income increased faster than anywhere else in Europe. Italian capitalism included some of Europe's most sophisticated producers of the new consumer goods—not least FIAT—with complex workplace hierarchies of managers, engineers, researchers and marketing, alongside large sectors of small-scale production in often low-value-added industries with paternalist power relationships. Massive migration from South to North and from country to city (9 million between 1955 and 1971) meant new generations not yet resigned to the rhythm and discipline of the factory and open to new forms of struggle. Meanwhile cyclical migration to West Germany and elsewhere combined with media images of the U.S.A. and the new pop culture to shape new forms of working-class identity among the young.

Education, with the promise of a position in state employment, had always offered a generational fix displacing some of the problems of the South. The near-doubling of university students between 1959 and 1969 placed huge pressure on the system, while the growth of new technocratic spaces of employment, and the development of subjects such as sociology, opened up new questions for discussion about the social purpose of education. Deeply authoritarian and pedagogically antiquated universities were ill-prepared to meet an expanded student population, both less privileged in their origins and less accepting of their social role.

The struggles of 1968 thus had a double face: a cycle of student activism in 1968 and one of working-class struggle in 1969, arising from different contradictions but in dialogue with one another. Italy's heterogeneity makes a single "national" narrative problematic, but in universities and schools, radical self-organization had developed from 1966, combining occupations and assemblies, challenging both the content and the power relations of the education system and connecting these to conflicts in the wider society. The Battle of Valle Giulia in 1968, when students defeated police in Rome, marked a highpoint, after which the working class increasingly took the stage.

In the workplace, the "hot autumn" of 1969 saw a massive revival in conflict which continued in many areas for much of the next decade. This involved a refusal to restrict demands to pay and conditions alone and a shift to more radical aims and forms of action and organizing within and outside the factory. Strikes and sabotage were combined with demands for radical reductions in the working week or for a single wage for everyone, with rank-and-file organizing winning substantial power within the factory. Unions were able to integrate many of these gains, leaving some activists now turning either to party-building or to struggles outside the workplace.

These conflicts had seen growing independence from the framework of the PCI, particularly after the events in France and Czechoslovakia. The general trend in education, factories, and neighborhoods to bottom-up organizing and direct action entered into dialogue with these new trends within the radical left to form a new "extra-parliamentary left," including Potere Operaio (Workers' Power), Lotta Continua (Continuing Struggle), and the group around the radical newspaper *il manifesto* among many other, often regionally distinctive, groups with tens of thousands of committed activists. Their very closeness to the movements meant that these movements often changed orientation, from Leninist to autonomist or from political parties to activist networks.

In Italy, the "years of lead"—the combination of right-wing violence, lethal state repression and armed struggle—formed less of a spectacular diversion from movements on the ground than in countries like France

Figure 8.1 "Lotta continua" (Continuing Struggle). Banner image from the newspaper of the far left Lotta Continua. 1969.

or West Germany. The "strategy of tension" followed by the far right with the collusion of elements of the security services directly targeted popular movements (over 4,500 incidents from 1969 to 1975). Bombings started in 1969, notably the December bombing in Milan which killed 17 people; December 1970 saw a failed coup involving the far right and military. Police and carabinieri killings of activists at demonstrations and otherwise, meanwhile, were far from uncommon. Together with the state's lack of legitimacy, this helps explain why non-violence was not an issue of principle on the left but rather one of tactics and strategy; "urban guerrilla" actions drew not only on the legitimacy of the Resistance but on family traditions and access to weapons, and often developed around grassroots struggles, not least workplace conflicts.

The attack on established power relations and cultural forms was particularly explosive in Italy, and less easy to absorb within new forms of consumerism. Women's struggles for divorce and abortion, for contraception and childcare, along with struggles for gay and lesbian rights directly challenged the dominant Catholic subculture and were hard to integrate within the conservative reality of much orthodox communist organizing. The "wages for housework" campaign, meanwhile, challenged even broader aspects of capitalist patriarchy.

More broadly, the challenge to hierarchical power relations in education, health, and mental health—here driven first by radical practitioners and then increasingly by patients and user groups—and other branches of the welfare state meant a new form of struggle within workplaces, communities, and services. This went together with an extensive counterculture, in dialogue with Anglo-American peers, going beyond drugs, music, and clothes to environmental struggles (not least after the Seveso chemical disaster of 1976) and radical forms of regional cultural revival.

Unlike most other countries, the cycle of mass participation in struggle continued past the early 1970s, with one movement succeeding another. The massive wave of 1977, responding to recession with new organizing styles, continued the process, whether this is seen as a second peak of the "long 1968" or a new wave of struggles. One reason for the strength and duration of struggles in Italy was the politicization of the Italian working class and the common cause which could be made not only between students and young workers on cultural grounds but between the radical left and older workers on political grounds.

The polycentric nature of Italian politics meant that movements increasingly expressed themselves in a wealth of alternative institutions: most notably "self-organized social centers," large-scale squats acting as activist bases, along with alternative newspapers, pirate radio, guerrilla theater, rent

Figure 8.2 "Workers and Students—Together We Will Win!" Bologna, 1968. Image from Archivio storico Marco Pezzi, Bologna.

strikes, and "auto-reduction" of prices, as well as new forms of working-class and feminist activism.

The struggles of the late 1970s met huge countervailing pressures: the PCI continued its move toward what became the "historical compromise" with Christian Democracy in 1976–8, facilitating a new wave of repression against movements (tanks in Bologna in 1977). Repression intensified after the Red Brigades kidnapped and executed former Prime Minister Aldo Moro in 1978. The right-wing bombing in Bologna in 1980 and the defeat of FIAT workers later that year marked the end of a period in which revolution seemed possible; economic restructuring and right-wing governments with Socialist involvement followed. Yet the scale and depth of movements continued to shape Italian society, and the after-effects of Italy's long 1968 could be felt well into the twenty-first century.

THE SAPIENZA THESES (1967)
Developed Collectively by the Occupiers of
the Sapienza University, Pisa

In early 1967 the Italian student movement was well underway, with actions in secondary schools as well as university occupations. The Gui plan, involving greater restrictions on university entry and higher fees, provided a particular point of reference. In this context the student movement in Pisa, one of the homes of Italian workerism, invited activists from Florence, Bologna, Milan, Cagliari, Turin, Camerino, Siena, Bari, Urbino, and Catania to help formulate a shared analysis. The "Sapienza Theses" critiqued a model of higher education as simply professional training for future employees. The selection here highlights how the movement's organizational structures—assemblies and occupations—were theorized as a model of grassroots democracy. In the short term, the implication was a self-organized movement operating outside the conventional structures of existing student unions. In the longer term, such orientations lent themselves to a wider struggle for democratization within social institutions far beyond the university.

*   *   *

A) The theses

1. These theses are proposed to the faculty assemblies by the delegates who have gathered in Pisa with a mandate from their base in order to clarify the directions of the student movement.

2. They were worked on in the occupied Sapienza in Pisa and, after the rector called the police against the delegates, in the institutes of the occupied faculties.

3. The work took place in an occupied university building, because the base has the right for its representatives to work in the place which more than any other belongs to students. Furthermore, theoretical work has no meaning if it is not put to the test of practice, and practice in this case is the struggle against everything which makes up the present university system, primarily expressed in the Gui plan and the recently passed laws.

4. These theses were developed while we were occupying the Sapienza to protest against the rectors' conference in Pisa [...]

5. The main aspect of the occupation of the Sapienza is not protest, and it would be a mistake to see its achievement as the public relations success created by the police intervention. The main aspect is the theses, and the only way to test to what extent what was done in Pisa was right comes from the base's discussion of the theses.

6. The occupations of university buildings must be institutionalized, and this can be done in the future quite separately from specific reasons for protest. The reasons for this institutionalization are as follows:

    a. The university belongs to the university base [...], and this must be affirmed against the existing structures which deny it;

b. The base and its representatives have to constantly study and discuss the situation and the line of action, and the place for this work is the university;

c. Within the university, we should experiment with the kinds of teaching and research based on group work which current structures prevent and which the base considers indispensable.

7. An essential activity of the movement is the systematic demolition of its opponent's theses, and the practical and theoretical demonstration of its superior rationality.

B) The current state of the movement

8. The movement consists of the assemblies and the students who contribute to the debate and to the practical action promoted by the assemblies.

[...]

"Progetto di Tesi del sindacato studentesco," February 7–11, 1967, republished by the University of Pisa at pisaeil68.unipi.it. Translated by Laurence Cox.

This text reproduces the typed version in the University of Pisa's historical archive, under "Occupazioni 1967–68," file "Pratica provvedimenti disciplinari" (33 pp.) Page 2 includes the following handwritten list of signatories: "Representatives of the assemblies of Letters and Physics at Pisa; Letters, Mathematics, Physics, Two-year Engineering, Biological and Natural Sciences at Florence; Physics and Mathematics at Bologna; Architecture, Milan; delegates from the Assemblies at Cagliari; Presidents of the Representative Organs at Turin and Camerino." These excerpts are a faithful reproduction which respects the original layout.

MANIFESTO FOR A NEGATIVE UNIVERSITY (1967)
Movement for a Negative University/Renato Curcio

The small northeastern town of Trento represented a key site in the development of Italian student radicalism. Up until 1962, sociology had been unavailable in the Italian university: radical Catholic academics then opened an experimental institute for sociology in Trento, which (unlike other university degrees) was open to students with a technical, rather than academic secondary-school education. Trento was the site of two occupations in 1966. The first successfully defended the right to earn a diploma in sociology. The second sought the democratization of the institute and student involvement in deciding the content of their education. The

"Manifesto" would have a powerful impact on the student movement: this first draft, written by Renato Curcio, draws on C. Wright Mills, Max Horkheimer, and the Berkeley Free Speech Movement, as well as Herbert Marcuse, mentioned in this excerpt.

* * *

Ideas for a Negative University

The ideas of the administrators of the present economic-social formation have a falsely dynamic character; or rather, they are qualitatively static and simulatory.

They can be summarized as follows:

A. Maintenance of the status quo (absorption of every potential capable of leading to a qualitative change of the system)
B. Elimination of antagonistic forces, without eliminating the roots of the antagonism, which are the conditions of power. (The contradictions of capitalism remain, but are carefully hidden through a careful effort of manipulation)
C. Unidimensional reduction of thought and political behavior (abandoning the objective aspect of reason, and its simultaneous formalization as a flattening of the contrast between the given and the possible)

The tools used to achieve these goals are, in the last analysis, technical instruments.

The technological apparatus substitutes itself for "terror" in taming centrifugal social forces. Indeed, it provides the groups who use it (own or control) with an immense superiority over the "rest of society."

[...]

University and Society

Today the university presents itself as an organization whose function is to satisfy the various technical needs of society. In other words, it provides the latest instruments in order to bring the organization of domination ever more up to date.

Students, like "things," are reshaped within it in order to fulfil this function tomorrow. The capital invested in the university both enables its existence and imposes a model of development on it, a one-way track which it is impossible to leave. [...]

Within the university, students personify impotence. Like Pavlovian
dogs, they are gradually taught to drool. Their reward will be a profession
(and those who don't learn meet the same fate as damaged goods: they are
not put on the market!)
The process of socialization within the university is complete.
"The student has no place in the university as a human being seeking to
enrich themselves intellectually. On the contrary, they become a mercenary
paid with grades, prestige, and degrees, things which in the future can be
exchanged for ready cash on the labour market."
Society needs the goods produced by the university (the graduate) only
insofar as these goods do not discuss the market.
[...]
Social change, indeed, must be prevented. But can we assume *tout court*
Marcuse's view that "the most characteristic success of advanced industrial
society is precisely its capacity to contain social change, its capacity to
integrate opposites?"
We prefer to formulate the general hypothesis that there is still the *concrete
possibility* for a radical overthrow of developed capitalism through *new forms
of class struggle* internally and externally (national and international) and we
propose the idea of a NEGATIVE UNIVERSITY which within the official
universities affirms the need for theoretical, critical, dialectical, negative
thought; which denounces what the mercenary salespeople call "reason" and
thus lays the basis for political work which is creative, antagonistic, and
alternative.
[...]

Concluding and Provisional Proposals

Utopias—says Marcuse—can be imagined without realism, but not the
necessary conditions for the creation of a free society. We believe that the
negative university must be seen as a necessary stage, and as the principal
political-cultural alternative to the university's further development toward
technocracy.
We believe therefore that the most urgent demands must focus on the
following points:

 – In the short term:

A) Achieving freedom of speech and of the press within the university
B) Achieving freedom of political activity and debate within the
   university

 – In the long term:

A)   Faculties to govern themselves politically and culturally
B)   Administrative control

These goals can only be achieved through a struggle that involves all the "democratic" and "revolutionary" forces of society.

Indeed, the student body cannot be considered equivalent to a "class." [...]

We therefore hold that it is only when the connection between *"revolutionary students"* and *"other revolutionary forces"* is effective and translates into joint actions that the effective conditions will be created for a free University and a non-repressive society.

For this reason we propose the project of a Negative University, which expresses—in new forms within Italian universities—that revolutionary tendency that alone can lead our society from "prehistory" to "History."

Università negativa, new series no. 1, 1967. Archivio Primo Moroni. Translated by Laurence Cox.

THE STRUGGLE CONTINUES (1968)

March 1968 marked the highpoint of the student movement in Italy, after which the initiative would pass increasingly to workplace struggle. By this point students had generalized demonstrations and occupations while conflicts with the police and university authorities were everyday occurrences. On February 29, 1968, the rector had called the police to evict students from the occupied University of Rome. The next day, this leaflet called on students to return. It highlights the unusual fact that the eviction had not been simply a one-way battle with police injuring students, but that students had fought back. When students met police on March 1, they would break through police lines and successfully retake university buildings. This "Battle of Valle Giulia" would become famous both through Paolo Pietrangeli's song, with its refrain "We didn't run away any more," and through the communist Pier Paolo Pasolini's poem, "The PCI to the young," which expressed his support for the police, the "children of the poor," and opposition to the students, who he called "Daddy's children"—the same language that Georges Marchais of the French Communist Party would use against Parisian students two months later.

* * *

YESTERDAY THE POLICE INTERVENED VIOLENTLY TO CHASE THE STUDENTS FROM THE UNIVERSITY: THEY ATTACKED WITH JEEPS; THEY BEAT, CLUBBED, AND INJURED PEOPLE

For the last month in Rome, like everywhere in Italy, the Student Movement has been in struggle, with occupied faculties, discussions, and assemblies in various schools.

Yesterday we were working in the occupied faculties. We were discussing the problems of the student condition. We were organizing the struggle against a situation of subordination and against the authoritarian structure of education. We had achieved a victory: that *exams would be held in the occupied faculties, with supervision and public discussion by all the students.*

Seeing that the Student Movement was *broadening out and growing stronger in struggle,* rather than becoming exhausted and dying of its own accord, the university rector and the government turned to force.

BUT STUDENTS RESPONDED WITH FORCE. This time they reacted, they blocked the circling jeeps with barricades and reaffirmed their decision to continue the struggle and return to the faculties.

But education doesn't start in the university.

The battle has to involve all students, because ALL STUDENTS HAVE TO SAY NO TO THE BOSSES' EDUCATION.

THE STRUGGLE CONTINUES:

THIS MORNING AT 10 AM IN PIAZZA DI SPAGNA

Republished on movimentostudentesco.it. Translated by Laurence Cox.

THE LESSONS OF THE REVOLT IN FRANCE (1968)
Potere Operaio

Potere Operaio here is not the slightly later political group, but a Pisa-based political group organized around the periodical of the same name, which would later form a key base for the formation of Lotta Continua. This text highlights the parallels between the conservative role of the French Communist Party (PCF) and its associated trade union federation (the CGT), and their Italian sister organizations (the PCI and the Italian General Confederation of Labour, CGIL). Along with the call to organize independently at the grassroots—which by mid-1968 was already starting to happen in a range of factories across the industrial North—the call for a new "revolutionary organization to direct the proletarians" is striking in retrospect. The Gestetnered text fit on one side of an A4 page, making it ideal for mass production and distribution at factory gates and elsewhere.

* * *

The revolt which is now breaking out across the whole of France is fundamentally important to us, because it grows out of a situation shared by all the
European countries (i.e. the growing exploitation of the proletarians and the
ever-harsher authoritarianism of the bosses). If today it is exploding in France,
tomorrow it can explode in Italy, in Spain, in Germany, and in England.
A regime which retains the form of parliamentary democracy, but where
decisions are only taken by the big industrialists and finance, whose greatest
representative is de Gaulle. A very harsh incomes policy, with high unemployment, intensified productivity, and the longest average working week in the
ECM [European Common Market] countries (45–46 hours). A class-based
school where one is taught to think what suits the bosses, and where only
bourgeois children complete their studies. The last few months have seen a
constant explosion of working-class struggles, particularly among metal and
textile workers, of department and workshop committees which have formed
spontaneously—struggles organized from *below*, struggles which the trade
unions keep separate and try to extinguish with compromises and defeatist
deals, but which often restart as soon as the agreement has been signed,
with wildcat stoppages, marches inside departments, passive and sometimes
organized forms of sabotaging production. Often particularist struggles turn
into massive struggles in the streets, with fierce battles with the police and
attacks on police stations: at Quimper it is the peasants, at Caen it is the
young metalworkers. Lastly, in Paris, it is the students who, starting from
the struggle to reform education, have quickly arrived at a political language,
a revolutionary one, and at the struggle for socialism. 15,000 demonstrators surround the barricades of the Latin Quarter, tear up the streets with
pneumatic drills and hold off thousands of police in battle gear throughout
the night. The ferocity of the CRS (the French riot police) is incredible:
whole apartment blocks searched using the SS approach, Red Cross first
aid stations assaulted, with doctors and wounded attacked with batons, girls
beaten and stripped in the middle of the street to humiliate them. Then a day
of demonstrations in all the French cities together with the workers (800,000
in Paris), and the regime concedes on the issue of education: amnesty for the
arrested students, freedom to occupy universities and schools, an immediate
start to reforms. But at this point all the working-class categories join the
struggle: the factories are occupied, transport shuts down, electricity and gas
are at the bare minimum. This is the *total paralysis of the country*. The workers'
committees, the real leaders of the struggle, multiply, with youth in the lead.
In many factories management has been taken prisoner; at Sud Aviation the
office doors were even welded shut, and management was fed through the
windows. The movement is still growing, and returning to the streets: while
general de Gaulle tries to propose the old referendum trick, Paris and other
cities fill up with barricades, and *on the barricades students and workers fight*

with an ever more explosive violence, which is destined to grow and will not be easily smothered. In the countryside the peasants are starting to move, they block the streets with tractors, cut down the telegraph poles, threaten to enter into the heart of the struggle. In the face of all this, the official organizations of the workers' movement, led by the PCF, keep talking about reforms and democracy, disavow the "extremists" and the "anarchists" who lead the student movement; the trade union bureaucrats stop the students in front of the Renault works saying loud and clear that they don't want to hear about revolution, that they want improvements to pay and conditions only; in Lyon they refuse to send pickets to strengthen the barricades, but the workers go anyway. Two national leaders of the CGT (the left-wing trade union federation) resign in protest against the treason of the CGT leadership, which clings to minimal issues of redistribution while the revolt catches fire across the country.

ALTHOUGH THE WORKERS' STRUGGLES ARE LED FROM BELOW, BY THE GRASSROOTS WORKERS' COMMMITTEES, ALTHOUGH EVER MORE WORKERS ARE COMING INTO THE STREETS TO FIGHT BESIDE THE STUDENTS, *THERE IS NO REVOLUTIONARY ORGANIZATION TO DIRECT THE PROLETARIANS TOWARD THE DESTRUCTION OF THE BOURGEOIS STATE AND TOWARD A SOCIALIST SOCIETY.*

[...]

THE REVOLT WHICH IS EXPLODING IN FRANCE IS FULL OF LESSONS FOR US.

IF WE WANT THINGS TO CHANGE, WE HAVE TO RADICALIZE OUR STRUGGLE AGAINST THE BOSSES, AND WORK TOGETHER TO FREE IT FROM BEING BRAKED AND CAGED BY THE REFORMIST PARTIES. TO DO THIS, WE HAVE TO ORGANIZE AT THE GRASSROOTS, BRANCH BY BRANCH, FACTORY BY FACTORY, SCHOOL BY SCHOOL.

IF WE WANT THINGS TO CHANGE COMPLETELY, WE HAVE TO HAVE THE CLARITY AND THE COURAGE TO SAY OPENLY THAT OUR GOAL IS REVOLUTION AND TO WORK FROM THIS PERSPECTIVE.

THE COMRADES OF POTERE OPERAIO

Republished on nelvento.net. Translated by Laurence Cox.

ONE YEAR LATER: PRAGUE STANDS ALONE (1969)
Lucio Magri

il manifesto *started as the voice of the dissident left within the PCI, published briefly in 1969 before their expulsion. The party leadership had condemned the*

1968 invasion of Czechoslovakia but remained aligned with Moscow, while operating an increasingly moderate line within Italian politics. The manifesto *left were less concerned with these* raisons d'état *and more with supporting radical and working-class struggles, whether this disrupted rapprochement with the Italian state or loyalty to the Soviet Union. This call for the working-class overthrow of the Soviet leadership represented a challenge which led to their exclusion from the PCI. This editorial shows an international perspective as an organic aspect of politics rather than, as at times in 1968, a rhetorical flourish aimed at a national audience.* il manifesto *became a political organization briefly but continued as a daily newspaper close to social movement struggles, still in existence today despite many changes.*

*   *   *

Czechoslovakia no longer evokes any real emotion. A few newspaper headlines and sonorous declarations from the leaders are not enough to hide this acceptance of the given situation.

Everyone is playing their own angle, trying to gain the greatest advantage or suffer the least damage from what is happening in Prague, without feeling they have to think or to act. This is true for all political forces, including the left. For years they have shared the expectation of a gradual but effective "democratic" evolution of Soviet society and the other European socialisms, under the pressure of economic development and through the actions of their leaderships. No one expects great ruptures, in one direction or the other. This conviction goes back to 1956.

[...]

Togliatti, who fell for the euphoria of the Twentieth Congress less than any other, was the first to recognize the possibility of steps backward and of rips in the fabric, but still within a positive overall direction. The formula of "unity in diversity" was derived from this conviction, to which Czechoslovakia's "new course" in 1968 brought undeniable support. It is true that it constituted a new and dramatic denunciation of the past, twelve years after the Twentieth Congress, and thus cast a shadow of doubt on the progress made in the meantime. And it is true that it expressed contradictory forces and centrifugal pressures and could thus entail the danger of a capitulation to the West. But once again this was a renewal pushed by the Communists and directed by their leading group. Thus it seemed to show that in that party and in that country, despite the mistakes which had been made, there was a wealth of people and ideas that could guarantee a constant correction of the process of renewal. And, in fact, within a few months working-class and popular participation was replacing the technocratic and third-force hegemony of the "new course" with a different and far richer inspiration.

218 VOICES OF 1968

The military intervention of August 1968 was a rude awakening. [...] There was still the pride, the good sense, the "socialist" character of Prague's resistance. One could still see, in the first months after the invasion, the expression of a political potential, of a social maturity which the party, or part of it, could still have held, up to a certain point: in other words, the existence of a line, losing for now but which could have recovered once Soviet pressure was lifted. When the Italian Communists condemned the Soviet intervention without starting a radical discussion about the direction of the current leading group of the U.S.S.R. and the Warsaw Pact countries, they were still betting, with some justification, on this last card.

The End of the "New Course"

1969 now forces us to reconsider. What is striking in the Czechoslovak events since April is the definitive liquidation of the forces which gave birth to the "new course." If mass resistance continues, however, it seems to lack a political expression or perspective.

[...]

Two Alternatives

One point seems fixed: the fragility of the technocratic alternative, and its offshoots in the intellectual opposition. These may be too weak, too tied to their own privileges or too subordinated to capitalist ideology to direct a block of progressive forces. They seek, and sometimes they find, mass support on the basis of incentives for consumption, but they are fated to break with it around the organization of work and democracy. [...]

A contrasting alternative had been sketched out precisely in the Czechoslovak experience: that based on the workers and the progressive, radical wing of the intellectuals. It is from here that the explosion of participation and of the maturity of the masses came, their natural hostility to privilege, their unexpected capacity for elaborating ideas and self-organization.

[...]

The real challenge for these countries, having now reached a certain level of development, is the same we have to face in the West: a radical discourse about inequality, direct democracy, overcoming individualism and alienated work, the critique of bourgeois science and technology, but in forms suited to societies which are now developed, complex, rich in individuality, capable of using the whole heritage of knowledge and capacities accumulated in centuries of struggle for the emancipation of humanity. [...]

For Resistance

The first point is a clear position toward the political choices of the leading groups of the U.S.S.R. and the other European socialist countries. It is no longer possible to hope for them to correct themselves: we have to aim for their defeat and their replacement, by a new block of social forces directed by the working class, a socialist renewal which challenges the political structures and is capable of genuinely expressing the enormous possibilities unleashed by the October Revolution. [...]

The Western proletariat has only one way to become a point of global reference, an active and effective moment of internationalism: to carry forward its own revolution; to become capable of proposing a different kind of socialism because it is bringing it about. The discussion of Czechoslovakia thus brings us back to Italy. With a new awareness: that if the crisis which is now open in the West closes again with a defeat or a non-event, we would pay with a severe retreat on the whole international revolutionary front. There is perfect coherence between those who forgive Brezhnev's politics and those who ask us for a policy of compromise. If the Communists in the West enter into this, we can only expect a conservative freezing in the socialist societies. It would be the internationalization of resignation.

il manifesto, September 4, 1969, 3–5. Translated by Laurence Cox.

AS WE WORK, WE WORKERS PRODUCE CAPITAL: HOW WE REPRODUCE CAPITAL'S RULE OVER OURSELVES (1969)
Workers' Committee of Porto Marghera

Porto Marghera near Venice was one of Italy's leading industrial zones, with 35,000 workers mainly in the chemical industry. During the long 1968 it was well known for its political activism. The reference here to Gianni Agnelli, head of FIAT, shows the connections with struggles in Turin, not least via Potere Operaio, active in Porto Marghera since 1963. This does not mean that these ideas are simply intellectual imports: self-educated activists in the Workers' Committee like Italo Sbrogiò—described by Toni Negri as his "Virgil," introducing him to working-class activism—had their own traditions of struggle and ways of reading the world, reflected in the pamphlet's conversational style and reference to key moments in working-class popular memory. The argument is closely linked to actual workplace struggles, such as the struggle to reduce working time (and maintain or increase pay) rather than use increased productivity to sack workers (and increase profits).

*   *   *

What does it mean to destroy the bosses' power? Who are the bosses and what do they want?

These seem stupid questions, but in fact they are fundamental in order to establish what our political line should be against them.

What we have to say first of all is that the cliché that the boss exploits the workers to get richer is wrong. This aspect certainly exists, but the bosses' wealth is in no way proportional to their power.

For example Agnelli, relative to the cars he produces, should go around wearing gold, but he is happy with his boat and his private plane—things which another boss, with a factory much smaller than FIAT's, can easily afford. What interests Agnelli is to keep and develop his power, which coincides with the development and growth of capitalism. In other words, capitalism is an impersonal system and capitalists act as its agents, to such a point that bosses are no longer even necessary for capitalism (in Russia, for example, there is capitalism without capitalists). What shows the presence of capitalism in Russia is the presence of profit. We must overthrow a social system which forces people to work. This should also be the yardstick for evaluating the experiences of the Chinese and Cuban revolutions.

Capitalism is fundamentally oriented, above all, to preserve this power relation against the working class and uses its development to reinforce this power even more.

This means that all the machines, the technological innovations, the development of industries, the very under-development of some areas, are used to control the working class politically.

Some examples of this capitalist behavior have become classic. For example, the introduction of the assembly line around the 1920s was a response to the revolutionary wave which shook the world in the years immediately after the First World War.

The goal was to make the kind of skilled working class which had made the Russian Revolution in '17 and the movement of factory councils across the whole of Europe disappear.

[...]

We must impose the working-class logic, according to which many kinds of machines must be invented in order to continually reduce working time to the point where it tends to disappear. At this point we can no longer talk about socialism. Socialism is what exists in Russia (a new organization of work), but the workers don't want this: the workers want to work less and less until there is no real compulsion to work.

When everyone is freed from the necessity to work, because they can feed themselves, clothe themselves and fulfil their desires without working, then there will be freedom! We believe that even today, with the technology that exists, many such things which sound like science fiction could be achieved. [...]

But what are the means for abolishing all this? We must break the mechanism of control that capital has set up for the workers. Nobody can predict the concrete actions through which this break will occur, let alone answer the questions of those who ask us what we want to replace that which we must destroy.

This is not the real problem. In none of the great revolutions of history did people know a priori what would replace that which was being overthrown, because the changes in people's character in the relationships between the classes go so deep in revolutionary periods that they make any historical prediction impossible.

[...]

Because of this we say that the workers are against society, in that society is entirely structured against them. The working class' struggle is indeed, as we have seen, the primary incentive for capitalism's development. Think of the French May, where small factories went into crisis because of the wage raises workers achieved through their revolutionary struggle—and this favored the concentration of capital and the development of monopoly. Think of the Soviet Union, where the revolution of '17 accelerated capitalist development so much as to transform a backward country like Tsarist Russia into one of the world's most powerful capitalist countries. In short, capitalism is a power which reproduces itself beyond the best intentions of individuals.

Republished on chicago86.org. Translated by Laurence Cox.

COMMUNIQUÉ NO. 3 (1970)
Red Brigade

Violence from police, carabinieri, and fascists was a common experience in Italy. In 1969–70, activists from various left groups, including Renato Curcio, started to collaborate, initially as the "Metropolitan Political Collective" and subsequently as the "Red Brigades" (BR). One of several armed struggle organizations, these began as autonomous local groups closely connected to movements (hence the singular.) The huge Pirelli rubber plant in Milan was a center of workplace struggle, with coordinated go-slows and other innovative tactics combined with bottom-up organizing. This statement following an action at Pirelli is notable both for the detailed information involved—showing real shop floor links—but also the general tone of humor and confidence. This "armed struggle"—burning two cars—came a year after a right-wing bomb in Milan had killed 17 people. Subsequently the Brigades would be less connected to popular struggles, culminating with the 1978 kidnapping and execution of former Prime Minister Aldo Moro.

* * *

Della Torre, mechanic

A good comrade: one of our own, 50 years old, 2 children. A leading organizer in the CGIL. 25 years of trade union activity. A partisan commander. He drove the struggles. They fired him. They did it together: first the bosses, then the unions. This sacking matters to us all. It is not a private matter: IT IS A COWARDLY POLITICAL LINE which aims to affect all workers in struggle.

If this goes through without a determined response from the whole factory, united, if it goes through on the basis of a cheap surrender by the trade unions and at our expense, Pirelli and Co. will have the green light, from now on, to get rid of whoever lifts their head to assert their rights.

In the first communiqué we distributed, we said "For every comrade they strike during the struggle, one of them will have to pay."

A comrade has been struck.

And so one of them, more precisely "the first one on the list" (as many workers in the factory suggested) has found his car destroyed.

But it is not over.

In fact we said "two eyes for an eye," and the spy *Ermanno Pellegrini's* [FIAT] 850 … is for us much, much less than an eye. Without taking into account that his real car is a white Giulia 1300 Junior GT which he has "inexplicably" kept carefully guarded in his garage for a while now.

But we are patient …!

Unless the spy Pelligrini RESIGNS; then the People's Tribunal might grant him a pardon. In any case Della Torre has to come back, come back to work to continue the struggle of all the exploited against the bosses.

Whip-rounds, lawyers kindly offered by the union, charity, aren't enough. Therefore until Della Torre is back with us, the contest between all of us workers and the boss' servants and petty tyrants mustn't finish and won't finish. The list is a long one, and we aren't short of imagination.

For the communist revolution.

RED BRIGADE

Originally issued December 1, 1970, republished in *Re Nudo* 4, April 1971. Translated by Laurence Cox.

FIRST DOCUMENT (1971)
Padua Women's Struggle Movement/Mariarosa Dalla Costa

This "first document" was written by the activist and theorist Mariarosa Dalla Costa as the basis for discussions which led to the foundation of a feminist group in Padua. The "Women's Struggle" group would soon become "Feminist Struggle" (Lotta Femminista). Dalla Costa developed an original perspective through her encounters with Toni Negri and Selma James, but also from her activism in Potere Operaio with the working-class housewives of Porto Marghera. All this enabled her to develop a new theoretical and political approach, linked to the women's struggles starting to develop across Italy. She would later rework this text as "Women and the Subversion of the Community," the key essay in The Power of Women and the Subversion of the Community *(written with Selma James in 1971). In 1972 Dalla Costa co-founded the International Feminist Collective with Selma James, Silvia Federici, and Brigitte Galtier, launching the wages for housework movement on an international scale.*

*   *   *

These observations attempting to define and analyse the "women's question" locate this very question within the "women's role" which the capitalist division of labor has produced.

In these pages we stress the figure of the "housewife" as the central figure of this role, assuming that fundamentally all the women who work outside the home also continue to be housewives.

In order to do this, it was indispensable first of all to analyse briefly how capital has produced the family and within it the housewife, destroying the kind of family group or community that existed previously. [...]

In recent years, particularly in the advanced countries, a series of women's movements have developed, with different connotations ranging from seeing the women's question as located within an atavistic struggle of man against woman understood as a struggle between species, to the women's question as a specific articulation of class exploitation.

Hence, although (especially for women who have had or have the experience of activism within the overall political struggle) the first of these positions seems generally ridiculous, I feel it worth noting that these women, who are part of the overall women's movement, constitute an extremely important indicator to understand the exasperation which many women have arrived at, within and outside the movement.

They themselves define their lesbianism in these terms (I am referring to what has been said at the movement's congresses in England and the U.S.): "It is not that women attract us more than men, but that we cannot put up with relationships with men any more."

Now to understand this exasperation we must see clearly how, if in precapitalist society women's autonomy was (like men's) more or less compromised by the overall conditions of production, never before have the conditions of production destroyed women's autonomy so absolutely as in capitalist society.

In other words, in precapitalist society the woman, like the other members of the family or the group she lived in, took part in social production and her work was *always skilled*—insofar as there was no wage, her position was not substantially different or separate from the man's. The advent of capitalist production expelled her from social production.

Capital destroyed the family and the community as the productive center; on the one hand, this moved and centered all social production in the factories and offices. On the other hand, it essentially removed men from the family, making them *waged workers*, while it placed women, children, the old, and the unwaged sick behind them; and more exactly from that moment it sent *children* to school. In this sense the earlier family or community ceased not only to be a productive center but also an educational center. *Children* were separated from *adults*, as *men* were separated from *women*.

[...]

The analyses of school which have emerged in the last few years, particularly with the arrival of the student movement, have well understood the school as a place of ideological discipline and the formation of labor power.

What perhaps has never come out, or at least not fully, is precisely what comes before all this, which is the *desperate crying* of children on the first day of *creche* when they find themselves left in a classroom and their parents leave.

And yet the whole story of school starts precisely here.

[...]

But something is happening in the newest cohorts of children and older kids, meaning that explaining to them when you become an adult is ever harder. Because it is them who are explaining things to us: six-year-old children have already fought against police dogs. In the South of Italy, revolts have always seen children do the same as adults.

[...]

At this point, if instead we denounce housework as productive work, a series of questions arise around the goals of the struggle and the forms of struggle.

The immediate demand which would follow from this—in other words *pay us a wage*—runs the risk of appearing to want to institutionalize the condition of slavery which was produced together with the condition of housewife and thus hardly to work as a mobilizing demand—even leaving aside the few illusions we can have about a domestic wage corresponding other than symbolically, given that those economists who have paid most attention to the oddities of today's movements have estimated the level of such wages at around 150 billion [lire].

The challenge is thus to follow forms of struggle which do not simply leave housewives alone in the home, at most available for the odd demonstration in town, waiting for a wage which would never pay for anything—forms of struggle which immediately break this whole structure of domestic work, directly refusing it, refusing to be housewives and refusing the home as a ghetto for one's own existence. Because the problem is not so much and not only to stop doing all this work, but to break this role.

[...]

Precisely because all capitalist organization presupposes the home, every site of struggle *outside* the home is vulnerable to a possible attack by women: factory assemblies or student assemblies for example are just as much legitimate sites of women's struggle and thus of encounter or conflict if one wants between women and men, each as individuals, not as mummy, daddy and child—with all the possibilities this represents to blow up the contradictions, the repressions, the frustrations which capital has sought to accumulate within the family.

[...]

Archivio di Lotta femminista per il salario al lavoro domestico, Donazione Mariarosa Dalla Costa, Biblioteca Civica di Padova, no. 1, series 1, section 1. Translated by Laurence Cox.

Further Reading

Balestrini, Nanni. *The Unseen.* Translated by Liz Heron. London: Verso, 2011.

Catanzaro, Raimondo, ed. *The Red Brigades and Left-Wing Terrorism in Italy.* London: Pinter Publishers, 1991.

Edwards, Phil. *More Work! Less Pay!: Rebellion and Repression in Italy, 1972–77.* Oxford: Manchester University Press, 2017.

Ginsborg, Paul. *A History of Contemporary Italy: Society and Politics, 1943–1988.* Basingstoke: Palgrave Macmillan, 2003.

Ginzburg, Carlo. *The Judge and the Historian: Marginal Notes on a Late-Twentieth Century Miscarriage of Justice.* London: Verso, 2002.

Hilwig, Stuart J. *Italy and 1968: Youthful Unrest and Democratic Culture.* Basingstoke: Palgrave Macmillan, 2009.

Lotringer, Sylvère and Christian Marazzi, eds. *Autonomia: Post-Political Politics.* Los Angeles: Semiotext(e), 2007.

Lumley, Robert. *States of Emergency: Cultures of Revolt in Italy from 1968 to 1978.* London: Verso, 1990.

Magri, Lucio. *The Tailor of Ulm: Communism in the Twentieth Century.* Translated by Patrick Camiller. London: Verso, 2011.

Passerini, Luisa. *Autobiography of a Generation: Italy, 1968.* Translated by Lisa Erdberg. Middletown, CT: Wesleyan University Press, 1996.

Portelli, Alessandro. *The Battle of Valle Giulia: Oral History and the Art of Dialogue.* Madison: University of Wisconsin Press, 1997.

Rossanda, Rossana. *The Comrade From Milan.* Translated by Romy Giuliani Clard. London: Verso, 2010.

Wright, Steve. *Storming Heaven: Class Composition and Struggle in Italian Autonomist Marxism,* second edition. London: Pluto Press, 2017.

Zamponi, Lorenzo. *Social Movements, Memory and Media: Narrative in Action in the Italian and Spanish Student Movements.* London: Palgrave, 2018.

9
Britain

By the 1950s, Britain was well on its way to postwar recovery. In the immediate aftermath of the war, a resurgent left built a welfare state that included the National Health Service, expansion of secondary and higher education, and developments in pensions, public housing, and welfare. Rationing formally ended in 1954, unemployment was brought under control, and new consumer goods found their way into shops across the country. As elsewhere in Western Europe, Britain awoke to a new age of affluence. In 1957, Prime Minister Harold MacMillan could boast that "our people have never had it so good."

Despite these real successes, life in postwar Britain was not without its anxieties. No one could ignore the relative decline of British power. Once the greatest modern empire, ruling over 150 million lives after World War II, by the early 1960s the British empire was in full crisis, as colony after colony asserted its independence.

Ruined after the war, deprived of its empire, and sandwiched by the new Cold War, Britain's future in the world seemed uncertain. The Suez debacle in 1956, in which the United States threatened to punish Britain for invading Egypt without consulting the White House, revealed Britain's clear subordination to the United States, now the leading capitalist economic power.

The British economy, though still strong, was not what it once was. The preeminent economic power of the nineteenth century, Britain now struggled to keep pace with its neighbors, like West Germany, France, and Italy, which saw much more robust growth rates. Britain's share of the world market continued to shrink, the government borrowed heavily, and the pound sterling came under significant pressure.

Moreover, despite the incredible changes of the postwar years, the stuffy atmosphere of the past continued to cast a long shadow into the early 1960s. As Labour leader Harold Wilson explained, the British were now "living in the jet age," but still "governed by an Edwardian establishment mentality." In response, he called for a "new Britain." In 1964, the Labour Party won a narrow parliamentary victory after 13 years of opposition, giving Wilson his chance to put his vision into practice.

Once in power, the Labour Party embarked on a broad program of social democratic modernization that encouraged state ownership, indicative planning, and scientific research. The consumer society continued to grow, with nearly nine out of ten British citizens owning television sets in the 1960s. In addition, Labour passed a wave of progressive legislation, in some respects not unlike the Great Society in the United States at the same time. It rapidly expanded the educational system, abolished the death penalty in 1965, ended the indictment of homosexuals in 1967, legalized limited abortion the same year, and ended censorship.

Yet Labour fell short. Wilson's economic policies did not mark a radical break with the past. Although Labour remained committed to reducing wealth inequality, 10 percent of the United Kingdom's population still possessed around 80 percent of all personal wealth in the 1960s. The push to broaden educational opportunities generated social mobility but not equality of outcomes. While the Labour Party paid lip service to leftist ideals, when it came to foreign policy, Britain remained a loyal American ally in the Cold War, vocally supporting the U.S. war in Vietnam. Even its social reforms were limited. The age of consent remained higher for non-heterosexuals, racism pervaded British society, women's opportunities were still relatively limited, and mainstream culture had not noticeably liberalized. It was in this context that Britain witnessed a wave of contestatory politics beginning in the mid-1960s.

To be sure, this wave was made possible by several earlier movements. The first was the formation of a New Left in the wake of the Soviet invasion of Hungary in 1956, which tried to create the intellectual foundations for a different kind of leftist politics. One of its leading voices was the *New Left Review*, whose first editor was Stuart Hall. In addition to the new intellectual ferment, the late 1950s and early 1960s saw the rise of youth subcultures, a few of them working class, that challenged mainstream society, making possible the subsequent counterculture. Lastly, social movements of the late 1950s, the most important of which were the Campaign for Nuclear Disarmament (CND) and the direct action-oriented Committee of 100, also set a precedent for a new round of activism. This anti-nuclear activism provided a crucial bridge to the more radical movements of the late 1960s. In fact, many of the activists of the later antiwar movement had cut their teeth in the CND.

Activism in the later 1960s focused on several core issues, but universities—with a new generation of students from less privileged backgrounds—were central. Although less militant than in Italy, West Germany, or later France, the British student movement saw its fair share of radical actions, especially at the London School of Economics. Here, protests, sit-ins, pickets, and even a hunger strike broke out when the administration suspended two student activists for organizing a demonstration against the new director's ties to Ian Smith's racist regime in Rhodesia, one of Britain's former colonies.

Another major source of discontent was the cultural conformity of the period. In response, British youth spearheaded one of the most vibrant counterculture scenes in Europe. What became known as the "underground" developed not only an alternative way of dressing, behaving, and being together, but a rich ecosystem of publications, such as *International Times*, an art magazine with columns on drugs and homosexuality. In the 1960s London became a global countercultural capital, and British music, art, literature, and theater spread far and wide.

The Vietnam War figured as one of the most divisive issues of the time. Although Britain did not send combat troops, the government did lend both logistical and rhetorical support. Opposition to Britain's role in the war gave rise to several antiwar organizations, such as the Communist-affiliated British Council for Peace in Vietnam, and the more radical Vietnam Solidarity Campaign (VSC). In the late 1960s, the VSC organized a series of actions, including a militant demonstration at the American Embassy on Grosvenor Square in London on March 17, 1968, and a massive demonstration on October 27, 1968.

Racism represented another dimension of Britain's post-colonial hangover. Between 1961 and 1964, Britain's Black population grew from about 300,000 to 1 million. Anti-immigrant sentiment gained ground,

Figure 9.1   Front page of the Left paper Black Dwarf. June 1, 1968.

perhaps best captured by the popularity of Conservative MP Enoch Powell's infamous "Rivers of Blood" speech. In this context, immigrants set to work building an anti-racist movement. The Campaign Against Racial Discrimination, founded in 1964, fought the discriminatory legislation and social inequality that immigrants, or children of immigrants, from the country's former colonies, confronted. The anti-racist movement would develop a more radical current, unsurprisingly heavily influenced by Black Power in the United States.

The linkages were deep. In 1965, Malcolm X traveled to London, where he met Michael de Freitas, a Trinidadian-born activist who soon adopted the name Michael X and went on to found the Racial Adjustment Action Society. In 1966, Nigerian-born playwright Obi Egbuna visited the United States, met American Black radicals, and returned home to found Britain's first self-declared Black Power movement, the Universal Coloured People's Association in 1967. That same year, Stokely Carmichael traveled to Britain for the Dialectics of Liberation conference. By the late 1960s and early 1970s, Britain boasted several Black radical groups, including the British Black Panthers, formed by Egbuna in 1968, and the Black Unity and Freedom Party.

The anti-racist movement ran alongside a revival of feminism in Britain. As elsewhere, women's liberation in Britain was very heterogeneous in terms of ideology, campaign issues, and forms of struggle. One of the most significant actions was a three-week long strike in 1968. Sewing machinists at Ford Motor Company's Dagenham plant in London staged a walkout in response to their grading as "less skilled" and thus paid less than their male colleagues. The strike would lead to the formation of the National Joint Action Campaign Committee for Women's Equal Rights and, eventually, to the Equal Pay Act 1970.

As in most other countries reviewed in this book, the 1970s in Britain witnessed the flowering social movements centering on gay liberation,

Figure 9.2   Black Power march in West London. 1970. Courtesy of The National Archives UK.

environmentalism, and animal rights, to name only a few. A small number of British radicals turned to armed struggle, such as the anarchist Angry Brigade. Meanwhile, the developing war in Northern Ireland was also felt in Britain, not least through anti-imperialist activism tied to the Irish immigrant population.

The 1970s was also a decade of growing labor militancy. In 1972, the National Union of Mineworkers went on a national strike for a pay raise. The action ended in victory, emboldening the labor movement, and initiating a long decade of labor activism. This activism, coupled with the oil shocks, soaring inflation, and the unraveling of the postwar Fordist compromise would create a crisis of capitalism. But as in the United States, it was not the radical left that ultimately benefited from this breakdown, but a new right under the leadership of Margaret Thatcher.

WHY VIETNAM SOLIDARITY? POLICY STATEMENT BY THE INTERNATIONAL COUNCIL OF THE VIETNAM SOLIDARITY CAMPAIGN (1966)

Britain's vocal support for the American War in Vietnam galvanized antiwar sentiment in the country. The most dynamic of the British antiwar organizations was the Vietnam Solidarity Campaign (VSC), founded in June 1966. Organized by radicals, and backed by the philosopher Bertrand Russell, the VSC organized several actions in the late 1960s. Below, we reproduce the VSC's founding policy statement. As against the more moderate antiwar organizations of the time, which preached neutrality, the VSC called for active solidarity with the National Liberation Front of South Vietnam as well as North Vietnam in their joint struggle against the United States. For the VSC, antiwar activism meant a commitment to criticizing British complicity, building international solidarity, and recognizing the Vietnamese people's right to self-determination.

* * *

Preface

The Vietnam Solidarity Campaign has only been in existence a few months but in that short time it has provoked a wide political discussion. For the first time in the left wing and peace press there has been a discussion as to what attitude the antiwar movement in this country should take to the national liberation struggle. We have received a very wide measure of support and sympathy from many sections of the movement. On the other hand some well-meaning people have felt themselves unable to take a solidarity position because they felt that this meant being in favour of prolonging the war. Others have felt that the only correct moral position to take is that of neutrality. More weighty arguments have come from those who argue that taking a solidarity position narrows the scope of opposition and thus makes it less effective.

The Vietnam Solidarity Campaign is convinced that, on the contrary, all those who oppose the war in Vietnam are morally bound to take a solidarity position. We are convinced, moreover, that this is the most effective way to oppose the war in Vietnam, that the existence of a powerful solidarity movement will stiffen all resistance to the American war of aggression. Having said this we do not dismiss lightly the arguments of those who take a different view. These vital questions will only be resolved by a thorough and detailed discussion. It is to this end that this pamphlet is devoted. [...]

The Basis of the Solidarity Campaign

The Vietnam Solidarity Campaign is the only campaign in Britain which seeks to build a united front of organizations and individuals offering full support to the Vietnamese people in their struggle against foreign aggression and domination.

We are a united front of individuals and groups, holding diverse political views and diverse estimates of the world political situation, but we unite together to declare our solidarity with the Vietnamese people because we judge their struggle to expel the foreign forces of the United States and its allies to be a wholly just struggle deserving of our full support. In other words, we base our solidarity with the Vietnamese, and with their organs and organizations of struggle, the National Liberation Front and the Democratic Republic of Vietnam, on the unconditional defense of the Vietnamese people's right to self-determination, to choose their own programs, their own leaders, their own organizations, to pursue their own national destiny, free from foreign intervention and aggression. [...]

We hold that a just solution to the Vietnamese war is the unconditional withdrawal of the aggressor's forces, the removal of his military bases from Vietnam, and the restoration of Vietnamese sovereignty to the Vietnamese people. *We are ready therefore to support any and only those conditions for peace which are acceptable to the Vietnamese themselves, to the Democratic Republic of Vietnam, and the National Liberation Front.* [...]

The Campaign's Attitude Toward the Existing Antiwar Movement in Britain

The Vietnam Solidarity Campaign has been organized because no other group in Britain has sought to build a united front of support for the

Democratic Republic of Vietnam and the National Liberation Front, based on the principle of self-determination.

The principle of self-determination is a fundamental democratic right which has been fought for by all oppressed people; it is the foundation stone of any just international order, and the most basic legal element in the structure of any stable international peace. Yet, the major existing antiwar organizations in Britain have each consistently compromised this principle with respect to the war in Vietnam. They have thereby weakened the antiwar struggle, both with respect to Vietnam in general, and they have as a consequence strengthened the position of the aggressor.

Whereas the main demand now advanced by the American antiwar movement is unconditional withdrawal of U.S. forces from Vietnam, the demand still put forward by British peace organizations is that negotiations between the parties be opened. It is precisely this call to *both* sides to negotiate, however, that compromises the basic principle of self-determination. For to demand that both parties to the conflict stop fighting is to equate the struggle for liberty and self-determination with the criminal actions of the aggressor. [...]

The history of appeasement in the thirties (also through negotiations) provides an awful lesson to those who would deny to small countries full support in their resistance to aggression. We who have joined together to form the Vietnam Solidarity Campaign are persuaded that solidarity with the Democratic Republic of Vietnam and the National Liberation Front now is not only the sole just and moral position to take with respect to this particular war, but that it is the only hope of preserving *world* peace as well.

Join the Vietnam Solidarity Campaign

The Vietnam Solidarity Campaign brings together representatives of those in Britain who have consistently and energetically combatted successive governments' support of American aggression.

Our President is *Bertrand Russell*; and our Chairman, *Ralph Schoenman*. [...]

If you wish to support the struggle of the Vietnamese people, your place is in the Vietnam Solidarity Campaign. [...]

Retrieved from the Red Mole Rising Archive: redmolerising.wordpress.com/vietnam-solidarity-campaign.

THE OCCUPATION OF LSE (1968)
Dave Slaney

England saw its own share of university actions in the long 1968. As elsewhere, the student movement was closely intertwined with other struggles, above all the antiwar movement. In fact, the two often overlapped in terms of people, ideology, and physical space. This was clearly seen in the occupation of the London School of Economics (LSE), which took place in conjunction with a mass antiwar demonstration on October 27, 1968. With nearly 100,000 people marching, it was the largest demonstration in postwar Britain to that date. Below, we publish a report on the occupation from the Vietnam Solidarity Campaign's Bulletin, *which described the occupation as, among other things, a kind of "socialist experience" that affected everyone involved.*

* * *

On Thursday, October 24, students of LSE began to occupy their school in open and explicit solidarity with the National Liberation Front of South Vietnam. The school was kept open until the evening of October 27, after the demonstration, in spite of the attempt of the Director to close it. As an example of local action on the issue of Vietnam, the occupation deserves at least a brief analysis.

The occupation, as originally conceived, had three purposes. The first was to mobilize the maximum number of students in LSE for the demonstration on the 27th. The second was to make available to the demonstration and the demonstrators whatever physical assets LSE had to offer. And the third was to increase the level of consciousness of LSE students. All of these purposes were achieved, but with varying degrees of success. [...]

The third purpose in occupying the school was well realized. This occupation and the debate surrounding it, provided an opportunity for intensive political education. At the largest students' union meeting ever held at LSE (1,200 students came to discuss the occupation), the case for the occupation was put with tolling arguments. Speakers related Vietnam to LSE (directly, by pointing out the complicity of some of the Governors; and indirectly, by showing that the ideas and theories taught at the LSE mystified and obscured the real causes of the Vietnam war, supported by the status-quo of imperialistic neo-capitalism, and hence perpetuated a system in which Vietnams are inevitable.) Speakers argued that the issue at LSE was the same as that in Vietnam: do people have the right to control their own lives and their own institutions? If people opposed American aggression in Vietnam (and no one at the LSE has ever publicly supported it) then they must do all they can to convert pious resolutions of opposition into active expressions of solidarity. It was our school, and we should use it to express our feelings. At the end of the meeting, 600 students supported this radical program.

Events then conspired to reinforce the lessons learned at the union meeting. On Friday morning, the director, acting in the name of the Court of Governors, attempted to close the school. The administration had exposed itself; it showed that it, and not the students, was the small and dangerous minority. By its arbitrary and revealing action, the administration convinced hundreds of doubting students of the correctness of the occupation. By the time the occupation was over, students had increased their awareness of the nature of capitalist society and of the role of LSE in that society. Support for the Vietnamese in their struggle against American aggression became more meaningful as it was linked with the students' own struggle within the LSE.

The final success of the occupation is less tangible than those successes listed above, but it is perhaps the most important. It concerns the effect which the occupation had upon those who took part. To have been inside LSE during that weekend was to participate in a socialist experience. There was a feeling of solidarity, of comradeship quite unlike anything which capitalism engenders.

There were the continuous discussions and debates on the real issues that concern us, in place of the stale academic rhetoric about unreal situations that characterize education in this society. There was the feeling that we were, in a small way, taking control of our own lives, that we were "liberating" a part of our lives. It is true that there was much to be criticized in the occupation: the low explicitly political level of much of the weekend; the failure to organize many of those LSE students who were engaging in their first political act, that lack of a clear idea as to what to do after the 27th. But in spite of these faults, the occupation of LSE still stands as a model for political action. By taking control of their own institution, on a revolutionary (rather than reformist, or economist) basis, the LSE students showed the way for students and workers in all the capitalist institutions.

Vietnam Solidarity Campaign, *Bulletin* 19, November 1968, 3–4. Retrieved from the Red Mole Rising Archive: redmolerising.wordpress.com/vietnam-solidarity-campaign.

NETWORK: OR HOW WE BEAT THE GALLERY SYSTEM (1968)
J.W.

On May 28, 1968, students and staff occupied the renowned Hornsey College of Art in North London. What was intended as a one-day teach-in turned into a six-week occupation in which students and staff assumed total control, inspiring actions at other art and design colleges elsewhere in the country. At the core of the Hornsey occupation was the desire for a more free and horizontal art education, an approach captured by the term "network system." The following text was originally published in a 1969 book bringing together documents produced by students and staff during the occupation. The text offers a humorous take on what the "network" might look like in practice and the quotidian nature of its setting— the toilet—mocks the "gallery system" and "art historians" of the conventional art world at the time.

* * *

There had been much talk about the "network system" in the long discussions and seminars at Hornsey, but there was little tangible evidence of such a system in operation.

Whilst talking to Dave, a fellow industrial designer, I decided to put such a system to the test. We both desperately wanted to paint, and finding the necessary materials available we set about fulfilling our aims. We both agreed instantly on our first combined project—we would paint the loo! The men's toilet—I must add, for our deliberations on the network had not yet reached the stage where we could tackle the women's.

A coat of white emulsion was soon applied to the walls and there was already evidence of some considerable technique and brush work in our efforts. Not knowing in which direction to proceed we sought the help of a third-year painter, Colin, who was evidently inspired by our work and immediately transformed the numerous water pipes in the area into a multi-coloured organic structure. Together we then began to work on the individual toilet doors, and using large areas of flat colour we achieved a perfect balance in the total work, by contrasting them subtly with the bare urinals that stood opposite.

All of this operation must have caused much favour in the College for we were paid many visits by photographers, onlookers and people we believed to be art historians who came and stood facing the wall in a line and inspected the white emulsion closely. There are rumours that we have started a new school of painting, known affectionately as the "cubicle" school. If this is true the network structure cannot be *all* bad.

Students and Staff of Hornsey College of Art, *The Hornsey Affair* (London: Penguin Books, 1969), 89.

"PEOPLE ROUND ABOUT LIVING IN FEAR" (1970)
International Times

The counterculture, or underground, figured as a core element of Britain's long 1968. Rock music festivals, in particular, emerged as a rallying point for counter-

cultural youth in the 1960s, and by the early 1970s, young people were enjoying so-called "free festivals." One of the first of these was the Phun City festival, which took place near Worthing, England, from July 24–26, 1970. Organized by Mike Farren, a key figure in what he himself termed the "psychedelic left," it was intended to be a non-profit festival, complete with free music, free food, and free drugs. Phun City set an example. A month later, guests at a monetized festival at the Isle of Wight refused to pay and tore down fences. More free festivals soon followed. The following article, originally published in the seminal International Times, *gives a chronological account of the exhilarating, though chaotic event.*

* * *

TUESDAY, July 14: Lawyers acting for West Sussex County Council inform Phun City's solicitors that an injunction is being sought to prevent the festival taking place. News of this action is carried by most national press & TV news.

WEDNESDAY, July 15: *Backers withdraw remainder of finance from project.*

THURSDAY, July 16: West Sussex County Council withdraw application for injunction, but information is not carried by any nationals. Finance is by now thoroughly scared off.

FRIDAY, July 17: *Ronan O'Rahilly is contacted with a view to replacing vital finance. Negotiations continue through weekend.*

MONDAY, July 20: Construction crews move onto site & start work with what little bread is left in bank & Ronan O'Rahilly investigates possibility of his company, Mid Atlantic Films, filming the event. Freaks begin to arrive at site & set up commune in the woods.

TUESDAY, July 21: *Woodland commune grows: work on site slows down as cash reserve dwindles. Ronan provisionally agrees to put in finance, to film the event, & generally help with organization.*

WEDNESDAY, July 22: Final details are worked out with Mid-Atlantic. Certain contractors begin demanding cash in advance and in some cases inflating prices.

THURSDAY, July 23: *Work on site resumes in earnest although it is now about 48 hours behind schedule. Woodland commune has by now constructed an independent festival village. Local Water Board refuse to accept Mid-Atlantic cheque & inform site manager McDonnell that water will not be connected unless paid cash. Sympathetic local councillor personally guarantees payment & water is turned on. Announcement is made that in view of deal with Ronan that no fences will be erected & that the audience will be put on trust to pay for admission. National press see no news value of idea of People's Festival.*

FRIDAY, July 24: Heavy rain all morning slows down construction work, & festival opens at 6:00 p.m. with toilets only half constructed. Health officials put deadline on having toilets completed or they will close festival. Staff have to be drawn off cash collection to work on toilets. Rain stops mid-afternoon but by then the crowd has been reduced to around 3,000. Some contractors begin to heavy organizers for full payment which leaves less than enough to pay all bands. Despite this, Stray, Wildmouth, J.J. Jackson & the Pretty Things all play. J.J. & the Pretties both do historic sets. Free, however, are appalled by the conception of the event & demand cash before they will consider playing. While this is being arranged they split, so the Pretty Things finish the evening.

SATURDAY, July 25: *Saturday dawns overcast & showery. Buttons & the London Hells Angels arrive in force & put in an amazing amount of hard work on behalf of the organization. Red Umbrella Caterers' boss, Alan Carter, begins threatening anyone who he feels is cutting across his franchise in any way. Friends' stall is one of these, & Carter threatens to drive a truck over their stall if they go on selling coffee. The afternoon's weather brightens & the music starts with Cochise, Mighty Baby & Demon Fuzz. Edgar Broughton offers to play free, providing he isn't filmed & heavy situation takes place between Peter Jenner & the film crew, although the tension is dispelled by a fine set by Edgar & Kevin Ayers playing together. The amazing Pink Fairies strip show follows, with Russ & Twink rolling naked on the stage. The Poetry Festival & Sci-Fi Conference get off to a bad start as the inflatable domes they're supposed to be happening in are still lying flat on the grass. The poetry starts in the Christian tent, but is evicted after complaints from the missionaries about obscenity. The BIT & Radio Geronimo newspapers are distributed around the ground. The two inflatables finally inflate & as the sun sets the MC5 start into their truly amazing set. As darkness falls, the lightshows go into full action for the first time & the ground becomes a mass of colour. For the first time a festival is a real environment. Legs Larry Smith & Steve Took's new band, Shagrat, follow MC5 & when the music finishes the audience retire to various holes & nooks for sleep & narcotics.*

SUNDAY, July 26: Heavy rain & the money has totally run out. Free beer is handed round by the Angels, who, although fearsome in regalia & carrying massive clubs, were in the main helpful & one of the main factors in holding the event together. The Jesus bunch hold what they call a People's Service. A couple of local bands fill in until the rain stops. Sunday's action, although damp & cold, is one happy togetherness. Virtually nobody gets paid anything above expenses & only Matthews Southern Comfort leave without playing. Quiver, Honks (ex-Junior Eyes) new band start the day's serious music. Black radical band Noir play a really excellent set, as does Mike Chapman who has the audience on its feet for a 20-minute "Hey Jude" which surpasses Paul McCartney. The Liverpool 8 Friendly Society follows, then Pete Brown, also excellent. The crowd gives a standing ovation to Sonia, a virtually unknown folksinger, after an impromptu spot. Roger Ruskin, robots, and the reporter from The People take part in a piece of weirdness. Mungo Jerry provide the final spot—very professional down home jug music. Finally they are joined by the organizers, the film crew and sundry musicians who close the event with a 15-minute anthem in plain E specially composed by Mick Farren. The audience once more repair to the woods and dome to consume narcotics and sleep.

MONDAY. July 28: *Clearing up, taking down tents and watching rain. About 100 people sit around in the woods smoking, talking, cooking up stews in Elsan buckets. Early afternoon, Councillor Flower and Health Inspector Rossiter arrive, chat to hippies, walk dogs and things, all dead amiable. Incensed by the rumors of common land, stay forever in our permanent commune, etc. etc. 100 pigs descend in three columns of trucks and proceed to clear the woods with enthusiasm, kicking over stews and councillors throwing clothes and gear on campfires and busting three people for dope.*

On attempting to placate all parties, organizers get told by head pig, Chief Inspector Somers, "you are responsible for this and our investigations will be along the lines of charging you with allowing the premises to be used for the smoking of cannabis resin." Very uptight over the treatment of his narcs during the past three days. Ha, Ha.

I THINK WE MUST HAVE LOST ABOUT FOUR GRAND, IT'S TOO EARLY TO SAY YET. IN TERMS OF MONEY IT WAS A DISASTER, BUT THE PEOPLE GOT IT ON .
– Mick Farren on behalf of Phun City Ltd

[...]

International Times 1, issue 85, August 13–27, 1970, 8–9. Retrieved from the *International Times* Archive: internationaltimes.it/archive.

THE OPPRESSED OF THE OPPRESSED (1971)
Black Women's Action Committee

As in the United States, Britain saw the rise of several Black radical formations in the long 1968, such as the Black Unity and Freedom Party, an initially Marxist-Leninist organization founded in England in 1970. Women within this group in turn created the Black Women's Action Committee to combat not only racism, but also sexism. As the group's history shows, British Black feminism often emerged from within the Black Power movement, rather than just as a response to white feminism. Below, we reproduce a text they wrote for International Women's Day in 1971. The text comments on equal pay, free abortion, and free nurseries, while referring to the limited demands discussed at the first national Women's Liberation Movement conference in 1970. Offering an account of what many today would call "intersecting" forms of oppression, the text is a strikingly early example of the kind of thinking that continues to shape many political struggles and conversations today.

* * *

Black women are the oppressed of the oppressed. They are oppressed as being part of the working class, as being black and as being women.

True equality between the sexes can *never* be achieved in a capitalist society, for inequality based on national, racial, and sexual differentials is an integral part of the mechanism of capitalist exploitation. Even in the most liberal bourgeois state, the rulers can grant reforms such as free day nurseries, free abortions etc., but what they cannot and are incapable of doing is to grant equality in the decisive spheres of social life, for it would weaken the very basis of their system which depends on a source of cheap labor.

Therefore, women must struggle to change this exploitative structure from its economic foundations, thereby transforming the social relations which result. For without a thorough-going revolution in which women play a decisive role, the bourgeois state will continue to dominate the lives of all the oppressed and exploited.

In the meantime, women as workers must fight for equal pay and status at the point of production.

However, the struggle for freedom by women cannot be separated from the world's anti-capitalist, anti-imperialist workers movement—black and white. History has shown that it is only a socialist revolution that can create and guarantee the conditions for eliminating all types of social inequalities, not least among these the status of women.

Therefore, women must struggle side by side with the other sections of the oppressed and exploited people to overthrow capitalism/imperialism and all other forms of oppression and exploitation. For only a unified struggle waged by all sections of the oppressed and exploited will bring capitalism and its evils to an end.

In this struggle, it is necessary for white women to understand the necessity to raise demands which will speak directly to the problem of black women who are, in addition to the problems faced by women, racially oppressed under capitalism.

Experience has shown that if any oppressed group in society is to win its rightful place in society it needs disciplined organization, steeled in struggle, and armed with revolutionary ideology and guns.

"EVERYTHING REACTIONARY IS THE SAME –
IF YOU DON'T HIT IT, IT WON'T FALL."
MAO TSE TUNG.

UNIFY THE STRUGGLE! STRIKE AT THE MAIN ENEMY!

[…]

Published on International Women's Day, March 6, 1971.

Black Unity and Freedom Party, *BLACK WOMEN SPEAK OUT: a B.U.F.P. pamphlet*, March 6, 1971, 4. Black Cultural Archives, Brixton, United Kingdom.

MANIFESTO (1971)
Gay Liberation Front

Inspired by the Gay Liberation Front (GLF) in the United States, a homonymous organization held its first meeting at the London School of Economics in October 1970. Soon after, GLF would host weekly meetings attended by hundreds; launch a number of initiatives, such as the Anti-Psychiatry Group, a Street Theater Group, and a Youth Group; and organize a series of direct actions, like disrupting the 1971 Festival of Light, a right-wing Christian campaign concerned about the "moral pollution" of the time. In its Manifesto, *reprinted here, GLF asks why and how gay people are oppressed, calls for the need to overcome oppression within the gay community, and outlines the aim of overthrowing "male supremacy" and*

Figure 9.3   The first major gay demonstration in Britain, organized by the Gay Liberation Front, London. August 1971. Courtesy of Peter Tatchell.

the "gender-role system" of "straight society." Like other radical texts of the long 1968, the GLF Manifesto argues not simply for reforms, but for a revolution.

* * *

Introduction

Throughout recorded history, oppressed groups have organised to claim their rights and obtain their needs. Homosexuals, who have been oppressed by physical violence and by ideological and psychological attacks at every level of social interaction, are at last becoming angry.

To you, our gay sisters and brothers, we say that you are oppressed; we intend to show you examples of the hatred and fear with which straight society relegates us to the position and treatment of sub-humans, and to explain their basis. We will show you how we can use our righteous anger to uproot the present oppressive system with its decaying and constricting ideology, and how we, together with other oppressed groups, can start to form a new order, and a liberated lifestyle, from the alternatives which we offer.

HOW we're oppressed

[...]

Self-oppression
The ultimate success of all forms of oppression is our self-oppression. Self-oppression is achieved when the gay person has adopted and internalised straight people's definition of what is good and bad. Self-oppression is saying: "When you come down to it, we are abnormal." Or doing what you most need and want to do, but with a sense of shame and loathing, or in a state of disassociation, pretending it isn't happening; cruising or cottaging not because you enjoy it, but because you're afraid of anything less anonymous. Self-oppression is saying: "I accept what I am," and meaning: "I accept that what I am is second-best and rather pathetic." [...]

Self-oppression is the dolly lesbian who says: "I can't stand those butch types who look like truck drivers," the virile gay man who shakes his head at the thought of "those pathetic queens." This is self-oppression because it's just another way of saying: "I'm a nice normal gay, just like an attractive heterosexual."

The ultimate in self-oppression is to avoid confronting straight society, and thereby provoking further hostility: Self-oppression is saying, and believing: "I am not oppressed."

WHY we're oppressed

Gay people are oppressed. [...] [W]e face the prejudice, hostility and violence of straight society, and the opportunities open to us in work and leisure are restricted, compared with those of straight people. Shouldn't we demand reforms that will give us tolerance and equality? Certainly we should—in a liberal-democratic society, legal equality, and protection from attack are the very least we should ask for. They are our civil rights.

But gay liberation does not just mean reforms. It means a revolutionary change in our whole society. [...]

Reforms may makes things better for a while; changes in the law can make straight people a little less hostile, a little more tolerant—but reform cannot change the deep-down attitude of straight people that homosexuality is at best inferior to their own way of life, at worst a sickening perversion. It will take more than reforms to change this attitude, because it is rooted in our society's most basic institution—the Patriarchal Family.

We've all been brought up to believe that the family is the source of our happiness and comfort. But look at the family more closely. Within the small family unit, in which the dominant man and submissive woman bring up their children in their own image, all our attitudes toward sexuality are learned at a very early age. Almost before we can talk, certainly before we can think for ourselves, we are taught that there are certain attributes that are "feminine" and others that are "masculine," and that they are God-given and unchangeable. Beliefs learned so young are very hard to change; but in fact these are false beliefs. What we are taught about the differences between man and woman is *propaganda*, not truth.

The truth is that there are no proven systematic differences between male and female, apart from the obvious biological ones. Male and female genitals and reproductive systems are different, and so are certain other physical characteristics, but all differences of temperament, aptitudes and so on, are the result of upbringing and social pressures. They are not inborn.

Human beings could be much more various than our constricted patterns of "masculine" and "feminine" permit—we should be free to develop with greater individuality. But as things are at present, there are only these two stereotyped roles into which everyone is supposed to fit, and most people— including gay people too—are apt to be alarmed when they hear these stereotypes or *gender roles* attacked [...]

By our very existence as gay people, we challenge these roles. It can easily be seen that homosexuals don't fit into the stereotypes of masculine and feminine and this is one of the main reasons why we become the object of suspicion, since everyone is taught that these and only these two roles are appropriate.

Our entire society is build around the patriarchal family and its enshrine-ment of these masculine and feminine roles. Religion, popular morality, art, literature and sport all reinforce these stereotypes. In other words, this society is a *sexist* society in which one's biological sex determines almost all of what one does and how one does it; a situation in which men are privileged, and women are mere adjuncts of men and objects for their use, both sexually and otherwise.

Since all children are taught so young that boys should be aggressive and adventurous, girls passive and pliant, most children do tend to behave in these ways as they get older and to believe that other people should do so too.

So sexism does not just oppose gay people but all women as well. It is assumed that because women bear children they should and must rear them and be simultaneously excluded from all other spheres of achievement.

However, as the indoctrination of the small child with these attitudes is not always entirely successful (if it were, there would be no gay people for a start), the ideas taken in by the young child almost unconsciously must be reinforced in the older child and teenager by a consciously expressed male chauvinism: the ideological expression of masculine superiority. Male chauvinism is not hatred of women, but male chauvinists accept women only on the basis that they are in fact lesser beings. It is an expression of male power and male privilege, and while it's quite possible for a gay man to be a male chauvinist, his very existence does also challenge male chauvinism in so far as he rejects his male supremacist role over women, and perhaps particularly if he rejects "masculine" qualities.

It is because of the patriarchal family that reforms are not enough. Freedom for gay people will never be permanently won until everyone is freed from sexist role-playing and the straitjacket of sexist rules about our sexuality. And we will not be freed from these so long as each succeeding generation is brought up in the same old sexist way in the patriarchal family.

[...]

[S]exism is not just an accident—it is an essential part of our present society and cannot be changed without the whole society changing with it. First, our society is dominated at every level by men, who have an interest in preserving the status quo; second, the present system of work and production depends on the existence of the patriarchal family. Conservative sociologists have pointed out that the small family unit of two parents and their children is essential in our contemporary advanced industrial society where work is minutely subdivided and highly regulated—in other words, for the majority *boring*. A man would not work at the assembly line if he had no wife and family to support; he would not give himself fully to his work without the supportive and reassuring little group ready to follow him about and gear itself to his needs, to put up with his ill temper when he is frustrated or put down by the boss at work.

Were it not also for the captive wife, educated by advertising and everything she reads into believing that she needs ever more new goodies for the home, for her own beautification and for the children's well-being, our economic system could not function properly, depending as it does on people buying far more manufactured goods than they need. The housewife, obsessed with the ownership of as many material goods as possible, is the agent of this high level of spending. None of these goods will ever satisfy her, since there is always something better to be had, and the surplus of these pseudo "necessities" goes hand in hand with the absence of genuinely necessary goods and services, such as adequate housing and schools. [...]

[...] We believe that work in an advanced industrial society could be organized on more humane lines, with each job more varied and more pleasurable, and that the way society is at present organised operates in the interests of a small ruling group of straight men who claim most of the status and money, and not in the interests of the people as a whole. We also believe that our economic resources could be used in a much more valuable and constructive way than they are at the moment—but that will not happen until the present pattern of male dominance in our society changes too.

That is why any reforms we might painfully exact from our rulers would only be fragile and vulnerable; that is why we, along with the women's movement, must fight for something more than reform. We must aim at the abolition of the family, so that the sexist, male supremacist system can no longer be nurtured there.
[...]

A New Life-style
In the final section we shall outline some of the practical steps gay liberation will take to make this revolution. But linked with this struggle to change society there is an important aspect of gay liberation that we can begin to build here and now—a NEW, LIBERATED LIFE-STYLE which will anticipate as far as possible the free society of the future.

Gay shows the way. In some ways we are already more advanced than straight people. We are already outside the family and we have already, in part at least, rejected the "masculine" or "feminine" roles society has designed for us. In a society dominated by the sexist culture it is very difficult, if not impossible, for heterosexual men and women to escape their rigid gender-role structuring and the roles of oppressor and oppressed. But gay men don't need to oppress women in order to fulfil their own psycho-sexual needs, and gay women don't have to relate sexually to the male oppressor, so that at this moment in time, the freest and most equal relationships are most likely to be between homosexuals.

But because the sexist culture has oppressed us and distorted our lives too, this is not always achieved. In our mistaken, placating efforts to be accepted and tolerated, we've too often submitted to the pressures to conform to the strait-jacket of society's rules and hang ups about sex.

[...]

Compulsive Monogamy

[...]

It is especially important for gay people to stop copying straight—we are the ones who have the best opportunities to create a new lifestyle and if we don't no one else will. Also, we need one another more than straight people do because we are equals suffering under an insidious oppression from a society too primitive to come to terms with the freedom we represent. Singly, or isolated in couples, we are weak—the way society wants us to be. Society cannot put us down so easily if we fuse together. We have to get together, understand one another, live together.

[...]

The way forward

Aims

The long-term goal of Gay Liberation, which inevitably brings us into conflict with the institutionalized sexism of this society, is to rid society of the gender-role system which is at the root of our oppression. This can only be achieved by eliminating the social pressures on men and women to conform to narrowly defined gender roles. It is particularly important that children and young people be encouraged to develop their own talents and interests and to express their own individuality rather than act out stereo-typed parts alien to their nature.

As we cannot carry out this revolutionary change alone, and as the abolition of gender roles is also a necessary condition of women's liberation, we will work to form a strategic alliance with the women's liberation movement, aiming to develop our ideas and our practice in close inter-relation. In order to build this alliance, the brothers in gay liberation will have to be prepared to sacrifice that degree of male chauvinism and male privilege that they still all possess.

[...]

Free our Heads

The starting point of our liberation must be to rid ourselves of the oppression which lies in the head of every one of us. This means freeing our heads from self-oppression and male chauvinism, and no longer organizing our lives according to the patterns with which we are indoctrinated by straight society. It means that we must root out the idea that homosexuality is bad, sick or immoral, and develop a gay pride. [...] The aim is to step outside the experience permitted by straight society and to learn to love and trust one another. This is the precondition for acting and struggling together.

By freeing our heads we get the confidence to come out publicly and proudly as gay people, and to win over our gay brothers and sisters to the ideas of gay liberation.

Campaign
Before we can create the new society of the future, we have to defend our interests as gay people here and now against all forms of oppression and victimization. [...]
[...]
We do not intend to ask for anything. We intend to stand firm and assert our basic rights. If this involves violence, it will not be we who initiate this but those who attempt to stand in our way to freedom. [...]

[...]

Gay Liberation Front, *Manifesto*, London, October, 1971.

Further Reading

Ali, Tariq. *Street-Fighting Years: An Autobiography of the Sixties*. London: Verso, 2005.
Angelo, Anne-Marie. "The Black Panthers in London, 1967–1972: A Diasporic Struggle Navigates the Black Atlantic." *Radical History Review* 103 (Winter 2009): 17–35.
Callaghan, John. *The Far Left in British Politics*. Oxford: Basil Blackwell, 1987.
Carr, Gordon. *The Angry Brigade: A History of Britain's First Urban Guerilla Group*. Oakland: PM Press, 2010.
Green, Jonathon. *All Dressed Up: The Sixties and Counterculture*. London: Pimlico, 1999.
Dworkin, Dennis. *Cultural Marxism in Postwar Britain: History, the New Left and the Origins of Cultural Studies*. Durham, NC: Duke University Press, 1997.
Kenny, Michael. *The First New Left: British Intellectuals After Stalin*. London: Lawrence and Wishart, 1995.
McKay, George. *Senseless Acts of Beauty Cultures of Resistance since the Sixties*. London: Verso, 1996.
Robinson, Lucy. *Gay Men and the Left in Postwar Britain: How the Personal Got Political*. Manchester: Manchester University Press, 2011.
Rowbotham, Sheila. *Promise of a Dream: Remembering the Sixties*. London: Penguin, 2001
Smith, Evan, and Matthew Worley, eds.. *Against the Grain: The British Far Left from 1956*. Manchester: Manchester University Press, 2014.
Thomlinson, Natalie. *Race, Ethnicity and the Women's Movement in England, 1968–1993*. Basingstoke: Palgrave Macmillan, 2016.

10
Northern Ireland

Created in 1921–2 as part of the settlement of the Irish War of Independence, Northern Ireland—"The North" or "The Six Counties" to many nationalists and republicans, "Ulster" to many unionists and loyalists—comprised the northeasterly part of the island of Ireland. The North—which would remain part of the United Kingdom while the South became independent—included much of the island's industrial base and hence of its urban working class along with some deeply rural areas. Crucially, the new mini-state contained a Protestant majority, largely comprised of the descendants of seventeenth-century settlers from Scotland and England, together with a sizeable Catholic minority. Most Protestants (primarily Presbyterians and Episcopalians) were unionist—supportive of the union with Britain—and most Catholics were nationalist—preferring reunification with the Republic of Ireland, as the South became in 1937.

There were reasons for these preferences: Northern Ireland had its own devolved rule from Stormont, "a Protestant parliament for a Protestant people" as it was approvingly put. As we shall see, this depended on a restricted franchise and gerrymandering to maintain power at the various levels; a power which was also massively represented in the Royal Ulster Constabulary (RUC) and the B Specials, the reserve police. This establishment, and the dominant Unionist Party, were also underpinned by the fraternal Orange Order, containing perhaps one in five adult Protestant men and organizing annual marches of a sectarian kind.

These very unequal ethnic power relations sustained strong economic inequalities, with discrimination and segregation commonplace, most visibly in employment and housing. In a society whose signature industries—farming, the shirt trade in Derry, and shipbuilding in Belfast—had long been in decline, these inequalities were intensely felt, despite strong class differentials within both communities and often parallel forms of patriarchy. Although trade unions were on occasion capable of making links across community lines around wage issues and the Northern Ireland Labour Party had some significant support, not least among Protestant workers in Belfast, most working-class Protestants valued the status differentials separating them from Catholics, while working-class Catholics usually expressed their radicalism through support for nationalist politics. Thus before the civil rights movement and the "Troubles," as the conflict from the later 1960s until the 1990s peace process was called, the political division between unionism and nationalism was the central one in Northern Irish politics.

By the late 1960s, the radical all-Ireland Sinn Féin party had undergone a substantial change of direction. The "Border Campaign," which its paramilitary wing, the Irish Republican Army (IRA), had led in the late 1950s and early 1960s, had ended badly, with little popular support in the North and a new wave of repression from both the Northern Irish state and the Southern. In the aftermath, traditionalist republicans had been defeated within both organizations by those arguing for a more Marxist approach, emphasizing class struggle rather than paramilitary action as the main road to an all-Ireland socialist republic but with limited capacity, able to support developing popular movements but not to initiate them.

What became the civil rights movement was thus a new departure in Northern Irish politics, focusing not on the "national question" but on discrimination against Catholics within Northern Ireland. The by now decade-long struggle of the U.S. civil rights movement provided a model and a language for thinking about this: ordinary people could be mobilized, and the central state might be forced into action, by nonviolent struggle aimed at highlighting injustice and inequalities. The city of Derry (to Catholics)/ Londonderry (to Protestants) was a key battleground for this; the Derry Housing Action Committee was already campaigning actively on injustices in public housing. The texts in this chapter focus particularly on Derry as a way into the complexities of Northern Irish movements in the period.

Since Derry had a large Catholic majority, gerrymandering could only produce a Protestant-dominated council with difficulty. However, votes in local elections were allocated to householders (including those in public housing), meaning that discrimination in local authority housing was not simply another form of injustice, but necessary for the continuation of unequal power relations. When the Northern Ireland Civil Rights Association was founded in 1967, its demands thus focused on equal voting rights, an end to gerrymandering, and to discrimination in state jobs and council housing, to the Special Powers Act, and to the B Specials.

In this context these demands challenged Unionist power in the state, ground-level inequalities between Protestants and Catholics, and the symbolic relationship of domination between the two. Unsurprisingly in retrospect, their expression was met with violence. A series of key events marked this progression. On October 5, 1968, a march led by the Derry Housing Action Committee was first banned and then attacked by the police despite the presence of MPs and media. This led to the formation in Belfast of the more student-oriented People's Democracy, whose march from Belfast to Derry was attacked with stones and iron bars by a loyalist mob at Burntollet Bridge on January 4, 1969, with the visible collusion of the RUC. In April, police attacked 42-year-old Samuel Devenney and his children in their home; when he died of his injuries in July, 15,000 people attended the funeral.

The conflict extended and radicalized across the North, with the now-famous sign, "You are now entering Free Derry", painted on the gable end of a house at the entrance to the Catholic working-class Bogside neighborhood. The marches both of civil rights supporters and of the Orange Order and similar Protestant groups (in Derry, the Apprentice Boys) increasingly finished in rioting, with the RUC attacking Catholics. In August 1969, conflict between the RUC and Bogside residents around an Apprentice Boys march turned into the "Battle of the Bogside." Residents organized barricades and petrol bombs and successfully kept the police out for three days. In Belfast, loyalist mobs attacked Catholic areas of west Belfast, burning houses, and shooting broke out between the RUC, IRA, and loyalists, leaving eight people dead.

On August 14, the Northern Irish prime minister requested and received British troops. Initially welcomed by many Catholics, these soon became an integral part of the militarization of the conflict, which continued to escalate with the formation of multiple loyalist and republican paramilitary groups and the intensification of state violence and repression. In these years too, Northern Ireland experienced the largest forced population movement in Europe since the end of the Second World War, with perhaps as many as 60,000 refugees in 1969–71. The war would continue until the 1990s, with around 3,700 deaths and 45,000 injured in a population of 1.5 million, where extended families and close communities meant that each death or atrocity acquired resonance far beyond those immediately affected.

The militarization process would overwhelm the strategic visions and options of the civil rights movement. More generally, popular movements were increasingly shaped by the "Troubles," and groups were rapidly labeled as "Catholic" or "Protestant," "Unionist" or "Nationalist." It is not that genuine cross-community organizing was impossible: it continued in trade union contexts and developed between feminists, ecologists, or peace activists. It is that the shadow of the conflict, and the strains it placed on organizing, weakened other movements considerably; thus, for example, with the mid-1970s campaign against the Westlink dual carriageway in Belfast; the small number of active feminists in the same period struggled to maintain organizations which were not dominated by the pressures of the war; and so on.

In the wider society, the Protestant working class remained stony soil for any kind of radical left, and the increased tendency toward independent organizing of an aggressive "loyalist" kind did nothing to change this.

On the other side of the divide, the events of 1969 in particular led to the emergence of the Provisional IRA and Sinn Féin at the expense of the old ("Official") organizations, with a renewed emphasis on the logics of armed struggle and Catholic nationalism.

This does not, however, mean that Northern Ireland missed out on "1968" and its longer-term consequences in terms of movements and ideas altogether, even if they were expressed differently. One often under-remarked aspect of the war was the extent to which it forced embattled communities—particularly working-class Catholics in Belfast and Derry—to self-organize outside and beyond the state for long periods. This was expressed through the occupation of territory ("Free Derry"), the collective rebuilding of burned-out houses, the creation of Irish-speaking schools, and so on.

Figure 10.1 Free Derry Corner. Late 1969. Copyright unknown; courtesy of the Museum of Free Derry.

Another and more immediate effect was to raise the question of state legitimacy within movements. If in many West European countries the immediate defeat of the revolutionary aspirations of 1968 had left a split between a radicalized and increasingly criminalized minority of activists and a wider movement field which accepted this defeat, in Northern Ireland the long-term loss of state legitimacy for Catholics in particular enabled movements to think differently about the nature of power and social change.

LONDONDERRY: ONE MAN, NO VOTE (1965)
Campaign for Social Justice in Northern Ireland

The Campaign for Social Justice in Northern Ireland (CSJ) was founded in 1964 in Dungannon by Patricia and Conn McCluskey, who had previously founded the Homeless Citizens Action League. The League had organized local women in 1963 to occupy unused buildings and hold a protest march. This pamphlet is characteristic of the CSJ's use of well-researched material to draw attention to the same issue on a wider scale. The choice of Derry as a focus reflects not just this move beyond the local, but also the city's combination of blatant injustice in the allocation of public housing and the political effects of this discrimination. The use of the name "Londonderry" fits with the address to the Westminster parliament at the end of the document: by analogy with the U.S., intervention from the central state might be hoped for where the regional state was hostile. The McCluskeys would go on to be involved in the foundation of the Northern Ireland Civil Rights Association (NICRA) in 1966–7, and NICRA's first march would be to Dungannon, in conjunction with CSJ.

*   *   *

[...]

Gerrymander

In the three Ulster counties where the Conservatives are in a minority, control is still maintained by the manipulation of electoral boundaries in a very undemocratic way known as "gerrymandering."

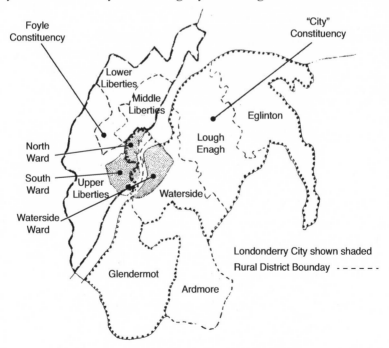

Figure 10.2   Londonderry parliamentary constituencies

There was a separate seat for the city of Londonderry in the early years of the Stormont parliament.

Because of the preponderance of Catholics the constituency returned a Nationalist (Catholic) member.

In order to neutralize the seat, the electoral division was re-arranged. The city itself was cut into two, Foyle returning a Nationalist.

The boundary of the "City" was stretched eight miles into the country [...] [T]he planners of the new boundary of the City constituency found it necessary to reach out to include pockets of Conservative (Protestant) voters, without reference to natural geographical features, in order to scrape together a Conservative and Unionist majority.

It is in local government franchise, however, that the "gerrymander" injustice is seen at its worst.

In local elections in Britain all adults over 21 have a vote. In Northern Ireland only a householder and his wife can vote. In addition limited companies are allotted six votes each. Catholics are denied houses and therefore lose voting strength. This is Conservative policy.

Here are the 1964 figures for Londonderry:

Roman Catholic adults over 21	19,870
Roman Catholics with local Government vote	14,325 (inc. 257 company votes)
Conservative adults over 21	10,573
Conservative adults with local Government vote	9,235 (inc. 902 company votes)

The wards are "gerrymandered" as to size and composition. The surplus Catholics are found in one large ward. The final result for Derry can be seen in the diagram on the back page.

The minority Unionist vote is thus able to elect the Mayor of Londonderry, who ex officio is a member of the Northern Ireland Senate, the salaried Upper House.

TOTAL POPULATION OF LONDONDERRY:
Census of Population Northern Ireland 1961 (H.M.S.O., Belfast)
Roman Catholic 36,049
Protestant 17,695

Housing Injustices

The housing situation causes most misery. The result of the housing qualification is that the Conservative and Unionist dominated Council will build and grant houses to Catholics more readily in the South Ward but, to preserve Conservative voting majority, only a small proportion of North and Waterside Ward houses are allotted to Catholics.

All the land in the South Ward has been used up, yet the corporation refuses to extend the city boundary.

All local authority houses in the city are allocated by one man, the Lord Mayor. The housing committee does not function. [...]

The backlog of people waiting to be housed after World War II had a large preponderance of Catholic families.

Housing needs at that time were so desperate that hundreds of families, nearly all Catholic, "squatted" into Nissen huts which had just been vacated by the American Army.

Even now, more than 20 years later, many of these people have not yet been re-housed (the precise number at this moment is 59 huts, housing 90 families), in spite of the fact that the huts are in a tumbledown condition and rat-infested.

Springtown Camp, as it is called, has been owned and administered during all this time by Londonderry Corporation. [...]

The British taxpayer keeps the Northern Ireland state in existence with an annual grant of over forty-six million pounds.

Then there are the national and diplomatic services of the United Kingdom, The Royal Mint, Civil List, National Debt, United Kingdom Parliament and other Imperial expenditures. If the Northern Ireland

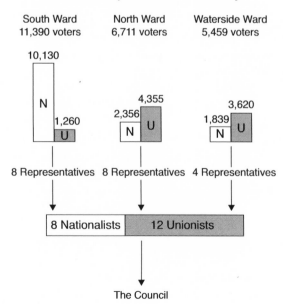

The Wards System in Londonderry

Parliament was paying its share of all these expenses it would have to find in addition something like 55 million pounds.

Because of what Northern Ireland is costing Britain, coupled with the fact that The Government of Ireland Act 1920 gives the Westminster Parliament complete authority over the Parliament at Belfast, do you not at least feel you owe it to yourselves to investigate matters in Northern Ireland, and if you find injustices to put things right?

This diagram [above] takes into account the restricted local government franchise. If everyone over 21 years had a vote, the position would show up even worse.

Republished on CAIN (cain.ulst.ac.uk).

'68 D.H.A.C. '69 (1969)
Derry Housing Action Committee

Alongside the constitutional agitation of civil rights activists, local organizing around housing issues in Derry built up across 1968 in the Derry Housing Action Committee (DHAC). DHAC was formed following the success of the Dublin Housing Action Committee's squatting campaign, and shared the former's orientation toward direct action and co-organizing with those affected. Reality *was DHAC's periodical and this 1969 piece explicitly draws the link between its early housing activism and the October 1968 march discussed in the next piece. The people of Derry, it writes, were arising from "50 years of slumber," in other words since its involvement in the Irish War of Independence.*

* * *

On a cold February day last year four women and two young men sat in the Corporation Housing Dept. discussing the housing position in the city, and in particular the case of the four women present, all of whom lived in flats at 8, Limavady Road. Their landlord within the past few days had knocked off their electric light and they had to live in candle-lit rooms. Their family doctors were concerned at the dangers of such and they hoped for action from the local council.

This was the beginning of the Derry Housing Action Committee, which grew from that small group of people, which included Mrs. McNamee, Dillon, Olphert and Quigley. The two young men were Derry man Danny McGinley and a Magee University College lecturer, English-born Mr. Steward Crehan.

Meetings to organize the homeless were held at Limavady Rd., and at Mr. Crehan's flat at 98, Beechwood Avenue. The inaugural meeting was held at the City Hotel on St. Patrick's Day weekend at which it was decided to go to the March monthly meeting of Derry Corporation to read a prepared address and to disrupt the proceedings. This type of activity remained a monthly date for the D.H.A.C. even up to the last Council meeting in March 1969.

For a period of almost three months the committee's activities were, as one might put it, strictly within the law. Many members thought that such protests to date were mild but it was not until June that the first really militant act had taken place. At 11:00 a.m. on the morning of the 22nd, at the caravan home of the Wilson Family in which a young child had died, directly linked to their living conditions, members assembled. The caravan was dragged across the main Lone Moor bus-route at the Hamilton St-Ann St junction. It remained there for some hours on the 22nd and blocked the road again on the 29th and 30th of the same month.

Eleven people appeared before the Bishop Street Court in July. [...] All were bound over for a period of two years to keep the peace and Melaugh, McCann, White and Wilson were fined £10 each, and Mitchel and Ms. Wilcock £5 each.

The Wilsons have since been given a home at 417 Bishop Street.

During the court hearings one of the most militant D.H.A.C. protests took place during the Official Opening of the lower deck of Craigavon Bridge. J.J. O'Hara, Tony O'Doherty, Roddy O'Carlin, Neil O'Donnell and Sean McGeehan sat down to block the first vehicle, the Mayor's official car. The R.U.C. moved in and removed the protestors while a few other members led the homeless in singing "WE SHALL OVERCOME"... All were taken away in police cars and in the less "comfortable" tenders to the "VIC".

In Bishop Street Court once again the R.M. [resident magistrate] sat with a puzzled face as the defendants entered their seats. The case ended with Lafferty and the sit-down protesters being bound over for two years to keep the peace and O'Doherty was fined £5 for "conducting" and prompting the singing of "WE SHALL OVERCOME"—which the court considered to be disorderly behavior.

[...]

Regular picketing of "Rachmanists" [slum landlords] and public buildings continued all the time and *Reality*, the official organ of the D.H.A.C. was being published so as to keep the funds of the organization capable of fighting for the city's estimated 1,650 homeless families. Public meetings were held to increase membership and to keep the homeless informed as to what action the committee intended to take next as part of our militant campaign.

Rent strikes were also organized so as to force Rachmanists to install fire escapes and issue rent books. Many it seemed would never give in to these demands but as time passed each broke down rather than end up without their weekly rents from the homeless. Repairs were also demanded and one landlord had to put £1,100 out for just one of his houses.

In the month of August the call was made by the D.H.A.C. to the Northern Ireland Civil Rights Association to hold the first ever civil rights march in the city. In a matter of weeks plans were being made with the NICRA executive for a march on October 5th. The first meeting was held in the upstairs of a bar in William Street and others in local hotels. At one meeting only 57 stewards attended and the funds for organizing the march came out of the organizers' own pockets in the first weeks of organizing. Some organizations which promised financial support failed to keep their promises and so the bulk of the finance which was required to defray expenses was collected chiefly in the Creggan Estate and from local shop owners. Placards were made by a subcommittee in a house on Long Tower Street, sometimes into the early hours of the morning.

Little did the organizers and those who were making the preparations for the march realize that October 5, 1968 would be entered in the pages of history and that at long last the local people of Derry would arise from 50 years of slumber.

Reality 7, 1969.

THREE EYEWITNESSES REPORT ON LONDONDERRY (1968)
Russell Kerr, John Ryan, and Anne Kerr

After the Northern Ireland Civil Rights Association's first march, from Coalisland to Dungannon, the Derry Housing Action Committee sought NICRA support for a civil rights march in Derry. The organizing committee also included the Northern Ireland Labour Party, the Republican Clubs, and the James Connolly Society. Under pressure from the Northern Irish Minister for Home Affairs, the march was banned. NICRA sought to cancel the march but the Derry organizers held firm, and ultimately several hundred people marched, to be met by riot police. The police attack, starting with Belfast West MP Gerry Fitt and then extending to the whole march, was filmed by TV cameras, drawing international attention to the civil rights movement. This report was compiled by three British Labour Party MPs who acted as legal observers at the march. It escaped nobody that the Labour Party, under Harold Wilson, was in government at the time.

* * *

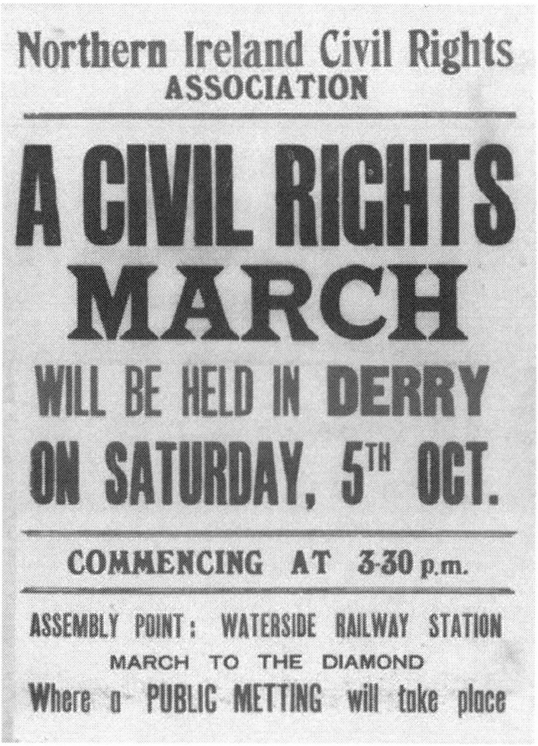

Northern Ireland Civil Rights
ASSOCIATION

A CIVIL RIGHTS
MARCH
WILL BE HELD IN DERRY
ON SATURDAY, 5TH OCT.

COMMENCING   AT   3-30 p.m.

ASSEMBLY POINT : WATERSIDE RAILWAY STATION
MARCH TO THE DIAMOND
Where a PUBLIC METTING will take place

Figure 10.3   Poster for the Duke Street march, Derry.
October 5, 1968. Courtesy of the Museum of Free Derry.

At the request of the Northern Ireland Civil Rights Association, we attended the march in the city of Londonderry on October 5th. At the outset we should stress that we took no part in the demonstration other than acting as observers. [...]

The demonstrators assembled from about 3:20 p.m. onwards at the open space beside the railway station at the waterside in Londonderry. They formed up and left the site at 3:45. They marched along Duke Street toward Craigavon Bridge. As to the composition of the march, we can say that the march was extremely orderly in its early stages, with a substantial number of stewards, mainly provided by the Derry City Labour Party. [...]

Among those present on the march were senior representatives of the Northern Ireland Labour Party, including the Chairman, Mr. Paddy Devlin. There were Republicans, the most notable of whom was Mr. Kevin Agnew of Magh[e]ra, a solicitor and Republican politician. There were also Nationalists, in particular Mr McAteer, the Leader of the Nationalist Opposition at Stormont, and there were members of the Republican Labour Party, in particular Mr. Gerry Fitt, M.P. for Belfast West. In addition to these, there were representatives of the Liberal Party from Belfast, and of the Belfast Trades Council.

[...] In general, although judgement of numbers is never easy, we would say there were around 3,000 people present and, in the main, they were elderly and middle-aged people. There was no particular preponderance of students or young people.

The march proceeded along Duke Street. There is a photograph in the *Irish Times* of the 6th of October which shows the position quite clearly. At the end of Duke Street, near the junction with Craigavon Bridge, the R.U.C. had positioned two large tenders to block the road and there were three lines of policemen positioned in front of them. At the very front of the march were Mr. McAteer, Mr. Devlin, Mr. Fitt and Mr. Cooper.

The marchers approached the police and when they were about a yard from the police ranks and obviously slowing up, the police opened up a passage into which were pulled Mr. Devlin and Mr. Fitt. Mr. Fitt was struck twice with a baton and Mr. Devlin was struck twice as well. They were then taken away, Mr. Fitt to have three stitches inserted in a head wound.

Meanwhile, police with sticks came in from both sides and began to belabor the leading marchers and to seize their banners and placards. There was some scuffling at this point and the police across the roadway drew their batons and forced the crowd back a short distance. Physical contact between the police and the crowd stopped after several minutes.

Duke Street is a narrow street of shops, in the main commercial or industrial properties with housing above. Some minutes after the above action, some dozens of policemen were positioned across the road behind the marchers, about 100 yards from the head of the march, thereby effectively preventing a retreat and resulting in people who had nothing to do with the march being trapped inside—people shopping or people normally resident in the street, for example.

The incident involving Mr. Devlin and Mr. Fitt took place at 4:03. From this point, until 4:34, the crowd settled down in Duke Street and there was a series of speeches [...]

[...]

The police then charged the crowd, using their batons vigorously and indiscriminately. At the same time the police at the bottom of the street moved up to separate the crowd so that instead of the crowd being sandwiched between the police they were now hemmed in on the pavements and in the shops on either side of the roadway.

[...]

In the second baton-charge at 4:34, another policeman was seen by Mr. Ryan to strike a man in the testicles with a baton. The man was already bleeding from head wounds. He immediately collapsed and was carted off. He also saw a woman around 60 who was hysterical on the pavement after having been hosed down by the cannon. A policeman approached her, removed her spectacles with one hand and hit her over the head with his baton with the other.

[...]

Regarding the use of the water cannons, which were used quite indiscriminately against all and sundry, we witnessed one incident where the jet was aimed through the open window of a house on the first floor, apparently at a television camera. [...]

[...]

House of Commons/PRONI Public Records HA/32/2/30, October 8, 1968. Published with the permission of the Deputy Keeper of Records (Public Records Office of Northern Ireland).

BURNTOLLET (1969)

Bowes Egan and Vincent McCormack

People's Democracy was founded at Queen's University Belfast in October 1968 in response to the RUC attack on the Derry march that month. It would become a key organization in radicalizing the civil rights movement, with figures like Bernadette Devlin, Eamonn McCann and Michael Farrell taking part. In January 1969 it organized a march from Belfast to Derry, which NICRA dissociated itself from. The march was explicitly modelled on the U.S. civil rights movement's Selma to Montgomery marches of 1965, which had been attacked by local troopers and police but ultimately secured federal protection. In Northern Ireland, no such protection was forthcoming; after a series of attacks in which the RUC failed to intervene, the march was ambushed at Burntollet Bridge near Derry by loyalists, including off-duty B Specials. The obvious police collusion led to a loss of faith in strategies depending on the good faith of the Northern Irish state.

*   *   *

[...]

The march continued slowly along the road, the walkers catching glimpses of the higher ground and police detachments through irregularities in the hedge. The next field disclosed about 50 people standing around in groups. Of these, Chief Constable Patterson and his policemen, came first in contact with a group of sturdy young men. Each of them carried a cudgel or some other weapon. The conversation between the groups seemed to be of quite an amiable sort; the young men moved casually ahead, now walking parallel, and a little in advance of the march, each one still fully armed. The policemen remained slightly behind them. [...]

The junction of the next two fields is obscured by an overgrown trough area surrounded by trees. A very young girl, perhaps fourteen or fifteen, appeared, jumping up and down and screaming, "Paisley, Paisley, Paisley." Then the bombardment really started. Bottles, bricks and stones rained down. One marcher noted: "I am not speaking of chips or pebbles. These were quarried stones, some of them several pounds in weight." His assessment was good. The field past the trough ran beside the road for more than a quarter of a mile. At approximately eight-foot intervals just behind the hedge, and at rather longer intervals further back on the higher ground, heaps of newly quarried stones had been deposited. "These certainly could not be found anywhere on the land," the owner, Tony Gormley, tells, "and nothing of the sort was there on the evening of January 3rd."

The use of these stones is well illustrated by John Gilmore, another Belfast student:

"I saw people, including one man who was standing with an armful of stones against his chest on the lower ground to the left of the field. Suddenly, I heard screams coming from behind, and looking around saw a shower of stones in the air. The march scattered in some panic; then I saw a girl being put onto a police tender with blood pouring from her head. Then I saw a television cameraman with blood streaming down his face."

[...]

At this stage, a number of walkers sought escape through a gap in the hedgeway, and moved into the field to mingle with throwers. There were shouts from the attackers as they saw that the newcomers wore no white armbands. And Chief Constable Patterson's policemen descended, batons drawn, to drive them from the field, back into the main injury area. "I have no doubt at all," says one of these men, "that the police in that field were there not to protect the marchers from the stoning which they must have known all about in advance, but to protect the attackers from any possible retaliation." Another local man survived the first shower of stones and tells:

"As we came near the Bridge the police were herding a few stragglers across the field. [I] recognized a man called Cooke from the Killaloo district. He was holding a large stone or brick in his left hand. I heard a cry of 'get the bastards,' and stones and bottles rained down."

The large field where the throwers were situated tapers to an end where a small laneway meets the main road at a sharp angle. Concealed from the marchers up this pathway were more than 60 men armed with cudgels, crowbars, iron bars, lead piping, and much more elaborate instruments of chastisement.

[...] As the riot-clad police at the head of the march came to the road junction, ambushers emerged from both sides. [...]

"The major portion of the C.R. [civil rights] procession was cut off and left at the mercy of the attackers. A fusillade of stones and bottles was followed by the full weight of the attack against the young men and women who had pledged themselves to a policy of non-violence.

"The attackers showed no mercy. Men were beaten senseless. Girls tore their way through the hedges screaming: 'No! No!' Shouting, club-waving, men pursued them."

[...]

By this time a number of overloaded ambulances were carrying the injured toward Altnagelvin Hospital in Derry. One injured marcher tells how he was carried into one of these vehicles then:

"About 50 yards ahead a group of men armed with sticks and bars formed a road block. One carried a hatchet, another a billhook. For a few minutes it seemed that they were going to drag us from the ambulance. But then the leader contented himself by saying, 'you got a lot less than you deserved. Next time we see you, it will be the last rites, as you call them, that you'll need. We'll kill each last one of you that turns up in this area again'."

Bowes Egan and Vincent McCormack, *Burntollet*, London: LRS Publishers, 1969. Retrieved from CAIN: cain.ulst.ac.uk.

BRITAIN AND THE BARRICADE (1969)
"A Republican in the Civil Rights Movement" (pseudonym)

September 1969 was a crucial moment for the Irish Republican Army (IRA). August had seen multiple attacks by RUC, B Specials, and unionist mobs on Catholic areas in Belfast and Derry. Several areas were barricaded and defended by residents' committees, but many were burned or otherwise forced out of their homes, often becoming refugees in the Republic. The question of military support for these areas would become a crucial one for IRA strategy, exacerbated by the development of what would in December become the Provisional IRA, rejecting the old ("Official") IRA's Marxist approach for an overtly Catholic and nationalist one. The arrival of British troops in August, and hints of willingness to intervene from Dublin, complicated the question further. This article in Sinn Féin's United Irishman, *by implication from an active IRA member, reflects what would become an "Official" perspective. It reflects the complex nature of the crisis and an activist understandings of the possibilities and limits of the self-organized areas.*

*   *   *

British long-term strategy clearly is to get back control over all Ireland. To do this it must (a) win Catholic support; (b) neutralize extreme-Unionist feeling and disarm the UVF [Ulster Volunteer Force] and B-Specials; (c) prevent the build-up of nationalist feeling in [the] 26 Counties from undermining the cosy capitulationist, free-trade, property dealing set up that has been carefully nurtured over the years of national defeat.

To achieve this, she must prevent the further development of a pogrom situation, by defending the Catholic population from the Specials successfully enough to prevent a resurgence of popular militancy in the South.

However in order to contain the unionists and prevent militancy spreading to the moderates, she must be seen to attempt to remove such arms as are considered to be available to the Defence Committees.

This she dare not do as long as the Defence Committees retain the support of the residents, so that to search for alleged arms would require the assumption of military control.

Thus the defensive organization of the people in the barricaded areas is a strong card that can be used in bargaining.

Brute force

Clearly in a brute force situation no-one would win. [...]

Policy for defence areas

The key to the whole situation is to concentrate on raising the political understanding of the defence areas and using them as *educators* for the nation at large.

The political analysis among the leadership of the defence areas would possibly evolve as follows:

(1)   Unionism by its "hard-line" on civil rights has shown that its ascendancy leadership realizes that its very existence under C.R. conditions would be threatened by loss of control by patronage of its protestant working-class basis. If they relied on religion alone, why should they worry?

(2)   The Catholics however are insisting that Civil Rights be granted and are prepared to establish well-defended enclaves until this occurs, realizing that this is the only way that they can defend themselves against armed extremists.

(3)   *Within the Stormont framework these are inconceivable.* Some therefore say "rule from Westminster".

(4)   Under a Tory Government in London, Westminster could *re-impose* *the Specials*, as they originally imposed them in 1920 before Stormont existed. Such indeed would be a likely backlash from a Tory Government advised by the Orangemen.

(5)   Therefore some strengthening of Irish control over the situation *must* be the objective. *The demand now for direct rule from Dublin however presents difficulties.*
Successive Dublin governments have a record of neglect of the Six County people, to the extent that they are in some way as remote as Westminster.

[...]

(9)   Parliamentary reform therefore in the North means the *replacement* of the present structure by a *new* one within which Catholics will be protected from discrimination and the advocacy of the politics of national unity will not be subversion.

The civil rights demands:

(a)   One man, One vote of equal value;
(b)   Outlawing of discrimination in jobs and housing;
(c)   Disarming and disbanding of the Specials and the disarming of the R.U.C.;
(d)   Abolition of the Special Powers Act.,

therefore need to be augmented by the democratic *political demands*.

(1)   Proportional Representation in all elections.
(2)   The right to secede to join a 32 county republic should the reformed parliament so decide.

Twenty six county reforms

Corresponding parliamentary reforms in the 26 counties must include:

(1)   Abolition of those articles in the Constitution which show special regard for the Canon Law of the Roman Catholic Church.
(2)   *Northern elected representatives to have the right to sit as observers in Leinster House and to participate in All-Ireland constitutional consultation.*

[...]

Revolution or training-ground?

The defence-enclave[s] must not be regarded as control or revolution in themselves: they are far from it. They are however powerful educators, catalysts whereby the political situation can be transformed in a direction beneficial to the mass of the Irish people. The political solution which emerges must retain *as much power in Ireland as possible*, and must make possible the development of an *all-Ireland consciousness* among the people. Note that this is already beginning via the relief work. The mode of organization of relief work is the key; *it must be used to build up contact between like organizations, north and south.* The pattern has been set by the Dublin Trades Council, which has started a fund which is to be administered by the Belfast Trades Council, thus emphasizing the 32-county nature of the Trade Union Movement, and also involving Protestant trade unionists in the relief work.

The present situation is a *training-ground* for revolution. It is likely that the radical organizations will emerge from it strengthened, with some minor but significant victories. Let those who think that this is the revolution beware; to act on this belief prematurely could lead to the smashing of all radical organization for years to come; a further fifty years "carnival of reaction."

United Irishman, September 1969, 3, republished on Irish Left Archive.

SPEECH TO THE NATIONAL ASSOCIATION FOR IRISH JUSTICE (1969)
People's Democracy/Eilish McDermott

The National Association for Irish Justice (NAIJ) was NICRA's U.S. voice. With its large Irish diaspora, the U.S. was important to Irish nationalists for organizational support and foreign policy pressure. NAIJ organized speaking tours for People's Democracy's (PD's) parliamentarian Bernadette Devlin and others, and held protests and events around Northern Ireland. Its first and only conference included speakers from NICRA and PD along with (Official) IRA Chief of Staff Cathal Goulding. This speech by Belfast student Eilish McDermott, a leading PD activist, shows the challenges of identifying a viable strategy in the new climate. It also shows concern for connections beyond the Irish diaspora to student movements and other struggles. McDermott visited the Black Panthers and was made an honorary Panther. Devlin, who was given the keys of New York in 1969, gave them to the Panthers in 1970—a move not appreciated by New York's conservative Irish establishment.

* * *

Chairman sir, ladies and gentlemen, as you heard, I am a member of the People's Democracy, and what I'd like to tell you about this morning is the role which the People's Democracy is now attempting to play in the struggle for civil rights, North and South.

People's Democracy, as you will know, has been active in the struggle for civil rights, for more jobs and houses and against toryism, North and South. It believes that its objectives can only be obtained by the ousting of both Tory Governments and the setting up of an Irish Workers Republic. We arrived at this decision after considering three basic factors, all of which occurred post-August this year. The first factor which we considered, was the Protestant backlash and the threat of Orange fascism. The second one considered by us was the use of eight and a half thousand British troops in Northern Ireland. The third factor was the necessity for support for our cause from the South. To start on the first one then, the Protestant backlash and the threat of Orange fascism, the People's Democracy recognized long ago that an end to discrimination was not enough. Slum and unemployment would remain breeding violence and misery. Our struggle would have to continue; now it has become very urgent.

[...]

To press ahead with purely civil liberty, the demands will lead to more programs [pogroms] and inevitably, to a sectarian response from the Catholics. To drop the campaign now would disillusion and demoralize the people who have been supporting us for so long; not only the people in Northern Ireland but the people throughout the world, the people in America, the people here in this hall.

[...]

The only conceivable Southern intervention in a Northern problem which would not plunge the area into an even bloodier civil war than we saw last summer would be an intervention designed to secure a Socialist Republic. Not to submerge the Protestant workers in a state where their standard of living would be lower and where the Catholic Church would have the ruling hand over them. The People's Democracy have already formed links in the South, in Galway, Cork, Dublin and Limerick, and they have found the results there very encouraging.

[...]

I want you to tell me what you think of these sort of propositions so that I can bring back your reply to the people in the People's Democracy in Belfast.

Now is the time, though, let us remember, to consider and plan future action. We can't go on putting it on the long finger, it isn't that sort of struggle anymore. It's no longer the sort of struggle that you can play by ear, it's the sort of struggle that you have to sit down and work out and think about and work at. We hope that you will be able to contribute and I know that you have financially contributed enormously during the past months. I

know that the people in Ireland are terribly ... not terribly grateful to you, but I don't know what they would have done without you.
[...]
[I]f there are any students in this hall, let me say to them and say to them also on behalf of the students in Belfast, first of all that we extend our greetings to you and secondly, if you can do in America as much as the students did in Belfast, and I don't mean that in a boastful sense, I just mean it to say that it is possible for young people to do this sort of thing. To take the initiative, perhaps, and I think that all support should be given to students in their own fight, in their fight for civil rights and human dignity in no matter what part of the world they live.

Republished on Irish Left Archive.

Further Reading

Aretxaga, Begoña. *Shattering silence: Women, Nationalism and Political Subjectivity in Northern Ireland*. Princeton: Princeton University Press, 1997.
Devlin, Bernadette. *The Price of My Soul*. London: Macmillan, 1969.
Dooley, Brian. *Black and Green: the Fight for Civil Rights in Northern Ireland and Black America*. London: Pluto Press, 1998.
Hanley, Brian and Scott Millar. *The Lost Revolution: The Story of the Official IRA and the Workers' Party*. London: Penguin, 2010.
McCann, Eamonn. *War and an Irish Town*. Chicago: Haymarket Books, 2018.
McClenaghan, Pauline, ed. *Spirit of '68: Beyond the Barricades*. Derry: Guildhall, 2009.
Ó Dochartaigh, Niall. *From Civil Rights to Armalites: Derry and the Birth of the Irish Troubles*, second edition. London: Palgrave, 2005.
Ó Dochartaigh, Fionnbarra. *Ulster's White Negroes: from Civil Rights to Insurrection*. Edinburgh: AK Press, 1994.
O'Keefe, Theresa. *Feminist Identity Development and Activism in Revolutionary Movements: Unusual Suspects*. London: Palgrave Macmillan, 2013.
Purdie, Bob. *Politics in the Streets: Origins of the Civil Rights Movement in Northern Ireland*. Belfast: Blackstaff, 1990. Now free at cain.ulst.ac.uk/events/crights/purdie/index.html.
Reynolds, Chris. *Sous les Pavés, the Troubles: Northern Ireland, France and the European Collective Memory of 1968*. Bern: Peter Lang, 2014.
The CAIN archive at cain.ulst.ac.uk/index.html includes a wealth of useful material.

11
Yugoslavia

As in other countries, communism grew in popularity in Yugoslavia during World War II, and the country became home to history's second successful communist revolution. Significantly, Yugoslavia was also one of the only countries to liberate itself from Nazi rule without the direct military leadership of the Red Army. As such, Yugoslavia remained fiercely independent, even as the world began to polarize with the onset of the Cold War. After a series of disagreements between Joseph Stalin and Yugoslavia's leader, Josip Broz Tito, the two countries parted ways.

Yugoslavia soon embarked on its "own path to socialism," centered on the ideal of self-management. In the workplace, this referred to the idea that workers should have democratic say over the production process, and that the working class should be autonomous from the centralized power of the state. At the national level, this meant granting greater power to the country's many nationalities. A federal state, Yugoslavia was composed of six constituent republics – Bosnia and Herzegovina, Croatia, Macedonia, Montenegro, Serbia, and Slovenia – and two autonomous provinces – Vojvodina and Kosovo. Despite these lofty aims, autonomy for the working class and the country's many nationalities fell short of expectations, causing serious problems later.

Isolated, Yugoslavia had little choice but to find friends elsewhere. Tito increasingly turned to the Global South. Along with a host of other countries trying to chart an independent course in the Cold War, Yugoslavia helped initiate the Non-Aligned Movement, formally established in Belgrade, the capital of Yugoslavia, in 1961. At the same time, Yugoslavia opened up to the United States. In the 1950s, the U.S. began sending economic and military aid to Yugoslavia. Unsurprisingly, Yugoslavia became one of the most Western-oriented Communist-led countries in what came to be known as the "East." Yugoslavia produced goods for export; well over half a million Yugoslavs, the majority Croatian, worked abroad, sending remittances home to boost the domestic economy; and the country became a prime tourist destination. In 1966 alone around 12 million tourists, mostly from Western Europe, visited the country.

As in many other countries, the 1960s were a time of economic growth in Yugoslavia. In 1965 and 1966, liberal forces within the country's ruling party, the League of Communists of Yugoslavia (LCY), pushed for a "socialist market economy." Yet the new reforms widened wealth inequality, felt especially by young people, and the liberalization of the economy was not parallelled by democratization. Both issues would trigger discontent. The country did, however, see increased freedom of expression. Dissidents, like Milovan Djilas, were rehabilitated. Beat music, performance art, and other artistic expressions gained popularity among the new generation. In 1964, professors from Belgrade and Zagreb founded *Praxis*, a journal of innovative Marxist philosophy that would play an important role in the movements to come. Yugoslav students, youth, and intellectuals were also very connected to developments abroad, reading foreign books and even meeting thinkers like Herbert Marcuse or Ernest Mandel, who visited an annual summer school on the island of Korčula.

From the mid-1960s, a student movement took shape. The issues were widespread, but in some ways similar to those in other countries. Students criticized the lack of democracy in universities, inadequate conditions, the poor physical state of academic buildings and dormitories, and the lack of capacity of these universities. Youth unemployment and emigration also became big issues, discussed even within *Susret*, the Youth League of Serbia's magazine. As elsewhere, Vietnam was central. The Student League of Yugoslavia, for example, organized demonstrations and sit-ins not only against the Vietnam War, but the regime itself for not being more critical of the United States. The protesters were violently repressed by riot police, which only made students resent the authorities further.

The LCY hoped to use the Student Leagues to contain the growing discontent, but these organizations soon gained a degree of autonomy, becoming vehicles for student discontent. In the 1960s they demanded actual self-management in the universities. Significantly, the students did not oppose socialism as such, only what passed for socialism in Yugoslavia, which they felt fell far short of the LCY's stated goals. Students were especially critical of the LCY's recent "liberal" turn. They feared that Yugoslavia might end up with the worst of both worlds, the empty consumerism and class divisions of the West and the authoritarianism of the East. They called instead for a kind of democratic socialism, and targeted the new ruling elite in the country. As one of their slogans put it: "down with the red bourgeoisie."

The student movement climaxed in June 1968, immediately after the May events in Paris. On June 2, police attacked a student protest, triggering a riot. The next day, the students marched. During negotiations with party officials, the police opened fire, wounding several. The same day, hundreds of students occupied the Philosophy and Sociology Faculty at the University of Belgrade. The University Committee of LCY voted in favor of a week-long solidarity strike. The Committee, which had for some time

Figure 11.1   Student occupation, Belgrade. June 1968.

worried about "spontaneous activity," thus took a first step co-opting the student movement. LCY-loyal professors warned the students about the risks of isolation, urging them to communicate their grievances via official channels. Following this advice, students drafted the somewhat moderate "Political Action Program." But fearing of co-optation, some radical students rejected the agreement that the University Committee had made on their behalf with the City Committee of the LCY.

The student uprising quickly spread to other cities, notably Sarajevo and Zagreb. Across the country, students continued to demonstrate, write letters of solidarity to allies at home and abroad, organize rallies, occupations, sit-ins, and assemblies, and form democratically elected Action Committees to organize strike activities. As for their demands, in addition to student issues, they focused on local problems in their respective cities, called for freedom of the press and assembly, and even criticized state centralization and bureaucracy. The student movement's internationalism contrasted sharply with the various ethnonationalist currents that were starting to rear their heads.

But Belgrade remained the center of the student movement in Yugoslavia, with an estimated 40,000 students participating in the movement there, and the Philosophy and Sociology Faculty remained the center of the center, so to speak, especially for the movement's radical wing. Its courtyard became something of a "student commune," a space for speeches, teach-ins, and sharing food. And it was from here that students planned other occupations.

Students also tried to build ties with workers, arguing that they were part of the same struggle, that they all had a common interest in self-management. The students thought unity between students and workers could create a new revolutionary force to take over where the revolutionaries of Yugoslavia's 1940s had now failed. However, partly due to the interference of the LCY, these efforts were largely unsuccessful.

As for the LCY, it played a most ambiguous role in these movements. Unlike almost all other ruling parties, the LCY not only supported, but encouraged the global unrest of the 1960s. Its papers reported on revolts abroad, its editors published texts from other movements, and some leaders openly sympathized with the international protests. Revolts in the "West," especially France, where the idea of "autogestion" was so prominent, as well as revolts in the "East," especially Czechoslovakia, which was attempting to build "socialism with a human face," were seen by some as confirmation of the validity of Yugoslavian ideas of self-management. Tito himself was so supportive of these developments that he personally traveled to Prague in early August, just before the Soviet invasion.

But while the LCY may have supported movements abroad, and in so doing unintentionally encouraged a spirit of activism, it grew nervous when serious protests broke out in its own backyard. Solidarity actions for movements abroad were one thing; protesting against the ruling order at home was another. But the LCY had to walk a fine line: outright repression at home would completely tarnish Tito's vision of Yugoslavia as a progressive socialist force in the world.

As the students pinned their struggle on the ideology of socialism and self-management, so too would the regime eventually use the same ideological reference points to contain the movement. In June 1968, after a week of student action and police repression, all in the defense of self-management, Tito surprised everyone by delivering a televised speech in which he praised the students for their commitment to the ideals of self-management. But he simultaneously condemned the more radical students as disloyal, characterizing them as at best poor imitators of students abroad and at worse foreign agents. He promised to introduce reforms according to the "Action Program," saying he would resign if he did not live up to his word.

Although Tito's speech had a demobilizing effect on the movement, not everyone was convinced, especially the students and professors in the Philosophy and Sociology Faculty. Activism continued, but so did the LCY's mixture of co-optation and repression: the League expanded its student membership to show support for the students' cause, while at the same time punishing the more radical elements of the movement. On July 20, the League officially shut down the Philosophy and Sociology Faculty.

This marked the beginning of a period of increased repression that characterized the first half of the 1970s.

Yet activism did not end. The counterculture lived on. Yugoslav activists became concerned with other issues, like the environment. In 1970, students in Belgrade protested in solidarity with miners in Bosnia. The early to mid-1970s also saw the emergence of another wave of feminist engagement. Driven by the contradiction between the government's rhetorical commitment to women's emancipation and the realities of "actually existing socialism," and taking inspiration from women's liberation movements in other countries, Yugoslav feminists organized their own movement, which reached a high point in 1978 with the first international feminist conference in the country.

Most significantly, and perhaps ominously given the fate of Yugoslavia, the wave of activism in the late 1960s and early 1970s gave way to revived nationalist sentiment. In Croatia, for example, protests in 1971 called for more rights to self-determination. The "Croatian Spring," as it came to be called, was harshly repressed by Tito, but the nationalist tide did not vanish. Quite the contrary, nationalism increasingly came to dominate the political horizon.

HONORED PROFESSOR (1968)
Ivica Percl

Zagreb folksinger Ivica Percl sang the ballad reproduced below in 1968, just as Yugoslavia's unofficial student movement was gathering force. Surviving footage shows a 23-year-old Percl, clad in a workers' cap and sporting long hair and sideburns, performing the song on a guitar and harmonica among the ruins of an old factory. The atmospheric setting within the remnants of Yugoslavia's earlier industrialization poignantly conveyed many young people's conviction that the existing structures of power, at home and abroad, were decayed and unresponsive. As the song shows, much of the country's youth were not content to simply support what they saw as their elders' shortsighted and misdirected interpretation of the country's mounting problems.

* * *

Honored professor, director,
Esteemed citizen—city dweller,
Politician of the days gone by,
And the lot of you trying to do away with hooligans.

Recall at times our working-class generation
The brave brigadiers with mattocks in their hands.
You cannot say we've lost our boldness,
Cos bravery must strive towards noble ends.

Tell me if you've ever really pondered
Where the youth spends its idle hours?
While the vast majority studies diligently
The rowdy minority shouts vigilantly.

Going round in circles day in, day out
Your petty little talk no longer sounds smart
"How come hooligans don't change and are all the same?"
Your questions and answers we always know by heart.

Can you reflect upon your own action?
You compete with each other who's got more to say,
About mop-top hairstyles and fashion of the day,
While the pressing issues remain at bay.

You never wondered how we felt
Watching our harbingers of hope melt.
Working against your people was least expected,
Something which amongst you had never been reflected.

Honored professor, director,
Esteemed citizen—city dweller,
Politician of the days gone by,
And the lot of you trying to do away with hooligans.

Courtesy of family Percl. Postovani profesore (Ivica Percl) © 1968 Croatia Records. Translated by Zoran Vučkovac. Introduction by Madigan Fichter, adapted from "Yugoslav Protest: Student Rebellion in Belgrade, Zagreb, and Sarajevo in 1968," *Slavic Review* 75, no. 1 (Spring 2016): 99–121.

RESOLUTION OF THE STUDENT DEMONSTRATION (1968)

On June 2, 1968 a cultural event took place in a small theater in a suburb of Belgrade. The authorities decided the event would only be open to members of the LCY-controlled Youth Action organization. Students protested and were thrown out by the police. Incited by a rumor that a student had been killed, 3,000 students took to the streets. Fights broke out, protesters torched a fire truck, the police attacked, and the students built barricades. Most of the students that took to the streets on the night of June 2 lived in the Student City dormitories in the suburb of New Belgrade, close to where the confrontation had erupted. The following day, they issued the following Resolution. While some of the demands focused on university conditions, the resolution issued a broad critique of the existing Yugoslavian system. Notably, the students criticized the existence of "social inequality," which they found unacceptable in a country claiming to be socialist.

* * *

Figure 11.2   University of Belgrade students take to the streets. June 1968.

Over the course of yesterday and today, students have, among other things, expressed their disagreement with the following phenomena in our society and raised the following demands:

1) We deem social inequality our fundamental domestic problem. In that respect, we demand:
   — consistent distribution according to work,
   — energetic action against acquiring wealth contrary to the tenets of socialism,
   — that the social structure of the student population be a representational reflection of the general social structure,
   — an abolition of each and every privilege present in our society.
2) High unemployment rate is another cause of student outrage. Hence we demand:
   — abolition of contract work,

— decrease in managerial staff without adequate qualifications and their replacement with young experts,

— faster implementation of the Law on obligatory internship and a stimulative action toward young experts in order to prevent them from going abroad.

3) The existence of strong bureaucratic influence in our society requires:

— democratization of all socio-political organizations and especially the League of Communists,

— democratization of all print and electronic media and means of forming public opinion,

— freedom of assembly and demonstration.

4) Students are especially embittered by the state of our universities. Therefore we require:

— improvement of the universities' material position,

— equal participation of students in forums discussing important societal issues and above all those directly or indirectly related to students,

— we condemn the emergence of clans and monopolies within some departments and demand fierce action against it,

— we demand a total and democratic (re)electability of all teaching staff,

— we demand free admission for students.

Student City,
June 3, 1968

Demonstrators' Action Committee
and Students' Assembly
in Student City

Reprinted in *Praxis*, nos. 1–2, "Marx i revolucija. Jun–lipanj 1968: Dokumenti" (special issue), Zagreb, 1969, 62–3. Retrieved from Rudi Petrović's Library: praxis. memoryoftheworld.org. Translated by Zoran Vučkovac.

LETTER FROM STUDENTS TO WORKERS (1968)

As in other countries in 1968, Yugoslav students tended to see themselves as a new revolutionary vanguard; but, also like students abroad, they made efforts to build alliances with the working class, the revolutionary subject canonized in the country's official socialist theory. In the following letter, written on June 4, two days after the uprising began, students report on worker support, while recognizing that they needed to do more to directly address the public, which they claim has been "insufficiently informed" by the LCY-loyal media. The letter argues that students and workers share common interests, for bottom-up self-management and shared ownership and against the top-down liberalizing economic reforms and state bureaucracy. Remarkably, the students insist that they do not oppose the official LCY ideology, but only wish for the League's program to be more consistently implemented.

* * *

Comrade Workers, Citizens, and Youth,

We have been receiving telegrams from the working collectives regarding the latest events at the University. We are happy to hear that workers from numerous collectives know and understand the aims and significance of our action and support our demands. However, due to an insufficiently informed public, the truth about our action has not reached all of them. We aim to inform you about our goals with this letter.

Comrades!

We are not fighting for our narrowly defined, material interests. We are embittered by the existence of enormous social and economic stratification in our society. We stand against the fact that the working class must single-handedly bear the brunt of economic reforms. We stand for bottom-up social self-management, unattainable without the producers being directly represented in self-governing and representational bodies. We stand against the increasing accumulation of wealth by individuals at the expense of the working class. We stand for social ownership and against attempts to set up capitalist shareholding companies.

It hurts us to see thousands of our people leaving to serve and work for global capital. We want to use our knowledge, zest, and love in building our socialist society.

We resent seeing how narrow bureaucratic interests strive to break up the brotherhood and unity of our peoples. We will not allow attempts to create rifts between workers and students. Your interests are also our own, those being the only true interests of socialism. We do not have a special program. Our program is that of the most progressive forces in our society—the Programme of the LCY and the Constitution. We demand its consistent implementation.

June 4, 1968

LONG LIVE THE SOLIDARITY BETWEEN WORKERS AND STUDENTS

Reprinted in *Praxis*, nos. 1–2, "Marx i revolucija. Jun–lipanj 1968: Dokumenti" (special issue), Zagreb, 1969, 83. Retrieved from Rudi Petrović's Library: praxis. memoryoftheworld.org. Translated by Zoran Vučkovac.

POLITICAL ACTION PROGRAM (1968)

Issued by both students and administrators at the University of Belgrade on June 5, three days after the start of the June events, the following "Political Action Program" became the most important semi-official document of the student uprising in Yugoslavia. But not everyone approved of the document. The radical students and professors at the Philosophy and Sociology Faculty at the University of Belgrade initially dismissed the Program as not being radical enough. For example, the emphasis on "social inequality" and "equal participation," which was so key to the more radical Resolution issued two days before, have been watered down here. When President Tito gave his televised speech on June 9, he promised to deliver on the demands set forth in the Program. To some extent, then, the Program can be seen as part of the state's strategy to co-opt the student uprising instead of relying exclusively on physical repression.

* * *

The Program is composed to help solve the central issues of our socialist society as a self-managed community of free and equal peoples and nationalities faster and more efficiently.

I.

We find that it is urgent to:

1. Take measures in order to rapidly reduce the great social disparities in our community. In this regard we demand: consistent application of the socialist principle of distribution according to work; clearly and accurately defined criteria for determining personal income; determining lowest and highest personal income and reversing income differentiation based on monopolistic positions; energetic action against non-socialist acquisition of property and nationalization of the property thus far unjustly acquired.
   Privileges in our society must be eradicated.
   Urgent measures are needed to progressively tax those whose income breaches the wage ceiling.
2. A long-term concept of economic development is needed for a faster and more efficient solution to the unemployment issues, which, fundamen-

tally, means securing the right to work for the entire working population of our country. Hence, a corresponding program of investment policy is needed, one that would secure the existence of employment programs along with the constant improvement of material and cultural living conditions of our people.

Measures need to be adopted for securing work for young qualified workers.

Therefore, it is necessary to solve the issues of internship and mandatory employment for all young professional staff, as well as the issue of part-time work. This needs to be either reduced to its minimum or abolished altogether.

The personnel policy demands a consistent implementation of the principle that vacancies requiring certain qualifications be filled by people in possession of those qualifications.

3. Actions are required to expedite the establishment of self-managing relations in our society that would eradicate the bureaucratic forces hindering the development of our communities.

The system of self-managed relations should be developed consistently not only in workers' organizations but also on all levels of our society, from municipal to federal, in such a way that within each self-managed entity the majority is comprised of direct producers. The starting position for the development of real self-management is independent decision-making by self-managers regarding all important conditions of their labor, especially the distribution of surplus labor.

Each self-managing entity should bear responsibility for accomplishing the tasks within their purview and should be held socially accountable in case they fail to accomplish their tasks.

It is necessary to pose the question of personal responsibility.

4. Democratization of all social and political organizations, especially the League of Communists, should be more thorough and quicker, in accordance with the development of self-managing relations. It should especially cover all the means of forming public opinion. Finally, democratization should enable the exercise of all rights and freedoms prescribed by the Constitution.

5. Vigorously prevent attempts to fragment social property or its degeneration into shareholding property.

Prevent individual and group tendencies to capitalize on individual labor, and subdue these tendencies using the constitutional framework and positive legal regulations.

6. Promptly amend the Law on Housing Relations in order to prevent speculation on socially and privately owned apartments.

7. Cultural relations should strive toward preventing commercialization while creating such conditions in which cultural and creative facilities are accessible to everyone.

II.

1. Immediately undertake educational reform in order to harmonize it with the developing needs of our economy, culture, and self-managing relations.
2. Realization of constitutionally guaranteed rights to equal conditions for education of all young people.
3. Pass a new law on the autonomy of the University.
   We also emphasize the need to implement the following concrete measures:
   a) Organize the University as a self-managed institution where progressive and critical scientific thought develops freely. In that respect it is necessary to develop the actual self-managing relations at the University faster and to creatively construct those self-managing forms compatible with the University environment.
   b) The social structure of students should correspond with the structure of society.
   c) The material position of students should be improved while the work on building student institutions should be intensified. And these institutions should be given to students to manage following the self-managing principles of our society.
   d) Strengthen the impact of science, the University and students on formulating the basic understanding about the paths and forms of our social and economic development.
   e) Introduce the principle of reappointment for all vocations while preventing its formalization and open the doors of the University to young people capable of scientific and pedagogic work.
   f) Revoke regulation concerning tuition in all educational institutions.

Belgrade, June 5, 1968

PLENUM OF THE UNIVERSITY COMMITTEE OF THE STUDENT
UNION AT THE UNIVERSITY OF BELGRADE
UNIVERSITY COMMITTEE OF THE LEAGUE OF COMMUNISTS AT
THE UNIVERSITY OF BELGRADE
STUDENT ACTION COMMITTEE OF ALL FACULTIES, COLLEGES, AND
ACADEMIES IN BELGRADE

Reprinted in *Praxis*, nos. 1–2, "Marx i revolucija. Jun–lipanj 1968: Dokumenti" (special issue), Zagreb, 1969, 139–41. Retrieved from Rudi Petrovič's Library: praxis.memoryoftheworld.org. Translated by Zoran Vučkovac.

PROCLAMATION OF THE REVOLUTIONARY STUDENTS OF THE SOCIALIST UNIVERSITY "SEVEN SECRETARIES OF THE YOUNG COMMUNIST LEAGUE OF YUGOSLAVIA" (1968)

While Belgrade emerged as the epicenter of the Yugoslav student uprising, activists not only organized in other Yugoslav cities, they worked hard to build networks of solidarity across the country's diverse Socialist Republics. This stood in striking contrast to the ethnonationalist currents that would intensify in later years. Written by students in Zagreb, Croatia, the following text speaks to the pan-Yugoslav scope of the movement, demanding, for example, that the authorities re-open the University of Belgrade. Following students in West Germany, who renamed Frankfurt University the "Karl Marx University," students in Belgrade renamed theirs the Red University "Karl Marx" in Belgrade. The Zagreb students followed the example, renaming their university the Socialist University "Seven Secretaries of SKOJ (the Young Communist League of Yugoslavia)," a reference to the communist secretaries who were tortured and killed under the reign of King Alexander I in the late 1920s and early 1930s.

* * *

At a rally of socialist-revolutionary democratic forces of the University of Zagreb, organized by students and teachers on June 5, 1968 at the Student Center in Zagreb, the following was concluded:

1. Forming an Action Committee comprised of student and teacher representatives;
2. Providing unreserved support for those tendencies in our Republic and Yugoslavia that seek consistent implementation of the main objectives of the social and economic reform as a meaningful stage of our socialist revolution. Hereby the primary theoretical criteria must be the introduction of eminently communist solutions into all of our social processes and relations;
3. We vigorously demand a genuine economic liberation of the working class which, alongside the Marxist intelligentsia, must become the actual bearer of the key socio-political decisions, ranging from the level of labor organization to national and federal levels. In this respect, we demand identification of the bureaucratic obstructionists in the pursuit of the aforementioned objectives of socio-economic reform;

4. We condemn the demagogic claims of those politicians who create an artificial gap between the students and the working class;

5. We demand the replacement of the secretaries of internal affairs of the Federation, the Socialist Republic of Serbia, and the city of Belgrade, investigation into their responsibility and the punishment of those elements guilty of brutal actions against students and teachers during the demonstrations in Belgrade;

    We demand condemnation of conduct of the political officials who failed to prevent the savage attack on the procession of students and teachers;

6. We request that the Parliament of the Socialist Republic of Croatia receives a delegation of students and teachers that will put forward demands for further democratization of our society and remove obstacles for international relations based on principles of full equality;

7. We demand that all forms of privileges allowing personal enrichment and ideological monopoly be abolished; we demand immediate establishing of full freedom of the press, assembly, agreement, manifestation and demonstration, swift implementation of measures to reduce unemployment, as well as measures aimed at improving the position of the working class and consistent application of the self-management principles and distribution according to work;

8. We demand freedom of the press and that the public be objectively informed regarding all revolutionary events in the whole society;

9. We demand the reopening of the Red University "Karl Marx" in Belgrade. In this respect, we demand that the Constitutional Court of the Socialist Federal Republic of Yugoslavia takes immediate action;

10. We express our support for the revolutionary student movement in Poland, Germany, France, Spain, Italy, and other countries;

11. From this point on the University of Zagreb is renamed the Socialist University "SEVEN SECRETARIES OF SKOJ";

12. We will distribute this proclamation to the press, radio, and television, and demand its publication, but we will also forward it to the Executive Board of the Socialist Republic of Croatia, the Parliament of the Socialist Republic of Croatia, and the Central Executive Committee of the Central Committee of the League of Communists of Croatia and request a public statement from them concerning students' demands.

Zagreb, June 5, 1968

Reprinted in *Praxis*, nos. 1–2, "Marx i revolucija. Jun–lipanj 1968: Dokumenti" (special issue), Zagreb, 1969, 188–9. Retrieved from Rudi Petrović's Library: praxis. memoryoftheworld.org. Translated by Zoran Vučkovac.

DISCUSSION HELD BY THE GENERAL ASSEMBLY OF
THE PHILOSOPHY AND SOCIOLOGY FACULTY (1968)

D. Plamenic

The students and professors of the Philosophy and Sociology Faculty at the University of Belgrade constituted the radical core of the uprising. Although President Tito's speech demobilized many students, effectively ending the occupation, many of these students and professors maintained their radical stance in the period that followed. This is clearly seen in the following text, which captures a discussion with a journalist loyal to the LCY. Soon after, on July 20, the League grew tired of the continued radicalism, and the police closed down the Faculty, and its Committee—home to several Praxis *professors who supported the movement, and were denounced for allegedly conspiring with Western forces— was expelled from the League of Communists. The text below was originally published in the British* New Left Review, *again indicating the strong transnational dimensions of the movement.*

*   *   *

The General Assembly began by describing the enemy as "everyone who has something to lose through equality." Following this, during a discussion of their enemy's total monopoly of the means of communication, it was noted that the most important reporter of the largest Yugoslav newspaper was present. As the reporter was one of the most vicious spokesmen for their enemy, they asked him to explain his opposition.

Reporter: "Well, I'm afraid I can't right now remember all the remarks I've written and as I didn't bring any material with me ... (jeering from the students) ... you must realize ... I'm not responsible for what is printed in the paper. The final decision is out of my hands. (laughter)

I guess if you like, I can give you my general opinion of what you people are doing. Essentially you are senseless agitators. You're not going to agree with that! You believe you've grounds for your movement, but the fact is you are operating out of only a petit bourgeois abstract humanism.

It is true that there are deformations in our socialist society, but these problems must be examined scientifically and so they are by all our institutions and, in fact, as you have seen fit to ignore, already many new laws have been passed to correct them. But you simply skip lightly over these difficult problems that our leaders are presently facing, in order to disqualify *in toto* everything about our self-management socialist institutions, together with our leaders."

Assistant Professor: "Please, would you give us a more precise definition of what you mean by 'abstract humanism'."

Reporter: "Abstract humanism, yes I can do that. One only has to glance at your literature to erase any doubt as to the nature of your ideology. The analysis that you make of the real difficulties facing our society is based on a simple-minded confusion of the various social, economic and technological problems on the one hand with the nature of management of the means of production on the other. This forces you to overlook the basically socialist nature of our society and the socialist motivation of our leaders. Instead, you strike out blindly at technology, against commodity relations, and even at self-management. But out of this sort of abstraction comes nothing more than more abstraction. This is why the content of your movement is of no value, unless you consider interruption of normal social activity as being of value."

Student 1: "You jump at the chance to attack our movement as nonsocialist; as it attacks you, and as you are by definition and membership and law a socialist, then of course we cannot be socialist—by definition (laughter). But I ask, if you stand for socialism then why have you ignored that last article by our ambassador to the United Nations on Vietnam published in your paper. In short he said that the Viet Cong and United States are equally guilty in Viet Nam. I am insulted by that! A more reactionary view of the world revolution one could not imagine. Yet you have not jumped at the chance to attack this position. Is it because you were not paid to attack it?"

Reporter: "Listen, I'm a simple reporter, my powers are limited. It would have done no good to attack that article. I can't change all our leaders' views. I'm just a little man with little ideas."

Student 2: "That sort of stuff doesn't go with us here. We don't rank people by their party functions, but by their contribution to society."

Reporter: (angry now) "I have defined for you abstract humanism in quite precise terms and you have nothing in reply but platitudes. You are silent too on commodity production, is it that you cannot defend your position?"

Professor 2: "Yes, you are quite right, we do attack commodity production and we find it diametrically opposed to socialism. But we may not be strong enough to move our society toward socialism. Nevertheless, we say that you are building capitalism. We demand Marxist criticism of the class you are building and the class which you represent. No, we don't want any more of this empty so-called socialist propaganda. You have systematically divided and neutralized the power of the working class and in so doing you have created power and privilege for yourselves. What you happen to find opportunistically convenient you call socialism.

Call what you have created what you like, but don't call it socialism. We here are for the real power in the hands of the working class, and if that is the meaning of self-management, then we are for self-management. But if self-management is nothing but a facade for the construction of the competitive profit mechanism of a bureaucratic managerial ... why don't I say capitalist, class, then we are against it. No you are not socialist and you are not creating socialism. Perhaps we have no way to stop you. But we will attempt to build a truly critical university to help the working class to understand what you are doing in its name. Yes, you are an avant-garde, but not of the working class. Print that if you like!"

D. Plamenic, "The Belgrade Student Insurrection," *New Left Review* I/54, 1969, 71–3.

Further Reading

Allcock, John B. *Explaining Yugoslavia.* New York: Columbia University Press, 2000.
Fichter, Madigan. "Yugoslav Protest: Student Rebellion in Belgrade, Zagreb, and Sarajevo in 1968." *Slavic Review* 75, no. 1 (Spring 2016): 99–121.
Gruenwald, Oskar. *The Yugoslav Search for Man: Marxist Humanism in Contemporary Yugoslavia.* South Hadley, Mass.: Bergin & Garvey Publishers, 1983.
Kanzleiter, Boris. "Yugoslavia." In *1968 in Europe: A History of Protest and Activism, 1956–1977,* edited by Martin Klimke and Joachim Scharloth, 219–28. New York: Palgrave Macmillan, 2008.
Kanzleiter, Boris. "1968 in Yugoslavia: Student Revolt between East and West." In *Between Prague Spring and French May: Opposition and Revolt in Europe, 1960–1980,* edited by Martin Klimke, Jacco Pekelder, and Joachim Scharloth, 84–100. New York: Berghahn Books, 2013.
Lampe, John R. *Yugoslavia as History: Twice There Was a Country,* second edition Cambridge: Cambridge University Press, 2000.
Pervan, Ralph. *Tito and the Students: The University and the University Student in Self-Managing Yugoslavia.* Nedlands: University of Western Australia Press, 1978.
Ramet, Sabrina P. *The Three Yugoslavias: State-Building and Legitimation, 1918–2005.* Bloomington, IN: Indiana University Press, 2006.
Rubinstein, Alvin Z. *Yugoslavia and the Nonaligned World.* Princeton: Princeton University Press, 2015.
Rusinow, Dennison I. *The Yugoslav Experiment 1948-1974.* Berkeley and Los Angeles: University of California Press, 1978.
Sher, Gerson S. *Praxis: Marxist Criticism and Dissent in Socialist Yugoslavia.* Bloomington, IN: Indiana University Press, 1978.

12
Czechoslovakia

As they set about rebuilding their country after World War II, Czechoslovak citizens searched for a vision for the postwar future. Many turned to communism. In their view, domestic communists had proven themselves in the Resistance, the Red Army liberated Eastern Europe from Nazi rule, and the U.S.S.R. seemed to promise an effective model of development. Communism's newfound popularity soon made itself felt at the polls. In March 1946, in the first free election since the war, the Communist Party of Czechoslovakia (CPCz) scored a whopping 40.17 percent, by far the strongest showing by any party in the country.

Although Joseph Stalin was initially happy to let communists in Czechoslovakia pursue their own path to communism, the onset of the Cold War led him to impose a single model across all of the East. With the support of local collaborators, Stalin curtailed Czechoslovak autonomy, purged thousands of dissident communists, and forced the country to adopt a command economy, single party rule, and collectivization.

But after Stalin's death, life began to change. In 1960, Czechoslovakia adopted a new constitution that declared an end to class war. While the country remained committed to central planning, the reformist turn brought about modest attempts at liberalization through the early and mid-1960s. Eventually, this constitutional shift created a space for the expression of new ideas. Indeed, the 1960s witnessed a revitalization of public debate, literary discussion, and cultural production.

Despite these real changes, hardliners in the Party, led by First Secretary Antonín Novotný, were reluctant to go any further, prompting criticism from intellectuals who intended to take full advantage of the new opening. In June 1967, for example, many of the country's leading writers gathered for the Fourth Congress of the Union of Czechoslovak Writers, where they called for reforms to the existing system.

In addition, while youth discontent had not prompted the initial reforms of the 1960s, it did push them further. With about half of the population in 1968 either not born, or mere children, when the country turned communist in 1948, many youth felt they belonged to a distinct generation, one excluded from the establishment. They tended to be more educated than the older generations, but many were over-qualified for the jobs they held. Given the conditions in the country, their discontent at first took the form of cultural subversion, with many drawing on countercultural elements from the capitalist West, like wearing blue jeans, reading Allen Ginsberg, or listening to The Beatles.

As elsewhere, students played the role of catalyzers. On October 31, 1967 a blackout at the Strahov dormitories behind Prague Castle prompted students to march in protest, with chants of "We want light!" ringing out into the night. The authorities responded with tear gas and baton blows, even inside the dormitory courtyard, a space assumed to be police-free. Intellectuals, already critical of the establishment, supported the students, amplifying the push for formal political change. In addition to the students and the intellectuals, Slovaks also joined the chorus. Many Slovaks felt they were treated like a second-class minority, that Slovakia was less economically developed, and that the region deserved greater autonomy. Reform-minded officials saw which way the wind was blowing.

This pressure for reform pushed the Communist Party to appoint a new First Secretary, Alexander Dubček, a Slovak, on January 5, 1968. Once in power, Dubček commissioned an "Action Program" to right the wrongs of the past by reforming the existing system. "Socialism with a human face," as it was called, would chart a new path between Stalinism and Western-style liberal capitalism. Officially published in April, the Program mapped out a concrete plan for change, which included easing restrictions on travel, abolishing censorship, and reforming the economy.

These reforms proved immensely popular. Significantly, most Czecho-slovak citizens agreed with the Communist Party's project of reforming the socialist system rather than replacing it with capitalism. In June and July 1968, the Institute of Public Opinion found that 86 percent of respondents favored "a continuation of socialist development" with only 5 percent wanting to return to capitalism. As for democratization, while many hoped for a multiparty system, they remained committed to the goals of the Communist Party. Polls revealed, for example, that while 50 percent of respondents wanted more parties, 70 percent believed any opposition party should retain a socialist program.

Czechoslovak citizens made good use of the new openings. New journals appeared, the nuclei of new parties started to emerge, a plethora of new groups, clubs, and associations took root. There was a Society for Human Rights, women's rights groups, student clubs, religious organizations, and cultural associations for ethnic minorities, like Poles, Ukrainians, and Roma. Most significantly, groups of students, writers, intellectuals, and later workers, emerged to push the reforms even further.

Dubček recognized that Czechoslovakia's experiment troubled the U.S.S.R., but he assured the Soviet premier, Leonid Brezhnev, that he had the situation under control. After all, the reform process was deeply popular, the Party was firmly in control, and there were no signs of an uprising, as happened in Hungary in 1956. But Brezhnev was unconvinced. He feared that Czechoslovakia might leave the Warsaw Pact; he worried that the reforms might spiral out of control, leading to the restoration of capitalism; and he was increasingly anxious about the possible spillover effects. In fact, hardline Communists in neighboring countries like Poland and East Germany feared that the events in Czechoslovakia might incite their own people to demand similar changes at home. In Poland, for example, graffiti ominously declared, "Poland is Awaiting its Own Dubček."

After months of negotiations, the Soviet Union lost its patience. On August 21, 1968, Warsaw Pact forces from the U.S.S.R., Poland, East Germany, Hungary, and Bulgaria invaded. The Soviets, in collaboration with hardline Czechoslovak Communists, seized control, taking Dubček and other reformists into custody, where they were forced to sign an agreement surrendering control in Moscow. While they would later claim to have saved the reform project, the eight-month long Prague Spring ground to a halt.

Figure 12.1 "The Bare-Chested Man in Front of an Occupying Tank." Bratislava, August 21, 1968. © Ladislav Bielik. Courtesy of Peter Bielik.

Immediately following the invasion, reformers held a clandestine Communist Party Congress in Vysočany, promising to continue fighting for the people, but simultaneously urging them to remain calm, obey orders from foreign troops, and prevent bloodshed. While most people in Czechoslovakia remained peaceful, many did turn to civil resistance. Some people tampered with road signs and renamed towns to confuse the invading troops. Others protested the presence of Warsaw Pact troops. Over one hundred people died in the invasion, with several hundred more wounded. While the resistance failed to halt the invasion, it undermined the U.S.S.R.'s attempt to legitimize the operation. Both the French and Italian Communist Parties, for example, broke ranks by expressing disapproval of the invasion.

As for the Soviets, what they expected would be a brief operation ended up taking months. The people despised the pro-Moscow hardliners installed by the U.S.S.R. Workers' councils that proliferated following the invasion. A 21-year-old student named Jan Palach set himself ablaze in January 1969.

Riots broke out when the Czechoslovak national team defeated the Soviet Union at the Hockey World Championships in March. And Czechoslovak citizens demonstrated again on the first anniversary of the invasion in August.

The government responded with force, replacing Dubček with a hardliner, and initiating a process of "normalization" that aimed to not only overturn almost all the "counterrevolutionary" measures of Dubček and his comrades, but to erase the memory of the Prague Spring and instill new values. Reactions to normalization were varied, as many Czechoslovak citizens accommodated themselves to the new order. But dissent continued, albeit in different forms. Tens of thousands expressed their opposition by emigrating. Others turned to art, and Czechoslovakia witnessed the emergence of the "Prague underground," a countercultural movement that built on the energies of the 1960s. It was spearheaded by the rock band, The Plastic People of the Universe, and their artistic director Ivan Martin Jirous. Formed in September 1968, they were harassed from the beginning, and in 1976 finally found guilty of "organized disturbance of the peace" and sentenced to prison.

One of the most significant consequences of the invasion and the repression that followed was not simply the discrediting of the Soviet Union, but the idea that the systems in the East could be reformed. After the Prague Spring, some, though not all, future activists distanced themselves from the idea of communism as such, looking for different models of reform. Increasingly, they would turn to ideas of human rights. These impulses would lead to the formation of Charter 77, led by, among others, Václav Havel, who eventually became the first President of the Czech Republic in 1993.

Although similar in some respects, the events of 1968 in Czechoslovakia differed significantly from those in most other countries in the Global North. The Prague Spring was led not by a radical youth movement, but "from above," by reformers in the country's Communist Party. It aimed not to radically overthrow the existing system, but to force those in power to live up to their stated vision of creating a truly egalitarian society. And it was also immensely popular, pushed forward by a broad coalition that largely remained loyal to the Party, pledging to stand by the government in the face of Soviet repression.

ACTION PROGRAM OF THE COMMUNIST PARTY OF CZECHOSLOVAKIA (1968)

On April 10, 1968, the Central Committee presented the following "Action Program" as a statement of its political intentions, often summarized in Alexander

Dubček's words as "socialism with a human face." Although the Communist Party would still enjoy a leading role, and central planning would remain the organizational principle of society, power would be slowly decentralized, travel restrictions gradually lifted, censorship relaxed, those who had been purged would be rehabilitated, and spaces created for pluralistic discussion, both inside and outside the Party. Communist reformers spoke of reforming the economy, federalizing the Czech and Slovak lands, even multiparty elections in the future. Radicals often anticipated these changes in practice before they had been formally legalized, and pushed them even further once they took effect.

* * *

[...]

The Leading Role of the Party: A Guarantee of Socialist Progress

At present it is most important that the party adopt a policy fully justifying its leading role in society. We believe this is a condition for the socialist development of the country. [...]

In the past, the leading role of the party was usually conceived of as a monopolistic concentration of power in the hands of party organs. This concept corresponded with the false thesis that the party is the instrument of the dictatorship of the proletariat. That harmful conception weakened the initiative and responsibility of state, economic, and social institutions, damaged the party's authority, and prevented it from carrying out its real functions. The party's goal is not to become a universal "caretaker" of society, bind all organizations, and watch every step taken in fulfillment of its directives. Its mission instead is primarily to inspire socialist initiative, to demonstrate communist perspectives, their modes, and to win over all workers by systematic persuasion and the personal examples of communists. This determines the conceptual side of party activity. Party organs should not deal with all problems; they should encourage others and suggest solutions to the most important difficulties. But at the same time the party cannot turn into an organization that influences society by its ideas and program alone. It must develop through its members and bodies the practical organizational methods of a political force in society. [...]

As a representative of the most progressive section of society—and therefore the representative of the prospective aims of society—the party cannot represent the full range of social interests. The National Front, the political face of the manifold interests of society, expresses the unity of social strata, interest groups, and of nations and nationalities in this society. The party does not want to and will not take the place of social organizations; on the contrary, it must ensure that their initiative and political responsibility for the unity of society are revived and can flourish. The role of the party is to find a way of satisfying the various interests without jeopardizing the interests of society as a whole, and promoting those interests and creating new progressive ones. The party's policy must not lead non-communists to feel that their rights and freedom are limited by the role of the party. [...]

For the Development of Socialist Democracy and a New System of the Political Management of Society

[...] We must reform the whole political system so that it will permit the dynamic development of social relations appropriate for socialism, combine broad democracy with scientific, highly qualified management, strengthen the social order, stabilize socialist relations, and maintain social discipline. The basic structure of the political system must, at the same time, provide firm guarantees against a return to the old methods of subjectivism and highhandedness [...] All these changes necessarily call for the commencement of work on a new Czechoslovak Constitution so that a draft may be thoroughly discussed by professionals and in public and submitted to the National Assembly shortly after the party congress. [...]

The implementation of the constitutional freedoms of assembly and association must be ensured this year so that the possibility of setting up voluntary organizations, special-interest associations, societies, and other such bodies is guaranteed by law, and so that the present interests and needs of various sections of our society are tended to without bureaucratic interference and free from a monopoly by any individual organization. Any restrictions in this respect can be imposed only by law, and only the law can stipulate what is anti-social, forbidden, or punishable. Freedoms guaranteed by law and in compliance with the constitution also apply fully to citizens of various creeds and religious denominations. [...]

Legal standards must also set forth a more explicit guarantee of the freedom of speech for minority interests and opinions (again within the framework of socialist laws and following the principle that decisions are taken in accordance with the will of the majority). The constitutional freedom of movement, particularly that of travel abroad for our citizens, must be explicitly guaranteed by law. In particular, this means that a citizen should have the legal right to long-term or permanent sojourn abroad and that people should not be groundlessly placed in the position of emigrants. At the same time it is necessary to protect by law the interests of the state, for example, with regard to a possible drain of some specialists, etc.

Our entire legal code must gradually come to grips with the problem of how to protect, in a better and more consistent way, the personal rights and property of citizens, and we must certainly remove statutes that effectively put individual citizens at a disadvantage with the state and other institutions. [...]

It is troubling that up to now the rehabilitation of people, both communists and non-communists, who were the victims of legal transgressions in previous years, has not always been carried out in full, regarding political and civic consequences. [...]

In the interest of the development of our socialist society it is absolutely essential to strengthen the unity of the Czechoslovak people and their confidence in the policy of the Communist Party of Czechoslovakia, to effect a crucial change in the constitutional arrangement of the relations between Czechs and Slovaks, and to carry out the necessary constitutional modifications. It is equally essential to respect the advantage of a socialist federal arrangement as a recognized and well-tested form of the legal coexistence of two equal nations in a common socialist state. [...]

Socialism Cannot Do without Enterprises

The democratization program of the economy places special emphasis on ensuring the independence of enterprises and enterprise groupings and their relative independence from state bodies; the full implementation of the right of consumers to determine their consumption patterns and lifestyles; the right to choose jobs freely; and the right and opportunity of various groups of working people and different social groups to formulate and defend their economic interests in shaping economic policy. [...]

Decision-making about the plan and the economic policy of the state must be both a process of mutual confrontation and harmonization of different interests, that is, the interests of enterprises, consumers, employers, different social groups of the population, nations, and so forth. [...]

The drafting of the national economic plan and the national economic policy must be subject to the democratic control of the National Assembly and specialized control of academic institutions. The supreme body implementing the economic policy of the state is the government. [...]

The Central Committee believes it is essential to raise the authority and responsibility of enterprises in the concrete implementation of international economic relations. Production and trade enterprises must have the right to choose their export and import organizations. At the same time it is necessary to lay down conditions that would entitle enterprises to act independently on foreign markets. [...]

The International Status and Foreign Policy of the Czechoslovak Socialist Republic

We will be implementing the Action Program at a time when the international situation is complicated. The development of that situation will influence the fulfillment of certain key aspects of the program. On the other hand, the process of socialist renewal in Czechoslovakia will make it possible for our republic to influence this international situation more actively. We stand resolutely on the side of progress, democracy, and socialism in the struggle by socialist and democratic forces against the aggressive attempts of world imperialism. It is from this viewpoint that we determine our attitude toward the most acute international problems of the present and our role in the worldwide struggle against the forces of imperialist reaction.

Taking, as a point of departure, the existing relationship of international forces and our awareness that Czechoslovakia is an active component of the revolutionary process in the world, the ČSSR (Czechoslovak Socialist Republic) will formulate its own position toward the fundamental problems of world politics.

The basic orientation of Czechoslovak foreign policy took root at the time of the struggle for national liberation and in the process of the social reconstruction of the country. It revolves around alliance and cooperation with the Soviet Union and the other socialist states. [...]

We will actively pursue a policy of peaceful coexistence vis-à-vis the advanced capitalist countries. Our geographical position, as well as the needs and capacities of an industrialized country, compel us to pursue a more active European policy aimed at the promotion of mutually advantageous relations with all states and with international organizations, and aimed at safeguarding the collective security of the European continent.

The Prague Spring 1968: A National Security Archive Documents Reader, ed. Jaromír Navrátil (Budapest & New York: Central European University Press, 2006), 92–5.

RUDI DUTSCHKE IN RECOVERY (1968)
Milan Hauner

In early 1968, German student leader Rudi Dutschke visited Czechoslovakia, where he met with students in Prague. On April 11, after his return to West Germany, an anti-communist shot him in the head in an attempted assassination. In May, a group of Prague students met with him and other student radicals from the Socialist German Student League (SDS) in Berlin. The account of this meeting, published on June 19, 1968, testifies to the transnational dimension of the long 1968. But it also shows how struggles varied across borders. Communist Czechoslovakia was vastly different from the capitalist Federal Republic of Germany, and the students brought different experiences to the table. Milan Hauner, who wrote the following piece for the radical Czech magazine Student, *left Czechoslovakia to visit Britain a few weeks before the Warsaw Pact invasion. He stayed, joined an organization that worked with Czechoslovak refugees, and later completed a doctorate at the University of Cambridge.*

* * *

A group of seven academics from the Humanities Faculty of the Charles University in Prague visited West Berlin at the end of May 1968 at the invitation of the SDS (Socialisticher Deutscher Studentenbund). We were supposed to take part in a discussion that Rudi Dutschke had arranged during his visit in Prague shortly before Easter when he returned to West Berlin to be shot by a right-wing extremist. Naturally, following the attempt on Dutschke's life and the student riots which followed, we were not met by anyone. We found radical students guarding round the clock their headquarters, known as Commune No. 2, in anticipation of an assault by right-wingers which, nevertheless, did not materialize. […]

On Sunday, June 2, a huge demonstration took place to commemorate the anniversary of Benno Ohnesorg, killed a year earlier. A colourful assortment of anti-authoritarian slogans shuffled along, with red flags and black banners. Nearby on Krumme Strasse in the entryway to House No. 66, was the spot where Benno Ohnesorg had been shot dead.

On Monday we were unexpectedly contacted by Gretchen Dutschke telling us that Rudi wanted to receive us. Within two hours we were welcomed in. We were greeted in a small hospital room by a young man in a bathrobe with a mustache and a closely shaved head à la Régis Debray. It was only when he squeezed our hands and we heard his voice that we realized it was Rudi. He sat down near us and we spoke right away. It was amazing to watch him. He was virtually bursting with energy and curiosity, that it was impossible to tell that he was struggling to find words as a result of sustaining a severe brain injury. Through intensive psycho-linguistic training, enabled by his indefatigable energy, Rudi has been gradually regaining his memory. Rudi literally escaped death only by a hairsbreadth. Had either bullet that entered his head penetrated but a millimeter further, he would not be among the living today. […] The pace of his recovery is beyond all precedent. Already he let it be known that he was not insisting that the attacker, who is recovering in the same hospital in Berlin Westend, pay any damages for his injuries. On the contrary, he was to demand his release because he did not consider Bachmann his enemy, but rather a victim of the irresponsible campaigns of the Springer press against student opposition.

We inquired into Rudi's immediate plans. Once released from the hospital, he was to make up for lost time and prepare for his trip to the United States. We expressed our desire on behalf of the Prague student body and our academic council of Prague students to invite him to convalesce in a Czech sanatorium, but he tried to convince us that it was unrealistic. With a laugh he rejected it as a quaint proposal, akin to going to a spa to sip mineral water with visiting Soviet apparatchiks. When we discussed the recent visit to Berlin by philosopher Herbert Marcuse, considered the intellectual father of the radical student movement in the West, Rudi revealed that Marcuse would like to visit Czechoslovakia in the autumn and speak to the student body.

What can be said of our general impressions during such a short stay? It was hard to conceal the fact that on the whole the student left in Germany was in a deep depression, taken aback by the enormity of the right's counter-offensive: the Emergency Laws imposed by the government and the rise of nationalist activism by the Sudeten Germans and the neo-Nazi National Democratic Party of Germany, etc. The Social Democratic Party of Germany was passing through a deep crisis following the assault on Dutschke. The Anti-Parliamentary Opposition (or APO) [should have been *Extra*-Parliamentary Opposition], primarily made up of students from the Free University, failed to make inroads among workers, or at least attain the kind of cooperation seen in the recent demonstrations in France. A bold experiment in academic critique was not enough. The APO has tried to reach out to other demographics, especially young workers, through the establishment of "grassroot groups" (*Basisgruppen*). Yet the prospect of educating workers was not particularly successful. Quite the opposite. Not long ago, a radical student march through "red Wedding," the Vysočany of Berlin, failed to make an impact and the students were attacked by workers.

During two improvised evening discussions it became evident that there existed a deep disagreement between our group and our interlocutors. We could not even agree on the topics of discussion beforehand. The differences were jarring and almost diametrically opposed between our two groups on the subjects of utopia and reality, aims and means, theory and practice. [...] We did not hide our deep skepticism towards the idea of some theoretical formula for a perfect utopia in the absence of the means, methods, assurances, and tools to achieve it.

Our German counterparts put great emphasis on creating an idealized type of *socialist democracy*, whose primary and indispensable precondition was the control of material production. They demanded furthermore consensus of all producers on the basis of an advisory system, consisting of individual workplaces as the breeding grounds of grassroots initiative. In principle, we seemed to agree on this point (otherwise socialism would not be achievable). However, disagreements emerged immediately when the discussion turned to concrete applications. The German radicals favored their orthodox concepts, though we presented them with a range of empirical examples from two decades of practical socialism—a beautiful utopia swiftly abused by human practice, that is to say degraded to the level of petty manipulations. Thus utopia was reduced to a distant image, gradually fading from the consciousness of the people, leaving behind only a bitter taste of a derailed revolution.

On the other hand, we were impressed by the theoretical mastery of the newest Marxist literature shown by our German colleagues—this literature of course not being available in university libraries at home. A novelty for us was the encounter with an unusual type of "students" only by name, who aspired to become professional revolutionaries of a kind. These individuals had been, for months and maybe even years, students in name only [...]

We returned home with many lessons and endeavors, both negative and positive. In the socialist camp only Czechoslovak students seem to have recognized that student movements have an international common denominator and should be recognized as a new phenomenon of social struggle in industrialized societies. We wished Rudi Dutschke a most successful recovery, and the same recovery to the APO. While the former was undergoing a miraculous recovery, the latter was showing signs of a weak body and irritated mind.

Student, June 19, 1968. Translated by Michael Vimont, with additional edits by the author himself (June 11, 2018).

TWO THOUSAND WORDS THAT BELONG TO WORKERS, FARMERS, OFFICIALS, SCIENTISTS, ARTISTS, AND EVERYBODY (1968)
Ludvík Vaculík

Although a member of the Communist Party, Ludvík Vaculík, a prominent Czech writer, consistently advocated for reforms in the 1960s. At the famous Fourth Congress of the Union of Czechoslovak Writers in July 1967 he openly criticized the Party. During the Prague Spring, Vaculík welcomed the "Action Program," but hoped to push the reform process even further. On June 27, 1968, a day after the Party abolished censorship, he published the following manifesto in several major newspapers. While it criticized the existing system, it nevertheless continued to uphold socialism as the end goal. Signed by prominent intellectuals and receiving a wide circulation, it proved very popular among Czechoslovaks.

*   *   *

The first threat to our national life was from the war. Then came other evil days and events that endangered the nation's spiritual well-being and character. Most of the nation welcomed the socialist program with high hopes. But it fell into the hands of the wrong people. [...]

After enjoying great popular confidence immediately after the war, the Communist Party by degrees bartered this confidence away for office, until it had all the offices and nothing else. [...]

Conditions inside the Communist Party served as both a pattern for and a cause of the identical conditions in the state. The party's association with the state deprived it of the asset of separation from executive power. No one criticized the activities of the state and of economic organs. Parliament forgot how to hold proper debates, the government forgot how to govern properly, and managers forgot how to manage properly. Elections lost their significance, and the law carried no weight. [...]

We all bear responsibility for the present state of affairs. But those among us who are communists bear more than others, and those who acted as components or instruments of unchecked power bear the greatest responsibility of all. [...] No organizations, not even communist ones, were really controlled by their own members. The chief sin and deception of these rulers was to have explained their own whims as the "will of the workers." [...] We all know, and every worker knows especially, that they had virtually no say in deciding anything. [...]

Since the beginning of this year we have been experiencing a regenerative process of democratization. It started inside the Communist Party, that much we must admit, even those communists among us who no longer had hopes that anything good could emerge from that quarter know this. It must also be added, of course, that the process could have started nowhere else. For after 20 years the communists were the only ones able to conduct some sort of political activity. It was only the opposition inside the Communist Party that had the privilege to voice antagonistic views. The effort and initiative now displayed by democratically-minded communists are only then a partial repayment of the debt owed by the entire party to the non-communists [...] The regenerative process has introduced nothing particularly new into our lives. It revives ideas and topics, many of which are older than the errors of our socialism, while others, having emerged from below the surface of visible history, should long ago have found expression but were instead repressed. Let us not foster the illusion that it is the power of truth which now makes such ideas victorious. Their victory has been due rather to the weakness of the old leaders, evidently already debilitated by 20 years of unchallenged rule. All the defects hidden in the foundations and ideology of the system have clearly reached their peak. So let us not overestimate the effects of the writers' and students' criticisms. The source of social change is the economy. [...]

In this moment of hope, albeit hope still threatened, we appeal to you. It took several months before many of us believed it was safe to speak up; many of us still do not think it is safe. But speak up we did exposing ourselves to the extent that we have no choice but to complete our plan to humanize the regime. If we did not, the old forces would exact cruel revenge. We appeal above all to those who so far have waited on the sidelines. The time now approaching will decide events for years to come.

The summer holidays are approaching, a time when we are inclined to let everything slip. But we can safely say that our dear adversaries will not give themselves a summer break; they will rally everyone who is under any obligation to them and are taking steps, even now, to secure themselves a quiet Christmas! Let us watch carefully how things develop, let us try to understand them and have our answers ready. Let us forget the impossible demand that someone from on high should always provide us with a single explanation and a single, simple moral imperative. Everyone will have to draw their own conclusions. Common, agreed conclusions can only be reached in discussion that requires freedom of speech—the only democratic achievement to our credit this year.

But in the days to come we must gird ourselves with our own initiative and make our own decisions.

To begin with we will oppose the view, sometimes voiced, that a democratic revival can be achieved without the communists, or even in opposition to them. This would be unjust, and foolish too. The communists already have their organizations in place, and in these we must support the progressive wing. They have their experienced officials, and they still have in their hands, after all, the crucial levers and buttons. On the other hand they have presented an Action Program to the public. This program will begin to even out the most glaring inequalities, and no one else has a program in such specific detail. We must demand that they produce local Action Programs in public in every district and community. Then the issue will suddenly revolve around very ordinary and long-awaited acts of justice. The Czechoslovak Communist Party is preparing for its congress, where it will elect its new Central Committee. Let us demand that it be a better committee than the present one. [...]

People have recently been worried that the democratization process has come to a halt. This feeling is partly a sign of fatigue after the excitement of events, but partly it reflects the truth. The season of astonishing revelations, of dismissals from high office, and of heady speeches couched in language of unaccustomed daring—all this is over. But the struggle between opposing forces has merely become somewhat less open, the fight continues over the content and formulation of the laws and over the scope of practical measures. Besides, we must give the new people time to work: the new ministers, prosecutors, chairmen and secretaries. They are entitled to time in which to prove themselves fit or unfit. This is all that can be expected at present of the central political bodies, though they have made a remarkably good showing so far in spite of themselves.

The everyday quality of our future democracy depends on what happens *in* the factories, and on what happens *to* the factories. Despite all our discussions, it is the economic managers who have us in their grasp. Good managers must be sought out and promoted. True, we are all badly paid in comparison with people in the developed countries, some of us worse than others. We can ask for more money, and more money can indeed be printed, but only if it is devalued in the process. Let us rather ask the directors and the chairmen of boards to tell us what they want to produce and at what cost, the customers they want to sell it to and at what price, the profit that will be made, and of that, how much will be reinvested in modernizing production and how much will be left over for distribution. Under dreary looking headlines, a hard battle is being covered in the press—the battle of democracy versus soft jobs. The workers, as entrepreneurs, can intervene in this battle by electing the right people to management and workers' councils. And as employees they can help themselves best by electing, as their trade union representatives, natural leaders and able, honorable individuals without regard to party affiliation.

Although at present one cannot expect more of the central political bodies, it is vital to achieve more at district and community level. Let us demand the departure of people who abused their power, damaged public property, and acted dishonorably or brutally. Ways must be found to compel them to resign. To mention a few: public criticism, resolutions, demonstrations, demonstrative work brigades, collections to buy presents for them on their retirement, strikes, and picketing at their front doors. But we should reject any illegal, indecent, or boorish methods, which they would exploit to bring influence to bear on Alexander Dubček. Our aversion to the writing of rude letters must be expressed so completely that the only explanation for any such missives in the future would be that their recipients had ordered them themselves. Let us revive the activity of the National Front. Let us demand public sessions of the national committees. For questions that no one else will look into, let us set up our own civic committees and commissions. There is nothing difficult about it; a few people gather together, elect a chairman, keep proper records, publish their findings, demand solutions, and refuse to be shouted down. Let us convert the district and local newspapers, which have mostly degenerated to the level of official mouth-pieces, into a platform for all the forward-looking elements in politics; let us demand that editorial boards be formed of National Front representatives, or else let us start new papers. Let us form committees for the defense of free speech. At our meetings, let us have our own staffs for ensuring order. If we hear strange reports, let us seek confirmation, let us send delegations to the proper authorities and publicize their answers, perhaps putting them up on front gates. Let us give support to the police when they are prosecut-ing genuine wrongdoers, for it is not our aim to create anarchy or a state of general uncertainty. Let us eschew quarrels between neighbors, and let us avoid drunkenness on political occasions. Let us expose informers.

The summer traffic throughout the republic will enhance interest in the settlement of constitutional relations between Czechs and Slovaks. Let us consider federalization as a method of solving the question of nationalities, but let us regard it as only one of several important measures designed to democratize the system. In itself this particular measure will not necessarily give even the Slovaks a better life. […]

There has been great alarm recently over the possibility that foreign forces will intervene in our development. Whatever superior forces may face us, all we can do is stick to our own positions, behave decently, and initiate nothing ourselves. We can show our government that we will stand by it, with weapons if need be, if it will do what we give it a mandate to do. And we can assure our allies that we will observe our treaties of alliance, friendship, and trade. Irritable reproaches and ill-argued suspicions on our part can only make things harder for our government, and bring no benefit to ourselves. […]

This spring a great opportunity was given to us once again, as it was after the end of the war. Again we have the chance to take into our own hands our common cause, which for working purposes we call socialism, and give it a form more appropriate to our once-good reputation and to the fairly good opinion we used to have of ourselves. The spring is over and will never return. By winter we will know all.

So ends our statement addressed to workers, farmers, officials, artists, scholars, scientists, technicians, and everybody. It was written at the behest of scholars and scientists.

The Prague Spring 1968: A National Security Archive Documents Reader, ed. Jaromír Navrátil (Budapest and New York: Central European University Press, 2006), 177–81.

PROCLAMATION ADOPTED AT THE OPENING
OF THE CONGRESS (1968)
Extraordinary Congress of the Communist Party of Czechoslovakia

On August 22, 1968, the day after the Warsaw Pact invasion, the Communist Party of Czechoslovakia held a secret congress in a factory in Vysočany, on the outskirts of Prague. This Extraordinary Congress, called by the Central Committee, reaffirmed the legitimacy of the existing leadership, repudiated the invasion and its internal supporters, and called for a one-hour general strike, but discouraged sustained resistance. While Czechoslovaks certainly protested, they largely heeded the call to avoid directly military confrontation. In contrast with the Soviet invasion of Hungary in 1956, which led to over 2,500 Hungarian deaths, and hundreds of executions afterwards, the Warsaw Pact invasion of 1968 left around 135 Czech and Slovak deaths. Following the Congress, a Czechoslovak delegation, dominated by pro-Moscow hardliners, was sent to Moscow. Under duress, the reformers in the delegation agreed to readjust the country's policies, change personnel, and repudiate the Extraordinary Congress.

* * *

Comrades, citizens of Czechoslovakia,

Today, on August 22, 1968, began the Extraordinary Congress of the Communist Party of Czechoslovakia, attended by its properly elected delegates. The Congress adopted the following proclamation:

Czechoslovakia is a free and sovereign socialist State, founded on the will and support of its people. However, its sovereignty was infringed on August 21, 1968, when it was occupied by the armed forces of the Soviet Union, Poland, the German Democratic Republic, Bulgaria, and Hungary.

This act is explained away by assertions that socialism was in danger and that certain leading Czechoslovak representatives had asked for the intervention. As was made clear [...] no responsible Party or constitutional body had asked for troops to be sent.

There was no counter-revolution in Czechoslovakia, nor was her socialist development threatened in any way. The people and the Party were perfectly capable of resolving the problems that had arisen by themselves, as was borne out by the tremendous trust enjoyed by the new Party leadership headed by Comrade Dubček. On the contrary, Czechoslovakia was about to put into practice Marx's and Lenin's fundamental concepts of socialist democracy. Czechoslovakia did not violate her obligations towards her allies, nor has she the slightest interest in hostility towards the socialist States and their people in the future. However, these obligations have been violated by the armed forces of the occupying powers.

They have trampled on Czechoslovakia's sovereignty and on their own obligations as allies, as well as on the Warsaw Pact and the agreements signed at Čierná and Bratislava. Several leading Czechoslovak representatives have been wrongfully arrested, isolated from the people and prevented from carrying out their duties. A number of government and Party offices have been occupied. All this amounts to a grave injustice.

The Congress categorically demands that normal conditions be created immediately for the work of Czechoslovak constitutional and political organs and that the arrested representatives be released without delay, so that they may return to their duties.

At this time of crisis, the unity of all our people, the unity of our two nations and the unity of both with our Party has become the most urgent problem of the day. Not even armed intervention has prevented the Czechoslovak people from remaining the one and only rightful and sovereign ruler of its own country. The defense of freedom in our socialist homeland is not the concern of the communists alone, but of all the Czechs and Slovaks and the other nationalities, of all workers, farmers, members of the intelligentsia, and of the young, of all who have the dignified and free life of our socialist country at heart. The communists can play their leading part by becoming the most active and self-sacrificing organizers of the campaign. for the withdrawal of foreign troops. They can achieve this aim in the closest unity with all patriots and with all the active democratic forces in our society.

The situation that arose in our country on August 21 cannot last. Socialist Czechoslovakia will never resign itself to being administered by the military occupation authorities, nor will it accept any collaborationist regime dependent on the armed might of the occupants.

The Extraordinary Fourteenth Congress declares that it recognizes only the lawfully elected constitutional representatives of this country [...]. It refuses to recognize, even as Party members, those members of the former Central Committee who fail in this difficult test.

Our basic demand must of course be the withdrawal of foreign troops. Should the above demands not be complied with; if, in particular, negotiations for the departure of foreign troops are not started within 24 hours with our constitutional and Party representatives, these being again free men; and if Comrade Dubček does not within that time-limit announce this to the nation; then the Congress asks all workers, led by members of the Communist Party, to carry out a one-hour protest strike at twelve noon on Friday 23 August. At the same time the Congress has resolved that if these demands are not met it will continue to take all necessary measures, and once the new Central Committee has been elected will entrust the carrying out of such measures to the Central Committee as the only lawful representative of the Party.

The Congress appeals to all communists and all Czechoslovak citizens to maintain law and order, to keep calm and behave in a disciplined fashion, thus ensuring that we on our side do not provoke incidents that could result in serious loss of life and damage to property. [...]

The Secret Vysočany Congress: Proceedings and Documents of the Extraordinary Fourteenth Congress of the Communist Party of Czechoslovakia, August 22, 1968, ed. Jiří Pelikán (New York: St. Martin's Press, 1972), 88–90. Translated by George Theiner and Deryck Viney.

INFORMATION FROM THE LOCAL COUNCILS OF THE COMMUNIST PARTY OF CZECHOSLOVAKIA, THE MUNICIPALITY, AND THE NATIONAL FRONT TO THE CITIZENS OF THE TOWN (1968)

Like the proclamation of the Vysočany Congress, this one-page flyer was also released by the official resistance immediately after the Warsaw Pact invasion. It restates the legitimacy of the reformist leadership and seeks symbolic support of two kinds: from the workers at Brandýs, 25 kilometres outside Prague, and from the people of Prague, who are asked to sign a petition against the invasion and to refuse cooperation. The hope was to rally popular support behind the leadership and force the Soviets and conservatives in the Party to rethink the invasion, without risking a bloodbath. Such attempts at resistance had limited coordination and were largely ineffective.

* * *

Dear Citizens,

The first day and night of the occupation of our land by the Warsaw Pact armies has come to pass without violent action, thanks to the reasonableness of our citizens and workers. It is our understanding that where disruptions occurred there was gunfire and loss of life. Therefore, it is necessary, also today, to maintain level-headedness, calm, and security by ensuring that workers immediately take up their duties to reduce economic losses.

City authorities are tracking developing events alongside you, and seek compliance with the views of the majority of citizens to ensure a civic life in accordance with our legitimate authority. We still stand for comrades Dubček, Svobada, Černik, Smrkovský, and Císař. Like the employees of the state company Brandýs' Machine Works and Foundry, we thus demand the following:

1. an immediate end to the unlawful occupation of our country,
2. an immediate withdrawal of foreign armies from our sovereign national territory,
3. respect for the sovereignty of our nation-state,
4. immediate release of the leaders of our legitimate government (the National Assembly and the Central Committee of the CPCz),
5. withdrawal of all occupying forces from radio, television, print media, and transport plants,
6. apologies to our people from all usurping governments and payment for all damages caused by the occupation.

These demands will be presented in a declaration for all citizens of our town to sign. We will announce the location of the signing center to you via public radio as soon as we overcome technical difficulties (broadcasting issues etc.).

At the same time, we ask that you, alongside city authorities, refuse to cooperate with occupiers and collaborators. [...]

We call on all factories and workers of the city to lend their support against these challenges.

The local councils of the CPCz, the Municipality, and the National Front will keep citizens informed of further developments.

Retrieved from the University of Michigan Special Collections Library's exhibit "The Soviet Invasion of Czechoslovakia: August 1968: Materials from the Labadie Collection of Social Protest Material": web.archive.org/web/20050204102745if_/ http://www.lib.umich.edu:80/spec-coll/czech/index.html. Accessed via the Internet Archive's Wayback Machine: archive.org/web. Translated by Michael Vimont.

RUSSIANS, GO HOME! (1968)
Aktual/Milan Knížák

Alternative music was an important part of the period, and often closely linked to movements. Musician and performance artist Milan Knížák played a key role in introducing the counterculture to Czechoslovakia in the 1960s. His art group, Aktual, became a major band in the underground scene. Not only was their music highly experimental (they would use hand sirens, electric saws, or motorcycles as instruments), the band's lyrics were, unusually for the time, overtly political and sung in Czech. Knížák wrote this song on August 21, immediately after the Warsaw Pact invasion; Aktual busked it on the streets of Marienbad that same day and later in pubs and on street corners. Their songs were often "on the borderline between irony and seriousness" (Knížák)—but this one is very straightforward, and of course politically risky.

* * *

Figure 12.2   The countercultural band Aktual on stage. Courtesy of Milan Knížák.

I had a strange dream last night
a stranger yet morning woke me up
under my windows canons and tanks
a friendly red visit—so I heard

Russians go home
we don't want you near
Russians go home
just get the fuck out of here

Back to Siberia your tanks you take
there you have your own stinky garden to rake
stick your communism right up your asses
watch out—your brother Hitler may still be awake
Russians go home
we don't want you near
Russians go home
just get the fuck out of here

Aktual, *děti bolševizmu* (Louny: Guerilla records, 2005). Translated by Karolína Dolanská.

WORKERS' COUNCILS: THE GUARANTEE OF
DEMOCRATIC ADMINISTRATION AND
MANAGERIAL ACTIVITY (1969)

Hoping to build a more democratic form of socialism, the "Action Program"
encouraged the formation of workers' councils in order to give workers a greater
say in the production process. Still, the power of the councils remained limited—
they did not, for example, have final say in economic matters—and few councils
actually emerged during Prague Spring. After the Warsaw Pact invasion in
August, however, worker militancy surged. The number of workers' councils grew
from around 19 in September to over 250 by the end of the year, and they pushed
the state-sanctioned boundaries of self-management. With the Warsaw Pact
invasion having blocked the formal political channels, workers' struggles became
all the more important for national reform. On January 9–10, 1969, delegates
from the various workers' councils met in Plzeň to coordinate and strengthen the
movement. Below, we reproduce excerpts from the minutes of the meeting, as well
as the final resolution.

* * *

A consultative meeting of representatives of the workers' councils and the
preparatory committees for the establishment of workers' councils, together
with representatives from the factory-level committees of the ROH [Rev-
olutionary Trade Union Movement], was held in Plzeň on January 9–10,
1969 in the Works Club of the Škoda Plzeň ROH.
[…]
The consultative meeting was tape-recorded, which has made it possible
for us to put these documents together. We have endeavored to give the
fullest possible picture of the consultative meeting. If in certain cases we
have not succeeded in conveying completely accurately the tenor of the
discussion, we apologize: it was not done deliberately. We were limited by
the technical means at our disposal and by shortage of time while dealing
with the overall scope of our plans and execution. […]
[…]

Comrade Lesyk, Engineer, Slovnaft Bratislava Workers' Council

May I also be allowed to say a few words? Slovnaft Bratislava was one of
the first enterprises to participate in the establishment of workers' councils.
Theirs was practically the first council in Slovakia. As early as May we
began to prepare for it: then came August 21, and immediately after the
Moscow agreement we set up our council. This was done because we wish
to clearly demonstrate our support for the course of action adopted by our

government after January. It was therefore as much a political act as an economic one. We based ourselves on the same principles as our comrades at Škoda, although there were no links between our places of work and we had no contacts with each other. In fact the statutes of the two councils are most identical. ...

The director's understanding of our efforts in this area was so great that we were able to set up the council without any real difficulty; we were so bold that we did not even ask the permission of the general management. ...

[...]

Comrade Bousa, Chairman of the Workers' Council, CSAD, Ustinnad Labem

To the best of our knowledge our workers' council, set up on October 18, 1968, is still the only existing council in the transport sector. ... In order to prevent the idea of self-management from being discredited, we propose that the majority of representatives on the councils of the public enterprises be elected by the workers themselves, and not just one third as has so far been suggested. ...

We propose that the transitional period be ended by the speedy enactment of the bill on socialist enterprises, and by the prompt establishment of complete autonomy for the national enterprises. As for ourselves in the CSAD [the Czech Road Haulage Company], we demand complete self-management without the limitations envisaged for the special or state enterprises.

[...]

Comrade Baxant, Engineer, Fruta Canning Factory, Prague

Our preparatory committee was composed of representatives of the factory's trade-union committee, of the enterprise management and of the factory's party organization. ... A workers' council was elected at the end of September. It consisted of 17 members, of whom five were manual workers, seven technicians (three of them with higher education qualifications) and five economists (one with higher education qualification).

[...]

Resolution Adopted by the Meeting of Representatives of Workers' Councils and Preparatory Committees

The consultative meeting of the delegates of the workers' councils and preparatory committees, representing 182 enterprises of the Czech Socialist

Republic and Slovak Socialist Republic, that is, some 890,000 workers, is determined to convey its views to the government of the Republic and to the National Assembly.

(1) We are pleased that the work of the bill on socialist enterprises will soon be completed. We appreciate the fact that the final draft, of which we have taken note, legalizes the position of the councils and gives them a future context to work in. Thus an important part of the Action Program of the CPCz and the government, as well as the December resolution of the plenary meeting of the Central Committee of the CPCz, has been put into practice. At the same time, we feel that during the final stages of the formulation of the law, the experiences and observations that were reported at our consultative meeting at Plzeň should also be drawn upon.

(2) It is our firm belief that it will not be possible to restore initiative to the enterprises, accomplish the economic reform and develop the power of the people without the formation of democratic organs of management. We consider the right to self-management as an inalienable right of the socialist producer. Thus we believe that all enterprises should as a principle have the right to elect councils to act as the supreme managerial organs, charged in particular with deciding the economic policy of the enterprises and with appointing, dismissing and assessing the senior management in their capacity as executive organs. Exceptions to this rule should only be made for exceptional reasons, and must be ratified by the Federal Assembly. In principle there is no enterprise within the economic system that cannot be self-managing. [...]

(3) We propose that extra-economic intervention in the area of responsibility of these councils be reduced to a minimum. The general interest of society and the public interest should as a matter of principle be assured by economic policies which guarantee that what is profitable for the state is equally profitable for the enterprise.

(4) We propose that the principles of self-management for the enterprises should as far as possible be adopted in general terms, so that the articles of the individual workers' councils may be adapted to suit the particular requirements of the enterprise. In the same way, the law should not prevent the long-term extension of the principle of self-management to all management bodies. [...]

(5) We are convinced that workers' councils can help to humanize both the work and relationships within the enterprises, and give to each producer a proper feeling that he is not just an employee, a mere working element in the production process, but also the organizer and joint creator of this process. This is why we wish to reemphasize here and now that the councils must always preserve their democratic character and their vital links with

their electors, thus preventing a special caste of "professional self-management executives" from forming. [...]
[...]

Workers' Councils in Czechoslovakia, 1968–9: Documents and Essays, ed. Vladimir
Fišera (New York: St. Martin's Press, 1978), 50, 65–6, 69–71.

A LETTER FROM JAN PALACH ADDRESSED TO THE UNION OF CZECHOSLOVAK WRITERS (1969)

*On January 16, 1969, a 20-year-old student named Jan Palach walked to
Prague's Wenceslas Square, doused himself in gasoline, then set himself on fire.
Palach's suicide was meant to protest not only the Warsaw Pact invasion, but the
demoralization he felt was setting in across the country. With normal channels of
protest closed down, Palach and his friends opted for something more dramatic.
His heroic death sparked a student hunger strike, about 750,000 people turned
his funeral into an act of protest, and several other activists, like the student Jan
Zajíc, followed his lead and self-immolated. Below we reproduce his publicly
circulated letter.*

*   *   *

Seeing that our nation finds itself on the brink of despair and surrender, we
have decided to voice our protest and awaken the conscience of our nation.

Our group consists of volunteers who are determined to give ourselves up
as kindling to be set ablaze for our cause.

I have had the honor to draw the first lot, and thus the right to write the
first letter and take up my place as the first torch.

Our demands are: 1) immediate revocation of censorship, 2) halting
the distribution of *Zprávy* [an occupation journal printed in the German
Democratic Republic]. As can be seen, our demands are not excessive, quite
the opposite.

If our demands are not met in five days, that is by January 21, 1969, and if
they are not met with sufficient support from the people (in the form of an
indefinite strike), another torch will be set aflame.

Torch No. 1

P.S. I do not believe that our nation will require more light. January 1968
started from the top. January 1969 must start from the bottom (if it is to
begin).

National Security Archive, Prague. Republished on Jan Palach: Charles University
Multimedia Project: janpalach.cz. Translated by Michael Vimont.

Further Reading

Bren, Paulina. *The Green Grocer and His TV: The Culture of Communism After the 1968 Prague Spring.* Ithaca: Cornell University Press, 2010.

Dubček, Alexander with Jiří Hochman, ed. *Hope Dies Last: The Autobiography of Alexander Dubcek.* New York: Kodansha International, 1993.

Fišera, Vladimir, ed. *Workers' Councils in Czechoslovakia, 1968–9: Documents and Essays.* New York: St. Martin's Press, 1978.

Golan, Galia. *The Czechoslovak Reform Movement: Communism in Crisis 1962–1968.* London: Cambridge University Press, 1971.

Golan, Galia. *Reform Rule in Czechoslovakia: The Dubček Era 1968–1969.* Cambridge: Cambridge University Press, 1973.

Kusin, Vladimir V. *Political Grouping in the Czechoslovak Reform Movement.* New York: Columbia University Press, 1972.

Mlynář, Zdeněk. *Nightfrost in Prague: The End of Humane Socialism.* New York: Karz Publishers, 1980.

Navrátil, Jaromir, ed. *The Prague Spring 1968: A National Security Archive Documents Reader.* New York: Central European University Press, 1998.

Nebřenský, Zdeněk. "Early Voices of Dissent: Czechoslovak Student Opposition at the Beginning of the 1960s." In *Between Prague Spring and French May: Opposition and Revolt in Europe, 1960–1980,* edited by Martin Klimke, Jacco Pekelder, and Joachim Scharloth, 32–48. New York: Berghahn Books, 2013.

Oates-Indruchová, Libora. "Unraveling a Tradition, or Spinning a Myth?: Gender Critique in Czech Society and Culture." In *The Routledge Handbook of the Global Sixties: Between Protest and Nation-Building,* edited by Chen Jian, Martin Klimke, Masha Kirasirova, Mary Nolan, Marilyn Young, and Joanna Waley-Cohen, 234–56. New York: Routledge, 2018.

Pauer, Jan. "Czechoslovakia." In *1968 in Europe: A History of Protest and Activism, 1956–1977,* edited by Martin Klimke and Joachim Scharloth, 163–77. New York: Palgrave Macmillan, 2008.

Pelikán, Jiří, ed. *The Secret Vysočany Congress: Proceedings and Documents of the Extraordinary Fourteenth Congress of the Communist Party of Czechoslovakia, 22 August 1968.* New York: St. Martin's Press, 1972.

Skilling, Gordon H. *Czechoslovakia's Interrupted Revolution.* Princeton: Princeton University Press, 1976.

Williams, Kieran. *The Prague Spring and its Aftermath: Czechoslovak Politics, 1968–1970.* Cambridge: Cambridge University Press, 1997.